PENGUIN  ACADEMICS

NEW NEW MEDIA

PENGUIN ACADEMICS

NEW NEW MEDIA

SECOND EDITION

PAUL LEVINSON

Fordham University

PEARSON

Boston Columbus Indianapolis New York San Francisco Upper Saddle River
Amsterdam Cape Town Dubai London Madrid Milan Munich Paris Montréal Toronto
Delhi Mexico City São Paulo Sydney Hong Kong Seoul Singapore Taipei Tokyo

Editorial Director: Craig Campanella
Editor-in-Chief, Communication: Karon Bowers
Senior Acquisitions Editor: Melissa Mashburn
Editorial Assistant: Megan Hermida
Senior Marketing Manager: Blair Zoe Tuckman
Managing Editor Production: Central Publishing
Production Project Manager: Romaine Denis
Manufacturing Buyer: Romaine Denis
Production Editor: Raegan Heerema
Senior Digital Editor: Paul DeLuca
Digital Editor: Lisa Dotson
Project Coordination, Text Design, and Electronic Page Makeup: Abinaya Rajendran, Integra
    Software Services Ltd.
Creative Director: Jayne Conte
Cover Designer: Bruce Kenselaar
Cover Images: Shutterstock Image
Printer/Binder: STP/ RR Donnelly Harrisonburg
Cover Printer: STP/ RR Donnelly Harrisonburg

Quote from Bob Dylan's "With God On Our Side": © 1963 by Warner Bros. Inc.; renewed 1991 by Special Rider Music. All rights reserved. International copyright secured. Reprinted by permission.

For more information about the Penguin Academics series, please contact us by mail at Pearson Education, attn. Marketing Department, 51 Madison Avenue, 28th Floor, New York, NY 10010, or visit us online at www.pearsonhighered.com/communication.

Library of Congress Cataloging-in-Publication Data
Levinson, Paul.
    New new media/Paul Levinson.—Second edition.
        p. cm.
    Includes bibliographical references and index.
    ISBN-13: 978-0-205-86557-4
    ISBN-10: 0-205-86557-7
    1. Social media.   2. Computer network resources.   3. User-generated content.   I. Title.
ZA4150.L48 2013
025.04—dc23

                                                                                            2012013641

10 9 8 7 6 5 4 3 2 1—V056—14 13 12

ISBN 10:   0-205-86557-7
ISBN 13: 978-0-205-86557-4

To Tina,
Simon and Sarah,
Molly and Carlos,
and Pooka—
always new to me.

contents

CHAPTER 5   WIKIPEDIA   65

CHAPTER 6   BLOGGING   81

CHAPTER 7   FOURSQUARE AND HARDWARE   118

CHAPTER 9   THE DARK SIDE OF NEW NEW MEDIA   161

CHAPTER 10   POLITICS AND NEW NEW MEDIA   172

preface to second edition and acknowledgments

Why You Need This New Edition

The blindingly fast pace of media evolution mandated this second edition of *New New Media*. Since the first edition was published three years ago, Myspace has shrunk to a tenth of its size, Facebook has blossomed to nearing a billion users, and Foursquare and Reddit have come on strong.

And these new new media, along with stalwarts Twitter, YouTube, and Wikipedia, have had game-changing new consequences. The Tea Party, the Arab Spring, and Occupy Wall Street were all made possible in one way or another by new new media, and the way they empower consumers of information to become producers. Further, as the use of smart phones and tablets has skyrocketed, the ability to write, take photographs, and make videos and send them out to the world is now literally in almost everyone's hands.

This revolution in communication encompasses all levels of society. The president of the United States and the pope now tweet, as does the person sitting next to you on a train or standing in back of you in a supermarket line. Four billion videos are viewed daily on YouTube, and these include not only Justin Bieber's, but the family's next door, and if that family happened to be baby Charlie's from "Charlie bit my finger, again," that neighbor's video would have been viewed more than 427 million times since it was uploaded in 2007. New new media empower people in all things, trivial and profound.

Acknowledgments

People have become the ultimate knowledge resource in this new new media world. You can ask a question on Facebook or Twitter and often get an answer within seconds. I was fortunate to have many sources of knowledge in preparing the first edition—you can see them in the Preface to the First Edition, which follows—and I thank them here again. In addition, for this new edition, I thank Scott Sandridge, Steve Thompson, Ted Ollikkala, and Joe Vito Moubry, whom I've never met, but who provided valuable leads to information, from their vantage points on Twitter and Facebook. Thanks also to Jonathan Sanders, my colleague at the time at Fordham University, for being the first to call my attention to the use of new new media in Russia's "White Revolution" in the Summer of 2011.

I also thank my editor, Melissa Mashburn, and her assistant, Megan Hermida, for their hard work on this second edition. Special thanks, as well, to Abinaya Rajendran, project manager at Integra Software Services, and Christine Clark, copy editor, for their superb work.

My wife Tina Vozick continued as an invaluable asset in all aspects of this book, from alerting me to important new new media developments in the news to detailed discussion of the themes of this book to carefully reading the first and other drafts. Tina's work on Wikipedia, where she's made more than 23,000 edits to various articles, was once again indispensable in my revision of the "Wikipedia" chapter. Our children, Simon and Molly—now joined by their spouses Sarah Seltzer and Carlos Godoy—were also constant sources of inspiration and information.

****

Enjoy this snapshot of new new media in early 2012. If the past three years have been any measure, it will already be a snapshot of the past by the time you read this, but enough will endure into the future to be recognizable and, one hopes, of value as you make your way in this world almost daily under new creation.

PAUL LEVINSON
NEW YORK CITY
MAY 2012

preface to first edition and acknowledgments

A new book is sometimes an expression of ideas that its author has been thinking about, researching, and developing for decades. Other books are just the opposite—an embodiment of insights that came to the author just before writing the book and drove the writing of every page. Given that some of the media considered in *New New Media*—such as YouTube and Twitter—did not even exist in 2004, this book is clearly a recent inspiration. But the themes addressed in *New New Media*—most importantly, the impact of media that make all of us producers as well as consumers of news, opinion, and entertainment—also draw upon fundamentals of human communication that have been with us for millennia.

The notion of new new media first occurred to me late in the Summer of 2007. In those days, I was Chair of the Department of Communication and Media Studies at Fordham University, where I still enjoy being a professor, and Lance Strate was my Associate Chair for graduate studies. Lance and I were discussing why our department's courses in "new media" were suffering from low enrollments, and it dawned on me that these courses, despite their appellation, were focused on topics that were old: how to use HTML, the general impact of the Web and email, and so forth. These subjects were "new" in the mid-1990s. In contrast, in the summer of 2007, students and people at large were eager to talk about blogging, Facebook, and YouTube, and we had noticed many a student logging on to a social medium during classes in the prior Spring and Fall semesters. I said to Lance that we should begin offering courses in *new* new media. The following Spring, I taught a graduate course that examined how the 2008 presidential campaign in America was being fueled by blogging, Facebook, and YouTube.

Lance Strate played another formative role in this book. In the Fall of 2007, he gave my name to Aron Keesbury, an acquisitions editor who was looking for new books for CQ Press. I pitched several books to Aron, and he seized on *New New Media*. I sent him a provisional table of contents, and, although we were not able to come to mutually agreeable contractual terms, Aron deserves credit for seeing the need for this book and thanks for providing stimulating conversations about its topics.

In the same week that I met Aron, Charles Sterin came to Fordham University to videotape me, all day, for the *Mass Media Revolution* multimedia textbook he was writing and producing for Pearson books. Several months later, Chuck suggested that his editor, Jeanne Zalesky, might be interested in *New New Media*.

Jeanne has been an ideal editor. An author writes a book, and an editor commends it to a publisher and, in turn, guides the publisher in commending the book to the world. Jeanne's spirited and savvy championing of *New New Media* has been invaluable in the publication of this book. Thanks as well to Danielle Urban of Elm Street Publishing Services for fine project management.

In my dual capacity as author and professor, every book that I write—even my science fiction—is to some degree indebted to the inspiration of my students, now and over the years, to the questions they asked and the stimulus they provided. But *New New Media* is especially a product of the undergraduate classes I taught at Fairleigh Dickinson University in the 1970s and 1980s, the graduate classes I taught at the New School for Social Research and for the Connected Education Online Program in the 1980s and 1990s and, most significantly, the undergraduate and graduate courses I have been teaching at Fordham University the past decade. I cannot possibly thank every student by name. But two in particular—Mike Plugh and Yulia Golobokova—made contributions so valuable that their names not only appear here in my acknowledgments but also in the pages of the book.

Thanks, as well, to several practitioners of new new media who provided valuable insights and information—Barna Donovan, Emon Hassan, Ken Hudson, and Mark Molaro.

One of the themes of *New New Media* that I have been exploring for years is how digital and mobile communication have been blending business and personal, family life. My wife, Tina Vozick, has been an indispensable discussant and reader of this book prior to publication—in fact, the only reader of the complete book prior to its reaching my editor's desk—and her work on Wikipedia was especially helpful to me in the writing of that chapter. Our children, Simon and Molly, now adults, have also been a continuing resource. Simon introduced me to Facebook in 2004, and Molly was the one who first alerted me to the degree to which people her age, in their early 20s, watch television online.

That was several years ago, and *New New Media* is a snapshot and analysis of the extraordinary revolution in communication, and thus our lives, that has occurred since then and is still occurring almost daily. Consider, for example, that just about a month ago the first tweet was sent from an astronaut in outer space....

PAUL LEVINSON
NEW YORK CITY
JULY 2009

CHAPTER 1

Why "New New" Media?

THE VERY LAST THING I WROTE FOR THE FIRST EDITION OF *New New Media*, in June 2009, was the following:

> Here is a timeline of some of the major clashes of new media with dictatorial governments in the 20th and 21st centuries:

> 1942–43: The White Rose uses photocopying to tell the truth to Germans about the Nazi government. Fails to dislodge the Nazis.

> 1979: Audio cassettes of Ayatollah Khomeini distributed in Iran. Succeeds in fomenting successful revolution against Shah.

> 1980s: Samizdat video in the Soviet Union criticizes Soviet government. May have helped pave the way for Gorbachev's perestroika and glasnost, and end of Soviet rule.

> 1989: Email gets word out to the world about Tiananmen Square protests. Fails to dislodge Chinese government.

> 2001: Cellphones help mobilize peaceful opposition to President Estrada in Philippines. The Second People Power Revolution succeeds.

> 2009: Twitter and YouTube get word out to the world about Iranian opposition to reported election outcome. Result: not yet clear as of this writing.

What is clear today—almost three years later, at the beginning of 2012—is that although the Green Revolution in Iran has not yet succeeded there, it has burst forth in the Arab Spring and Occupy Wall Street movements in the United States of America and around the world. These are expressions of direct democracy, a form of government that began in Ancient Athens, was soon supplanted by the empires of Alexander the Great and Rome, and that has not been seen in many places since then. Instead, the democratic societies of the world—in the United States, Europe, and, increasingly in the 20th century, in other parts of the world—have been indirect or representative democracies, with elected officials expressing, in principle, the will of the people.

These representative democracies have been facilitated by what we today call "old media"—first, the printing press, and then, in the 20th century, radio and then television, the media of broadcasting. In these older media, which in the case of radio and television still hold almost as strong a position today as in the past, a few people at the top—editors, producers, or what are known in media theory as "gatekeepers"—make all the decisions about what information, news, and entertainment appear on their pages, airways, and screens. Their audiences—including us—can thus easily receive and consume information, but not publish it.

In contrast, the most recent, current media of the 21st century allow consumers to just as easily produce and disseminate as receive and consume information. But this is not true of all information on the Web. *The New York Times* website is as subject to its editorial control as the physical newspaper. Even Amazon and iTunes work with publishers, not consumers, for the sources of most of their books and music, although the ease with which authors can directly publish a book as a Kindle edition is beginning to change that. But on Facebook or Twitter, on YouTube or Google+, on Wikipedia or a blog, which anyone can create, the reader and the publisher are often the same person— a consumer/producer who now numbers in the high hundreds of millions around the world. This is why I call these media not just "new" but "new new" media, to distinguish the lack of power that new media such as Amazon and iTunes and *The New York Times* online give to producers versus the enormous power that "new new media," including Facebook, Twitter, and YouTube, put in everyone's hands.

The central theme of this second edition of *New New Media* is how this empowerment of everyone as producers and disseminators of information is continuing to change the ways all of us live, work, and play. The change ignited and facilitates not only Occupy Wall Street, but also the Tea Party—in many ways at the opposite end of the political spectrum in the United States—because the Tea Party stems from the same dissatisfaction with representative government, in a digital age in which new new media can give everyone a much more direct voice in decisions about society. And the change pertains not only to politics, but also to how we live our daily lives in the real offline world, where the restaurants in which we are dining can be known by everyone with whom we socialize—who "follows" us in some way on Facebook, Twitter, Foursquare— instantly and wherever we and they may be. Indeed, so integrated have our online and offline lives become, that it makes increasingly less sense to even use those terms. Wherever we may be, whether online or offline, whether tweeting about our actions in the real world or about something we just encountered online, we inhabit a new new media world in which both the digital and physical are close at hand.

Why "New New" Rather than "Social" Media?

Twitter, Facebook, and YouTube are regularly called "social media," so why use the term "new new media" to describe them and other media we examine in this book?

The media that allow consumers to become producers are undoubtedly social, and far more interactive than older, one-way media such as television. We tweet not only about what we do and think, but also in response to the tweets of others, whom we may or may not already know online or in person. "Friends"—much more likely digital than flesh-and-blood—are one of the primary components of new new media, and will receive considerable attention in this book.

But older media—whether just plain "new" such as Amazon and iTunes, or just plain "old" such as broadcasting and print—have significant social components as well. People always talk about the books they read, the music they listen to, the movies and television shows they see. Indeed, this often is done totally offline. If not social components of these older media, what are bookstore reading groups and watercooler talk about political candidates seen on television? Even conversing with a friend about what you're watching on television or reading in a newspaper is an example of the intrinsic social quality of media. To communicate, in other words, even to receive information one-way from a page or a screen, is to socialize.

So the social aspect of new new media, though crucial, and in much greater evidence than the social aspect of older media, is not unique enough in new new media to warrant our use of the terms "social media" and "new new media" interchangeably. In addition, other primary elements of new new media—such as the consumer becoming a producer—can easily be practiced by one person working alone, not socially, for example, writing a blog post or recording a video.

It is far too late to change the "social media" appellation that we hear daily, incessantly, in the older mass media to describe YouTube, Twitter, and Facebook. But we can try for a more discerning terminology in this book.

Guiding Principles of New New Media

But what are the distinguishing characteristics of these media—the common denominators of Facebook, Twitter, YouTube, Wikipedia, blogging, and the other media addressed in this book—that set them all apart, in different but overlapping ways, from older media?

Every Consumer Is a Producer: This is the central, underlying characteristic shared by all new new media. Anyone reading a blog can start a blog nearly instantly. A blog on MSNBC.com or on NYTimes.com is an example not of new new media but of new media. MSNBC's blogs are on the Web, which makes them new media. But their readers at most have a secondary, indirect impact on the words in the blog—they may be able to comment on the blog, but they cannot alter a blog post or create a new post or create a new blog on MSNBC.com. In contrast, a blog you create allows you to amend and remove any post, to create new ones, and to decide whether or not comments will be allowed—in other words, the blogger has all the powers of the traditional publisher over her or his blog. In the case of Wikipedia, not only do reader/editors have the power to edit the articles at any time, they, in fact, do this all the time.

But that is not the only defining characteristic of new new media. Other characteristics include the following:

You Get What You Don't Pay For: New new media are always free to the consumer and sometimes to the producer. Amazon and iTunes therefore again are examples not of new new media but new media, because the books and other items on Amazon, and the songs on iTunes, are for sale. In contrast, a video with a song on the new new medium YouTube is free. Blog host sites such as Blogspot and Wordpress are free to the blogs' producers. Wikipedia relies on funding drives (much like the Public Broadcasting Service) and is free to its readers/editors (who are often one and the same). Twitter relies on venture capital and advertising, and is free to its reader/writer users. Facebook has extensive advertising, has become a publicly owned corporation, and is free to its users. YouTube not only runs ads on its site, but also offers revenue-sharing options to anyone who uploads a video that does not infringe on someone else's copyright—the same Google AdSense system available to bloggers on any site—and YouTube is free to both viewers and uploaders of videos.

Traditional broadcast media have always been and continue to be free, having this significant characteristic in common with new new media, and making them more akin to new new media than Amazon and iTunes, which charge their customers. Cable television, however, on which traditional broadcast television is now available, charges its customers. Traditional print media also charge—even though they, like broadcast media, also rely on advertising—and some of them, such as *The New York Times*, have adopted a pay wall model for their online services (readers have to pay), with mixed results.

Competitive and Mutually Catalytic: As I detailed in *Human Replay: A Theory of the Evolution of Media* (Levinson, 1979; see also *The Soft Edge*, Levinson, 1997), media compete with one another for our time and patronage and live or die much as do living organisms in the Darwinian biological world. But as in the natural world, where organisms live in symbiotic relationships—bees feed on plants and pollinate them, and we enjoy the flowers and the honey—media in general, and new new media in particular, not only compete with one another but also work to each other's benefit. A post on a blog with an embedded YouTube video can be automatically sent to Twitter, which generates a one-line message with the blog's title, first line, and link, which in turn can be set to show up on Facebook and LinkedIn, and via widgets or special applications on other blogs. Each of these new new media supports the others, even as it competes with all the others for our attention. Further, new new media are similarly competitive and synergistic with older media. Bloggers take readers away from books and viewers away from television, but can write books and appear on television themselves, or at the very least review books and television shows on their blogs. And newly created media can also spur older media to change. A "ton" of privacy alterations were instituted by Facebook due to Google+, commented New Movement Media (Bodnar, 2011).

More than Search Engines and Email: Google and similar search engines and email systems are the nervous systems of the Web, the online equivalents of Microsoft Internet Explorer, Firefox, Chrome, and other systems on our computers that we use to traverse the Internet. Email and searching are essential to new new media, but they are not new new media themselves. Web-based money systems such as PayPal also can be crucial to new new media but similarly work as their service systems rather than as new new media in their own right. Although Google and PayPal are free—and users can customize the operation of their email, searching, and, in the case of PayPal, banking procedures—these systems cannot be fundamentally created or even tailored by their users in the way that readers can be writers and editors of Wikipedia or can choose what to put on their Facebook Timelines, and decide what varying level of access to give current and potential Facebook readers. In the same way, although group members can write to Yahoo message boards, the moderators of these groups have complete, old-media control over the discussions, with the power to remove any given message. Applications such as Google's AdSense can play specific supporting roles for new new media—in the case of AdSense, earning money from blogs and YouTube videos—and we will examine the value and impact of those applications for the new new media they support. Google+ is a Twitter/Facebook-like system, or a new new medium that is operated by Google, and we will look at it as well in this book.

New New Media Ultimately Beyond the User's Control: But new new media do require underlying platforms beyond the control of their consumer/producers—whether Facebook mechanics, blogging systems, YouTube formats, Wikipedia editing procedures, and the like—even though the ratio of user input to a fixed system is much more in favor of the user in new new media than in infrastructures such as Google and Yahoo. When the new new medium is operating well (no glitches) and as expected (no changes from the last time we used it), we tend to forget that the medium is under someone else's control. But as soon as a medium changes any aspect of its interface, as Facebook has done several times a year, we become aware that we are not in charge, and painfully aware if we do not like the change. The same occurs when a medium ceases operation (as Vox did in 2010), or when it is purchased by another organization that puts the acquired medium out of business. (Google purchased Aardvark, the question-and-answer medium, in 2010, and shelved it in 2011.)

New New Media Encompass Prior New Media Principles

One of the defining characteristics of even the oldest new media—what has been clear since they arose over a decade ago in the mid-1990s—is that people can use, enjoy, and benefit from them on the user's rather than the medium's timetable, once the content has been posted online. This provided and still offers a big advantage over having to wait for the delivery of your morning newspaper, for a radio station to play your favorite song, or for the weekly broadcast of a series you like on television. Those "media by appointment" were and are characteristic of all old media, and the freeing of users from some of this appointment bondage by TiVo and DVR represents a significant step in the evolution of television from old to new medium.

New new media give their users the same control over when and where to get text, sound, and audiovisual content as provided by new media. Indeed, new new media continue all the advantages that new media have over old media. But new new media do more. Unlike new media, where the user has to wait for the content to be produced by someone else—whether a book written by someone else that has to be ordered or downloaded on Amazon, whether a song written and recorded by someone else that has to be downloaded on iTunes—the true or fully empowered new new media user also has the option of producing content, and consuming content produced by hundreds of millions of other new new media consumer/producers. This constitutes a de facto worldwide community of consumer/producers that did not exist with older media.

The Order and Content of the Chapters

The order of the chapters in the first edition of *New New Media*, completed in June 2009, provides a snapshot of the comparative importance and impact of the new new media back then:

1. Why "New New" Media?
2. Blogging
3. YouTube

Alexa, a free online service that ranks specific Web media with an algorithm that takes into account number of visitors, links on other websites, and so forth, had the following ranking in December 2008 for new new media examined in the first edition of this book: YouTube #3, Facebook #5, Myspace #7, Wikipedia #8, Digg #294, Twitter #669, and Second Life #3354 (Yahoo was ranked #1, and Google #2).

The order of chapters in this second edition of *New New Media*, completed in early 2012, is a story of how dramatically and quickly the different new new media themselves have comparatively evolved in under three years. Other than this opening chapter, no chapter in this edition is in the same place as in the first edition. Further, some chapters have been removed as standalone chapters and compressed, and others—new chapters—have been added. The new chapter order and reasons for these changes are as follows:

"Facebook" (born in 2004) is the subject of the second chapter in this new edition of *New New Media*, moving from 7 to 2 in chapter order (but because both editions have the introductory chapter as 1, Facebook has really moved from 6 to 1), and from #5 to #2 in Alexa ranking as of December 2011. (Google as a whole moved up from #2 to #1 in Alexa, and Yahoo dropped from #1 to #5.) At the time the original edition was written in 2009, Facebook had just pulled ahead of Myspace in number of users, but the two were pretty much the same in terms of impact on the world. Today, in 2012, Facebook is in a new new media class of its own. With more than 800 million active users as of July 2011, 4.27 billion U.S. dollars a year revenue in 2011 (1 billion of which was profit), and a highly successful, award-winning movie (*The Social Network*) released in 2010 about its creation and development, Facebook towers over all other social media and has become, along with Twitter and YouTube, all but synonymous with social media (i.e., new new media) in the public mind. Further, Facebook more than any social medium has finely attuned, defined, and refined the notion of an online "Friend" and its relation to in-person friends, and continues to do so with all manner of tinkering and changes on almost a monthly basis. "Friendship" in new new media is one of the central themes of this book.

"Twitter" (2006), the eighth chapter in the original edition of this book, jumps to chapter 3 in the current edition, and has soared from #669 to #10 in Alexa. At more than 300 million users as of 2011, it is less than half the user-size of Facebook, but with 1.6 billion search queries a day on the Web—searches for something that was tweeted— Twitter is in many ways just as prominent as Facebook, and in some ways more important, because it provides easy access to the tweets of friends as well as prominent politicians and celebrities. Google+, launched in June 2011 by Google, has characteristics of both Facebook (extensive profiles) and Twitter (ease of posting with and without links), but is more like Twitter, and will be discussed in the Twitter chapter.

"YouTube" (2005) moved from the third to the fourth chapter in this book, holding steady at #3 in Alexa, even though it has become far more significant in the world at large than it was in 2009. It is in fourth place in this edition of *New New Media* only because Facebook and Twitter have become even more important. With more than three billion videos viewed daily at the end of 2011—in contrast to 1.2 billion a day as of June 2009—YouTube is arguably bigger than Facebook and Twitter together. But it is bigger in a different way—videos engage the viewer in a manner that is very different from the written word—and I place it as the third leg of the overarching triad of new new media that are changing our world.

"Wikipedia," moving from chapter 4 to 5, but up from #8 to #6 in Alexa ranking, opened online shop in January 2001, which makes it the oldest specific new new medium considered in this book. Like YouTube, Wikipedia has increased in importance and usage since 2009, and was placed a bit further back in this edition of *New New Media* only because of the more extraordinary growth of Facebook, Twitter, and YouTube. But Wikipedia is unique among new new media in ways that reach beyond its age and number of users: (1) First, although blogging competes with older media such as newspapers, and YouTube with television, the new new medium of Wikipedia is a head-on challenge to one of the most venerable media in the past few hundred years: the encyclopedia. As a repository of authoritative information, an encyclopedia such as the *Britannica* operates (now online only) as the epitome of an expert-driven, top-down, vetted media system. In contrast, Wikipedia is literally written by its readers (100,000 reader/writers out of 365 million readers who could be reader/writers if they wished, in 2012; see Wikipedia, 2012, for current statistics). (2) Although Wikipedia's readers daily write new articles (a total of 20 million in 283 different language editions independently written worldwide as of 2012) on a wide variety of topics, most of the writing on Wikipedia is editing—correcting, expanding, tightening—of previously written articles. This vetting by the world at large is another one of the prime principles of new new media. (3) Wikipedia is also the most consistent in its denial of the old-media, professionally produced method of generating articles. Although reader/editors work in a loose hierarchy, with some editors having more power than others, there are few articles on Wikipedia in which even the newest reader/editor can have no input. In contrast, many of the videos on YouTube are professionally produced, and traditional press media such as *The New York Times* publish blogs daily and more often.

In "Blogging" (1997 or earlier), formerly the second chapter in the book, now the sixth, we examine the first new new medium that is not a specific system but a general, new kind of writing and publishing. It also is the oldest new new medium—the only one that harks back to the 1990s. Its mechanisms, the ways it empowers the writer, are a blueprint for all subsequent new new media, which in one way or another can all be seen as derived from blogging. This is the reason blogging was put at the front of the first edition of this book. Its movement further into the book reflects, again, not a diminishing of its importance, but the greater rate of growth of Facebook, Twitter, and YouTube. More than 165 million blogs were active in 2011, up from 130 million in 2008. Blogging—written and video—also brings to the fore the question of what and who is a journalist, and therefore entitled to First Amendment protections. If we agree with Marshall McLuhan that "the medium is the message," then the practice of reporting the news makes the practitioner a journalist, whatever the specific medium of expression, be it paper press, broadcast television, blog, or video streaming and upload to YouTube. Such issues have relevance to the role of new new media in Occupy Wall Street.

"Foursquare" (2009), currently ranking #782 in Alexa, makes its premiere appearance in this second edition of *New New Media* as chapter 7, with 10 million users in 2011. As a "location-based" medium, in which users let their "Friends" know where they are by "checking in" from the store, restaurant, movie, or even street corner they may be standing on, Foursquare can be seen as an offshoot of the "I'm at Tony's Pizza" aspect of Twitter—or the use of Twitter to tell the world nothing more interesting than where you are. But because Foursquare is devoted exclusively to announcing your location in the real world, it represents the most evolved form of digital/real-world integration, in contrast to Twitter, which consists mostly of digital-only or digital-about-digital or digital-about-other-media communication. Further, Foursquare is the first and thus far only major new new medium to require a smart phone or tablet such as an iPad—you cannot "check in" from a desktop or even a laptop—which underscores its connection to physical place and travel through the real world. The cutting-edge hardware of new new media—iPhones, BlackBerrys, Androids, iPads, Kindles, and so forth—were assessed in their own chapter 13 in the first edition of *New New Media*, but will here be examined in the Foursquare chapter.

"Smaller Potatoes" is the title of chapter 8 of this edition of *New New Media*, and it is not the name of any new new media system. Rather, we consider in this chapter several new new media that have diminished in importance since the first edition, but still warrant analysis in this book. Myspace (2003) now serves as a textbook example, literally, of the decline and fall of a new new medium in our still nascent new new media age. Myspace had the greatest number of visitors to social media sites from 2005 through the beginning of 2008, and had its own chapter 6 in the first edition of this book, ahead of Facebook. But Myspace had already dropped below Facebook by the time the first edition of *New New Media* was published in 2009, and it has since dropped to 30 million users (from #5 to #138 in Alexa rank), and now functions primarily as a music site. We will look at the reasons for Myspace's decline—selling for 35 million dollars in 2011 in contrast to the billions of dollars Facebook is expected to raise in 2012 from public investors—and compare Myspace to other music sites such as Reverbnation and Soundcloud. Digg (2004) had its own chapter 5 in the first edition of this book—ahead of both Myspace and Facebook—with some 236 million visitors in 2008, and a top 20 Alexa ranking at the height of its influence in the U.S. 2008 presidential election. As a news site in which users vote stories up and down ("digg" and "bury") with the most successful stories getting on the Digg front page, Digg represented and still represents another way in which consumers (readers) are becoming producers (editors) in the new new media age. But for a variety of reasons that we will explore, Digg fell to 50 million users a year in 2011, dipping below its long-standing rival Reddit, which has played a significant role in the dissemination of information about Occupy Wall Street, and which we also look at in this chapter. (Digg had already fallen to #294 on Alexa by the end of 2008, and is currently up to #194, with Reddit surpassing it at #114.) Second Life (2003), the system in which people play, buy and sell products, and engage in online social activities via their avatars, was not too large even in 2009 (#3354 in Alexa), when it was given its own chapter 9 in this book, and it had more than 82,000 concurrent users online ("in-world") at the beginning of that year. Second Life's number of concurrent users began dropping that year and by 2010 averaged 54,000, with no figures available for 2011 as of this writing. But its Alexa ranking has risen to #2608, and Second Life remains the best example of complete immersion in a digital realm. It is in that sense at the opposite end of the new new media spectrum from Foursquare. Podcasting, which can be considered an acoustic or audio form of blogging, was accorded its own chapter—10—in the first edition. Since 2009, however, audio podcasts have increasingly given way to videos or vidcasts, for dissemination on YouTube or other video new new media sites. The many qualities that podcasting and vidcasting have in common will be discussed in the YouTube chapter. The uniquely acoustic elements of podcasting will be assessed in the "Smaller Potatoes" chapter.

The general position of both the original and current editions of this book is that new new media provide significant, often revolutionary, benefits to the burgeoning number of people in the world who employ these media for work, play, and education. But new new media, like all human tools, can also be put to personally and socially destructive purposes, including criminal and lethal actions. These range from new, digital renditions of long-practiced bad behavior, such as cyberbullying and cyberstalking, to the straightforward use of social media for facilitation of crimes, including robbery and murder. We explore some of these abuses and crimes, as well as possible remedies that arise from new new media, in chapter 9, "The Dark Side of New New Media." We also examine some uses of new new media, such as Wikileaks, which are deemed by some to be destructive to society but by others to be bona fide expressions of the press, protected by the First Amendment.

The first edition of this book was conceived in the Fall of 2007, when the campaign that elected Barack Obama president of the United States was already underway. Obama at the time was called the first "cybergenic" president (Saffo, 2008; see also Levinson, quoted in Zurawik, 2008), but since then the knack of using new new media has been learned by all political persuasions in the United States and the world at large. The concluding chapter of this new edition—chapter 10, "Politics and New New Media"— examines the use of new new media by the Tea Party, Republican as well as Democratic candidates in the American election campaigns of 2012, and what in the long run may be even more important: Occupy Wall Street, the Arab Spring, and the resurgence of direct democracy around the world. We also continue to discuss in this chapter the role of the First Amendment in protecting new new media journalists and their coverage of Occupy Wall Street events.

Speed in the Evolution of New New Media and Hardware

The sheer speed in the evolution of new new media is evident in the previously noted shifts in importance and existence of new new media systems and sites. YouTube and Twitter, which played such an important role in the U.S. presidential election in 2008, given the relative lack of use of these media by the McCain campaign in contrast to Obama's, did not even exist in the election of 2004. The role they will play in the 2012 election is therefore not predictable except in the very general sense that they will have major, likely decisive, impact—with tweets heralding breaking political news; YouTube bringing video coverage for first sight and review 24 hours a day; and Facebook, blogging, Wikipedia, and the rest providing context and elaboration of rapidly changing stories and events.

But the evolution of new new media is happening so fast that the constellation of the media themselves will change between the time I am writing this second edition of *New New Media* and the time you are reading it. Myspace faded from the central picture between the first and second editions—between 2009 and 2012. Foursquare did not exist when most of the first edition was written. Facebook and Twitter, highly significant already in 2009, have exploded in size and impact since then.

Pinterest, founded in limited closed beta (not open to the public) in 2010, did not even exist when the first edition of *New New Media* was published. It was not in my early drafts for this second edition in 2011, but "has skyrocketed since mid-2011" in number of users and their level of engagement (MarketingProfs, 2012), and is now in chapter 6 in the photographic blogging section. It could well have its own chapter in the third edition of this book.

Meanwhile, the hardware upon which new new media live has more than kept pace with the evolution of the systems. The iPhone, the breakthrough technology for reaching the Web and thus new new media in the palm of your hand, was just introduced in July 2007. It was soon joined by smart BlackBerrys and Android phones, and by a very different kind of new new media device, the iPad, in early 2010. iPads or tablets dispense with the smart phone model—built on the cellphone—and offer bigger screens, far more suitable for writing, reading, and viewing images, television shows, movies, and YouTube videos. Both smart phones and tablets continue to evolve, offering new models on almost a yearly basis.

The success of these new devices—15 million iPads sold by March 2011, when the iPad 2 was released, and 108 million iPhones sold by then—conveys at least one thing about new new media of which we can be 100 percent certain: they will continue to play crucial and increasingly important roles in our lives.

The Prime Methodology: Learning by Doing

As was the case for the first edition, most of the sources cited in this second edition of *New New Media* are articles on the Web, for the simple reason that books are inadequate to the task of assessing media which are evolving almost monthly to new forms and functions. *The Obama Victory: How Media, Money, and Message Shaped the 2008 Election* (Kenski, Hardy, Jamieson, 2010), for example, has no listings in its index for any of the new new media described in the previous sections, other than YouTube, which appears on just 6 out of 314 pages. Further, given that most books take the better part of a year or more from their writing to reaching readers on paper and screens, a book even when appropriately focused is inevitably a snapshot of the past, however recent. The same, of course, is true of this or any edition of *New New Media*, and the reader is advised to look at my blog post, "What's Newer than *New New Media*" (Levinson, 2009–2012), for a continuing update. Many of the developments discussed in the current edition were first highlighted on that blog, and this will continue for future editions.

Fortunately, all media on the Web—including old-fashioned, editorially driven articles—can instantly report and analyze new developments, in any area, including new new media. But beyond the use of the Web rather than books as a primary resource, the "research" conducted for this book is consistent with the reader or researcher becoming a producer in new new media, and with the American pragmatic philosopher John Dewey's principle (e.g., Dewey, 1925) that we learn best by practicing, working in, or doing the activity that we study. Indeed, the prime source of much of the information in this book comes from what I have learned and continue to learn in my excursions—my work as a writer, producer, and publicist—in all of the new new media considered in this book. There is, of course, always the possibility that my, or any individual researcher's, experience as a practitioner may not be representative of the world's at large. Where relevant, I have thus noted where my status as a professor and author of this and other books may have colored my experiences as a new new media practitioner. And the citations from other sources about the subjects considered in this book also serve as a check on the accuracy of my own program of researching this book by "doing" the new new media.

A brief list of initiations of my new new media experiences follows:

I joined Facebook in April 2005 on the advice of my son, Simon, who was then a student at Harvard (where Facebook began), and on the strength of my .edu account at Fordham University, where I was and still am a professor. In those days, only people with .edu email addresses could join Facebook.

Facebook long since changed that requirement, and, indeed, one of the hallmarks of all new new media is that anyone (at least anyone with a stated age of 13 or older) can join and then play or work on them. I joined Myspace in May 2005 but did not start participating there until the publication of my most recent science fiction novel, *The Plot to Save Socrates,* in February 2006. I put up my first blog post on Myspace that month. I had two reasons for participating on Myspace: research for the purpose of writing about Myspace, and promoting my novel. This dual purpose points to one of the other characteristics of new new media: their encouragement of multitasking, or doing more than one thing at the same time. As William James (1890, p. 462), another pragmatic American philosopher and psychologist, noted back in the 19th century, our brains are wired to embrace the "great blooming, buzzing confusion" of the world.

I've been appearing on the older media of national cable and network television since my appearance on Jesse Ventura's short-lived program on MSNBC in October 2003, and I began uploading video segments of my various appearances on television to YouTube in August 2006. I also discovered, that month, articles about me and *The Plot to Save Socrates* that had been posted on Wikipedia. I soon after joined it, and wrote Wikipedia articles on subjects and people ranging from *Village Voice* reporter and Pulitzer Prize winner Teresa Carpenter to Paul Feiner, town supervisor of Greenburgh, New York, and got involved in a heated debate about whether the podcast *Jawbone Radio* deserved to have an article. (I thought it should but lost that debate. But I soon after won a debate to retain an article about Podcast Pickle, a podcast-hosting service and message board.)

I had begun my own, first podcast—*Light On Light Through,* about popular culture, television, politics, "the works," as my blurb for it says—in October 2006. A month later I added *Levinson News Clips* for television reviews, and by the end of that year I had a third podcast, *Ask Lev,* which offers tips to writers.

I began *Infinite Regress,* my first and still primary independent blog—not associated with Myspace, Salon, and so forth—in November 2006. By January 2012, I had posted more than 1,900 entries on InfiniteRegress.tv, which attracted more than 900,000 readers. One of the ways of attracting readers is to post links and brief summaries of your blog posts on Digg and Reddit, which I joined in December 2006. Twitter is another way, and I began tweeting in the summer of 2007. Applications—"apps" or special programs—can be employed to send titles and links of blog posts, YouTube videos, or anything of interest on the Web directly to Twitter and other sites, which in turn can be automatically relayed to sites such as Facebook, LinkedIn, and Myspace.

In November 2007, I was invited by Ken Hudson to give a lecture about new new media in Second Life. I joined and discovered that I had to outfit my avatar with hair, body type, gender, and clothes, as well as make sure my microphone was working. I joined Foursquare in July 2010, and "check in" with my BlackBerry Torch. I began using Google+ in much the same way as Twitter and Facebook in September 2011.

I continue to maintain accounts on all of these systems, not only because I intend to draw upon them for updates to this book, but also because I enjoy and otherwise profit from my work and experiences on them. All are free and available to everyone—characteristic of all new new media. And anyone who gets an account on any of these systems can use them to produce as well as receive information. Readers who want to learn more about these new new media are advised to join and use them.

A good place to start would be Facebook, subject of the next chapter, in the unlikely event that you're not already a member.

CHAPTER 2

Facebook

"IF FACEBOOK WERE A NATION, IT WOULD BE THE WORLD'S THIRD largest behind only China and India. Hundreds of new people join every hour," Sally Deenan aptly observed in *Success* magazine in April 2011. A success indeed—more than 800 million users by July 2011, third in population after China and India but attained in just eight years rather than thousands of years. Facebook reported a profit of one billion dollars in 2011, and in February 2012, its long-anticipated "IPO"—initial public offering, or stock market launch—was expected to get Facebook at least five billion dollars in investment money from the public (Szalai, 2012), a lot more than the 1.7 billion dollars Google raised when it went public in 2004. Facebook is community writ large, new new media style.

In the Fall of 2011, Tiffany Shlain urged fans of her new documentary movie *Connected* to go not to the elaborate Web page set up for the movie, but to the movie's newly posted Facebook page. This good advice highlights the difference between a Web page, however attractive and detailed, and a Facebook page, however newly created. The Web page may offer better imagery, longer movie clips, and extensive control of the page for the creator, but it lacks Facebook's community and its potential for building communities. The professional Web page is an old new medium. Facebook is a new new medium par excellence.

Community is about human relationships—a group of people becomes a community when its members have some common, enduring connection. The two most profound kinds of connection in human life are family and friendship. Both can and do migrate or extend from the real world to the digital world—our offline family and friends can be part of our online communities—but new new media have also invented a new kind of friendship, one that never existed before, and indeed exists only online. Except "exists" is too weak a word for this phenomenon, because digital "Friends" flourish like wildflowers online—or like weeds, if you consider the online Friend secondary to in-person friends (I do not, I just consider them different). And no online environment has been more conducive to and defining of digital friendship than Facebook.

The Irresistible Appeal of "Friends"

Friendster, the oldest social medium (2002), put the word "friend" in its name (the rest of which comes from Napster, the highly popular, free MP3 music file-sharing site at the time). Friendster attracted three million users in its first three months of its existence, and continues today as a social gaming site highly successful in Southeast Asia.

Myspace opened its online doors a year later, in 2003. Like Friendster, Myspace was free. And its tagline was "a place for friends." Myspace had exceeded Friendster in number of users in 2004, the year that Mark Zuckerberg launched Facebook.

I joined Facebook in early 2005—not to find in-person friends online, not to make new online Friends, and not even to promote my science fiction novels. I joined because my son was an early Facebook enthusiast. He was a student at Harvard, where Zuckerberg was also a student in 2004. In those days, only people with .edu email addresses could get accounts on Facebook, and most of the people on Facebook were students at colleges and universities. I was able to join because, as a Fordham University professor, I had an .edu email address. So my Facebook membership was motivated by family and made possible by my profession. Friendship, offline and online, had nothing to do with it. But that would soon change.

Today, I have nearly 5000 Friends on Facebook (5000 is the maximum that Facebook allows). Some 25 of these are family members, 100 are former students, and 50 are colleagues at Fordham University or professors I have met at least once from other universities. Add to that maybe 75 people consisting of real friends in my life, and others who would better be described as acquaintances, including people I have met in person just once or twice. That's 250 out of 5000. And of those 4750, I interact with at most 20–25 in a given week, and at most another 75–100 once or twice in a given year. As I am writing this, on December 31, 2011, I just wished everyone a Happy New Year in my "Status." Of the 20 Friends who have already "Liked" that—"Like" is a formal signification of approval on Facebook, YouTube, and many social media—I have met only two in person, and just once for each (Michele Lang, science fiction author, at a convention two years ago, and David Sobelman, a filmmaker, at a screening of a film he made five years ago about Marshall McLuhan). Of the remaining 18 people I've never met in person, I consider two to be close online Friends. As the "Likes" continue to come in, I expect the ratio to tilt far more in the direction of people I not only never met in person but also barely know online.

Yet all of these people are my Friends on Facebook.

What Does Online "Friendship" Mean?

A purely online Friend, even one you interact with and have come to "know" online, has only one significant thing in common with offline, in-person friends—a sharing of one or more keen interests. Otherwise, I recall the response I received shortly after I began actively participating on Myspace in 2006 and invited someone with tastes in science fiction very similar to mine to be Friends. "Uh, are we, like, going to hang out?" he replied, sarcastically. I apologized, and said I regretted that the invitation to be a Friend implied a connection that went far beyond a coincidence of interest in science fiction.

In addition to sharing one or more interests with you—sports, clothing, food, shopping, relationships, whatever—you and your offline friends have this in common: you know what each other looks like, what you sound like. These key, profound character-istics are all effortlessly tied together in the package we call "friend," or person we know in person, in the flesh, in the street, wherever, but not necessarily online, and with no batteries or any sort of equipment needed.

Although Facebook "Profiles"—the calling cards of everyone on Facebook and other new new media—are filled with photos, and can have links to audio tracks with voices, there is no guarantee that these are really the images and voices of the name in the Profile. Indeed, the only way anyone can know for sure if an online Friend with a given name is really the same person with the offline name is to meet that online Friend in person (not recommended, except in very public places, for obvious safety reasons, which we will explore in detail in "The Dark Side of New New Media").

You even can receive Friend requests from "people" you know are not real, as I did from "Don Draper" from *Mad Men* and "Kate" from *Lost*. I have also been online Friends with several "people" by the name of Socrates, who died in 399 BC. And I've been not only a recipient but also a creator of such unreal online personas.

"Sierra Waters" is a lead character in my published works *The Plot to Save Socrates* (Levinson, 2006) and "Unburning Alexandria" (Levinson, 2008). I established accounts under her name on Facebook and Myspace in 2008. It was crystal clear to anyone who looked at the Profiles for Sierra that she was a character in my fiction. Nonetheless, "Sierra" received more than one email from men on Myspace—or accounts with male names—asking her for sexual favors.

Online friendship on Facebook and other new new media can therefore correspond to a continuum of offline characteristics: your online Friend is already your offline friend (or member of your family), or is already an offline friend of one of your offline friends, or has no connection whatsoever to anyone you already know in person, or is the name of an historical figure or a straight-up fictitious character.

Facebook more than any other social medium has grappled with the complex nature of online friendship, and has attempted to fine-tune online friendships to better correspond to their offline realities.

Fine-Tuning Online Friendship

As of January 2012, Facebook offered three options for online Friends—"Friends," "Close Friends," and "Acquaintances," as well as an impersonal "Subscription" option, and opportunity for individuals to set up "Pages" (or have a Page created for them) as an Author, Public Figure, Politician, even a book or a movie title, or whatever. Google+ offers similar "Friends," "Family," "Acquaintance," and "Following" (the equivalent of "Subscription") choices for its "Circles," as well as an option to set up pages for busi-nesses, books, and so forth. Twitter offers only a "Follow" option, which may or may not be mutual.

As mentioned earlier, Facebook has long had a limit of 5000 on the total number of "Friends" one could have (actually, the 5000 total includes number of "Friends" as well as number of "Pages" and so forth "Liked"), a de facto recognition of the obvious fact that no human being could have more than a fraction of 5000 friends in the real world. In contrast, there is no limit to the number of Subscribers an individual can have, nor is there a limit on the number of Likes a Public Page can receive. Subscriptions and Pages, then, serve as outer boundaries on the construct of Friends—"Friend"ly kinds of areas, where people can attach themselves to people of interest, or follow them, without maintaining the online fiction of friendship.

"Close Friends" and "Acquaintances" on Facebook, on the other hand, parse or divide the construct of online friendship into smaller, more apt groups. Just as in real-life friends, where some are close, and some are so casual that they might more accurately be called acquaintances, these same words describe the three intensities of friendship online.

Further, Facebook's extensive privacy settings allow users to specify and distinguish what Close Friends, Friends, and Acquaintances, as well as users identified as "family" (intended only for people who are real family members) can see of the user's photographs, Timeline posts, and other online activities. Given that anyone can capture photos and information from any Facebook Profile to which they have access, and distribute such information as far and wide as they please, such privacy settings are inherently porous.

The Facebook "Group" and Its Evolution

Community requires a coalescing of some number of individuals into a group, in which an interest or interests shared by friends on a one-to-one basis are shared, discussed, and furthered by the many, or the members of the group.

Groups on Facebook are focused on most of the interests known to humanity, ranging from popular culture passions such as movies, TV shows, and music to cutting-edge social and political issues.

The Facebook Group "Barack Obama (One Million Strong for Barack)" continued to grow even after the election in November 2008, and as of May 2009 had more than a million members. By January 2012, this Group had long been replaced by a "Barack Obama (Politician)" Page, with more than 24 million "Likes." The "Mitt Romney (Politician)" Page had more than one million "Likes," Rick Santorum's just 55,000 (the day after he came in a close 8-vote second to Romney in the Iowa Caucus, which later turned out to be a narrow win for Santorum), and Ron Paul (who came in third in Iowa) some 24,000.

Why a "Page" rather than a "Group" on Facebook? The "Page" represents an attempt to better define a "Group," in the same way that Facebook has tried to more accurately define and refine online "Friendship." A Group implies individuals who want to take some active role in promoting the Group's interest or purpose. But most members of big Facebook Groups did little more in the Group than express their general keen interest in the Group's theme or purpose. "Liking" a Page is a more accurate reflection of this passive participation.

But Facebook has long been more than just an American social medium, and its Groups serve as vehicles of social action all around the world. As Eric Shawn reported on Fox News in December 2008, twelve million people "took to the streets" in 190 cities around the world in February 2008 to protest Colombia's terrorist group FARC, all in response to Oscar Morales's organization of the event in the Facebook Group "One Million Voices Against FARC," in what can now be unmistakably seen in retrospect as a precursor of the Arab Spring and Occupy Wall Street. Jared Cohen of the U.S. State Department explained to Shawn that, on Facebook, "you can be an activist from your bedroom," but that misses the point that the new new media activist has a seamless interface between the streets and the screen. On New Year's Eve 2012 (that is, beginning December 31, 2011), I watched Tim Pool's video streaming of NYPD (New York Police Department) officers arresting protesters in Manhattan. He was in the street, I was at home, both part of the same OWS community.

Any user can set up a Group or Page on Facebook, at no charge, in just a minute or two. You come up with a topic, write a brief description, perhaps a paragraph or two about current developments, upload a picture, and start inviting your Friends.

To appreciate just how easy this is, whatever the subject, consider the following:

I returned home late on Friday evening of the Thanksgiving 2008 weekend, the third day of a terrorist attack and crisis in Mumbai, India, and was looking for the latest news coverage on my favorite all-news television station, MSNBC. What I got instead was MSNBC's "Doc Bloc"—in this case, canned footage from several years ago, called "Caught on Camera."

I posted several blogs about this problem, such as "MSNBC Runs Canned Doc Bloc as Mumbai Burns," on *Infinite Regress* (Levinson, 2008), and discovered, via comments posted and email, that many other people felt the same way. We all wanted MSNBC to provide 24/7 news coverage; our day and age and world require no less. (See chapter 9, "The Dark Side of New New Media," for a discussion of how Facebook and Twitter, in contrast to MSNBC, provided crucially important initial coverage of the Mumbai terrorist attack and its consequences.)

MSNBC had started in the 1990s as a partnership of the Internet and television, or a marriage of old (NBC) and new (Microsoft—MS) media. I decided to see if I could harness the social power of new new media—in this case, Facebook—to influence programming on television. On December 1, 2008, I created a Facebook Group called "Stop the Doc Bloc on MSNBC," provided a description much like the preceding—"I returned home late Friday . . ."—and concluded: "Let's see if we here on Facebook, perhaps just by joining this group, can get MSNBC to do what's best for its viewers and itself—stop the doc bloc—give us news! Tell your news junkie friends about this FB group!"

I invited close to 1500 of my then 1600 Friends on Facebook. Users are allowed to be in only a maximum of 300 Groups, which was the reason my other 100 Friends could not receive invitations. I downloaded a public domain image of a red stop sign, used the free GIMP program (which works much like Photoshop) to write the words "DOC BLOC" under the word "STOP" on the sign, and uploaded the image to the Group. Within two hours, the Group had more than 50 members. Twenty-four hours later, the Group had 150 members—at least 15 of whom were not on my initial invitation list. This is viral marketing in action—in this case, for a shared cause. Whenever someone on Facebook joins a Group, a "notification" about that is published on the joiner's Page and can be seen by all of his or her Friends in their "Ticker." If they find the Group of interest, they can join, and the cycle is reinitiated.

As of May 2009, "Stop the Doc Bloc" had expanded only to a little more than 300 members, and MSNBC had not changed its weekend programming one bit. As of January 2012, the inactive Group shrunk to 265 members—the last previous post was in October 2010—but MSNBC had cut back significantly on its Doc Bloc, especially on Fridays, when it now has live news programming through 10 p.m. Not every Group succeeds completely—or even partially.

But the power of Facebook Groups is nonetheless undeniable, so much so that the oldest media and their proponents also used Facebook Groups to further their causes. Mark Hunter pointed out the irony, in his *Podcastmatters Social Media* podcast (Hunter, 2009), of the "Don't Let Newspapers Die" Cause on Facebook (a "Cause" is a special kind of Group), with the motto "Save a Journalist, Buy a Newspaper." Ironic, yes, to employ one of the very new new media—though it's not clear how many people get their news from Facebook—that is putting the endangered object of your cause out of business. On the other hand, it cannot hurt, and the formation of this Cause-Group certainly reflects an understanding, on the part of newspaper advocates, of the power of new new media. As of May 2009, "Don't Let Newspapers Die" had a little more than 80,000 members. As of January 2012, the motto and cause had taken up residence on another new new medium—aptly named "causes.com"—where it has more than 100,000 members. Whether the cause will succeed is still not clear. (See chapter 6, "Blogging," for more on the prospects of survival for newspapers in the digital age.)

As a last example, for now, of the use of Facebook Groups for social and political causes, I was invited in November 2011 to a newly formed Group, "The Fordham 99% Club," by a Fordham University colleague, Mark Naison, whom I only knew in passing at the time. The Group had been formed at the suggestion of Ira Schor, Naison's colleague, who wanted to create a "place" for people who were unable to physically participate in Occupy Wall Street events, but wanted to play an active part in the movement (another example of the intermingling of the real and virtual worlds in new new media). The Group had close to 200 members in January 2012, after it began admitting users with similar interests who were not Fordham students or faculty, and serves not only as forum for discussion, but a repository of information about Occupy Wall Street events in New York and beyond.

Facebook Friends and Groups as Knowledge-Base Resources

Facebook has "status bars," which, as in the case of Twitter (see chapter 3), are usually used to tell the online world what you are thinking, doing, or feeling. "What's on your mind?" the Facebook status bar prompts you. They can also be used to get out word about publications and events, with links to places anywhere on the Web. And status bars can also be used to ask questions you can't otherwise find answers to on the Web. As fresh and continuously updated as Wikipedia is, it cannot possibly have an article or part of an article that answers every specific question someone might have about breaking news, or even about some arcane event in history. Aardvark, in operation from 2008–2011, was a new new medium entirely devoted to answering its users' questions by sending them to other self-identified "expert" users—but Aardvark was purchased and then discontinued by Google.

Here is how the status bar on Facebook can help with this job:

In the week of November 17, 2008, Keith Olbermann and Rachel Maddow were unaccountably absent from their MSNBC *Countdown* and *Rachel Maddow* shows. No explanation at all was given for Olbermann's absence; David Shuster simply said he was filling in for Olbermann. Maddow started each of her shows with an announcement that her replacements—Arianna Huffington (founder of *The Huffington Post)* the first night, Alison Stewart the second night—would be taking her place. The substitutes said at the end of each of Rachel Maddow's shows that she would be back "soon."

Not only was there was no announcement on MSNBC, but there also wasn't much about this on the Web, other than someone else (Arnold, 2008) who also was wondering what had happened to the two. I'd assumed they were on some sort of vacations, but...I posted a question in my "Status" on Facebook, and, sure enough, Mike Plugh, one of my most brilliant and knowledgeable former students, came back with an answer (see Levinson, 2008, "Where Have Olbermann and Maddow Disappeared To?"): "Vacation. They ran straight through the election without a break and I think Rachel is on the Air America Cruise with some lucky listeners. Olbermann may be in his basement hitting rewind and play on the Ben Affleck impression at SNL."

Mike not only answered my question with style, but, assuming the information he provided was correct, also offered an important lesson in the value of new new media as sources of information. When old media fail to keep us posted, and old-fashioned searches for information on the Web fail to give us answers, the new new media and their principle of readers becoming writers and providers of information sometimes can give us the answers we seek. In this sense, Facebook goes one step further than Wikipedia, by turning the whole new new media world into one big encyclopedia, in which any one of your online Friends can write the answer to your question.

Groups also have status bars that prompt members to "Write something"—"Write Post, Add Photo/Video, Ask Question." The advantage of the Group status bar, for questions about which Group members are presumably knowledgeable, is a much more targeted audience.

Facebook Friends as Real-Time Knowledge Resources

From the very beginning of online communication in the 1980s, it provided avenues for live or real-time exchanges, and asynchronous or time-delayed dispensing of information. Prior to digital media, all communication with the exception of the telephone and in-person conversation was asynchronous—that is, either one-way, or, if two-way, as in writing of letters, with a delay between sending and receiving the letter, and in return receiving a response. The printed book can be considered an archetypal asynchronous medium, in some cases conveying information that was first communicated hundreds or even thousands of years ago. Prior to the invention of the telephone, the only real-time communication was the face-to-face conversation (with smoke signals, semaphores, and scribbling a note to someone standing right next to you being minor exceptions—see Levinson, 1997, for more on the history of media).

Facebook and all new new media offer both options—real-time and asynchronous. The preponderance of communication on most new new media, however, is asynchronous—certainly for videos on YouTube, articles on Wikipedia, and blogging, where comments (and the talk sections on Wikipedia) are the only place for real-time exchanges. (Live tweeting and live blogging, which, as the names suggest, take place in real time, would be partial exceptions—live only if readers happened to be online at the time the tweets and blog were written.) Facebook, however, does have significant real-time components that can be used for a variety of purposes, from casual chat to serious pursuit of knowledge.

I was logged onto Facebook on November 21, 2008. James Winston, a Facebook Friend whom I had never met in person, asked me if he could ask a question or two for a paper he was writing. James was at the time a graduate student in Communication and Media Studies at Northern Illinois University.

His question was about "information overload"—did I think the Web was contributing to it, and did I think higher education was doing a good job in teaching students how to cope with it?

I replied that I do not think "overload" is the problem we face; the challenge is how to cope with "information underload," or not enough information to enable us to get the most out of new new media to successfully navigate the Web. Humans are, after all, inherently multitasking organisms. I referred James to William James (1890, p. 462; see also chapter 1 of the present book) and his observation about "blooming, buzzing confusion" of the world and our capacity to make sense of it. Updated to today's world and media, we could say that all we need is the right navigational information—that is why we do not feel too overwhelmed when we walk into a library or a bookstore, which have vastly more books than we could possibly read. We have learned, since we were children, how to navigate libraries and bookstores (see also Levinson, 1997, pp. 134–135, and Levinson, 2007, "Interview by Mark Molaro," for more on information "overload" as "underload").

As for higher education, I told James that I think it does a good enough job giving students some information about new new media, but the best way of learning how to use these media is to actually use them (as per John Dewey, 1925, whom we also encountered in chapter 1 of *New New Media*).

In the process of answering James, I realized that what we were doing—his asking me these questions, my answering him, on Facebook—was a good example of new new media employed as not just an interactive knowledge base but a live, real-time knowledge resource. I told him I might put this conversation into this book; he said that would be great. All of that happened just seconds before I started writing this section for the first edition of this book.

I also told James I would see that he received a complimentary copy of this book, which he did. By the time you are reading this, he will likely also have already received a copy of this second edition, which you now have in your hands or on your screen. James could be reading this section right now.

He asked me one additional question in 2008: Did I think the advantages and content of the Web were more useful to younger people—Generation Y? I told him I thought the Internet, as what I call the "medium of media" (*Digital McLuhan*, Levinson, 1999), had information relevant to people of all ages.

James then thanked me—for answering his questions and for promising the "shout-out" in this book—and asked if he could ask me additional questions in the future. I said sure.

And the conversation ended. My knowledge as a resource for James Winston was that easy. He was in Illinois, I in New York, but we could have been on opposite ends of the Earth. And the conversation could have taken place with equal ease between James and any other professor, or any other student and me, or any two people, professors, students, or otherwise. The world of new new media has made knowledge easier to obtain than at any time in history.

Indeed, I served as a real-time knowledge resource for Piotr Mach, who messaged me on Facebook on January 10, 2012:

> *I am a 'political science' student at University of Warsaw, Poland, specializing in political marketing and writing my master's on new media tools in Barack Obama's 2008 presidential campaign. Right now I'm reading your book "New New Media".... That's why I would like to ask for your opinion about mybarackobama.com and its fundraising tools in Obama's campaign in 2008. Would you categorize it as new new or just new media? I'm asking because users were normally just passive—they could either donate or not. But on the other hand they could put up the personalized fundraising tool on their profile and encourage their friends to donate.*

He was (of course) reading the first, 2009, edition of this book. I replied as follows:

> *I'd say mybarackobama.com was a transitory medium in 2007–2008—metamorphing (like a caterpillar into a butterfly) from a new to a new new medium. Passive donation was indeed, as you say, just a new media mode. But in effect deputizing users to become their own fund-raisers is a classic new new media move (equivalent to producing your own videos). Hope this helps—best of luck with your studies.*

Facebook has done its part to make this kind of knowledge acquisition even easier than in 2008. The Chat and Message systems on Facebook were in effect merged in 2011, so that any live chat automatically appears and stays in the user's message history, making it almost effortless to reference later. Piotr and I concluded our conversation via Chat. I told him I was revising this very part of *New New Media* when I received his question. He said, nice coincidence, he was reading that very part. I told him I would be putting our exchange in the second edition, as an example of Facebook as an international real-time knowledge resource. The synchronous and asynchronous have been literally integrated in this aspect of new new media evolution.

But what if I had given James Winston or Piotr Mach incorrect information, whether because of ignorance or malice? Had they any reason to think that, they could easily have checked my other writings available on the Web. As we will see in more detail in chapter 6 about Wikipedia, new new media provide not only resources of knowledge but the ready means to check and correct any knowledge in question or in need of confirmation or revision.

Meeting Online Friends in the Real World

The twofold initial logic of Facebook—either finding out more about classmates you already knew or keeping an eye out on the physical campus for someone you did not already know but whose face you had seen on Facebook—contained an assumption, an expectation, that people might be interested in jumping from online to in-person friendships and relationships. In a campus community, safety inside the campus was not a major concern. You could meet someone you first got to see or know on Facebook by going to a school cafeteria or other public place on campus with a real-life friend or two. That kind of environment was and is very different from the kinds of in-person meetings that came to be associated with Myspace, for example, in which two people, not part of any physical campus community, got to "know" each other online and then meet in the real world. Such meetings can obviously be fraught with serious danger, and we will examine them further in chapter 9, "The Dark Side of New New Media."

But the expansion of Facebook far beyond the campus has made it more like Myspace and its avenues for real-life meetings of online Friends, whether dangerous or beneficial. How can these dangers be kept at bay? The sensible way to meet safely with anyone you have not already met in person is to meet in a public place or, if appropriate, in a professional environment. A restaurant would be a good example of such a public place, just as a business office would be a good example of a professional environment that someone might visit for a job interview generated by an online exchange.

Leaving the safety considerations aside, what do we know about how online relationships fare when transferred to the in-person world, when transformed from digital code to flesh-and-blood? As I detailed in *The Soft Edge: A Natural History and Future of the*

Information Revolution (Levinson, 1997), there is a long history going back to the mid-1980s of people meeting online and falling in love (eHarmony, Match.com, Christian Mingle, and JDate would be current examples of social media devoted to initiating real-world romantic relationships), and people meeting online and progressing to successful in-person business relationships.

I have been a party, numerous times, to two kinds of business or professional in-person relationships that began online.

From 1985–1995, my wife, Tina Vozick, and I created and administered Connected Education, the first online program to offer courses for graduate credit and a complete MA in Media Studies, entirely online. Thousands of students from more than 40 states in the United States and 20 countries around the world registered in our courses for credit granted by the New School for Social Research, Polytechnic University, the Bath College of Higher Education (in England), and other colleges and universities (see Levinson, 1997, for details). I knew fewer than 5 percent of our students in person prior to their Connect Ed registration. I met fewer than another 5 percent of our online students—people I had never met before in person—at conferences I attended in various cities in the United States and abroad during the program, or when online students came to New York City for whatever reason.

I noticed something the first time I met someone in person whom I had previously known only online, which has held true for just about every other such online to in-person conversion meeting with an online student, friend, or associate: After an initial jolt lasting a few minutes at most, the online persona was clearly recognizable in the person sitting across from me at a table. Indeed, in those days—from 1985 to the early 2000s—most of the online communication was in text, with no images or photographs of the people with whom you were conversing online. So meeting someone in person whom you had gotten to know online was doubly strange: You were seeing a face for the person whose written words you had come to know, as well as getting a voice and in-person personality to go with those words. The potential was high for concluding that this person at the table or in the room with you was very different from the person you knew online. And, yet, the result was just the opposite.

The other professional situation in which I met a fair number of people in person whom I had first come to know online—as many as 50 percent of this particular online community—arose in the early and mid-1990s, when authors and publishers of science fiction began conversing on a variety of online systems such as CompuServe and GEnie (Levinson, 1997). I had just started publishing science fiction at that time, and in 1998 I became president of the Science Fiction Writers of America. In that capacity, as well as before and after (I served from 1998–2001), I met hundreds of authors and dozens of publishers and editors in person—at conventions and smaller meetings—whom I already knew from our online exchanges. As was the case with my online students, in all cases the in-person face, voice, and personality were completely in accordance with what I already knew of these authors and publishers from their words online.

Reconnecting with Old Friends Online

At the opposite end of the spectrum of meeting online friends in person is the experience of reconnecting online with in-person friends and acquaintances you have not been in touch with for years. This has been happening with me for more than 10 years, mostly when old friends, classmates, and former students see me on television and then contact me via email. On New Year's Day, 2000, I appeared as a panelist on Fox News' *The New Millennium: Science, Fiction, Fantasy* special. Shortly after, I received emails from Felix Poelz, a high school classmate whom I had not seen since 1963, and Peter Rosenthal, guitarist on my 1972 *Twice Upon a Rhyme* album (Peter and I had been out of touch since the mid-1970s). In the 1980s and 1990s, I received email from a handful of former in-person students. These were early indications of the power of cyberspace, prior to 21st century social media, to vanquish the time and distance that separate us from old friends and acquaintances.

The pace picked up a bit on Myspace when I became an active member in early 2006. But Facebook, likely because of its origins as a university community, has bumped up such online reunions to a new level. Of my 5000 Friends on Facebook, more than 100 are former students and friends I had not heard from in years. I receive about two to three Friend requests per year from old acquaintances. You can easily find on Facebook many people who went to your high school and college, sorted by their graduation year. Felix's name was not listed among the 1963 graduates of Christopher Columbus High School (he was not a Facebook member), but of the more than 150 people listed, there were a few whose names were familiar.

If the danger of meeting online "Friends" in person, when you do not already know them in person, is counted as one of the drawbacks and potential abuses of new new social media, then getting back in touch with an old, long-out-of-touch friend must be considered one of its great, soul-nurturing benefits. If we agree with Carl Sagan (1978) that we are the stuff of the cosmos examining itself, then the reunification of old, in-person acquaintances via social media is the cosmos's way of sewing itself back together.

Protection for the "Hidden Dimension": Cleaning Up Your Online Pages

The "hidden dimension" of all new new media self-productions is their endurance on the Web long after we have written or created them. I borrow the phrase from Edward T. Hall, who coined it long before the Internet, as the title of his 1966 book about the significance of interpersonal distance and space in human relations, which we usually take for granted, even though they can powerfully shape the course and outcome of a conversation. We similarly often pay no particular attention to the longevity of our blog posts, YouTube videos, and Facebook Profiles and Pages, which can be and are read by people long after we have posted the words and images, and can therefore have an effect not intended or foreseen by us at the time of the initial posting.

Although I did not start blogging until 2006, words that I wrote more than a decade earlier come up in Google searches today. Fortunately for me, everything that I have written or created online—including on Facebook Pages—has been for professional, not primarily personal, purposes. Thus, comments by me on GEnie (the General Electric Network for Information Exchange) in the early 1990s, usually about some aspect of science fiction (see Levinson, 1997), are no more likely to be embarrassing to me now than my first published scholarly article in 1976 ("Hot and Cool Redefined for Interactive Media" in *The Media Ecology Review*) or, for that matter, my 1972 album *Twice Upon a Rhyme* (which was reissued on CD in 2008 and on remastered vinyl in 2010, in addition to being available on iTunes, Amazon, eMusic, Spotify, and other MP3 outlets—see the "Myspace" section of chapter 8 for more about music online). I am, immodestly, proud of all of that.

Most people on Facebook, however, conceive of their Profiles as personal, not professional. And the danger that must be well known now to every student with a Facebook account arises: You post photos on your Facebook Page, photos taken at a party when you were drunk out of your mind or similarly indisposed. A year or two later, you apply for a job somewhere, and your would-be boss takes a look at those photos and decides not to be your boss—the drunk photos cost you that job. Indeed, employers and potential employers have controversially taken to requesting or requiring employees to provide access to their Facebook passwords and Twitter accounts, which would allow the employer to see not only what is publicly posted but privately communicated via messages (Madrigal, 2011).

In an ideal world, a potential or current boss would not care how you behaved at a party two years—or even two days—earlier. All that would count is how you performed in the workplace. (I made this point to Bill O'Reilly as a guest on *The O'Reilly Factor* on Fox News in 2004, when I defended the right of a local news anchor to take her clothes off in a wet T-shirt contest when on vacation; see Levinson, 2004.) No one other than your personal acquaintances or people of your choosing would be able to see your photos. Facebook does provide options for allowing less than complete access to everything on your account. But employer requests for access to new new media activity of employees, and repostings by even well-meaning Friends, along with the capacity to easily copy everything online from music to videos to photos, make the Facebook protections not very reliable. Human inquisitiveness usually sooner or later surmounts any barriers you've erected to protect your personal information online.

Thus, the best remedy you can apply for embarrassing photos and other new new media creations is the following: Do not post them in the first place. And, if you do, remember to remove them as soon as you are no longer happy with them in public view. Drunk posting need not equal drunk retention. But always remember that the viral dissemination of anything and everything online means that what you erase from your Facebook profile page today may endure for years on someone else's page, website, personal computer, or any device connected to the Internet or the cloud—constituting an ominous cloud forever above your head. If you have to clean up a page, in other words, there's always a chance that at least some of the cleanup may be in vain. On Twitter, member of the House of Representatives Anthony Weiner posted a photo and removed it a few minutes later—but not before someone had seen it, which triggered a chain of events that led to his resignation (see the next chapter, and the section "The Other Congressman Who Tweeted Too Much").

Subjective and Objective Differences Among New New Media

As we conclude this chapter about Facebook, and turn to Twitter, the next new new medium on our roster, a question inevitably arises: Which medium is better? The question, of course, is not as straightforward as it may seem, and might be better presented as the following: Which new new medium is better for what application or purpose?

But even that question admits to no simple answer, because our preference for one new new medium over another—for any media or activities in competition for our favor and patronage—depends on a combination of subjective and objective factors.

A subjective factor or criterion derives from our personal experiences with the medium, unique or pertaining more to us than the medium. We might prefer Facebook over Twitter, for example, because we met or came to know a good friend or romantic interest on Facebook, or because a connection on Facebook helped land us a job. If Twitter had 100 people you wanted to be in touch with, you obviously would find Twitter better, or of greater value, than would I, if I had interest in only a few people who were tweeting. Or, to put this in yet another way, a slower or less efficient social medium would likely be preferable to its faster, more efficient rival, if the slower system had users who were for any reason more desirable, helpful, or in any positive manner important to you.

As I mentioned earlier in the chapter, I joined Facebook in 2005 because my son had an early account there—a powerful, personal, subjective inducement to appreciate Facebook. In contrast, when I joined Myspace in 2005, I knew almost no one there, other than the student who had casually recommended that I join. I thus rarely logged on. When I returned to Myspace in 2006 to promote my new science fiction novel, *The Plot to Save Socrates*, I immediately began searching for people whose interests included "science fiction" or, better, "time travel." Within a few days, I had about 20 Friends— all of whom I had no knowledge of whatsoever in the offline, real world. Our mutual interest in science fiction led us to read each other's pages and blog posts on Myspace, and by 2007 I had more than 1000 Myspace Friends. About 40 had purchased my books by then, but that was no longer the main reason I valued their online friendship. Rather, I had come to feel as if we were part of a community—one that commented on political issues, on television shows and movies we had seen, that wished each other Happy New Year and Happy Halloween and Happy Birthday—a community even though, with just a handful of exceptions, we had never met.

Meanwhile, I rarely used my Facebook account at that time. This was because other than my son, with whom I was easily in touch via phone and email, and my students, with whom I was also in touch via email and, if they currently were my students, in the classroom, there was no one else I was interested in communicating with on Facebook in 2005–2007. At that point, I thought Myspace was a better system—for my needs—than was Facebook. But with the receding of Myspace in 2008 and the concurrent growth of Facebook, the fulcrum of new new media subjective value shifted for me again. A good number of my Myspace Friends continue to be my Friends to this day on Facebook, which has evolved to be both a professional as well as a personal port of call for me. The point, again, is that the subjective pros and cons of any social medium go with where the people who are important to you digitally reside.

Subjective factors also include what I call the "first love syndrome," found not only in what we most like in online systems but in movies, television shows, and novels. The principle is that we most love what we first experience. People who read the *Lord of the Rings* trilogy before seeing the movies told me they enjoyed the movies but thought the novels were better, providing the definitive treatment of the epic. On the other hand, people who first saw the movies thought the novels were good but sometimes meandered. I know some people who first saw the movies and did not even finish the novels. I have taken no formal survey, but conversations with many people over the years about which they preferred, book or movie, movie or television show of the same story, convince me that what people most prefer is what they first encountered and came to love.

And what of objective differences between Facebook and other new new media?

Some objective differences have to do with the control that users have over their Profile Pages. Myspace allows users to decorate their Profile Pages with all the colors, images, and sounds available through HTML (much like an independent blog page). Twitter allows the upload of an image to serve as background for the Profile Page. In contrast, Facebook permits only plain text, links (which can convey images and videos to the page), and smaller photos (which do not take up the entire page) on its Profile Pages.

Facebook's origins as a way for college students to "meet" each other—see what they look like, what their interests are—without having to physically meet has shaped its growth and given it a greater grounding, literally, in the real world than its competitors. In the beginning, Facebook communities consisted of students who could easily meet in person if they wanted, because they were attending the same college. When Facebook soon welcomed students from universities and colleges other than Harvard, the possibility of first meeting people online and then in person, or first in person and then online, continued. And as family members began to show up on Facebook, its communities took an even more profound turn to the real world. Subsequently, Facebook surpassed and eclipsed Myspace, which from its outset and years of expansion never had the grounding in in-person relationships that typified Facebook. We might therefore list grounding in real-life relationships as one of the key objective characteristics of Facebook.

This characteristic continues to define Facebook in comparison to other online systems. Twitter, which we will consider in the next chapter, certainly has real-life friends and family tweeting. But the Twitter accounts with millions of Followers are held by celebrities—politicians and movie stars—who likely know in person few or none of their Followers. In contrast, Foursquare, which we consider later in this book, is an intrinsically "place-based" system, consisting of "check-ins" mostly from all manner of real places.

The Facebook Timeline

One characteristic in which Facebook currently excels above Twitter, Myspace, and all new new media fueled by Friends and Followers is the opportunity on Facebook to read and act on any postings made by you and your Friends on your public space years after they first were posted. This public space famously had been called a "Wall." Its past was not easily accessible—until its name was changed near the end of 2011 to Timeline.

I'm looking at my first year on Facebook—2005—on my Timeline right now, in January 2012. All that was necessary to bring that year to my screen was clicking on "2005." There were just three entries on my Wall back then:

> from Diana Richter, April 17, 2005: " 'i always liked my perspective on life to be clear. thats why i never did drugs or wore sunglasses' -paul levinson"

> from Michelle Pastor, May 2, 2005: "unbelievable, inconceivable YOUUUUUUU!"

> from Loni Lichtman, December 10, 2005: "THE WALL!!!!!!!!"

Diana was and is a friend of my daughter Molly, and the quote from me comes from something I once or twice told Molly, and she shared with Diana. Michelle was an undergrad student in my "Intro to Communication and Media Studies" course at Fordham University. Her quote comes from my song "Unbelievable, Inconceivable You" (1968), recorded by the Vogues, and still up on my http://paullevinson.info Web page.

Loni was a graduate student in my "Targeted Writing" course at Fordham University, and her exaltation about "The Wall" shows how important it was back then on Facebook and as a topic of discussion in our class.

Taken together, these three posts on my Facebook Wall in 2005 summarize some of the crucial points made in this chapter. Facebook was used far less frequently then than it is today, and your Friends were people you already knew in the real world (my daughter's real-life friend, and two of my students). These Wall posts also bring home the longevity of anything posted online—the Facebook Timeline makes the trivial profound, at least insofar as endurance beyond the time of its creation.

Also noteworthy, but not yet mentioned in this chapter, is that, in the early days, people rarely posted on their own Walls. In contrast, by 2012 and for several years preceding, most Wall posts were made by the owners of the Wall, either about events they found of interest, or about their activities.

Loni's 2005 exclamation on my Wall about "The Wall" is also ironic to see on my Timeline, because the Timeline replaced The Wall in 2011. This underscores another crucial point. Not only do new new media evolve at lightning speed, but arguably the most important part of that evolution is beyond the user's, or the consumer/producer's, control. We might write mostly whatever we please on our Walls and Timelines, but Facebook has the right to replace the Wall with the Timeline any time it chooses. Facebook may choose to do this suddenly or gradually—as of January 2012, the choice to go from Wall to Timeline was still voluntary (transitioning to mandatory)—but Facebook nonetheless holds all the cards.

Not that Facebook is averse to censoring content, too. At the end of 2008, Facebook embarked on a campaign to cleanse its pages of all pornographic photographs. Not that they were ever encouraged or permitted in the first place, but no central system can possibly police the uploading of every single photo. The "objectionable" photographic content included women's naked breasts. But, as Lisa M. Krieger detailed in the *San Jose Mercury News* (2008), this policy resulted in the removal from members' Facebook Pages of certain photographs of mothers nursing babies, which were assessed as "obscene, pornographic or sexually explicit." This, in turn, resulted in online and real-world protests against Facebook, as well as a profusion of Groups and Causes on Facebook, for and against photos of breastfeeding. Facebook told Krieger, in its defense, that most photos of breastfeeding were not and would not be removed—only those in which the areola (that is, the darker skin around the nipple) is visible. But the damage to the ideal of a user-created medium was done.

As we will see in this book, different new new media play out this conflict between the old authoritarian and the new democratic in their own distinct ways. Wikipedia, for example, is far less "old school" in terms of what may be removed from its pages than is Facebook. Nonetheless, Wikipedia can still remove a phrase, an article, a photo, which you or I may write or upload, if a sufficient group of other reader/editors deem it unsuitable. Wikipedia, in other words, has to some extent replaced authoritarian, expert-driven control with democratic, group control, but it has by no means eliminated or even reduced control over individual expression. Indeed, the imperative or at least encouragement for everyone to edit on Wikipedia increases group control.

Nonetheless, as indicative as such policing of content is about how new new media can limit what consumers turned producers can actually produce, such limits are not as ultimately undermining of user control of new new media as is Facebook's or any medium's ability to suddenly change its fundamental architecture. The moral of this story for students of new new media is that, however much we may consider the new new medium an extension of ourselves, our lives, our desires (as per McLuhan's view of all media as human "extensions," 1964), new new media are at their very core not—not entirely. New new media do express individual expression far more than older media, but they maintain, like all media, crucial aspects of their operation that are irreducibly beyond our control. However much we may feel that a new new media system is ours, because of the extraordinary powers of production and self-projection the new new medium invests in us, the new new medium is actually never ours completely. In the case of Facebook, the new new medium is also Facebook's. In this profound, underlying, unalterable sense, there is no difference among old, new, and new new media. The deep differences between new new and older media that we have identified and are examining in this book are thus not the complete story of new new media.

We should bear in mind this iron underpinning, inflexible to the user, of all new new media as we proceed to look at the extraordinary flights of Twitter in our next chapter.

CHAPTER 3

Twitter

WOULD YOU LIKE EVERYONE IN THE WORLD TO KNOW WHAT movie you just saw or are going to see, what you really think of your teacher or boss or president, what you just ate for lunch or intend to eat, whether it's sunny or raining, or the police are pepper spraying the people next to you—any and all of those things, and more, whatever you might want the world to know—just a second or so after you had the thought or experience and the idea to broadcast it to the world? Twitter makes it easy for you to do all of that.

You can disseminate whatever information you please, to whatever portion of the world you like, as long as the people in that portion have accounts on Twitter. That would be more than 300 million people in the world at large as of 2011, up from some 30 million in May 2009, with Twitter growing faster at that time than any other social medium (Schonfeld, 2009), and the first tweet from outer space on May 12, 2009 (Van Grove, 2009). Twitter was still the fastest growing medium in 2011, second only to Facebook in total number of users (Bennett, 2011).

Further, the fact that you can do that from your smart phone, iPad, or any other mobile Web-connecting device at hand means that your access to the world, and its access to you, is as much a part of you, as close at hand, as your hand itself. This pertains to all new new media, but the simplicity of posting and reading on Twitter makes it almost as fluid as speech, and even more subject to impulse because it can be done silently, with no one nearby who can overhear and thus inhibit what you might want to say.

Concerned about your privacy? Worried that this ease of access will give unwanted eyes access to you and your thoughts? Like all online systems, you can tweet under a pseudonym or assumed identity. You can even adopt the name of a television character. Or you can choose not to tweet at all.

On the other hand, if you welcome publicity and need it for your profession, you can tweet engagingly under your real name. Don Lemon of CNN, Tamron Hall of MSNBC, and *Meet the Press* anchor David Gregory were actively using Twitter as early as the beginning of 2009. Now just about every television news anchor and commentator has a Twitter account. They work tweets they receive into their television news shows, in another example of old and new new media cooperation. Accounts of celebrities, politicians, and other high-profile users have blue verification check marks next to their account names—signifying that Barack Obama's account is really Barack Obama's and not someone else's using his name. A "beta" procedure in which any user could apply to have his or her account verified was discontinued in 2011 by Twitter, which now (2012) advises users to verify their accounts by linking to their blogs or official websites.

Ashton Kutcher (more than 9 million followers in January 2012) and Barack Obama (nearly 12 million) have Twitter accounts—though Obama's tweets, authorized by him, are mostly not his own, in contrast to Kutcher's. "This account is run by #Obama2012 campaign staff," the President's Twitter Profile truthfully advises, "Tweets from the President are signed -bo." Obama held the first presidential press conference on Twitter in July 2011 (Olander, 2011), but the tweeted questions presented to the president were "curated" rather than randomly selected, which weakened the democratic new new media potential of the event (see Levinson, 2011, "First Presidential Twitter press conference"; and the discussion of YouTube presidential debates in the next chapter). The pope will have his own Twitter account, the Vatican announced in February 2012, explaining that "though he may not al- ways write the tweets, he will approve each one" (Chansanchai, 2012; see also "The Pope's Channel" in the next chapter for the Vatican analysis of the pros and cons of new new media).

Tweeting was once called "microblogging"—long ago and far away, it seems, but that was only three years ago, in 2009—which, come to think of it, is indeed long ago and far away given the speed-of-light pace of new new media evolution. Today, tweeting is mostly just known, irrevocably and irreversibly, as tweeting.

Welcome, then, to this burgeoning world of tweeting, or the publication and dissemi- nation online of a line or two about yourself, or anything you might like to say, personally, professionally, or politically, anytime you please. Twitter is no longer the new kid on the media block, started as a project by Odeo podcasting people Jack Dorsey, Noah Glass, Biz Stone, and Evan Williams in March 2006. It grew so fast in just the first half of 2009— Twitter had a total of only about 6 million users in February 2009, in contrast to 30 million by May of that year—that an article in the February 8, 2009, issue of *New York* magazine (Leitch, 2009) advised, "If you're the last person in the world to not know what Twitter is, here's a simple explanation." By June 15, 2009, Twitter needed no introduction. It was, to nobody's surprise, the cover story of *Time* magazine (Johnson, 2009).

But as both articles go on to explain and we will detail in this chapter, there is much that is complex and profound about tweeting—even more so in 2012 than 2009.

The Epitome of Immediacy

Instant publication—whether of text, images, sounds, or videos—is one of the hallmarks of new new media. But the hallmarks are not distributed in new new media equally.

You can raise a phone and take a photo or grab a video, which is usually easier than any kind of writing. But editing a video is usually not as easy as editing text, and uploading it to an online site and publishing it can take much longer than writing, especially with the processing time required for lengthy videos. Further, because writing directly online to a blog or a page or a site is as easy or easier than writing offline, in contrast to photos and even the briefest videos, which need to be taken offline and uploaded, getting written words online is also a little easier than doing the same for photographs and videos.

The upshot, when all aspects of creation and publishing online are taken into account, is that text is easier to disseminate than photos and videos. And a line or so of text—140 characters is the limit on Twitter—moves the fastest of all. If you're an author who agonizes over every word, this very short form could take a long time to write. I was once asked to write a 200-character blurb—not 200 words, but 200 characters—about one of my novels for the Science Fiction Book Club, and it took about 15 minutes for me to write. That was because I wanted every word, and therefore every letter or character, to count—every word to attract potential readers to my novel. If all I was writing about was how much I enjoyed the slice of pizza I just bought on Fordham Road, or even what I thought, in a phrase, about First Amendment rights being violated, or about the president's latest speech, I could dash off that line in a few seconds with no problem.

All thoughts originate in the mind—or, if you want to be less metaphysical, in the brain. One kind of synapse or neurological pathway delivers the thought to our vocal apparatus when we speak. Another kind of synapse gets the thought to our fingers, with which we write or type. Presumably these two synapses or pathways to personal communication are the same length—the thought travels at the same speed to tongue or finger.

Prior to the advent of electronic media, immediacy of thought conveyed to the tongue only reached as far as anyone within hearing distance. Immediacy of thought conveyed to the finger was even more limited: It ended with the finger, because for anyone else to read what had been written, the parchment, papyrus, or paper had to be passed from hand to hand. Although this nonelectronic "digital" transmission—digital as in finger to finger—could happen quickly, it was slower than the speed of sound. Thus, speech had the edge over writing in immediacy. (See Levinson, *Digital McLuhan*, 1999, for handwriting as a form of "digital," or finger, communication.)

Electricity travels at the speed of light, which means that any message encoded and committed to electronic delivery—whether voice or written word—can be sent anywhere in the world instantly. Electricity travels at 186,000 miles per second, and the world is about 24,000 miles around at the equator. However, this did not mean that such messages would be received—heard or read—by any human being instantly. Equipment at the receiving end, whether turning on a television or walking to a ringing telephone, added seconds at the very least to the ultimate reception of information transmitted at the speed of light.

More than any other old, new, or even new new medium, Twitter's revolution is that it makes the sending and receiving of its brief messages nearly as instant as their conception and writing. Twitter is faster than blogging, because its tweets are shorter than blog posts. Twitter is faster than Foursquare, which consumes crucial seconds or more in verifying your location for the check-in. Twitter's one-liners can be created, sent, and received with the flick of a finger. Writing when tweeted has thus become as easy and effortless to communicate over vast distances as speech has always been to people within earshot.

Further, the messages conveyed via Twitter are readable by anyone who wishes to "follow" your tweets on the system—that is the default—or they can be sent to specific groups or just one person. This means that Twitter is not only the most immediate written medium in history, but it is also the most integrated combination of interpersonal and mass communication.

Interpersonal + Mass Communication = Twitter

The preceding title is about 45 characters, so it easily could have been sent via Twitter. And it would have been sent in ways that combine these two great branches of communication.

One of the basic lessons of communication is that it comes in two kinds. Interpersonal communication consists of one person sending a message to another person, in which the second person can easily switch from being a receiver to a sender. Examples would be in-person and video face-to-face communication, written correspondence, IMing on computers, and talking and texting on the phone. Mass communication consists of one person or source sending a message to many people at the same time, with these many receivers not having the capacity to become senders. Examples would be wall carvings, books, newspapers, motion pictures, radio, television, and Web pages and blogs that allow no comments. Interpersonal is thus pinpoint and two-way, whereas mass communication is broad (hence the word "broadcast," from the widespread or broad casting of seeds in planting) and one-way.

Sometimes people mistakenly say that interpersonal is nontechnological in contrast to mass media, which must be high-tech or at least use industrial technology such as a printing press. But talking on the telephone is an example of interpersonal communication that is technological, and a poster on a wall or writing on a blackboard is an almost no-tech, or very low-tech, kind of mass communication.

Apropos of blackboards, the classroom is one of few communication settings that can and does easily switch between mass and interpersonal communication. When I lecture in a class, the students are receivers of mass communication, or my message to many people. But as soon as a student asks a question and I answer, she and I are communicating interpersonally—while for the rest of the class, who continue as listeners, the communication is still mass communication. When I finish answering the first student's question and call on another student, the first student moves back into the mass communication audience, as the second student and I now engage in interpersonal communication.

Twitter takes the classroom to a global level. Although it is not without precedent in digital media—chat rooms and private IMs also swing between mass and interpersonal communication—Twitter is a chat room, classroom, or gathering that goes on 24 hours a day, 7 days a week. And although the messages on Twitter can certainly be educational, it is the communication structure of the classroom, not its content, that is catapulted into a worldwide conversation on Twitter.

Twitter expands the classroom communication structure in a second way, making group-to-individual communication as easy as individual-to-group (teacher-to-class). Groups of all sizes and purposes send out tweets—old media giants such as Fox News and CNN, which offer real-time tickers or updates of news stories; political campaigns for president and all manner of elected offices; and groups devoted to a particular cause or social purpose, such as TwitterMoms, which helped mobilize opposition to Facebook's ban on photos of breastfeeding, discussed in the previous chapter. Messages of 140 characters on such subjects, with links to bigger content in blogs, videos, and traditional news media on the Web, reach tweeters on the same smart phones, tablets, and laptops on which they see tweets such as "Just got to my dentist's office. Ugh!"

Tweets also allow effortless broadcasting of professional and personal information, such as this text from Karl Rove on February 14, 2009: "Back in Washington. Working on the book this weekend. Tune in to Fox News tomorrow AM. I'll be on Chris Wallace's 100 Day Special." Indeed, links to all of my blog posts and podcasts show up on my Twitter account and are seen by my 4700 (as of January 2012) "Followers," as are tweets about my TV and radio appearances and interviews in the old-media press, and off-the-cuff comments about baseball games and snowstorms.

The automatic sending to Twitter (via applications or "apps") of links to anything and everything on the Web, or anything and everything with a URL—blog posts, videos, news stories, the full gamut of new and new new media—and the instantly subsequent, automatic relay of these tweets (if the tweeter enables this) to Facebook, LinkedIn, Squidoo, Reverbnation, and "meta" or "aggregate" new new systems such as FriendFeed ("meta" because their content consists of links from Twitter, Facebook, YouTube, and other new new media activity) constitute a self-perpetuating, not entirely planned, expanding network that has much in common with living organisms and evolutionary systems (see Levinson, 1979 and 1997, for more on the organic evolution of media).

Twitter as Smart T-Shirt or Jewelry

But when Twitter functions as a statement of feeling—"I'm so bored in this class" or "I'm feeling really good tonight, don't know why"—Twitter is working as a kind of virtual apparel or jewelry. It becomes something we "wear" or send out to the world, like a dark hat or a bright necklace, to indicate our emotional disposition.

When messages on Twitter get more specific, such as "I just voted for Obama" or "I just voted for Romney," they move metaphorically from jewelry to campaign pins or T-shirts with messages. Back in 1970, when the personal computer revolution was more than a decade away, Gary Gumpert wrote about "the rise of mini-comm." He was talking about how people could "broadcast" their own personal messages, or messages tailored to their views and feelings, via words printed on their T-shirts, sweatshirts, and other clothing. As in all new new media improvements in the written realm, personal and political messages in the digital age via updates on Twitter do the "mini-comm" one big series of steps better, by allowing any words to be "printed" or published worldwide instantly, retweeted or RT'd by receivers to their Followers, and then revised or changed a split second later, with a new "tweet," if the writer so desires.

Messages on T-shirts, of course, can be commercial—promoting a given product— as well as political or personal. Twitter messages have similar diversity and can range far beyond reports of emotional states, political candidates, and public demonstrations. Furthermore, because such messages are all received on media already connected to the Web, Twitter messages are well suited for creating buzz about items and activities that live on the Web, with handy URLs or links.

URLs are a frequent component of Twitter messages sent by major news media such as Fox News and *The New York Times* with links to breaking stories on their pages. In that function, Twitter becomes a type of wire service, like AP or Reuters. "Followers" receive these messages but do not usually reply. In those communications, Twitter is working as a mass rather than an interpersonal medium, though receivers of those messages can certainly communicate among themselves via Twitter.

Twitter allows one-way Followers in which A gets all of B's tweets, but B does not get tweets from A, and mutual Followers in which A and B each see all of the other's tweets. One-way Followers are the equivalent of Subscribers on Facebook, and mutual Followers are the equivalent of Friends. Mutual Followers can send each other private messages (DMs or "direct messages"), unseen by anyone else on Twitter, in addition to public tweets directed at one another that everyone on Twitter can see. (Rep. Anthony Weiner thought he was sending a DM but instead sent a public or "mass media" message with sexually suggestive content to a Follower. See "The Other Congressman Who Tweeted Too Much," in an upcoming section, for what ensued.)

When Twitter works as a form of one-to-one interpersonal communication, it operates not only as a kind of jewelry but a neo-telegraph. Or, as I told Ken Hudson in our

November 2007 interview in Second Life, "the telegraph was much like microblogging." The telegraph also was indeed much like tweeting—not in the speed of delivery, but the succinctness of its telegrams, for which senders were charged per word.

Bloggers not only can send out links to their blog posts via Twitter, but also can automate this dissemination via free services such as TwitterFeed. In the second half of 2011, approximately 15 percent of all readers of my *Infinite Regress* blog arrived via links to my pages sent out automatically on Twitter (three times as many as the 5 percent in the second half of 2008). To return to the jewelry and T-shirt analogy, then, Twitter messages range from store-bought (news from CNN) to handmade (a link to a blog post by any individual). As is the case with all new new media, older media are not really obliterated but rather are subsumed and furthered on Twitter.

Google+, Twitter, Facebook, and Pownce

Thus far, less than a decade into the age of new new media—if we count this age as not fully starting until the arrival of Twitter in 2006—the main victims of new new media have been not old, off-line media but new new media themselves. Yes, newspapers have shut down (we will discuss the decline of newspapers in chapter 6, "Blogging"), but most printed newspapers continue in some diminished form. In contrast, new new media disappear from the Web with regularity, distressing or exhilarating, depending on your perspective. Since the publication of the first edition of this book, Odeo the podcasting host has gone, as have Aardvark the real-time expertise service, Adjix the Twitter-link shortener with embedded advertisements, and Google Buzz, which lasted about a year (2010–2011).

Pownce, developed by the Digg design team, was Twitter's only, and much smaller, competitor from 2007 through December 2008, when it closed shop. Its main advantage in comparison to Twitter was that files—images, music, and video—could be sent along with the messages, in contrast to Twitter, which sent just links. The Pownce receiver thus was saved the step of clicking on the link and could immediately enjoy the sights and sounds.

This advantage was not enough to save Pownce, but it is one of the main features that at first distinguished Google+ from Twitter. With the failure of Google Buzz—which was little more than another form of Twitter—already written on the wall by June 2011, Google launched Google+. It had more than 60 million users by the end of 2011, was adding more than half a million new users per day, and expected to reach 400 million users by the end of 2012—exceeding Twitter's 300+ million at the beginning of 2012, assuming that number doesn't grow by at least 33% (Guynn, 2011). (But see also Ferraro, 2012, "Google+ Defenses," for some weaknesses in Google+'s growth.)

Google+'s success is no doubt a result of it being not just a Twitter lookalike, but also an amalgam of Twitter and Facebook. Google+ has "Circles," the equivalent of Facebook Groups, but with much easier means of information targeting. A link posted on Google+ can be sent out to the entire public of Google+ users, or to specific Circles—for example, "media theory," "science fiction," "music," and "former students," in my case. These links give more of the original text or article or blog post than is available on Twitter, and there is no 140-character limit on the accompanying message or caption. Videos and photos are now embeddable in both tweets and Facebook status bars, and easily viewable on Twitter and Facebook without having to leave the sites, but

Google+ has a more seamless interface with YouTube, which is also owned by Google. Like Facebook, Google+ has Profile Pages for its users, as well as Pages for books and businesses (see Bodnar, 2011, for a detailed, comprehensive analysis and comparison of Twitter, Facebook, and Google+ features).

As in all aspects of the new new media universe, there is increasing convergence of systems. Google+ was created with full knowledge of Twitter and Facebook (and the failure of Google Buzz). Facebook's constant alteration of its architecture cannot help but take into account successful new features on Google+. Twitter has updated its system as well, making it easier to see who has made your tweet a "Favorite" (much like the + in Google+, and the "Like" on Facebook), who has retweeted your tweet (the equivalent of "Share" on Google+ and Facebook), and replied or responded to your tweets ("comments" on Google+ and Facebook). These three "newer" new new media are inevitably becoming more similar.

Will they eventually totally merge into one system—whatever its name—that combines the most successful characteristics of all three? Perhaps, eventually. In the meantime, Google+ clearly has the most immediate potential for growth—given its 60-million size— but Twitter remains the scrappy upstart, given its secondary position to Facebook, and the fact that it is not owned by a digital behemoth like Google.

Twitter Dangers: The Congressman Who Tweeted Too Much

The dangers of telling the world what you are doing via tweets should be obvious, especially if what you are doing is provocative and you are in a vulnerable, publicly accessible place. You might think that this applies to chatterbox—or, better, tweeterbox—kids, and it does. But consider the series of tweets sent by Rep. Peter Hoekstra (R-Michigan), on February 6, 2009: "Just landed in Baghdad..." And, later, "Moved into green zone by helicopter Iraqi flag now over palace. Headed to new US embassy Appears calmer less chaotic than previous here" (Donnelly, 2009). Hoekstra, a member of the House Intelligence Committee, had fallen prey to a dangerous illusion that has accompanied online communication since the 1980s—dangerous, in Hoekstra's case, because let's say a terrorist anywhere in the world had read his tweet, and forwarded it to people on the ground in a position to attack Hoekstra's party. The illusion comes from mistaking the screen in front of you—whether a computer on your desk in the 1980s or a BlackBerry in your hand today—as a personal device upon which you can record your thoughts, be they private, angry, whatever, for delivery only to the person or people you had in mind. After all, the device in the 1980s was called a "personal computer." Tweets can be even more misleading because you might think that they can be seen only by your Followers. Your tweets are indeed seen by your Followers but also can be seen by everyone else on Twitter, unless you chose to "protect" your Profile and make your tweets available only to your approved Followers and not to the Twitter world at large—which, as we've seen, now (in early 2012) numbers 300 million and counting. As an indication of how intrinsically public and global almost all Twitter activity is, less than 1 percent of Twitter users have "protected" or shielded their accounts (Shapiro, 2011).

In Hoekstra's enthusiasm for the new new medium, then, he neglected to check out all of its features and control mechanisms. This was an understandable, albeit potentially deadly, error. Adults become children—usually in the best sense of the word—when we encounter and adopt a new mode of communication, especially one such as Twitter, which with a few keystrokes can open new vistas for our personal and professional lives. It might also be worth noting that the average age of Twitter users, according to an unscientific, sample survey conducted via Twitter in February 2009, was 37 (Weist, 2009; see also the scientific sample survey by Heil & Piskorski, 2009, and its findings of 90 percent of all tweets by the 10 percent most active users, "an average man is almost twice more likely to follow another man than a woman," and other demographics of interest). New new media in general, including Twitter as one of its leading cutting edges in particular, are not just for kids anymore, and have not been for at least five years.

The Other Congressman Who Tweeted Too Much

Indeed, tweeting too much is a bipartisan hazard. Anthony Weiner, D-NY, Member of the House of Representatives until June, 2011, tweeted too much in a very different way— sending a sexually suggestive photo to a Twitter Follower (a 21-year-old woman not his wife). Weiner used yfrog, which, like Twitpic, stores photos for easy sharing through Twitter. His tweet was intended to be private (a "direct message"), but Weiner mistakenly sent it out via public message to his Follower. He quickly removed the tweet after it had been posted, but the damage was done—the tweet was seen by a conservative tweeter, who clicked on the link, saw the photo on yfrog, and promptly forwarded what he had found to Andrew Breitbart's popular blog (Breitbart.com—Alexa rank #3574). Weiner at first claimed his Twitter account had been hacked, but when additional photos, some sexually explicit, came to light, Weiner apologized, for lying as well as for sending the photos, and resigned (Weiner transcript, 2011).

Why would a congressman, someone in national public office and therefore the public eye, do such a private thing in such a public venue? The answer, as with Representative Hoekstra, was that, at the time of the tweeting, the tweeter didn't feel or realize that what he was doing was potentially very public—or, in Weiner's case, public at all. As with Facebook pages and all forms of communication with a screen right in front of you, on desk, lap, or in your hand, which no one who is in your physical proximity can see, Twitter engenders the deception that what you are communicating is entirely between you and the intended receiver or receivers. But unlike Las Vegas, nothing that happens via new new media stays in the new new media system in which it happens—or, if it does, that's just coincidence, because the deeper reality is that whatever happens online is intrinsically and pervasively connected to all other media and therefore all people in the world. Putting something online in any fashion is giving it the potential of being up in bright lights on Times Square, with cameras from every news operation in the world on it.

Yuri Wright, a promising high school football player with big college prospects, learned this lesson in January 2012, when his crude sexually explicit and racially charged tweets attracted public attention. As Andy Staples aptly put it in *Sports Illustrated* (Staples, 2012), "in most football locker rooms, the words recruit Yuri Wright used on Twitter tend to pepper casual conversation between teammates—provided no coaches are around." But on Twitter, not only coaches but also everyone and their grandparents are around, and Wright was expelled from Don Bosco Prep for his tweets.

High school student Emma Thompson's tweet heard 'round the world—or at least, around most of the United States—had a happier ending in November 2011. She tweeted that Kansas Governor Sam Brownback "sucked," with the hashtag "#heblowsalot." Brownback's staff took umbrage and contacted Thompson's high school administrators, who directed her to write a letter of apology to Brownback. She refused. Fortunately, Brownback, unlike the high school's administrators, apparently understood the First Amendment, and apologized to Thompson for his staff's overzealousness (Madison, 2011). This incident nonetheless brings home the same unavoidable lesson as in the Hoekstra, Weiner, and Wright episodes: Anything tweeted, whatever the intentions of the tweeter, can in principle be seen by anyone and everyone, including the last people in the world the tweeter would want to see it.

Far worse dangers of new new media, however, come not from their mistaken use but their savvy employment by people bent on bad deeds. In chapter 9, "The Dark Side of New New Media," we will consider the deliberate use of Twitter by terrorists.

But Twitter has also been a powerful enabler of democratic expression.

Twitter vs. the Mullahs in Iran

People took to the streets in protest about what they saw as the fraudulent presidential election in Iran in June 2009. This is an old story in dictatorial regimes—people protesting in public squares—and often has dashed hopes for democracy, as was the case in Tiananmen Square in China in 1989 (see Levinson, *Cellphone*, 2004, for more). But people and democracy had new tools at their disposal in 2009.

The Supreme Leader of Iran, who supported the reelection of Mahmoud Ahmadinejad, moved with like-minded mullahs to ban reporting of the growing objections to the election, the call for a new one, and the fact that protesters were being beaten and killed. The news blackout worked for eyewitness reporting by traditional, centralized media, such as broadcast facilities, and for professional journalists, who were easy enough to identify and expel or otherwise prevent from directly reporting on events. But YouTube, Facebook, and, most prominently, Twitter were not as easy to stop or even control in 2009 Iran.

Internet and cellphone service were intermittently restricted and partially shut down in Iran. However, cutting off all tweets and uploads of videos to YouTube would have required all Internet and cellphone service to be severed in that country, which its authorities were wary of doing, because that would have had ill effects for Iranian business and other essential exchanges of information. The result left protesters and citizen reporters with pipelines for their tweets and videos, which people outside Iran could also use to send tweets back into Iran via "proxies" that appeared legitimate to the authorities.

At the same time, of course, Iranian authorities could and apparently did use Twitter to send out misleading information. When I was asked on an interview on KNX Radio broadcasting from Los Angeles on June 16, 2009, how anyone could know if tweets coming out of Iran were true or disinformation, I replied that the aggregate of tweeters, just like the many reader/editors on Wikipedia, provided some checks and balances on the accuracy of the information (Levinson, 2009, "New New Media vs. the Mullahs"). And, indeed, tweets suspected of being planted by the government were identified and denounced on Twitter (see Grossman, 2009).

The protest in Iran did not succeed in 2009. The mullahs and Ahmadinejad are still in power as of January 2012. But it is worth noting that a new medium of the late

1970s, the audio cassette, was instrumental in the Iranian revolution of 1979 (Zunes, 2009), cellphones helped organize the successful Second People Power Revolution in the Philippines in 2001 (see Rheingold, 2003; Popkin, 2009), and the U.S. State Department thought Twitter was so crucial in the early days of the 2009 protest in Iran that it asked Twitter to delay a scheduled shutdown for maintenance until a time when most of Iran was likely asleep (Grossman, 2009).

The new new media techniques first used in Iran in 2009 had greater success in the Arab Spring of 2011 and after—ridding Tunisia and Egypt of their dictators, and Libya (with military assistance from the United States and Europe) as well. These same techniques also facilitated Occupy Wall Street across the United States and much of the world beginning in the Fall of 2011. We will consider these profound political developments in chapter 10, "Politics and New New Media."

Here is the timeline of some of the major clashes of newly invented media with governmental authority in the 20th and 21st centuries that I put on the first page of this book, updated now from the first edition of *New New Media*. Newly invented media are intrinsically difficult for governments to control, because they are usually too recent for people in government to fully understand. Further, even before the Internet and new new (social) media, the devices and systems listed in the following timeline were conducive to individual creation of messages, unlike mass media of similar vintage, in particular radio and television.

1942–43: The White Rose uses photocopying to tell the truth to Germans about the Nazi government. Fails to dislodge the Nazis.

1979: Audio cassettes of Ayatollah Khomeini distributed in Iran. Succeeds in fomenting successful revolution against Shah.

1980s: Samizdat video in the Soviet Union criticizes Soviet government. May have helped pave the way for Gorbachev's perestroika and glasnost, and end of Soviet rule.

1989: Email gets word out to the world about Tiananmen Square protests. Fails to dislodge Chinese government.

2001: Cellphones help mobilize peaceful opposition to President Estrada in Philippines. The Second People Power Revolution succeeds.

2009: Twitter and YouTube get word out to the world about Iranian opposition to reported election outcome. Fails to dislodge the Iranian government.

2010–ongoing: Twitter, Facebook, and YouTube help mobilize opposition to governments in Tunisia and Egypt, and help get word out to the world about these developments. Dictators are dislodged in peaceful revolutions. The Arab Spring spreads to Libya (regime overthrown via military force) and Yemen (prime minister resigns), and to Bahrain and Syria, with results inconclusive as of January 2012. Arab Spring protests in 12 other countries (see Wikipedia, "The Arab Spring," for current statuses).

2011–ongoing: Twitter, Facebook, and YouTube help facilitate protests in the United States, which soon spread around the world, known as Occupy Wall Street. Results inconclusive as of January 2012.

McLuhan as Microblogger

The short form of Twitter is not only a politically efficient and socially cool necessity; it had already been developed, long before Twitter, into a well-known literary form. Marshall McLuhan died on the last day of 1980—not only years before there was tweeting and blogging but a few years before email and more than a decade before easily accessible Web pages. But McLuhan was microblogging or tweeting in one of his most important books, *The Gutenberg Galaxy* (McLuhan, 1962), with chapter titles or "glosses" such as "Schizophrenia may be a necessary consequence of literacy" and "The new electronic interdependence recreates the world in the image of a global village." There were 107 such "tweets" in that book.

I first recognized the digital format of McLuhan's writing two decades prior to Twitter. In 1986, I wrote a piece for the *IEEE Transactions of Professional Communications* entitled "Marshall McLuhan and Computer Conferencing," in which I suggested that the pithy, aphoristic bursts that characterized his writing—his great works from the 1960s consisted of chapters often not more than a page or two in length—were actually a form of Web writing ("computer conferencing"), or what we today call blog posts, decades before the Web and online communication had emerged.

Fast-forward 21 years....I was browsing through a Twitter page, a few months after I had joined in the summer of 2007, and realized that the tweets bore a strong resemblance to the titles of those short chapters in McLuhan's books. If the contents of his chapters were blog posts, a page or two of thoughts, with no necessary connection between one chapter and the next, no fixed order, then the titles of those chapters were tweets, or an arresting phrase or two, at most. McLuhan's chapter "glosses," in other words, were tweets before their time (Levinson, "McLuhan," 2007)—fixed on paper, not floating on the screen. Of course, titles such as "Nobody ever made a grammatical error in a non-literate society" in *The Gutenberg Galaxy* were far more meaningful than most of the tweets on Twitter. So McLuhan's titles not only presaged Twitter, they also presaged the best that Twitter could be. (And to complete the transformation, there are now several Twitter accounts under McLuhan's name that tweet his aphorisms.)

But how did the real Marshall McLuhan manage to see the digital age? It was not that he had access to some sort of crystal ball that provided glimpses of the future. McLuhan owned no fantastical Prester John speculum that breached time. It was rather that McLuhan's mind worked in a way that our digital age, and new new media in particular, have captured and projected onto our screens and lives. If new new media express how human beings always wanted to communicate, all along, but could not, because our ancestors and parents lacked the technological sophistication (see my "anthropotropic" theory of media evolution for more; Levinson, 1979, 1997), then McLuhan understood and was in touch with this way of communicating, decades before it came to be. He wrote not about his age but ours, in a style that worked best not with the print media of his day but the new new media of our current time.

This, in turn, suggests that such a short form of writing was always part of our human capability, but, with the exception of graffiti and the telegram, our culture and education until the present served to limit or rule it out. McLuhan was able to break through those limits, and the short form is now becoming the norm in texting, IMing, status reporting, and tweeting.

The resurgence of the short—Shakespeare got it, when he wrote "brevity is the soul of wit"—also points to a more general historical dynamic between old and new new media. Retrieval of earlier communication forms by new technologies is an important part of McLuhan's media theory and was most developed in his "tetrad," or four-part model of what he referred to as media "effects." Every newly introduced medium "amplifies" aspects of our communication (radio, for example, amplifies sound across distance), "obsolesces" a currently widespread form (radio took the place of some reading), "retrieves" an earlier form (radio brought back the spoken word), and eventually reverses or "flips" into something else (radio becomes audiovisual television). *Digital McLuhan* (Levinson, 1999) provides more details and examples of tetrads, but, regarding Twitter, we could say it amplifies the short written phrase; obsolesces long blogs and phone calls; retrieves graffiti, telegrams, poetic phrases, and McLuhan's writing; and flips into ... well, that's yet to be seen.

But maybe we already have a glimpse of one of the new new media forms that Twitter is engendering or flipping into. Robert K. Blechman's *Executive Severance* (2012), described by the author as a "twitstery," is a novel written entirely on Twitter, once a day, one tweet at a time. Whereas Amazon, a new medium, engendered the Kindle (another kind of new medium with digital content in traditional book form), Twitter the new new medium has engendered a genuinely new kind of novel, one that could not have existed before Twitter. The novel created in tweets on Twitter completes the cycle started by McLuhan, who wrote in tweets before Twitter was born.

But most of Twitter plays not off fiction but the real world in which you and I exist. In chapter 7, we will see how Foursquare has pushed the integration of the digital and real world to a new, even more handy level. Next, we turn to the video new new medium— YouTube—part of the Facebook-Twitter-YouTube triad engine that most propels new new media in 2012.

CHAPTER 4

YouTube

IF TEXT IS CLOSEST TO THE OLDEST PERMANENT FORM OF HUMAN communication—the oldest form, period, if we include the cave paintings in Altamira and Lascaux as a kind of picture writing, or etchings on 60,000-year-old ostrich eggs as a form of writing (Lloyd, 2010)—then audiovisual recordings are surely the newest.

Even though the ancient Alexandrians knew about persistence of vision—the characteristic of human perception that keeps images in our vision a split second after they are in front of our eyes, and makes motion pictures possible—motion pictures themselves did not become a mass medium until the 1890s. The first movies back then were voiceless. Talkies arrived in the late 1920s, around the same time television was invented, which did not begin to have a major impact until the late 1940s. But commercial television grew quickly—it still holds the record for fastest rate of growth for a medium in the United States—and was being watched in nearly 90 percent of American homes by the end of the 1950s. VCRs were introduced in the mid-1970s, and cable as an independent source of programming in the early 1980s. The history of audiovisual media prior to YouTube, in other words, only goes back fewer than a hundred fast-moving years.

YouTube was created in February 2005—the work of Chad Hurley, Steve Chen, and Jawed Karim, who had been colleagues at PayPal—and publicly debuted in November 2005. It has certainly thrived on clips from network and cable television, a striking partnership of old and new media. But its most unexpected and long-lasting impact has come from videos made by nonprofessionals, or, rather, by people who are not cable or network television producers. Its trademark, along with the YouTube logo, is "Broadcast Yourself."

Consider, for example, the story of Obama Girl—a YouTube and new new media classic, seen nearly 24 million times as of January 2012, generating videos seen more than 120 million times, and chosen by *Newsweek* as one of the top 10 memes of the decade.

"Obama Girl"

The story of Obama Girl begins in December 2006 on an old medium. *Saturday Night Live*, on NBC television, aired an hilarious skit originally titled "My Dick in a Box." Thanks to the FCC, however, NBC was afraid to broadcast the comical routine with its original wording. "My Dick" was replaced by "Special Treat."

But the singing and dancing with the original wording somehow made its way onto YouTube, where it attracted millions of viewers, likely more in the long run than had seen the bowdlerized skit on television. (Congress has unsuccessfully tried to impose language restrictions on the Internet, and although Bill Clinton actually signed the Communications Decency Act of 1996 into law, it was struck down by the Supreme Court.)

Enter Ben Relles, who, with singer/songwriter Leah Kauffman, had an idea for an answer or a response video to "My Dick in a Box": "My Box in a Box." Answer videos or video responses are a YouTube equivalent of text comments on Facebook, and they give new producers a good way to attract attention by literally appending the response video (if the original video owner approves) to a video that already enjoys a big audience, or large number of views. YouTube also has a thriving text comment section. Popular videos generate thousands of comments, in contrast to a handful of response videos.

"My Box in a Box" did not do nearly as well as the original "My Dick in a Box," which received more than 24 million views in the first six months it was on YouTube (see *Catch Up Lady*, 2007). "Box in a Box" has been taken down and put back up numerous times since then, so its statistics as of January 2012 of nearly 5 million views since its posting in December 2006 are not strictly comparable to "My Dick in a Box." But the numbers were more than enough to get Ben Relles and his team, BarelyPolitical.com, interested in YouTube as a medium to showcase their productions.

Fox's *24* started a new season ("Day Six") in January 2007. Relles and company had an idea for a video, "I've Got a Crush on Jack Bauer" (the charismatic lead character on *24*, played by Kiefer Sutherland). That's the way Kauffman wrote the song. Barack Obama announced he was running for president in February 2007, and that gave Relles the idea that Obama would be an even more exciting object of a video crush than Bauer. Amber Lee Ettinger was brought in to act the smitten part, lip-synching Kauffman's voice. "I've Got a Crush on Obama" was put up on YouTube in June 2007. It received more than 2.3 million views the first month (Sklar, 2007). Obama Girl became a popular icon. Further video with Obama Girl followed, as well as a bevy of similar or answer videos for other candidates in the 2008 presidential election, including Hillary Clinton and John McCain. When Ben Relles and Amber Lee Ettinger visited my "Intro to Communication and Media Studies" class at Fordham University in September 2007, there wasn't a person in my 120-student class who had not already seen or heard about Obama Girl (Levinson, 2007). Obama Girl returned to YouTube in 2012, with a parody video of "You're the One That I Want" (from *Grease*), and a takeoff from *Glee,* in which she tells Obama that he'll have to work to win her vote this time (Hayes, 2012). "Glease" (Polipop, 2012) had 75,000 views within a week of its posting in February 2012.

Did Obama Girl have an impact on the 2008 election? Who would admit to voting for a candidate because of a saucy, funny video? But this much is clear: Obama did very well with the under-30-years-of-age voter—in the primaries and the general election—and this was precisely the group that did not go to the polls in the numbers needed by Democratic presidential candidate John Kerry in 2004, and the group that most watched Obama Girl on their computer screens in 2007. And the Obama Girl video went viral at a very early and therefore crucial time in the campaign, when many people were still first learning whatever they could about Barack Obama. The video, at the very least, showed Obama as someone cool, interesting, and attractive.

Linda Wertheimer reported on National Public Radio (June 24, 2008) that the number of voters under age 30 in the 2008 primaries and caucuses across America was two to three times greater than in 2004. Fifty-eight percent of these voters identified themselves as Democratic, and they voted for Obama over Clinton by 3-to-1 margins in states such as Georgia, which Obama won in the 2008 primaries, and 2-to-1 margins for Obama in states such as Pennsylvania, which Obama lost in the 2008 primaries.

The trend held through the November 2008 general election, in which at least 50 percent of 18- to 29-year-olds voted in America for the first time since 1972, and 66 percent of them voted for Obama, "up 12 percent from those who voted for John Kerry in 2004 and 18 percent from those who supported Al Gore in 2000" (Grimes, 2008; see also Dahl, 2008). As we will see throughout this book, and especially in chapter 10, the 2008 "Obama campaign was able to leverage many types of new and social media" (Baird, 2008)—techniques that Republicans as well as Democrats had well mastered by 2012.

YouTube 2008 Presidential Primary Debates

The 2008 presidential campaigns also saw the debut of YouTube primary debates in 2007, in which questions for the candidates were submitted via YouTube video clips. CNN, under whose auspices the candidates assembled to answer the questions, selected the video clips, making these debates a little less than a breath of totally direct democracy, or an example of completely new new media in politics. But the origin of questions directly from American citizens was a significant improvement over questions asked by news commentators, presumably asking questions on our behalf. No doubt some of the questions were coached and perhaps even prepared by surrogates for the candidates. But even with such inevitable abuses, the YouTube debates marked an important step forward in the democratization of the debate and thus the election process.

What follows are my blog posts, entered immediately after the Democratic CNN-YouTube primary debate on July 23, 2007, and the Republican CNN-YouTube primary debate on November 28, 2007:

> *The first YouTube/CNN Presidential Debate—this one with the Democrats—just concluded. I said I would wait until I saw it, to say how much of a revolution it was. Having seen it, I think it was revolutionary indeed—and, in fact, as much a leap forward in the debates and democracy as the first presidential debates on television in 1960.*
>
> *I don't ever recall seeing a debate in either party with such a refreshing, humorous, frank and incisive series of questions. The people asking the questions in the YouTube videos were far more on the money than any panel of experts.*
>
> *And the candidates rose to the occasion with honest and important answers.*
>
> *Barack Obama, when asked about whether he is a legitimate African-American candidate—given his access to power—quipped, "Ask the New York cabbies!" (African-Americans unfortunately have a tougher time getting a cab to stop for them and pick them up than Caucasian New Yorkers—I'm Caucasian, I've lived in New York all of my life, and maybe this problem has lessened a little, but it still exists.)*

Hillary Clinton, responding to a question about the election of Bush in 2000, responded that, actually, Bush was not elected president.

John Edwards, on health care, gave an impassioned plea for the need for all Americans to have it—he did this even though he had exceeded his time, and Anderson Cooper was trying to cut him off.

Joe Biden answered a YouTube question about gun control, asked by someone who was armed with an automatic weapon, which he called his "baby." Answered Biden: if that's your baby, you need help....

And that's just a sampler.

Even Anderson Cooper, who did seem to unfairly cut off the minor candidates—such as Mike Gravel—more than the major candidates, was in fine form tonight. The final questioner asked each candidate to cite something liked and disliked about the candidate to the left. Kucinich quipped that there was no one standing to his left on the stage (true). Cooper replied—we tried to find someone to your left but there was no one....

There's nothing like the fresh air of democracy to energize a debate and give people clearer choices. There was concern, before the debate, about CNN exercising too much control in choosing the YouTube questions to be shown—I agree that CNN should not have selected the questions, but I don't see how the choices could have been any better.

I'm looking forward to the Republican rendition of this fine experiment—which will become the norm—in September.

But on July 27 I added, with link to new blog post: "Republicans Now Thumb Noses at YouTube as Well as Evolution."

The last line was added because, as of July 27, 2007, only John McCain and Ron Paul had committed to a Republican primary CNN-YouTube debate in September 2007, so CNN was obliged to cancel it. The Republicans eventually did see the YouTube light, and their YouTube debate took place on CNN on November 28, 2007. I posted the following on my blog immediately after the debate:

I didn't find tonight's Republican YouTube/CNN debate as refreshing and provocative as the first YouTube debate among the Democratic contenders for president a few months ago. Possibly the YouTube bloom is off the rose. More likely the questions weren't as humorous or provocative tonight as those received via YouTube for the Democrats.

Otherwise, it was a good, punchy debate, which showed most of the candidates off to their best advantage. McCain, in particular, was more eloquent and forceful than usual in his support of the war and his denunciation of torture. Romney was on the receiving end of McCain's torture lecture—Romney falling back on his all-too-typical letting the experts decide—but Ron Paul had a fine moment in his cogent explanation, back to McCain, on the difference between being an isolationist and a noninterventionist (Ron Paul is the latter). And Ron Paul also spoke truth about why violence has decreased in southern Iraq—that it happened because the British left.

But Romney was excellent in knocking down Giuliani's attack on Romney's alleged employment of illegal aliens—Romney reasonably replied that he contracted with a company to work on his home, he did not directly hire illegal aliens.

I should note here, however, that although I admired Romney's rhetoric in this exchange—a rarity—I think most of the Republicans and many of the Democrats are making too big a deal about illegal aliens (not that terminology matters all that much, but I can't help thinking of people from outer space whenever I hear that phrase). One of America's greatest strengths has always been its openness to people from other countries and cultures.

Huckabee was probably the best on stage about this issue, refusing to back down from his funding of education for children of illegal immigrants.

Giuliani, other than the exchange with Romney on the employment of illegal immigrants, was pretty much on top of his game, and Fred Thompson was a little more animated than usual tonight, too.

So where do we stand: Huckabee is personable and gaining in the polls and could conceivably pull an upset in Iowa. Even if he comes close, he could be a good running mate for Giuliani. I'd say it's too late for McCain and Thompson, whatever they do or say from now on. Romney is still Giuliani's major competition.

And Ron Paul still has by far the best positions. He alone among the Republican candidates continues to speak the truth to authority about war. We'll soon find out how many votes this translates into in the primaries.

Huckabee went on to win in Iowa; McCain was not too late to win the Republican nomination; Ron Paul, in fact, did very poorly in actual primary voting—even though articles in favor of his candidacy were "Dugg up" to the front page of Digg every day in the primary campaigns, and phone-ins after presidential debates frequently declared him the winner. We will explore in chapter 8 in the section on Digg why this was so—why Ron Paul, who in 2008 did so well in new new media, did so poorly in the primaries. We will also look at why Ron Paul did somewhat better in the Republican primaries in 2012.

Barack Obama did very well in new new media in 2008, and won not only the nomination but also the general presidential election. Part of the reason is that Obama also looked very good on the older medium of television.

Telegenic + YouTube = Cybergenic

Barack Obama was first described as "cybergenic" by Paul Saffo in June Saffo, 2008, an observation Mark Leibovich picked up in *The New York Times* in August Leibovich, 2008. The logic of the appellation is that just as FDR was a master of radio (see "Radio Heads" in Levinson, 1997, for more on FDR's as well as Churchill's, Hitler's, and Stalin's—political wielding of radio), and JFK was a natural for television (in contrast to Nixon), so was Obama a perfect Internet candidate in 2008, especially in comparison to his opponent John McCain.

The historical analogies, however, are not completely apt. FDR and his advisers understood and harnessed the power of radio, whereas JFK merely looked better than Nixon on television. On the other hand, Kennedy and his advisers knew after the debates that he had performed well on TV—a majority of people who heard the debates on radio thought Nixon did better, in contrast to the majority of television viewers who liked Kennedy (see McLuhan, 1964, p. 261)—and televised press conferences became a hallmark of his administration. Indeed, JFK's press conferences are still the high watermark for élan and style of a president talking to the media, though historians may conclude that Obama and Ronald Reagan came close.

But, more important, the designation of Obama as cybergenic, in contrast to telegenic, misses the crucial role that looking and sounding good on television plays in making a candidate cybergenic.

In fact, the synergistic, mutually catalytic relationship between old and new new media can be easily missed when focusing on the revolutionary impact of new new media. In the case of blogging, for example, investigative reporting from old print media fuels much of the reporting and commentary on new and new new media such as *The Huffington Post* and *Daily Kos* (see chapter 6, "Blogging," for more). And successful television series beginning with *Lost* have vigorously enlisted the viral Internet for promotion. In the case of the "cybergenic" candidate, most of the political video clips that appear on the Web, embedded from YouTube or directly from news sites such as MSNBC.com, originated on traditional cable television.

This means that a candidate must look good on television to look good on the Web. No matter how good I may look in a television appearance, thanks to expert lighting, I am not going to look like George Clooney. Similarly, Obama's YouTube superiority over McCain in 2008 flowed from Obama's looking and sounding better on television. For all the magic and power of YouTube, it cannot make a new new media silk purse out of a TV sow's ear.

The relationship of new and old media, of new new media to the preexisting real world, is one of the main areas of focus in this book. The gist, politically, is that success in new new media is not in itself enough—or is not really success unless it is aided and abetted by older media, and reflected in the world offline.

YouTube Undeniability and Democracy

At the opposite end of the professional production spectrum, we have YouTube clips not taken from a television talk show or news show and not even created by non-network producers such as Ben Relles. We have clips taken via cellphone, smart phone, or other lightweight, handheld video cameras that could be in the hands of...well, anyone.

And though the producers of such clips taken on the fly can be anonymous or completely unknown, the subjects of the videos could be the same politicians and celebrities we see on traditional television.

Senator George Allen (R-VA), for whatever reason, called on a questioner at a public event on August 15, 2006, and referred to him as "Macaca." The term is a racial epithet in some parts of the world. Allen denied that he uttered the term; he said he had no recollection of saying it. YouTube knew better. A clip of George Allen saying "Macaca" was up for all the world to see—which they did, one by one, hundreds of thousands of times (more than 625,000 views as of the beginning of 2012). Allen lost his bid for reelection to the Senate that year and, along with it, his position as a likely contender for the Republican presidential nomination in 2008. *Rolling Stone* aptly titled an article, shortly after the incident, "The First YouTube Election: George Allen and 'Macaca'." The subtitle was "George Allen: Digital Foot in Twenty-First Century Mouth" (Dickinson, 2006).

Michael Richards, the comedian who played Kramer on *Seinfeld*, also discovered that cellphone videos and their dissemination on the Web were no laughing matter. Richards' response to a heckler at the Laugh Factory in West Hollywood on November 16, 2006, was to refer to the heckler as a "nigger"—six times (TMZ staff, 2006). Richards later apologized but will always be something more—and worse—than a funnyman in the public eye.

Jonathan Alter (then of *Newsweek*), on Keith Olbermann's *Countdown* on MSNBC on June 9, 2008, captured this facet of the YouTube revolution early on—what it means for politicians, and, by extension, anyone in the public arena. In 2000, Alter said, a videotape of a politician talking would be in some vault in some network backroom somewhere, after its airing on television. (This was the case in 2004, as well.) But by 2008 and thereafter, anything a politician said could be up in the bright, unblinking lights of YouTube minutes later, out of the custody and control of both the network and the politician.

Alter was talking about John McCain's claim that he had never commented on the media's impact on politics and elections—a claim refuted by McCain's statement just a few days earlier that the media had been unfair to Hillary Clinton in her race for the Democratic nomination. "The media often overlooked how compassionately she spoke to the concerns and dreams of millions of Americans" McCain had declared (2008), in a speech widely available on YouTube.

And a politician's words not only can be posted on YouTube a few minutes after they have been spoken, but they also can stay on YouTube for years—in effect, forever. Words in a YouTube video clip are not only undeniable, they are indelible. The lights are not only bright and unblinking but permanent. They and any video can be removed from YouTube, but the lights do not burn out on their own. Unlike a television broadcast, which must be recorded via TiVo or DVR to last beyond the moment, the YouTube video is inherently in the longevity zone.

The political consequences of this indelibility pertain not only to live events such as George Allen's, but also to appearances on television that show up on YouTube. Republican 2008 vice presidential candidate Sarah Palin's response on the *CBS Evening News* to Katie Couric about what newspapers Palin read—she could not name a single one—was first broadcast on September 30, 2008. It soon was on YouTube, where it had received nearly 2 million views by November 2008 (more than 2.5 million as of January 2012). It is impossible to ever know what precise impact this had on the election results in 2008, but it certainly could not have helped the Republicans. In the Republican presidential primary campaign of 2011–2012, the repeated surge and collapse of some half a dozen candidates—Michele Bachmann, Rick Perry, Herman Cain, Newt Gingrich, Rick Santorum—was no doubt fueled by video clips of embarrassing, damaging statements on YouTube. Rick Perry's November 2011 infamous "oops" moment, for example—when he could not name in a televised debate the three federal cabinet departments he wanted to abolish—was still enjoying a brisk viewership in early 2012, with more than half a million cumulative views on several video clips.

Anything recorded via any audiovisual device is a candidate for universal and long-lasting dissemination on YouTube—and that includes not only what politicians and other celebrities are saying now but also what anyone said or sang or otherwise communicated since the invention of motion pictures in the 1880s and the phonograph in 1877, if a motion picture or a recording was made of that communication. YouTube now (January 2012) has recordings of U.S. presidents Benjamin Harrison (1888–1892), Grover Cleveland (second term, 1892–1896), and William McKinley (1896–1901). (See the upcoming section, "'My Guitar Gently Weeps' Through the Ages," for more on YouTube immortality.)

YouTube Usurps Television as a Herald of Public Events

By all accounts, including mine (e.g., Sullivan, 2008; see Suellentrop, 2008, for a summary of blog reviews; Levinson, "Superb Speeches by Bill Clinton and John Kerry," 2008), 2004 Democratic nominee for president John Kerry gave one of the best speeches of the 2008

Democratic Convention in Denver, and probably the best speech of his life, on August 27, 2008. Unaccountably, the speech was carried in its entirety on none of the three major all-news cable television networks. Instead, MSNBC, CNN, and Fox News went for their own talking heads. As Andrew Sullivan aptly noted, "Cable believed their pundits were more interesting than this speech. They made the wrong call."

Or perhaps we can indeed account for why the cable television networks cut Kerry. Driven by the need to attract a maximum of viewers, required in turn to attract a maximum amount of revenue from advertisers, the program directors at the networks probably figured that John Kerry, not known as an electrifying speaker, might well lead viewers to other channels with more scintillating talking-head programming. Or, the networks at least thought that Chris Matthews, Wolf Blitzer, and Brit Hume—on MSNBC, CNN, and Fox News, respectively—would bore fewer viewers than Kerry.

C-SPAN and PBS, not beholden to advertisers, did broadcast John Kerry's speech. My wife and I had C-SPAN on as an inset on our television screen—we were watching MSNBC—and we switched to get an idea of what Kerry was saying. We kept our television on C-SPAN for the rest of Kerry's speech.

Noncommercial television thus saved TV as an instant herald for John Kerry. Beyond that, the speech was posted on YouTube within an hour. It attracted thousands of viewers in a few hours (more than 170,000 views by January 2012). Television increasingly counts only in the immediate run—in the short, medium, and long runs, YouTube has become the medium of record.

The relationship of YouTube to television in the coverage of public events complements the relationship of blogging to newspapers and helps pinpoint the position of new new media in our culture. Blogging provides commentary far faster than the op-eds of any printed newspaper. YouTube provides audiovisual records of events on television that would otherwise be gone the instant they concluded—or, in the case of John Kerry's 2008 speech, incompletely broadcast or not at all. Television, of course, can replay parts or all of any programming, but such replays are not accessible 24 hours a day, from most places in the world, as is any video on YouTube. Anything on television can be captured on TiVo or DVR, but those records are private, not publicly accessible. The new new media herald of events is thus faster in the case of blogging and more reliable in the case of YouTube than their old media counterparts. For the time being and near future, newspapers will continue because they do not require batteries to read, and television because it is still often an effortlessly accessible first word. But the better heralds of new new media are likely to continue to supplant and replace newspapers and television, especially as old and newer media—newspapers, blogs, television, YouTube videos—are all available on the same smart phone or tablet screen, which makes moving between the old and newer medium, between television and YouTube, that much easier.

YouTube Is Not Only Omni-Accessible and Free to Viewers—It's Also Free to Producers

Barack Obama paid $5 million for a 30-minute address (Sinderbrand & Wells, 2008), carried by most of the major television networks, a week before the presidential election of 2008. Some 33 million people saw his address (Gold, 2008), so the money was well spent.

But YouTube charges nothing for placement of videos on its site. As Joe Trippi remarked, Obama "can do a half-hour YouTube address every Saturday, addressing millions. The networks would never give the president that much television time each week, but the press is still going to have to cover what he says on YouTube" (Fouhy, 2008). A presidential candidate would certainly not get 30 minutes free of charge every Saturday to talk to the nation via network television, but Trippi astutely observes that likely neither would a president. Broadcast media have become more protective of income earned from their rented time in the 21st century than back in the first part of the 20th, when FDR delivered 30 "fireside chats" to the American public in prime time via radio from 1933 to 1944 (Dunlop, 1951).

Trippi, author of *The Revolution Will Not Be Televised: Democracy, the Internet, and the Overthrow of Everything* (2004), first came to America's attention as the manager of Howard Dean's unsuccessful campaign for the Democratic nomination for president in 2004. Trippi chronicles and assesses the Dean campaign in his book. Dean became known as the "Internet candidate," and Trippi was the Internet mastermind, but new new media back in 2004 were not what they were in 2008 and 2012. Blogging was thriving in 2004, but Facebook was in its infancy and YouTube and Twitter were still a year or two away.

Obama as the New FDR in New New Media as Well as the New New Deal?

The November 24, 2008, cover of *Time* magazine depicted Barack Obama as the new FDR—the then president-elect in specs, gray suit and hat, sitting in a car, cigarette jutting jauntily upward—and was captioned "The New New Deal."

The comparison, of course, was to FDR and Obama both first taking office in the throes of financial crises and catastrophe, and to Obama's plans for public works projects—"infrastructure" in 21st-century parlance—to help Americans get back to work and lay the foundations for more efficient commerce, just as FDR did in the Great Depression of the 1930s.

But the announcement—a day after the *Time* cover became public on November 13, 2008—that Obama's radio address on November 15 would also be made available on YouTube showed that Obama was trying to be the new FDR not only in New Deal economic terms but also in the employment of the newest media to communicate to the American people.

Roosevelt's "fireside chats" had used the new medium of his day, radio, to communicate directly to the American people, as no president had ever done before. Roosevelt and his advisers understood the advantages of new radio, which allowed anyone talking through it, including the president, to sound and seem as if he were talking directly to Americans, in their living rooms, bedrooms, or in whatever room their radio was situated. The effect was powerful, unprecedented, profound. My parents, who grew up in the Great Depression, often told me how they regarded Roosevelt as almost a kind of father—which makes sense, for whose deep voice would otherwise be talking to you in the inner sanctums of your home, if the economy and then the war were making you feel almost as helpless as a child? When World War II came, my parents, in their late teens and early 20s, felt especially comforted by Roosevelt's voice. They felt that, as long as FDR was talking to them and all Americans, the country would be okay. (See Levinson, 1997, *The Soft Edge* for more on radio and FDR.)

Americans stopped listening to radio that way in the 1950s, when television became the predominant political broadcast medium, and radio became a vehicle of rock 'n' roll. By 1960, people who saw the Kennedy-Nixon debates on television thought Kennedy won, in contrast to those who heard the debates on radio, as we considered previously. Unfortunately for Nixon, 87 percent of American households had televisions in their homes by 1960 (Roark et al., 2007). And by the election and its aftermath in 2008, YouTube was replacing television as the predominant political audiovisual medium—though, as discussed in the "Cybergenic" section, this by no means indicated that television had become unimportant in politics. To the contrary, a lot of what is on YouTube comes from television.

Obama's YouTube addresses, however, certainly did not have the same success as FDR's fireside chats in the 1930s and '40s—certainly not as of early 2012 for Obama, when his prospects for reelection were by no means assured. Roosevelt was the first four-term American president (and the last, due to the term limits set in the 22nd Amendment to the Constitution); Obama, in contrast, as of early 2012, is just in his first term and on a popularity roller coaster in the polls. The reasons for FDR's and Obama's different receptions surely reside in more than the media—for example, the de facto current need for majorities of 60 in the Senate making passage of new legislation more difficult than in the 1930s—but YouTube, for its part, may not be as comforting to viewers in the 21st century as radio was to its listeners in the 1930s. In place of the voice in the home, the fatherly reassurance that radio conveyed for FDR, YouTube plays to people on the move, in a peripatetic society in which everything, including the words of the president and the Congress, is subject to high levels of distrust. If new new media facilitated Occupy Wall Street and the resurgence of direct democracy, then the flip side of that, what comes along with it, is a bounding dissatisfaction with elected officials of all parties. Indeed, not only has YouTube played a major role in bringing the world an ongoing eyewitness record of Occupy Wall Street, but the need that YouTube unleashed to see these events as they're happening led to real-time video new new media such as UStream (founded in 2007), which exceed YouTube in being on the literal cutting edge of news (see chapter 10 for more).

Amateur YouTube Stars and Producers

Because YouTube is fed by anyone with a video camera or camera phone, the people in the video—the subject of the clip—can just as easily be unknown as famous. The amateur or unknown YouTube producer can point the camera at himself or herself, friends, the general public, or celebrities (if they're close at hand) with almost equal facility.

Kony 2012—a 30-minute documentary about the depredations of Ugandan Joseph Kony—became the fastest-growing video in the history of YouTube in March 2012, with more than 75 million views in its first week. Although the movie's director Jason Russell had some prior professional experience—he sold a script for a dance movie to Steven Spielberg, to help finance *Kony 2012* (Greene, 2012)—he certainly was not known to many people prior to 2012. The documentary has what have become some of the standard winning ingredients for a YouTube video, including Russell's five-year old son, and a call to action to make Kony and his villainy infamous (see Vamburkar, 2012, for a critique, and Levinson, 2012, "In Defense," for defense of the movie).

As of April 2012, Justin Bieber's "Baby" had the most all-time views on YouTube—more than 725 million—and *Kony 2012* more than 85 million. "Charlie bit my finger—again!" was in sixth place (formerly in first place), with more than 440 million views (see MacManus, 2012, for the history). What "Baby" and "Charlie" both have in common is their stars were discovered on YouTube—Bieber by his would-be manager in 2008, and Charlie and his older brother by their parents, who put up their video in 2007. Bieber went on to become a pop icon in the music world beyond YouTube, while Charlie and his family continue to hold forth only on YouTube. Comparing the numbers of viewers for both YouTube stars to television, the 2012 Super Bowl was the most watched broadcast in TV history, attracting 111.3 million viewers, which means the two total amateurs (baby Charlie and his slightly older brother) have attracted almost four times the number of viewers of the most watched show ever on television, and amateur-turned-professional singer Bieber has six times as many viewers as the Super Bowl on his lead video. (But in a good example of old and new new media synergy, the Super Bowl also set a record for greatest number of tweets per second, or TPS, for an English-language event—10,245—see Horn, 2012, for details.) Of course, the Super Bowl broadcast was live, over several hours, while the YouTube views accrued over several years. So the comparison of YouTube and television viewers is not completely equivalent, although it nonetheless shows that YouTube and television are both in the same huge audience ballpark, and you need not be a superstar to play in it. The extraordinary success of then-unknown-vocalist Susan Boyle in April 2009, first appearing on television's *Britain's Got Talent*, but with video clips receiving more than 100 million views on YouTube within a month after, provides another example both of the power of YouTube in contrast to television and the symbiotic relationship of these two media. Boyle was brought to public prominence by both television and YouTube.

Meanwhile, Chris Crocker, a total unknown when he first uploaded his video in 2007, had attained more than 42 million views for his hilarious "Leave Britney Alone" clip as of January 2012. His video is in effect an amateur/celebrity hybrid, with the producer or creator an amateur prior to the making of the video, but the subject already a big star (Britney Spears). "Obama Girl" would be another example (Ben Relles, little-known producer, about Barack Obama).

"Food Fight" provides a more purebred example of how lack of previous fame is no impediment to success on YouTube—much like Charlie and his brother, though a little more artistic. The YouTube description tells us that the video presents a short history of wars since World War II from the American perspective, as seen through the best-known foods of the warring nations. It was produced, written, and animated by Stefan Nadelman, at the time also a complete unknown, as the Dylan line goes. And, indeed, nothing about the animated video was well known beforehand—no stars, no voices, just animated. It was uploaded to YouTube in February 2008, had attained more than 3.6 million views by February 2009, and twice that amount, more than 7 million views, by February 2012. How could such a video, however superb, but with such utter lack of celebrity status, attract millions of viewers? I first saw "Food Fight" when a friend and colleague at Fordham University—Professor Lance Strate, who was also a "Friend" on Myspace—placed it in a comment he entered on my Myspace profile. Such nonprofessional promotion, which now typifies Facebook and Twitter, can be every bit as effective as a multimillion-dollar publicity campaign. Indeed, most public relations and publicity firms these days spend a lot of money in attempts to simulate such word-of-mouth, in-the-street marketing, a/k/a social media promotion.

This is best known as viral marketing, and it is the unpredictable, wildly successful promotional engine of the new new media age. "Charlie Bit My Finger—Again!" and "Food Fight" are archetypal examples of the unadulterated viral video on YouTube.

Viral Videos

Viral marketing, viral videos—viral any product or activity relating to popular culture—operates via one person who loves a song or video or whatever on the Web or elsewhere letting another person know of this enjoyment. When millions of people let millions of other people know about such a video, it can become enormously popular—as much as or more so than a video promoted by old-media advertising and publicity.

Once called "word of mouth," "viral" is something more, because digital word of mouth can reach anyone, anywhere in the world, and millions of people, instantly, in contrast to old-fashioned spoken word of mouth, which can reach only the person right next to you or, in the days of just landline telephone, at the other end of your phone connection (nowadays, cellphones and smart phones, especially when texting, are part of viral communication).

But why "viral"? In the biological world in which we and our physical bodies reside, a virus spreads by hitching a ride on or infecting a host cell; every time that host cell reproduces, the new cell takes a piece of the virus along with it. The viral video does much the same, by infecting or hitching a ride in the mind of every viewer who may see it. When these minds have access to new new media, where they can talk about, link, and even edit the video, the viral dissemination can become epidemic. Whether in the world of biology or popular culture, the virus or viral video sells itself.

Richard Dawkins was the first to apply this viral metaphor to human mentality in his discussion of "memes" in his 1991 essay "Viruses of the Mind." Human beings become hosts—happy, unhappy, conscious, or otherwise—of ideas. And the words all humans speak, and the books and articles that authors, reporters, and now bloggers write, and the links to videos and whatever anyone puts on Facebook and Twitter, then proceed to spread these ideas, these "memes," to other people, just as viruses disseminate their genetic materials from cell to cell, and just as DNA perpetuates itself through the reproduction of living organisms. Dawkins is here picking up on Samuel Butler's famous observation (1878) that a chicken is just an egg's way of producing more eggs—in Dawkins' schema, living organisms are machinery used by DNA to make more DNA. Dawkins first presented this perspective on DNA in his 1976 breakthrough book, *The Selfish Gene*, some 15 years prior to his equation of memes or infectious ideas with biological viruses. We could now say that DNA, viruses, memes, and viral videos all operate on the same hijack-the-host basis—to the general betterment of the host with DNA, detriment of the host with biological viruses, and either betterment or detriment depending on the specific meme or viral video.

Prior to Dawkins' "Viruses of the Mind," and well before the advent of the Web as a major fact of life, the virus analogy became prominent in the computer age in the popular designation of certain kinds of destructive computer programs as "computer viruses." (Dawkins prominently acknowledged and built upon the computer virus metaphor in his 1991 paper.) Attached to a computer program or code that did, or was purported to do, something useful—something the computer owner desired—the virus, once set loose on the computer, would erase files and do all manner of things that interfered with the user's work, to the point of shutting down the computer. This virus analogy obviously has a lot in common with the biological virus (more than does the virus metaphor in viral marketing), because both biological and computer viruses can result in the breakdown of their hosts—illness and possible death in humans and animals, uselessness and incapacity of computers.

The migration of the analogy to popular culture memes, however, resulted in "virus" not necessarily signifying anything bad. A viral video, after all, may be instructive and humorous—as is "Food Fight"—with no damage done to any of the hosts. (As an aside, the very growth and expansion of the use of the adjective "viral" has been viral, and not at all in a bad way, because the term indeed helps us understand how YouTube, new new media, and popular culture in general increasingly work together in the 21st century.)

Nonetheless, an abuse does occur on YouTube in which videos of beatings and other mistreatment of people and animals are uploaded for the perverse satisfaction of their creators and the perverse enjoyment of some viewers.

Viral Videos Gone Bad

The inevitable drawback of all open systems, the trade-off for the democratic benefits of all new new media, is that open systems can admit bad eggs. In the case of Wikipedia, which we will look at in the next chapter, the damage done by disruptive writer/editors is to the words in Wikipedia—its online articles. Such despoiling is easily discovered, removed, or otherwise remedied.

A video portraying a beating, or "beat down," can be easily removed from YouTube. But because real people are being beaten, the damage is to far more than information, and removal of the offending video cannot reverse or undo the beating or other depredation. The one upside of the ubiquitous video in such cases is that there is a permanent record of the crime, which makes it easier for the offenders to be brought to justice. But YouTube is nonetheless open to the question: Did the culture it created, in which anyone can be a star given the right (i.e., massively attractive) viral video, provide too easy an invitation to mentally unbalanced or ethically vacant people?

This is a question that arises whenever people as a whole are empowered by a new technology. The new device rarely creates the appetite for the evil deed. I recall kids in my schoolyard, alas, being beaten up by what the teachers called "toughs" back in the 1950s (when I was a student, not yet a teacher). Would people who toss babies across rooms (see O'Brien, 2008) and puppies over cliffs (see Wortham, 2008), just so they can be videotaped and see themselves on YouTube, not be likely to do similar things in the absence of YouTube?

We will examine the beat downs and other abuses conducted via or on behalf of YouTube and other new new media in more detail in chapter 9, "The Dark Side of New New Media." For now, we might well consider *Salon*'s Farhad Manjoo's (2008) thought that "the idea that the Web has desensitized kids to beatings and that MySpace has given rise to teen brutality is extremely dubious....despite high-profile news stories, we've got no evidence that that's the case—that bullying, fighting, or generalized teen angst has worsened during the MySpace era. Also, doesn't it seem just as plausible that headline-making incidents like this could deter, rather than provoke, violence in kids?"

Manjoo's last point suggests that kids with any brains will see that a beating that features them as the beaters, on YouTube, will provide both legal evidence against them and continuing shame in the future. Whether this would restrain all potential abusers eager for publicity, we don't know, but we can nonetheless assume that they would probably sooner or later do something deplorable, with or without YouTube, and YouTube in general contributes a lot more to the public good than to its undermining. We will continue to consider some of those beneficial effects in this chapter, but we should not lose sight of the abuses, and always stay on the lookout for ways to reduce or remove them, while maintaining and increasing the benefits.

The YouTube Revolution in Popular Culture

It was Harold Innis (1951), one of Marshall McLuhan's inspirations, who first wrote about how all media either space-bind or time-bind—that is, make communication easier across space or distance (as in the case of written documents carried across Roman roads), across time (as in the case of hieroglyphics carved on walls), or both (books produced by the printing press). As McLuhan (1962, McLuhan, 1964) noticed, new technologies in the 19th and 20th centuries continued to facilitate these kinds of "extensions," usually either across space or time, primarily, not both. The telegraph and telephone were space-binding extensions, while the photograph and phonograph were time-binding.

Here in our 21st century, all new new media are both space-binding and time-binding, due to the speed (across space) and retrievability (across time) of any information conveyed on the Web. But YouTube, especially, does both, par excellence.

A few years ago, I was watching a DVD of Martin Scorsese's 2005 documentary about Bob Dylan, *No Direction Home*. The movie has a clip of Dylan and Joan Baez performing Dylan's "With God on Our Side" at the Newport Folk Festival in July 1963. Baez takes Dylan by the hand out onto the stage, and they start singing.

After the movie, I searched on Baez and "With God on Our Side" on YouTube and found her complete rendition of the song in Stockholm, Sweden, in 1966. I embedded the YouTube video on my website, InfiniteRegress.tv, and commended it to people running for president—one line in the song in particular, "If God's on our side, He'll stop the next war."

There are as many examples of such discoveries as there are videos with music performances on YouTube, which has turned every computer, smart phone, and tablet screen into on-demand television at your 24-hour disposal—or, as Innis or McLuhan might have put it, had they lived to see this age, an easily accessible window across space and time.

Roy Orbison's Guitar

The Traveling Wilburys were—in my opinion and that of many critics and fans (e.g., Gill, 2007)—the best rock supergroup ever to have existed. Bob Dylan, George Harrison, Jeff Lynne, Tom Petty, and Roy Orbison recorded under that name from 1988 to 1990. Their best-known songs were "Handle with Care" and "End of the Line."

Roy Orbison died at the age of 52 in December 1988. When the time came to record a video of "End of the Line," the Wilburys put Orbison's rocking guitar in a rocking chair in the part of the song starting at 1 minute 44 seconds, where Orbison carried the lead. You also can see the rocking guitar at the very end of "End of the Line." (You can read all about this in the Wikipedia entry on the Traveling Wilburys.)

You can see the video and this moving tribute to Orbison any time you like on YouTube—in your home, office, or any place you happen to be with a smart phone or tablet.

YouTube, in other words, has robbed death of some of its meaning—at least insofar as it pertains to popular culture. The end of the line for audiovisual popular culture has become immortality on YouTube.

When I heard the news on February 11, 2012, that Whitney Houston had died, the first thing I did was watch her performance of "I Will Always Love You" from *The Bodyguard* (1992)—on YouTube. Millions of other people had done the same in the preceding years, and who knows how many million more will do this in the future. I did the same for The Monkees' "Daydream Believer," when news of Davy Jones's death broke on February 29, 2012 (see also Levinson, 2012, "Why The Monkees Are Important").

"My Guitar Gently Weeps" Through the Ages

Roy Orbison's is not the only immortal guitar on YouTube. George Harrison (1943–2001), another member of the Traveling Wilburys who is no longer with us, also has a guitar that plays across YouTube, in a way that brings home another one of YouTube's signature characteristics: presentation of numerous, slightly different takes of the same real-life event or numerous versions of the same song or creative work.

Slightly different takes of the same event can come from numerous people in a live audience with camera phones and other handheld vid-cams. Numerous renditions of the same song can also come from recordings of different performances throughout the decades.

YouTube has at least a dozen versions of George Harrison's "While My Guitar Gently Weeps," beginning with Harrison's performance at his 1971 Concert for Bangladesh, which also features Eric Clapton on guitar, and proceeding through the years to Eric Clapton and Paul McCartney's rendition of the song at the 2002 Memorial Concert for George, and the 2004 performance (my favorite) by Tom Petty and Jeff Lynne, with incandescent guitar work by Prince, when Harrison was posthumously inducted into the Rock 'n' Roll Hall of Fame for his solo work.

We see Harrison progressing through 20 years in these videos, Clapton through 30 years, with the song poignantly surviving its author. We see blurry videos with unclear sound taken by "bootleggers" at concerts, and we see top-of-the-line clips made for television broadcast. We see a de facto library, hear a record album through history, which we can add to or subtract from at any time, including—if perchance we happened to have recorded it—even adding a video clip of our own making.

We see, in short, the essence of YouTube and new new media.

We can also see on YouTube about 10 renditions of George Harrison's "All Things Must Pass," including one sung by Paul McCartney after Harrison's death. (My favorite, however—McCartney's performance at the Memorial Concert for George held at the Royal Albert Hall in London on November 29, 2002, one year after George's death—was gone from YouTube when I looked in November 2008. Indeed, when I looked at my list of more than 100 musical "Favorites" on YouTube in early 2012, seven had been removed, including videos by the Rolling Stones, David Bowie, and Langhorne Slim. The reason was copyright violation, which we will examine in the "YouTube's Achilles' Heel" section later in this chapter.)

"All Things Must Pass" is about the fleeting quality of all things, undesirable as well as desirable facts of life, bad as well as good states of being.

All things must pass. But it is tempting to now add to Harrison's perceptive lyric: except for performances lost in the night, now captured on video and added to what may well be the bright eternity of YouTube. For although YouTube itself, as it is currently configured, may well come to pass or be transformed or subsumed into something different, there is no reason to suppose that videos currently on YouTube, especially those of groups such as the Beatles and the Traveling Wilburys, or any great contemporary artist, will not be included in such post-YouTube media. And even when a video is removed from YouTube, it can be restored, and that removal cannot possibly erase the video already downloaded to users' computers, tablets, and smart phones. (See, however, Amazon's removal of George Orwell's *1984* from Kindles in 2009, discussed in the next chapter.)

YouTube Retrieves MTV

"Video Killed the Radio Star," the U.K. New Wave group The Buggles sang to everyone in 1979, heralding the success of music videos on MTV in the 1980s and being the very first video played on MTV when it began in 1981.

Here is what really happened:

To begin with, the enormous and rapid dissemination of television sets in the 1950s was thought by many observers to spell the end of radio. (A famous *New Yorker* cover in 1955, Perry Barlow's "Another Radio to the Attic," shows a radio languishing next to a crank-up Victrola in a dusty corner, as if it were an artifact from some long-ago era. Carl Rose's 1951 *New Yorker* cartoon similarly depicts a little girl and her mother in the attic, with the little girl pointing to a radio and asking, "What's that, Mama?") Television had co-opted radio's original and highly successful network programming of soap operas, serials, and news.

But radio did not fade away; it instead thrived and became the most profitable medium, dollar spent for dollar earned. Radio did this by playing rock 'n' roll records, supplied free of charge by record companies and sometimes even with payments (which the U.S. government soon investigated and prosecuted, calling this "payola"). And radio capitalized on the capacity of all acoustic media to be listened to when doing other things—in the case of radio, when driving, getting up in the morning, and so forth. Thus rock 'n' roll and multitasking propelled Top 40 radio in the 1950s and '60s, and FM radio in the 1960s and '70s (see Levinson, 1997, for details).

The debut of MTV in the early 1980s indeed diverted some of the limelight from radio to the television screen. But MTV hardly "killed" radio or the radio star, and by the mid-1990s, CDs and, even more important, MP3s were tipping the scale of attention and prominence in the popular culture back to acoustic media.

This was the situation when YouTube opened its virtual doors in 2005. But the music videos easily available on YouTube, from decades past to the present, have given the video a new, expanded lease on life in the popular culture.

In sum: video didn't kill the radio star in the first place. But YouTube has made the music video even more of a major player than it was on MTV in the 1980s—an example of a new new medium (YouTube) supplanting a newish old medium (MTV or cable television).

Will YouTube Put iTunes Out of Business?

As we have seen, new new media compete not only with old media but with new media on the Web, or media on the Web that charge for their information, operate via strict editorial control, and employ other procedures of old, mass media.

How long can iTunes, which as of January 2012 charges 69 cents, 99 cents, or $1.29 per song, survive YouTube's free competition? iTunes, Amazon.com, and newspapers online such as *The New York Times* and *The Wall Street Journal* that charge for subscriptions are classic examples of "new" in contrast to "new new" media. Old media exist offline. New media exist online but retain old media ways of doing business. Some new media retain more old ways than others. iTunes charges (but not for podcasts) and has strict editorial control over what appears on its pages. *The Huffington Post*, which can be considered about halfway between new and new new media, is free but still wields strict old media gatekeeping, or editorial control. New new media coexist with new media online but dispense with all old media confinements of payment and editorial control.

iTunes is still not without its advantages in comparison to YouTube—mainly in the great number of songs it offers and their easy organization. More than 10 billion tracks had been downloaded from iTunes as of February 2010. The quality of the music for sale on iTunes is likely better than the sound of most, but not all, YouTube videos, but as high-quality videos become more prevalent on YouTube, this difference is likely to vanish. Further, the accessibility of YouTube and videos on iPhones (and iPads) makes them competitive with MP3s played on iPods—ironic, because Apple is the maker of both iPhones and iPods, which means Apple succeeds whatever way the new new media cookie crumbles. But the pace of media evolution is so fast that it cannot help but generate competition even among products of different divisions of the same company.

Perhaps such concerns are what led iTunes to say in October 2008 that it might shut itself down if artists and record producers received higher royalties for sale of their songs on iTunes (Ahmed, 2008). The Copyright Royalty Board in Washington, D.C., was convinced by iTunes and supported its refusal to raise royalties from 9 to 16 cents per download (Frith, 2008).

But, again, Apple would have won in any case. If iTunes went out of business, Apple would still be doing well with its iPhones and iPads and their YouTube access. Meanwhile, iTunes continues to grow, as evidenced by the Beatles' catalog finally coming online at the end of 2010.

YouTube Refutes Lewis Mumford and Turns the Videoclip into a Transcript

Lewis Mumford (1895–1990) typified the attitude of many critics of television when he compared watching it with being in a state of "mass psychosis" in his Mumford, 1970 *The Pentagon of Power* (p. 294). Mumford's objection to television was that it provided no sense of past or future, allowing viewers no way to look back or skip ahead when they were watching a television series or news show, as readers easily could when reading a book or newspaper. VCR technology began to give viewers some control over the past and future in television as early as 1976. DVR and TiVo technologies have greatly expanded that control by allowing users to program the recording of episodes weeks in advance.

But YouTube ratchets up this viewer control a significant step by allowing people to watch what is on YouTube not only at any time but also from any place, if the viewer happens to have a smart phone or other portable, Internet-accessing device at hand. Via the combination of YouTube and mobile media, the audiovisual image is at last as controllable by the viewer as pages in a book are to a reader. (See my *Cellphone: The Story of the World's Most Mobile Medium*, 2004, for a history and current impact of mobility in media, and chapter 7 of *New New Media* for more on the impact of smart phones and other mobile media on new new media on the Web.) Mumford's hyperbole was incorrect in the first place. But YouTube has decisively consigned it to the attic of bygone intellectual error.

YouTube has made the online video as accessible and "readable" to the viewer as a written transcript online or in hand. Just as the reader of a written transcript can stop, go back, browse forward, or read a section again, so can the viewer of a YouTube video do the same with the moving images on the screen. From the point of view of the new new media user, there is indeed no significant difference between an online transcript and video, other than that one must be literate to read the transcript. We can make the following analogy: a transcript or book or newspaper in hand is to VCRs and DVDs as a transcript or book online is to a video on YouTube and other online video sites. The goal or target of all new new media—or, in Aristotle's terms, their "final cause"—is to make their worldwide contents as accessible as a book in hand.

Tim Russert, 1950–2008

YouTube has also made the immediate past unforgettable and universally retrievable. Tim Russert, *Meet the Press* moderator and NBC Washington News Chief, died unexpectedly on June 13, 2008. The story was covered all that day and most of the weekend on three all-news cable networks in the United States—MSNBC, CNN, and Fox News. YouTube played a different role, with more than 500 clips of Tim Russert added in the first 24 hours after his death. Tom Brokaw's report of Russert's death had more than 700,000 views nearly four years later.

The YouTube contribution underscores another significant difference between new media (cable television) and new new media (YouTube). Although CNN International is available in many parts of the world, it appropriately moved on to other stories in the days following Russert's death (MSNBC and Fox have much less international reach). In contrast, the YouTube clips of Russert were instantly available everywhere in the world and will continue to be instantly available for years to come—or, as indicated previously regarding the music videos of Roy Orbison and George Harrison, in principle, forever. Unless the videos violate copyright.

YouTube's Achilles' Heel: Copyright

The following has happened to many a blogger: You write a nice post about a favorite song or a musical performance—as, in fact, I did, in June 2008, about Paul McCartney's rendition of George Harrison's "All Things Must Pass" at the 2002 Royal Albert Hall Memorial Concert—and flesh it out with a video of the performance, via an embed from

YouTube. It looks and sounds great. You put links to your post on Twitter, Facebook, Reddit, and all the appropriate places. You receive complimentary comments. But a few months later, you also receive an email from a disappointed reader, who got a message that the video is "no longer available."

You check on your blog site, and then on YouTube, and, sure enough, you find that the video has been taken down from YouTube, because it violated its "terms of service"—or, in plainer English, some person or corporation told YouTube that the video violated its copyright. The hand of old media copyright enforcement, withered but not without power, has pulled the rug and the fun out from under your new new media blog creation. Or, to try another appendage metaphor, you have just encountered YouTube's Achilles' heel: copyright enforcement.

YouTube's one flaw is that, despite the potential immortality of every video on its site, there is no guarantee that any given video clip available today will be there tomorrow, or even five minutes from now. The immortality is the default condition, which can be deliberately broken at any time. This means there is no guarantee that any links to video elsewhere on the Web, and embeds of the video, will continue to work.

The Internet, on the one hand, has gone a long way to achieving even more stability and even permanency than paper—what I call "reliable locatability" (see Levinson, "The Book on the Book," 1998; Levinson, *Cellphone*, 2004; and Levinson, "The Secret Riches," 2007)—via "permalinks." But even permalinked text and videos can be taken down, and YouTube's vulnerability to copyright enforcement, in addition to the person who put up a video in the first place deciding to remove it for whatever reason, is a significant, retrograde old media step backward. The great asset of YouTube and new new media, which is that anyone can become a producer, finds its limitation in the reverse effect that stems from the same power, and makes every producer a potential deleter.

There is software readily available that allows users to download videos—not just link to or embed them—with the result that these users can then put the videos up on their own Web pages, without recourse to YouTube or other video storage and dissemination sites such as Blip.tv, Metacafe, and Vimeo.

But this might well be a copyright violation, also. And though the violation might never be discovered, its possibility keeps us on one of the prime battle lines of old and new media, on the one hand, and new new media on the other: the battle line of copyright.

Copyright—literally, the right to copy—started as a royal prerogative in Europe, after the introduction of the printing press in the middle of the 15th century. Monarchs gave printers the right to make copies and thereby controlled the output of written information in their realms. But in 1710, Parliament in England enacted the Statute of Anne, which made copyright a right to be claimed by authors and protected on behalf of authors by the government (see Kaplan, 1966; Levinson, 1997).

This is where copyright resides today. It protects the author's interests in three ways. The owner of the copyright determines who, if anyone, can (1) make copies of the work, (2) make money from copies of the work, or (3) use portions of the work in new creations, not of the original creator's making.

Details in the practice of copyright are complex and have evolved. At the beginning of the 20th century, authors had to formally claim copyright. By the end of the 20th century, copyright was accepted as a right belonging to authors, inherent in the authorship of the work (registration of copyright with the government makes enforcement of copyright easier but is not required for an author's assertion of copyright). A hundred years ago, the term of a copyright in the United States was 28 years, with one renewal possible. It is currently for the lifetime of the author plus 75 years. (The Berne Convention, of which the United States and 163 other nations are signatories, provides copyright protection for the life of the author plus 50 years. Signatories are free to provide longer protection.) "Fair Use" is a custom supported in U.S. courts of law, which allows inclusion of small portions of work for educational and similar uses, without obtaining the approval of the copyright holder. But all rights deriving from the copyright can be assigned, or bought and sold.

Someone who embeds on his or her Web site a YouTube video of someone else's creation likely has none of the preceding copyright factors in mind. The burgeoning millions of embeds on the Web—done without any attention to the copyrights that YouTube boilerplate says must be observed and adhered to—speak loudly of the reality that the traditional old media mold of copyright is irrevocably broken in the new new media age.

The controversy over SOPA—the Stop Online Piracy Act, introduced in the U.S. House of Representatives in October 2011, and shelved in January 2012 after online protests, including a one-day shutdown of Wikipedia and Reddit (see Levinson, "Is Wikipedia Wrong?" 2012)—is indicative of the rough sailing copyright faces ahead. Proponents of the bill wanted to prevent theft of intellectual property online—movies, music, the very content of YouTube. But the strong provisions of the bill would have held not only the uploaders of the pirated content responsible, but also the online systems such as YouTube on which the content was made available.

Unsurprisingly, Hollywood studios were the most vociferous supporters of the bill. But online sites—YouTube, Facebook, Twitter, Wikipedia, the prime movers of new new media—correctly pointed out that policing their sites for pirated content would cripple their operation. And supporters of the First Amendment, including me, noted that SOPA would violate the provision that says Congress can make "no law...abridging the freedom of speech, or of the press." (The Communications Decency Act was struck down by the Supreme Court in 1997, as noted earlier in this chapter.)

But is copyright completely shattered, or are some parts worth preserving and applying, if possible, to YouTube and new new media? The fundamental right to control who can make copies seems lost, and that is likely for the best. But the copyright holder's right to share in any income generated from the work—and, indeed, to determine whether another person or corporation can make money from the work—seems a reasonable right to preserve. Further, because income is more easily tracked than place-ment of embeds on a Web page, this commercial aspect of copyright is not impossible or even very difficult to enforce.

Plagiarism is also worthy of prevention and punishment. In its worst forms, the plagiarist takes work created by someone else and not only passes it off as his or her own but seeks to make income from it. Here the Web is not the plagiarist's best friend. The universal access that makes everything available to everyone on the Web means that, sooner or later, someone familiar with the original work will come across the plagiarist's version and report the plagiarism to the original author or current copyright holder.

The bottom line is that dissemination of copies of a work, whether an MP3 of a recording or a YouTube clip of a video, is impossible to prevent in the realm of new new media, and probably should not be prevented, unless money is made from the dissemi-nation or the work is plagiarized (disguising the original author's creation of the work), in which case the creator should be paid and/or the dissemination should be stopped, if possible.

In practical terms, the Recording Industry Association of America's (RIAA's) attempt to prevent dissemination of MP3s purely for the purpose of sharing and not for making money will not succeed in the long run (see Marder, 2007, and Levinson, 2007, "RIAA's Monstrous Legacy," for discussions of how the RIAA has alienated segments of the music-loving public). Neither will the Associated Press (AP) succeed in its attempt to require payment for posting of quotes from its articles in the free blogosphere (see Liza, 2008). As for the future of copyright, it will likely evolve to something closer to the "Creative Commons," in which the creator specifies what kinds of rights are given to the world at large—for example, right to copy but not commercialize (see creativecommons.org).

"Net neutrality" and "open source" systems are consistent with this post-Gutenberg, post-Marconi—or post-old media—approach to intellectual property. Net neutrality wants the digital architecture or operating systems and widgets of the Web to be entirely usable by any personal computer system, including nonproprietary, noncommercial systems, or those that may access the Web with programs other than Microsoft's or Apple's, or not protected by copyright and patent. Open-source systems permit anyone to see the code that makes a Web page work the way it does. The viewer can then capture and use this code to create new pages. Both net neutrality and open source approaches, which have yet to be universally realized and implemented, give the amateur, nonprofessional Web builder and programmer—that is, everyone—the same producer possibilities that new new media bestow to all readers, listeners, and viewers. Or we could say that net neutrality and open sourcing are to the structure or architecture of new new media as YouTube and everything else we are considering in this book are to the content of new new media, and the production and reception of this content.

Comments as Verifiers on YouTube: The Fleetwoods

As is the case with all new new media, the open invitation to everyone to upload video clips to YouTube means that some of the information that accompanies these videos—the brief descriptions of what is on the little screens, even the titles—could be wrong, intentionally or accidentally. Text and video comments, which can be written or uploaded by anyone (if the original video uploader allows this option), provide a mechanism for correction of such errors, just as text comments do in blogging.

Consider the case of The Fleetwoods. The California trio had two hugely successful No. 1 records in the 1950s, "Come Softly to Me" and "Mr. Blue," which featured mellow vocals and beautiful harmonies. The group was unusual in its membership, consisting of one male and two female singers: Gary Troxel, Gretchen Christopher, and Barbara Ellis. YouTube has a fine, vintage video of the group performing "Come Softly to Me" on *American Bandstand* in 1959. (I actually remember seeing that, with Dick Clark's introduction and all, when I was a kid.)

YouTube also has half a dozen other videos of The Fleetwoods, including performances in August 2007 on a PBS special and in November 2007 in Las Vegas. But, on closer inspection, these two performances are not quite by the original Fleetwoods. Gary Troxel is still singing a mellow lead in the PBS performance but with two other women. And Gretchen Christopher is the only original member of the group performing in Las Vegas.

But how would someone watching these video clips know this? Not from the titles or descriptions, which give only the name of the group, song, and venues. Fortunately, the comments entered by savvy viewers provided the clarifying details.

Of course, there is no guarantee that all or any comments for any video with misleading information will provide accurate corrections. But their capacity to do so—to draw upon the general wisdom of the millions of YouTube viewers—is an example of the self-corrective quality of new new media, which we will see in even greater prominence in Wikipedia, to be examined in the next chapter.

YouTube also added an "annotation" option in 2008, which allows uploaders of videos, at any time, to insert brief phrases of text (annotations) into the video. These can also help clarify who and what is seen in the video.

The Pope's Channel

January 2009 brought the news that "Pope Benedict XVI has launched his own dedicated channel on the popular video sharing website, YouTube" (BBC, 2009). A subsequent Associated Press article (Winfield, 2009) observed that, "The pontiff joins President Barack Obama, who launched an official White House channel on his inauguration day, as well as Queen Elizabeth, who went online with her royal YouTube channel in December 2007." The Vatican Channel, as it is officially called, had more than 1300 videos and 36,000 subscribers as of January 2012.

According to Winfield, the Vatican's embracing of what we are calling new new media is by no means free of proviso and controversy. On the one hand, "In his annual message for the World Day of Communication, Benedict praised as a 'gift to humanity' the benefits of social networking sites such as Facebook and MySpace in forging friendships and understanding." On the other hand, the pontiff "also warned that virtual socializing had its risks, saying 'obsessive' online networking could isolate people from real social interaction and broaden the digital divide by further marginalizing people." Pope Benedict reiterated and expanded this dialectic analysis in 2012—this time, about Twitter—observing that "in concise phrases, often no longer than a verse from the Bible, profound thoughts can be communicated, as long as those taking part in the conversation do not neglect to cultivate their own inner lives" (quoted in Golijan, 2012).

As we saw previously in "Viral Videos Gone Bad" and will see in more detail in chapter 9, "The Dark Side of New New Media," social media certainly have their dangers, ranging from cyberstalking and cyberbullying to even use by terrorists. But the concern about social media taking the place of real-life interactions and isolating people from in-person contact and their own deeper lives has been raised not only about new and new new media but as far back as motion pictures early in the 20th century (McKeever, 1910) and is the basis of concern about "bookworms," or people who spend too much time reading books and not enough in the "real," flesh-and-blood world (see Levinson, 2003, for more on the relationship of virtual and physical interactions). Not only is there no evidence of any such deleterious effect, but the use of Twitter and other new new media to bring together people in small and large groups for the Arab Spring and Occupy Wall Street in 2011 also refutes the proposition that social media get in the way of real-life meetings and interactions, or distract from pursuit of profound concerns. The Arab Spring and Occupy Wall Street similarly refute the notion of a burgeoning "digital divide," in which socioeconomic lower-income groups are locked out of the online process. YouTube, Facebook, Twitter, Wikipedia, and all new new media are, after all, free, and most are available via any kind of computer or smart phone, including older, less expensive models.

The Roman Catholic Church, indeed, has given a mixed reception to the new media of the day at least as far back as the introduction of print in Europe in the 1450s. Although writing was regarded as the "Apostolate of the Pen," the printed word was held suspect by some Church fathers as a debasement of the written manuscript, in which the hand that wrote was thought to be guided by the soul (see Eisenstein, 1979, for more). The dependence of the Protestant Reformation in 1519 on the printed Bible—Luther urged people to read the Bible for themselves, which would not have been possible without mass-produced printed Bibles—ironically substantiated the Church's concern about printing (see Levinson, 1997), but the Jesuit Counter Reformation was quick to recognize the pedagogic and propagandistic value of print. In the second part of the 20th century, the Church was once again a little slow to recognize the power of television, but the Vatican II Council from 1962–1965 rectified that. Like the Jesuit endorsement of print and the Vatican II's appreciation of one-way electronic mass media, Pope Benedict's YouTube channel demonstrates that, despite the Church's unwarranted misgivings, it is correct that in order to effectively disseminate its teachings in the 21st century, the Church needs to utilize the new new media of our day—in the case of YouTube, the ability to view a video message any time of day, from any place in the world, whenever one desires.

YouTube as International Information Liberator

Just as YouTube in America is available both to heads of state and to people on the street, as both consumers and producers, so, too, is YouTube internationally available to more than the Queen of England and the Pope.

Yulia Golobokova, my former student, is in her late 20s now. She was born in the Soviet Union and is presently a citizen of Russia. In December 2008—the last meeting of my fall 2008 graduate class "Media Research Methods" at Fordham University—Yulia presented a 10-minute summary of her final project, a proposal for research into some aspect of media or communication. Her topic was YouTube. Among the important points she made, many of which I introduced to the class and have discussed in this chapter, the one that struck me the most was this: YouTube, Yulia said, enabled her to find out what was going on in the world, find out the truth, when she was living in Moscow. Unlike television in her country, YouTube is not controlled by her government.

The beauty of YouTube is that it is not controlled by any government—neither Russian or American. I already knew that, and it is easy to take for granted, but the value of YouTube—and, indeed, of all new new media—to the world at large was brought home to me and became more than a theoretical point with a student from Russia standing up in my class and talking about it.

I first met Yulia in September 2008 when she walked into my office, a few days before our first class, and introduced herself. She said how happy she was to meet me and that I looked and sounded just as she had expected.

"How is that?" I asked, wondering how and why she might have some preconception of what I looked and sounded like.

"I've seen your videos in Moscow, lots of times, on YouTube," Yulia replied. In the realm of new new media, there is no difference between a computer screen in New York and in Moscow—they are equidistant on YouTube.

Of course, governments can attempt to ban YouTube, as Pakistan did for at least two hours in February 2008 because of "anti-Islamic content" (Malkin, 2008). The ban apparently caused worldwide problems with YouTube service, showing that the system is far from invulnerable and indeed is interconnected with and dependent on all kinds of other systems and servers and hence potentially weak or vulnerable links, as is the case with all new new media. Pakistan lifted the ban when informed that its "erroneous Internet protocols" had caused problems outside of Pakistan.

Fortunately, attempts of dictatorial governments to regulate media have had a poor record of success, as Nazi Germany found out with the "White Rose" anti-Nazi photocopiers (Dumbach & Newborn, 1986) and the Soviet Union discovered with its "samizdat videos" in the 1980s (Levinson, 1992). See the timeline in the previous chapter in the "Iran" section for the complete record of totalitarian regimes versus revolutionary media in the 20th and 21st centuries.

Resistance to authorities, whether in government or media, has never been easier in our age of YouTube and new new media. In the next chapter, we will look at how Wikipedia has overthrown the tyranny of the expert, at least insofar as the information and wisdom we expect to find in an encyclopedia.

CHAPTER 5

Wikipedia

We come from a tradition in which knowledge has to be vouched for, authorized, and approved by experts before it is allowed to reach us. Whether clerics or professors or newspaper editors, the effect is the same: Knowledge must be vouchsafed and deemed acceptable by professionals, before it reaches the eyes and ears of people in the world at large. Of course, all kinds of knowledge, information, facts, and falsities can be seen, heard, or discovered by anyone and everyone. But our tradition, common to both Western and Eastern and all cultures in between, with roots deep in the ancient world, requires that knowledge have the imprimatur, or seal of expert approval, to be considered worthy of study and further dissemination.

Before we scoff at this vetting, we should understand its logic. It is as easy to create and disseminate a falsehood as it is a truth. We might be flooded by such falsehoods, were gatekeepers not carefully regulating what can reach us.

On the other hand, is not our very rationality in the business of separating truths from falsehoods, lies, and distortions, and recognizing truth in the crowded field? Certainly John Milton thought so. In his *Areopagetica*, published in 1644, Milton argued that truth and falsity must be allowed to confront each other without restrictions in the marketplace of ideas. Milton was confident that truth would be recognized, unless censorship accidentally or otherwise kept some truth from entering this contest and thereby warped the results. Thomas Jefferson wholeheartedly agreed, which is why he and like-minded Founding Fathers from Virginia insisted on the First Amendment to our Constitution: "Congress shall make no law...abridging freedom of speech, or of the press." (See also Percival, 2012, for a brief on the power of rationality.)

Boards of experts that determined what went into encyclopedias prior to Wikipedia were certainly not governmental censors or in any way in violation of the First Amendment. But they nonetheless embodied and practiced a kind of censorship, or gatekeeping, that prevented the people at large from determining the truth or falsity of a factual statement, or the more complex question of its relative importance.

Wikipedia, which was brought online in January 2001 by Jimmy Wales and Larry Sanger—Wales continues to play a predominant role in Wikipedia's administration—and by January 2012 had nearly 4 million articles written in English (out of 20 million in 283 different language editions), overthrew that reign by philosopher-king experts. None of those articles was written by an appointed expert—or, if experts wrote the articles, the knowledge embodied in their Wikipedia writing, not their official expertise, was what decided whether those articles survived.

Pickles and Pericles

Almost anyone can write and edit entries on Wikipedia (the "almost" refers to people who have been banned, which will be discussed in detail in "All Wikipedians Are Equal, but Some Are More Equal Than Others" later in this chapter). Age, education, location, gender—none of this makes a difference, or is supposed to make a difference, on Wikipedia. Even intention to help with the writing of an entry, or the opposite intention—to destroy it—makes no difference, at first. Hence, entries on Wikipedia are teeming with the work of pranksters—deliberately introduced errors. These are quickly corrected by readers/editors (readers and editors are the same on Wikipedia). Indeed, there is an ever-waging war on Wikipedia, between those who attempt to make and keep entries truthful and those who seek for whatever reason to disrupt this process.

My favorite example, because it is so trivial yet instructive, comes from a few years ago, when a synopsis for an entry on Pericles made the front page of Wikipedia (the front page is controlled by administrators—see "All Wikipedians Are Equal"). In the first line of the entry, an alternate spelling of Pericles—Perikles—was given. When I logged on to that page, I immediately noticed that Perikles had been changed to Pickles by some anonymous vandal. I changed Pickles back to Perikles (in those days, I absent-mindedly did not even always use my account on Wikipedia—I was also an anonymous user, with just an IP, or numerical Internet address). Another vandal (or at least someone with a different IP address from the first vandal) soon changed Perikles to Pickles, and this pickle fight went on with various combatants for at least a few hours.

Of course, far more serious battles of this sort are being waged daily, even hourly, on Wikipedia concerning character assassinations of public figures and celebrities, calumnies (to use that great 18th-century term), and other misleading information posted about political candidates. Barack Obama being falsely described as a Muslim was among the most common of misrepresentations on Wikipedia in 2008. In all cases, trivial and profound, the dynamics are the same: Armies of light, or immune systems, or good cops—whatever metaphor appeals to you—fight armies of darkness, or infection to Wikipedia, or marauders of the truth.

The medical analogy might work best to underscore the difference between expert-driven, gate-kept encyclopedias such as the venerable *Britannica* and mass-intelligence-driven encyclopedias such as Wikipedia. In an expert-driven system, the only people who can write are those who have been certified as free from mental maliciousness or other incapacity. In the people-driven system, because anyone can write, all readers/editors serve as antibodies to correct infection—false information—introduced by harmful germs.

But the battlefield on Wikipedia is even more complicated.

Inclusionists vs. Exclusionists: Battle Between Wikipedian Heroes

Life would be simpler if battles between heroes and villains were the only kind that afflicted our world. But, in fact, battles—or at least disagreements—often break out in the ranks of defenders of the truth.

On Wikipedia, a battle is waged constantly between two kinds of readers/editors, who are both trying to make the online encyclopedia the best it can be. Both do their utmost to root out vandalism wherever they see it. But their battle is not primarily about vandalism but about what kind of truthful information should be allowed on Wikipedia. Their battlefield is thus not about truth but about relevance and worthiness to be included in an encyclopedia.

As their names suggest—names proudly touted by the two factions themselves—the "exclusionists," or deletionists, want to limit the entries on Wikipedia, while the "inclusionists" want to keep and expand entries. But there is a lot of room between no entries at all (which, of course, the exclusionists do not want) and anything truthful that anyone writes about anything, however unimportant (which, of course, the inclusionists do not really want, either). And there are subtleties and variations within the groups. "Deletionists" focus on removing complete articles deemed unworthy for an encyclopedia, while "exclusionists" are more concerned about removing irrelevant or unimportant sections of otherwise acceptable articles. "Mergists" are a school of deletionists who want to merge two or more articles into one, because some of the articles are deemed insufficient in importance to stand on their own or merit their own article. If these groups sound to you almost like religious or political factions, you would be right. Except the subject matter need not be political or religious and can indeed be any topic. What makes these factions seem religious or political is not the subject of their focus on Wikipedia but the intensity and specificity of their editing philosophies.

Expert-driven encyclopedias such as *Britannica*, which ended its printed edition in 2012 (the last printed edition was in 2010), were exclusionist, and, given the limitations of print on paper, had no choice but to be. After all, would anyone purchase an encyclopedia of 1,000 or 10,000 volumes? The *Encyclopedia Britannica* thus not only restricted the number of new entries but also removed or reduced the length of older entries that its editors deemed less relevant. (I pointed out in the preface of my novel *The Plot to Save Socrates*, 2006, the value of having access to a *Britannica* from the mid-1950s or earlier—entries on ancient history were shortened in the mid-1950s to make room for the enormous growth of scientific knowledge such as DNA in that era.) The *Britannica*'s digital editions survive the demise of the printed edition, but follow the same selective editorial policies (see Pepitone, 2012).

Inclusionists point out that an online encyclopedia labors under no such draconian paper master.

Among the most frequently debated issues between exclusionists and inclusionists on Wikipedia is the "notability" of possible subjects of articles—is the person, current or historical, important enough to warrant a Wikipedia entry? Among the many guiding principles used by editor/readers in making such decisions is one that holds that "notability is not inherited." For example, you will find no entry on Francine Descartes, daughter of the great philosopher. But a major entry, of course, is found on Wikipedia for John Stuart Mill, son of James Mill, who was also an important philosopher and has a Wikipedia article (though James Mill was not as significant in impact as his son). The point here is that John Stuart Mill would have merited an entry even if his father had been an unknown stable hand.

Incidentally, you or any reader can post an entry on Francine Descartes on Wikipedia any time you like. It would likely be put up for immediate deletion, however. (See "All Wikipedians Are Equal, but Some Are More Equal Than Others," later in this chapter, for much more on the process of deletion on Wikipedia.)

The "notability is not inherited" principle is not at all controversial or difficult to apply in the cases of Francine Descartes and John Stuart Mill. But it can be and has been highly contentious in many other cases.

Consider, for example, the article for Lolo Soetoro, Barack Obama's Indonesian stepfather. The brief history of the man, as it relates to Obama, is that Barack Obama's mother, Ann Dunham, married Soetoro after she and Obama's biological father (Barack Obama the elder) were divorced. Barack Obama the future U.S. president lived in Indonesia for four years, from ages six to ten. He returned without his mother or Soetoro to Hawaii, where he lived with his grandparents and completed his secondary education through high school.

So does Lolo Soetoro warrant a Wikipedia entry? "Notability is not inherited"—whether forward to descendants or backward to ancestors—would suggest not, but the question became contentious in the 2008 American presidential campaign, for reasons having little to do with traditional exclusionist/inclusionist debating points. Obama supporters on Wikipedia thought readers/editors in favor of a Soetoro entry wanted it as a way of drawing attention to Obama's Muslim upbringing in Indonesia and thereby painting him as an un-American candidate. This led some readers/editors who were usually inclusionists to oppose the article—that is, delete it, merge it, or redirect it (for example, to an article about Ann Dunham).

The Lolo Soetoro article was at first removed from Wikipedia, with searches for it redirected to a more general "Family of Barack Obama" article, which contains a section on Soetoro. (Technically, then, the article was not deleted but merged into the "Family" article.) But the Soetoro article was reinstated in June 2008 and survived at least one additional attempt to remove and merge it. (See Wellman, 2008, for a detailed account of the Wikipedia battles over the Soetoro article. My wife, Tina Vozick, who edits on Wikipedia as "Tvoz," was a "mergist" in these discussions, departing from her usual "inclusionist" perspective.)

A nonpolitical example of what exclusionists and inclusionists argue about on Wikipedia is the "category" about "Fictional Jews." A category on Wikipedia is a link that can pull together diverse articles. The category links appear at the bottom of articles and all together on compilation pages that display the titles of the articles, or the names of the subjects. Not all categories are controversial. "Fictional private investigators," for example, is accepted by exclusionists and appears on pages for Sherlock Holmes, Hercule Poirot, Sam Spade, Mike Hammer, and the like. This was not the case for "Fictional Jews," which once appeared on pages ranging from Shakespeare's Shylock, James Joyce's Leopold Bloom, *Law and Order*'s John Munch, and my barely known character Dr. Phil D'Amato. The category was removed in March 2008, but brought back to life in April 2010 after considerable discussion. (An article called "List of fictional Jews," however, continued without interruption. A "list" is a less dynamic component of Wikipedia than a category—the listed items do not appear at the bottom of articles about the people or items in the list.)

Aside from the easy come, easy go lesson about "categories" on Wikipedia—or maybe "difficult" would be a better adjective—the "fictional characters" story provides a textbook case of the ongoing inclusionist/exclusionist debate. On the exclusionist side, clearly, such a category has nothing essential—nothing not already available in the subject entries themselves, whether about Shylock, Bloom, or others. But on the inclusionist side, the category provided another way of accessing the information, another method of linking and learning. And because the storage and bandwidth capacities of Wikipedia are in effect infinite in comparison to words printed on paper, what harm was ever done by including such a category? Perhaps the exclusionists were concerned about ethnic stereotyping.

Neutrality of Editors and Conflicts of Interest

As the author of novels and short stories in which Phil D'Amato appears as a character (for example, *The Silk Code*, 1999), I have a professional interest in wanting any category in which he appears to continue on Wikipedia. I actually first found out about the "Fictional Jews" category after it had been deleted and did not take part in any of the subsequent online discussions pro or con, because the ideal editor on Wikipedia is supposed to be a reader who has no vested interest in the article or page he or she is writing or editing. This means the editor has nothing to gain or lose financially, personally, or professionally from the words on the page. Friedrich Engels, the Wikipedia guidelines on conflict of interest (COI) helpfully inform us, would not be the best person to edit an entry on Karl Marx.

But day-to-day, more current situations on Wikipedia may not be as clear-cut. Should someone who supports Obama refrain from editing pages about him and his work, or should Obama supporters, if they are known, be called out by other editors or warned by Wikipedia administrators not to edit Obama's pages? If this seems extreme to you, as it does to me, would you feel the same way if pages about Mitt Romney or Ron Paul were at issue? And staying in the political realm, but moving up the ladder of possible conflict of interest, what about a Democratic Party precinct captain? What about David Axelrod (a senior White House adviser) or Howard Dean (former Democratic National Committee chairman)? What about Michelle Obama? Should she be editing President Obama's Wikipedia page?

The last three people would seem, ipso facto, to be courting conflict of interest if they edited any Wikipedia pages in which Obama was the subject. But would it be fair for them to be banned from such editing?

Joe de Santis, Newt Gingrich's Communications Director in the 2012 presidential primary campaigns, in fact did substantial editing under his real name on Gingrich's Wikipedia pages in 2011–2012. He was alerted to the conflict-of-interest rules, stopped editing, and confined his contribution to comments in the "Talk," pages, where editors publicly discuss their work. Was any harm done to Wikipedia or the body politic?

In the end, the only objective way to enforce neutrality in Wikipedia entries might well be to limit the appraisal to the words on the page and not to the person who wrote them. As literary critic I. A. Richards warned us way back in 1929, the intentions of the writer are often inscrutable and have no real connection to the impact of the text. All that should count in analysis and criticism of a text, Richards wrote, is the text itself.

Furthermore, this problem of looking at the identity of the editor and assessing his or her neutrality is exacerbated on Wikipedia by the ease of creating pseudonymous accounts.

Identity Problems

Authenticity of users (readers, writers, and commenters) is a problem everywhere in the worlds of new and new new media, where setting up a false identity is as easy as creating an email account on Gmail or Yahoo, under any name you choose, and then using it as the verifier on Facebook, Twitter, here, there, and everywhere.

But the problem is especially vexing on Wikipedia, because it initially operates via consensus achieved in online discussions of readers/editors ("initially" meaning before a problem might be passed on to and reviewed by administrators, for discussion of which, see "All Wikipedians Are Equal, but Some Are More Equal Than Others" later in this chapter). Wikipedians even have a name for accounts created by individuals solely or mainly for the purpose of bringing additional support for their positions into consensus discussions: "sock puppets."

Creating accounts on Wikipedia is actually easier than on Facebook and most online systems; verification via email to an already-existing Gmail or other address is not currently required. Indeed, editors can work on Wikipedia with no Wikipedia account, in which case they are identified by their IPs. Wikipedia is in the business of encouraging and maximizing participation. As in all things participatory and democratic, the process works better with more participants.

But this ease of creating accounts also has the result of making sock puppetry easy to pursue. And a clever creator of sock puppets can be difficult to identify. The bogus accounts can be created on different computers, with different IPs, and can lie dormant for months or get involved in Wikipedia discussions that have nothing to do with the sock puppeteer's real motives. When the sock puppet eventually springs into action and begins writing on behalf of articles near and dear to him or her, urging their retention or deletion in any debates that may ensue, there is no reason for anyone to think that this reader/editor has a vested interest in the article. Used in its most intelligent and effective forms, the sock puppet is thus the new new media equivalent of a sleeper cell. A sharp-eyed participant in the discussion may suspect something amiss, especially if the sock puppet writes in a style that is in some way idiosyncratic, but such suspicions can be difficult to prove when based solely on similarities in writing style.

An interesting back formation from the sock puppet, which is actually very different, is the so-called "meat puppet"—or a real account, created by a real person, for the purpose of supporting a friend's or associate's project on Wikipedia. The problem with equating sock puppets and meat puppets, however, is that the motive of any living human can be unclear. If I come to the aid of a friend in a discussion about whether to delete or keep an article about whatever on Wikipedia, who other than I can know for sure whether I really support my friend's position, and would have had the same opinion if my friend did not exist, or whether I don't care at all about this issue and entered the online discussion only at my friend's behest? Or perhaps the truth is that I spoke up in the discussion because of a mix of the two factors: I believe in the issue but wrote what I wrote because my friend encouraged me.

Issues such as sock puppets versus meat puppets, and the difficulty of identifying and protecting against them, show that online life is by no means immune to the complexities and complications of real life. The two are both subject to vandals and troublemakers, who may be more or less difficult to deal with online. The saving grace of anything destructive online, however, is that it can in itself cause no physical damage in the real world—no damage, that is, unless we act on it or allow its misinformation to guide our actions in the real world. This is the case whether we are dealing with cyberbullies on Facebook or vandals of knowledge on Wikipedia. And we can add to that, as a cause for this real-world concern, a report that the U.S. government contracted for "software which could create multiple fake social media profiles to manipulate and sway public opinion on controversial issues" (Storm, 2011). It seems that sock puppets are not just for Wikipedia any more.

All Wikipedians Are Equal, but Some Are More Equal Than Others

Wikipedia is the most thoroughgoing, consistently user-driven system on the Internet. It is the pick of the new new media litter, at least insofar as its primary, revolutionary characteristic of allowing consumers to become producers. It is the closest to direct democracy in the actual operation of a major online system. But although all readers can indeed be editors of Wikipedia, a preliminary survey reported that 90 percent of Wikipedia edits were made by the top 15 percent of the most active Wikipedia editors (working paper by Mikolaj Jan Piskorski and Andreea Gorbatai, cited in Heil & Piskorski, 2009). This is an intrinsic shortcoming of all democratic processes, in which opportunity to participate (as in voting) only partially equates to actual participation. And although editors usually decide via discussion and consensus whether an article, or part of an article, is worthy of Wikipedia, what happens when editors cannot decide? Or what happens when an editor acts as a vandal or creates sock puppets to support his or her position? Or what happens when an entry is so controversial that it is rife with constant deletions and reinstatements to the extent that it changes back and forth every few minutes?

Enter the Wikipedia administrators, who are nominated and chosen by a public discussion and consensus of editors (an editor may nominate any other editor, including oneself). A special super kind of administrator—a "bureaucrat," also chosen by community consensus—determines if consensus has been reached in favor of promoting the editor to administrator and, if so, bestows the promotion. A few administrators also act as "checkusers"—they are given the authority to see the IPs of named or account-holding readers/editors (see "Transparency on Wikipedia Pages," later in this chapter).

One of the two prime powers of administrators is blocking the accounts of errant editors. Vandalism is one way to be errant but so is violation of the "three-revert" rule, which insists that no editor can revert changes—reinstate after something is deleted, delete after something is reinstated, and so forth—more than three times in 24 hours on a given page or entry. Administrators have the power to block an editor's account after fewer than three reversions, but three is the stated and usually followed number.

An account can be blocked for an hour, a day, a week, a month, or indefinitely. The blocked editor can appeal, and any other administrator can reverse the decision of the blocking administrator or reduce the sentence (the duration of the block). However, because part of the purpose of blocking is to reduce or defuse so-called "edit wars"—two editors undoing each other's work—administrators try not to initiate a similar war of their own by repeatedly blocking and unblocking editors (which constitutes a "wheel war," in Wikipedian parlance).

The second major power of administrators is "protecting" a page or entry—preventing any reader/editor other than an administrator from making further edits. As with blocking of accounts, the protection can be for any length of time, and any administrator can unprotect a page or open it for renewed editing. So "wheel wars," or administrators reversing one another's actions, are a pitfall to be avoided here, too.

The daily main or front page of Wikipedia, which contains a "featured article" (a synopsis of a longer article) selected by a single, specially appointed administrator, is always "read-only," or incapable of being edited by anyone other than an administrator. On that always-protected page, Wikipedia becomes perilously close to the organizing structure of the front page of *The New York Times*. In this straightforward method, Wikipedia gains reliability at the expense of its democratic process. All that readers/editors and even other administrators can do is make suggestions about what "Today's Featured Article" should be. And all that readers/editors can do about errors is point them out, so an administrator can correct them.

Protection of other pages, however, can be an especially tricky business. Let's say, for example, that on a given day, two groups of editors (reader/writers) with sincere, diametrically opposing political viewpoints, are busy "correcting" and "uncorrecting" a political candidate's page. This is not about straight-up vandalism, which can be corrected as many times as necessary (an important exception to the three-revert rule is that it does not apply to correction of obvious falsehoods and the work of vandals, but the falsehoods have to be obvious). But in a politically motivated edit war, where the page receives thousands of views an hour, the stakes can be much higher than in run-of-the-mill Perikles/pickles vandalism. An administrator who comes upon this battle might decide to protect the page, to give the warring editors a little time to cool off. But for this period of time, no one other than another administrator would be able to edit the page—thus depriving Wikipedia of its main mechanism of error correction. What if the administrator, either accidentally or otherwise, left an interpretation in the protected page, not because it was agreed by consensus that the interpretation was best, but because it most suited the administrator's political perspective? Thousands or more readers would see this interpretation on the page. Pages for Barack Obama, John McCain, Joe Biden, and Sarah Palin were indeed briefly protected on October 30, 2008, as edit wars and racist attacks escalated five days prior to that year's election. Rick Santorum's page was fully protected for almost three days in February 2012, over an edit war concerning contraception. The full protection, originally decreed for three full days, was changed to "semi-protection" after editors objected to the full protection (see Levinson, 2012, "Rick Santorum," for details).

In practice, full protection of pages for politicians or any subject is infrequent on Wikipedia—and the front page, always protected, is an obvious one-of-a-kind special case. But pages can also be semi-protected, or blocked from anonymous and new account edits (new account defined as more recent than four days and having made fewer than ten edits on Wikipedia), and this is a much more common practice. Obama's page has been intermittently semi-protected since 2007. (See Vargas, 2007, for discussion of vandalism on Obama's Wikipedia page.) Semi-protection is usually deployed to stop drive-by vandalism, which is far more common than political spinning. But even semi-protection ties at least one of Wikipedia's hands behind its back—the hand of anonymous and new accounts for correcting errors. Editors not blocked by semi-protection will, of course, be able to correct errors, but the pool of error correctors is still reduced.

But Wikipedia does have at least one additional, built-in defense against vandals.

Transparency on Wikipedia Pages

A major feature of Wikipedia that puts even the most diligent vandal at a disadvantage is the complete history of edits easily available on every page or entry. This means that any and all changes, additions, and deletions, profound and trivial, can be seen on the screen by any reader/editor. A vandal may seek to disguise an important piece of dirty work by bundling it with a lot of obvious vandalism, and a revision, helpful or destructive, may be missed by a casual reader of the History page, but every single revision is nonetheless listed. Wikipedia also shows what every page looked like before and after the edit.

The transparent History pages on Wikipedia make it radically different from most blogs on the Web, which at most indicate if and when a page has been edited, or, as in the case of Google's Blogspot (of which my *Infinite Regress* blog is an example), give no indication that a page has been edited at all. Facebook's Timeline provides a record of everything the user has done on Facebook, but the user can easily hide any actions from public view or remove them totally. Given that a page on Wikipedia can be edited by a myriad of people, in contrast to only the blogger being able to edit his or her blog, and only the account holder (user) on Facebook, this hypertransparency of editing history on Wikipedia makes sense.

This level of transparency on Wikipedia, however, pertains to pages or articles and not to readers/editors. As indicated earlier, one need not have an account to edit on Wikipedia, in which case, you are identified by your IP. An IP is unique to your computer connection to the Internet. If you take your laptop to a friend's house and log on via wi-fi available there, you will be using his or her IP. (Mobile media such as smart phones and tablets have their own IPs.) IPs are thus not a foolproof way of identifying a particular reader/editor.

If you register for an account (free) on Wikipedia, you are thereafter identified by your account name, not your IP. But this allows individuals to register for any number of accounts and serves as the basis for sock puppetry (though an individual may want to have more than one account for non-nefarious purposes). Only specially appointed administrators —"checkusers"—have the ability to see the IP of any given account, as mentioned earlier. These can be helpful in rooting out sock puppets, though the recalcitrant puppeteer can resort to different IPs for the puppets—for example, in libraries, Apple stores, schools, and indeed any wi-fi hot spot such as Starbucks, Panera Bread, or a hotel lobby.

Wikipedia vs. *Britannica*

So, with all of these potentials for error and safeguards, with the battles waging on Wikipedia between vandals and editors, between editors and editors, between editors and administrators, and sometimes between administrators and administrators—all for the purpose of making sure that the articles on Wikipedia contain only accurate and relevant information—how does Wikipedia fare as an accurate source of information? An error is easier to identify than an irrelevance. If Wikipedia's reader-written, constantly in-flux pages were as free from error as, say, the distinguished, expert-written pages of the *Encyclopedia Britannica*, that would tell us something very important about how the democratic antibodies of a new new media book of knowledge compare with the strict gatekeeping of our older, trusted reference sources.

The correct answer is that Wikipedia seems to be holding its own against the *Encyclopedia Britannica*—a remarkable accomplishment—but the jury is still not entirely in. *Nature*—one of the two leading science magazines in the world (along with *Science*)—reported the results of a study it conducted in 2005, in which experts examined 42 articles each from Wikipedia and the *Britannica* online edition (Giles, 2005). The experts found an average of four inaccuracies per Wikipedia article and three per *Britannica* article—in other words, not much of a difference at all. This result was widely publicized (for example, Associated Press, 2005) but drew an outraged objection from *Britannica*, which alleged that *Nature*'s investigators were the ones who got their facts wrong and, in other cases, offered mere opinion not expert judgment (Orlowski, 2006). *Britannica* called upon *Nature* to retract its report. *Nature* (2006) replied with a lengthy explanation of its methods and findings and concluded, "We do not intend to retract our article." Three years later, *Nature* stood by its 2005 findings (Giles, 2008).

The clearest lesson of these dueling experts may be that expert opinion is not as reliable as it holds itself out to be—either *Nature* was in error, or *Britannica* erred in its criticism of *Nature*, or both—which in itself provides another strong argument in favor of encyclopedia by democracy on Wikipedia, or what *Nature*'s study suggests works as well as encyclopedia by expert, oligarchic decree. (See also Messer-Kruse, 2012, for the travails of a recognized expert trying to edit on Wikipedia—or another example of conflict between the expert and the democratic editing cultures.)

Old vs. New New Media in Reporting the Death of Tim Russert

Wikipedia competes not only with old media encyclopedias but also with old media news reporting in newspapers, radio, and television. When *Meet the Press* moderator Tim Russert died unexpectedly, shortly after 2:20 p.m. on June 13, 2008, NBC and other traditional news media understandably waited until relatives were notified before informing the general public. That occurred at 3:30 p.m., when Tom Brokaw broke into the afternoon programming on NBC, CNBC, and MSNBC and announced Russert's death. ABC, CBS, CNN, and Fox News all waited for Brokaw's announcement to broadcast their own announcements and reports.

Wikipedia did not. According to a *New York Times* June 23, 2008, account of the events of June 13 (Cohen, 2008), Russert's page on Wikipedia was updated at 3:01 p.m. to reflect Russert's death. (You can see this in the history of Russert's page on Wikipedia.) Also according to *The New York Times*, the person who made the change on Wikipedia was "a junior-level employee" of Internet Broadcasting Services—an organization that supplies information to local NBC-TV stations and other companies—who was subsequently fired. (*The New York Times* put the story of Russert's death on its own Web site five minutes before Brokaw's announcement.)

The difference between Wikipedia's and television's treatment of the Russert story highlights the radical departure of new new media from the way old and new media operate. In the case of NBC and all the broadcast and cable media, an executive—a gatekeeping editor of some sort—made the call as to when the story would be aired. This is the procedure for any and every story we see on broadcast and cable TV, hear on the radio, or read in the newspaper. In contrast, no one in the employ of Wikipedia made such a decision, because that is not the way Wikipedia works. (The Wikimedia Foundation and lawyers who work for Wikipedia do not make initial publishing decisions.) An employee of a company totally unrelated to Wikipedia updated Russert's page. Anyone could have done that—you or I. Or we might have put up a completely false story about Russert or anyone.

It is not that Wikipedia has no standards for what is published in its online encyclopedia. It does, but the standards are applied, again, by you, me, anyone who happens to read an article. One of Wikipedia's primary standards is that facts need confirmation in other media before they stand on Wikipedia. Because no confirmation existed at 3:01 p.m. of Russert's death, the update announcing it on Russert's page was deleted 10 minutes later (according to *The New York Times*, by someone using another Internet Broadcasting Services computer). And, soon after, it of course was reinstated.

But would any new reader/editor know about this or any of the other many guidelines for articles on Wikipedia? Extensive, detailed descriptions, explications, and summaries of standards are posted on Wikipedia, and these are accessible in numerous ways (for example, see "Category: Wikipedia behavioral guidelines"). As is the case with any democracy, it can work only if citizens have easy, reliable access to its laws. As is also the case in any democracy, the laws or guidelines are constantly debated and refined.

Wikipedia Wrongly Reports the "Deaths" of Ted Kennedy and Robert Byrd

Indeed, the egregiously wrong Wikipedia report of Ted Kennedy's and Robert Byrd's "deaths" on Inauguration Day, 2009, led Jimmy Wales to urge a new level of editorial review, in which "trusted editors" would need to approve all biographical entries by new and anonymous editors (see Pershing, 2009; Kells, 2009). In reality, Ted Kennedy had a seizure and was taken out of the post-inauguration luncheon by medics. Byrd, age 91 at the time, was apprehensive and decided to leave the luncheon as well. Kennedy recovered, and Byrd was not really ill in the first place, but in the initial confusion, Wikipedia listed both senators as deceased. (Ted Kennedy died eight months later, and Robert Byrd the following year.)

Whether by accident or vandalism, such erroneous posts call into question the reliability of Wikipedia. They were removed within five minutes—a testament to the correcting power of numerous readers/editors—but numerous readers nonetheless saw the incorrect reports. Instating a layer of editorial review would certainly help with this problem, but it would also undermine Wikipedia's fundamental policy that anyone can write and edit and publish on its pages. Several proposals (including Wales's) addressing this issue have long been under discussion on Wikipedia. (Wikipedia in Germany already has such a review policy in place—for all articles, whatever the subject. See Wales, 2009, for preliminary details. And see also Perez-Pena, 2009, for how Wales and Wikipedia administrators kept news of a kidnapping off Wikipedia to help enable the victim's eventual escape.)

Encyclopedia or Newspaper?

The immediate announcement of Tim Russert's death on Wikipedia—and the erroneous reports about Kennedy and Byrd—raises another contentious issue: Is Wikipedia an encyclopedia or a newspaper? Publishing news as quickly as possible is, after all, what a newspaper does. But Wikipedia and newspapers are not the same.

News media, in general, are supposed to report events that are true and significant in some sense, and as soon as possible. Certainly an encyclopedia subscribes to the first two—everything in it should be true and significant—but instead of speed, an encyclopedia presumably wants to publish information that has some kind of enduring relevance. And the very definition of enduring means it cannot cohabit with immediate, unless one wants to take a leap of faith and predict or assume that an event that occurred yesterday will be of interest to general readers 10 years later.

Sometimes such predictions are easy to make with confidence: Regardless of who wins an election for president of the United States, we can rest assured that the results of that election will continue to be of at least some historical importance. But what about the unexpected death of a prominent news moderator such as Tim Russert?

In the days following Russert's death in June 2008, not only was his already-existing page on Wikipedia updated hundreds of times, but additional pages also were put up, with reactions to his death by famous people and other information. Was Wikipedia working as an encyclopedia or a newspaper with such entries?

Newspapers, of course, report not only immediate and breaking news but also publish follow-up and retrospective stories as well. To the extent that enduring Wikipedia articles are as well researched as stories in newspapers—assuming that the newspapers have researched their stories—then the Wikipedia article becomes less distinguishable from a follow-up newspaper story. Ironically, Wikipedia guidelines require stories to be sourced, and although no firm ranking of sources (which sources are preferable to others) is insisted on or provided, old media newspapers are held in higher regard as sources than blog posts, and world-renowned newspapers such as *The New York Times* are preferable to high school newspapers (see Wikipedia, 2012, "Identifying Reliable Sources," for more). This provides yet another example of the interdependence and love/hate relationship of old and new new media that we saw in chapter 2 about Facebook, where we encountered a group organized on that new new medium to help save the old medium of newspapers.

In the end, the dominant principle in determining whether Wikipedia is an encyclopedia or a newspaper or both is that Wikipedia editors and administrators really have little say in how the rest of the world sees and uses Wikipedia. If readers use Wikipedia as they would a newspaper—a more up-to-date version of *The New York Times*—then how can Wikipedians stop that?

This, once again, is a cardinal principle of new new media: Not only do consumers become producers, but consumers—not necessarily the same consumers but all consumers, in general—always determine how the new new medium is used. This gives a new meaning to the concept of user: not just one who consumes or uses a medium but, in that very use, helps determine what that medium is. John Dewey (1925), the American philosopher who argued that truth is best perceived and reached through real use and experience, not preexisting thought and analysis, would have approved.

Does Wikipedia Make Libraries Unnecessary?

If Wikipedia is not quite yet, but may be becoming, a kind of newspaper, how does the online encyclopedia, which in principle has an infinite number of articles, compare with book and brick libraries?

Colin Powell, Secretary of State in George W. Bush's first administration (2001–2005), was an early appreciator of Wikipedia. He told Fareed Zakaria on Zakaria's CNN *GPS* program in December 2008 that, when he arrived at the State Department in 2001, he advised everyone to "get rid of all the books in your office. You don't need them anymore, as long as you have a couple of search engines and Wikipedia. And then I challenged my people to try to keep up with Wikipedia in terms of changes in countries."

Powell—whatever history may say about his presentation to the United Nations, prior to the Iraq War in 2003, that Saddam Hussein had weapons of mass destruction when it turned out later he apparently did not—was alert to something significant about Wikipedia and its advantages over older media, and alert to this very early. Books on the shelf suffer from an utter inability to be corrected or updated. All print media, in which words are wedded to paper, are similarly unchangeable and no different in this crucial respect from hieroglyphics carved into a pyramid (see Levinson, 1997, for more).

Newspapers do the best they can in this rigid realm by putting out new editions daily—they did this even more often prior to the triumph of electronic media in the mid-20th century—and offering follow-ups and updates on stories, as well as corrections. But unlike last year's books, last month's newspapers are far more likely to stuff packing boxes than provide missing information.

Books in libraries, then—and even online or digitally delivered—carry the burden for reference media. But like the facts in printed encyclopedias, the information in such books and libraries may well be out of date, as Colin Powell noted back in 2001.

That's the argument in favor of Wikipedia over books in libraries. Yet Powell went a little too far when he said we "don't need" books anymore, whether in the State Department or the world at large, and such a statement still goes too far in 2012.

Wikipedia has two disadvantages in comparison with libraries in 2012. The first is that it no doubt does not have some information available in books, whether about international politics and geography or any subject. But this is a classic example of what I call a "caterpillar criticism" (Levinson, 1988)—assessing a medium's incapacity at a given time as if it were permanent, rather than a work in progress, just as we might note that one problem with a caterpillar as an insect is that it cannot fly. There is no reason to think that, in ensuing years, knowledge will exist in any book on any shelf that will not be on Wikipedia. Indeed, Colin Powell's advice about not needing books, though still not correct today, is more correct now in 2012 than it was in 2001. And we can expect it to become more correct every year, every day, every hour.

But Wikipedia suffers from a second disadvantage in comparison with books, which is far more chronic, with no solution presently in sight. As we considered in the previous chapter about YouTube, anything online, anything dependent on a link to a URL for retrieval, lacks what I call the "reliable locatability" of books. If you are currently reading these words on page 77—or the words on any page of this book, page 33, 63, any page—and the book consists of bound pages, those words will be there, on the same exact pages, tomorrow, next year, even a hundred or more years from now if you put the book in a safe place. The act of just putting the book on a shelf is usually enough to ensure that the words will be there for you the next time you look for them, in the exact same place in the book on the page. But anything on the Web, even a site totally under your control, does not have this reliability—you could decide to close the site at any time. Even e-books downloaded to your Kindle do not have this reliability, as Amazon's removal of George Orwell's *1984* from Kindles around the United States in 2009, over concern about copyright, demonstrates. Ironically, Orwell's book is about the total information control of a future nightmare society, a society consistent with Amazon's action (see Levinson, 2009, for more).

The exception to the expectation of reliable locatability in paper books would be a real bookworm that ate some pages, or some other unforeseen cause of damage to the pages of the book. Even a book on a shelf (see Petroski, 1999, for the history and impact of bookshelves) could be destroyed, the page may be torn out or obliterated, and this means reliable locatability is not an absolute guarantee that the text will survive in place. But the wedding of printed words to paper is permanent, and this means that their readers can have a much greater assurance than with anything on the Web, or any device like the Kindle that receives text from the Web, that the words and images will be where expected, remembered, noted, or cited for future reference.

Wikipedia, to be sure, is probably the most reliably locatable source of information on the Web. Its myriad readers/editors take great care to make sure any changes in links to articles are automatically redirected, often from more than one path or alternate spelling of a name or title of an article. And, as indicated previously in the chapter, Wikipedia maintains complete and accessible histories of every change or edit made on any of its pages. But the system is still not perfect. For example, an article that is completely deleted may be available only to Wikipedia administrators and not the general reading/editing public. And the sheer ease with which anything can be deleted online, if someone with the necessary access wants something gone, makes even the most secure online entry less secure than any old book. In fact, Wikipedia recognizes the inherent evanescence of Web sources in comparison with books and other old media sources by putting in its Web citations at the bottom of articles not just the date of the cited Web page's creation but also the date it was last checked by a Wikipedia editor to make sure it was still online at the indicated URL. For the same reason, I noted in the Bibliography to this book that the links supplied were good as of February 2012.

The bottom line is that a paper book on a shelf is more reliable—more likely to be there when we need it—than even the most dependable site on the Web: Wikipedia. On January 18, 2012, Wikipedia went dark for a day—shut itself off—in protest of SOPA (Stop Online Piracy Act), then under consideration by the U.S. Congress. The cause was just—SOPA was yet another proposed violation of the First Amendment (see Levinson, 2012)—but the lesson of the voluntary shutdown is disquieting for those who value and yearn for more reliable locatability on the Internet. No decision by any institution, whether reached by consensus as on Wikipedia or traditional corporate fiat as on Amazon, could possibly make the paper book in your bookcase go dark. As we saw at the conclusion of chapter 2 concerning Facebook, the deepest decisions regarding the new new media are not in the hands of the users on whom the new new media bestow unprecedented powers. These decisions, including whether the medium lives or dies, whether it is on or off for just a day, remain in the hands of the media themselves (and potentially the government). In this regard, new new media are no different from the oldest media in our midst.

The future of old-fashioned books and libraries thus seems under no near, total jeopardy from Wikipedia and other new new media, though we can expect the offline media to play a decreasing reference role in our lives. (In the realm of entertainment, Netflix has been offering an increasing number of movies and television shows streaming on its website, rather than DVDs in the mail.) And, although books have been banned and burned throughout history, the practical impossibility of rounding up all copies of a book, once printed and distributed, makes them invulnerable to complete banning by government, commercial, or religious directive.

That's not the case for anything online, including Wikipedia, as we will see for yet another reason in our concluding section of this chapter.

The United Kingdom vs. Wikipedia

An encyclopedia is about the last kind of text one would expect to be banned—the very word "encyclopedia" breathes something stodgy—especially in the United Kingdom, where the *Encyclopedia Britannica* was first published, in Scotland in the 1770s. On the other hand, encyclopedias have been politically troublesome to some regimes, but this was not the problem that Wikipedia encountered in the United Kingdom in December 2008 (Kirk, 2008).

It was an album cover posted on Wikipedia—*Virgin Killer* by The Scorpions, from 1976—that attracted the concern of the U.K.'s Internet Watch Foundation (IWF), which put the album on its blacklist due to the image of a nude young girl on its cover (the genital area, however, cannot be clearly seen, due to a cracked-glass effect in the image). The IWF is not affiliated with the U.K. government, but British Internet providers, whom the government expects to maintain standards of decency, take the blacklist very seriously. The result: Some 95 percent of British Internet users were blocked from Wikipedia for three days until the IWF lifted the ban (Raphael, 2008; Collins, 2008). That's right: British Internet users were blocked from all of Wikipedia on account of one album cover. Although the intent was to block the offending page, "The initial move last Friday by the IWF, which acts as a watchdog...for Internet content visible in the U.K. meant that some people could not see any pages on Wikipedia at all, while others were unable to edit pages on the user-generated encyclopedia" (Arthur, 2008).

As with Pakistan's ban of YouTube for several hours in February 2008, the blocking of Wikipedia in the United Kingdom over a questionable page highlights again the deep vulnerability in new new media—the stark reality that, for all the power they put in our hands, they are fundamentally not in our control. Although new new media may be outside the scope of the FCC (Federal Communications Commission) or other governmental supervision in the United States—for now—they are subject to control and banning in other parts of the world. In the case of Wikipedia, this can be especially destructive, because every reader unable to access Wikipedia is also an editor, unable to write or work to reach consensus in editorial discussions, which are the lifeblood of the online encyclopedia. (Collins, 2008, reported that the ban "left millions of Britons unable to make edits on the Wikipedia site.") And the interconnectedness of everything in new new media—in the case of Wikipedia, of all of its pages to one another—meant that the banning of a single page took the whole encyclopedia offline and beyond access to everyone attempting to access it via the Internet in the country where the ban was in effect. This is equivalent to putting a padlock on an entire bookstore or library, just to keep one book out of the public's hands.

Indeed, in the case of the Pakistani ban, not only was that country affected but so was access to YouTube around the world. Not just the bookstore was boarded up; bookstores around the world were behind the shutters, too.

Presumably, digital surgical techniques sooner or later will be able to take out just the offending page, or remove from public access what the censor considers a tumor, rather than shutting down a whole, vital new new media organ. But the fundamental problem remains: The current architecture of new new media and their conduits makes them all too easy to ban by central authorities. A glaring irony of new new media is that the digital engineering that makes them the most democratizing media in human history also gives governments and other authorities more power to ban them than the Catholic Church ever had over Galileo's books nearly 400 years ago.

The problem with the global village, from the perspective of combating censorship, is that the entire globe can be censored just by boarding up a few of the vendors of free information on Main Street. Had SOPA and its potential for government shutdown of Internet sites in the United States been enacted into law, the interconnected nervous system of the entire world would have been in jeopardy.

We turn in the next chapter to blogging, which, more than any other new new media activity, has been center stage in debates about freedom of the press.

CHAPTER 6

Blogging

BLOGGERS ARE OFTEN REFERRED TO AS "CITIZEN JOURNALISTS," to underline the fact that a blogger need not be a professional journalist to write and publish about the news. But the adjective "citizen" is still insufficient to convey the scope of liberation that blogging has bestowed upon us. The truth is that one need not be a citizen of this or any particular country, one need not be an adult, one need not have any attribute other than being able to read and write in order to blog.

Consider, for example, the following, and bear in mind that, although I am a professor of communication and media studies, I have no professional expertise in politics. I am just a citizen. But, even if I were not...

It was past one in the morning on May 7, 2008. Ninety-nine percent of the vote had finally come in from the Democratic presidential primary in Indiana. Hillary Clinton had won by just 2 percent. A few hours earlier, Barack Obama had won big in North Carolina. I wrote a blog post saying Barack Obama would be the Democratic nominee for president.

I posted it not only on InfiniteRegress.tv—my television review and politics blog—but on my Myspace blog as well. I put up links to it on Facebook and Digg. My blog on Amazon automatically posted it via a "feed." A link to my post also automatically appeared on Twitter.

My various "stat counters" reported that thousands of people had read my blog within an hour of its posting.

Just a few years earlier, the only possible recipient of my thoughts about such a decisive political development, moments after it had occurred in the middle of the night, would have been my wife. We could have talked about the results in Indiana. I could also have written about them and sent this to any number of online magazines, but my words would not have been automatically posted. Gatekeepers—otherwise known as editors, likely not at work until the next morning—would have needed to approve them.

From the beginning of the human species, from the very first time that two people spoke, speech has been as easy to produce as to consume. We switch effortlessly from hearing to talking. But speech lacked permanence, and we invented writing to safeguard what our memories might lose. The written word was also almost as easy to produce as to consume—writing well is more difficult than being able to read, but to be literate was and is to be able to write as well as read. As long as the written words remained personal, individual, and not mass-produced, the process of writing—at least writing something, however brief—was as widespread as reading.

The printing press changed all of that. It opened many doors. It made Bibles, reports of Columbus's voyages, and scientific treatises readily available to millions of readers. But it ended the equality of consumers and producers, and radically altered the one-to-one ratio in which just about every reader was also a writer. A sliver of the population contributes what goes into books, newspapers, and magazines.

And now blogging has in turn changed and reversed all of that. Although there are still more readers than writers of blogs, any reader can become a writer, either by commenting on someone else's blog or, with just a little more effort, by starting a blog of one's own. More than 165 million blogs were being written in 2011.

Although speaking is easier than writing, publishing of writing in digital form—online—requires less production than online publishing of audio or audiovisual clips of spoken words. In fact, publication of a written blog requires no production at all beyond the writing and initial posting of the writing. "Web-logging" has been known by the name "blogging" since 1997 (McCullagh & Broache, 2007; but see also Katie Hafner's 1999 *New York Times* review of Heather Anne Halpert's *Lemonyellow.com*, identified as an "on-line intellectual diary"). It has roots in the digital age in "computer conferencing" and message boards that go back at least 15 years prior (Levinson, 1997), and thus became the first big player in the new new media revolution.

A Thumbnail History of Electronic Writing

Writing always had some advantages over speaking as a mode of human expression. Not only was writing permanent, in contrast to the instantly fleeting quality of speech, but writing also allowed the sender greater control of the message. An angry, very happy, or extremely sad speaker can find it difficult to disguise those emotions in speech. But the same emotions can make no appearance at all in a written document, unless the writer chooses to make those feelings plain. This is one reason texting surpassed speaking on cellphones in the hands of people under 45 around the world (Nielsen Mobile report, discussed by Finin, 2008).

But after the enormous boost given to the dissemination of the written word by the printing press, the progress of writing in the evolution of media was slow. The telegraph in the 1830s gave the written word the capacity to be sent anywhere in the world—or anywhere connected by wires and cables—instantly. But the requirement of a telegraph operator to make this happen, as well as someone to deliver the telegram, not only worked against the immediacy of this electronic communication but also made it far more impersonal than written letters. It was one thing to declare your love in a letter and quite another to utter those words to a telegraph operator for transmission to the intended recipient.

The telegraph, however, revolutionized news delivery by allowing reporters to file stories instantly with their newspapers. Baron Julius von Reuter started his news service with carrier pigeons, which could convey news more quickly than via boats across the English Channel. But the baron's news agency soon came to rely on the telegraph. Its successful descendant was bought by the Thomson Company for $15.8 billion in 2008 (Associated Press, 2008).

Blogging takes the dissemination of news and opinion one big step beyond the telegraph by allowing "reporters"—that is, people, everyone—to file their stories instantly not with their newspapers but on their blogs and, therein, with the world at large. And because blogs are under the personal editorship of the writer, they can be about anything the writer pleases—unlike newspapers and magazines, where professional editors—not writers—usually decide the subject of the stories.

This personalization or "de-professionalization" of communication is one of the signal characteristics of new new media. It was not until the deployment of the fax in the 1980s, and the advent of email around the same time, that the writer finally reclaimed privacy and control over the written word. But the fax was primarily for one-to-one communication—much like the telegraph. And even emails sent to groups were less than a drop in the bucket in the reach of mass media such as newspapers. Blogging combines the best of both—the personal control of email and the long reach of mass media.

Blogging About Anything, Forever

The personal control that the writer has over his or her blog means that the blog can be about any subject, not just news. On the evening of May 29, 2008, my blog received 20,000 "hits" on a page (views of the page) I had written the year before, about the previous season's finale of *Lost* (Season 3 finale: "Through the Looking Glass"). This development, something that happens on blogs all the time, highlights two significant characteristics of blogging, in particular, and new new media, in general. The first is that anyone can blog about anything—I'm a professor and an author, not a professional television critic. The second is that the impact of a blog post, including when it will have its maximum impact, is unpredictable. My blog post about *Lost* received thousands of online visits shortly after it was written in 2007, but these were less than half of the visits or hits it surprisingly received on that one day a year later in 2008.

Permanence is one of the most revolutionary aspects of new new media and character-izes all new new media—as we saw with YouTube in chapter 4—not just blogging. One of the prime characteristics of old electronic media, such as radio and television, was their fleeting quality. Like the in-person spoken word, the word on radio and television was gone the instant after it was spoken. This evanescence led Lewis Mumford (1970, p. 294) to critique the viewers of television as in a "state of mass psychosis" in which "man" is confined to a "present time-cage that cuts him off from both his past and his future." Mumford apparently was not aware of the professional video recorders and "portapak" video cameras that were already giving television some permanence in 1970 (see Levinson, 1997, for more of my critique of Mumford), but he certainly was not wrong that the electronic media of his day offered information that was far less permanent than that conveyed by print. The first wave of new, digital media—the Web of the mid-1990s—began to invest its commu-nications with more permanence. But until the use of "permalinks" became widespread, a development that awaited the rise of blogging in the first years of the 21st century, items on the Web lacked anything remotely like the "reliable locatability" of words on pages of books on shelves discussed in the previous chapter (see also Levinson, 1998; Levinson, *Cellphone*, 2004; and Levinson, "The Secret Riches," 2007, for more).

Although blog pages still lack the reliable locatability of books—it is easier for a blogger to remove a post, or her or his entire blog, than it is to write a new post—their instant availability to anyone, anywhere, with a connection to the Internet may in one way give them a greater net durability (pun intended), a durability to more people, than any book. If a text is available online for 10 years to millions of people, is it more or less durable to the culture than 1000 books available for 100 years on library shelves? Indeed, it may well be that the ease of making permalinks, along with the sheer number of people who can easily access them, will make the contents of blogs more permanent, in the long run, than printed books—even though, in the short run, printed books are still the best bet for durability.

The blog post is thus not only immediate and universally accessible, but, like the YouTube video, the blog post can last forever. Indeed, whether photograph, video, or text, once it is committed to the Web, it is not only easily deletable on a given page but in principle all but impossible to delete everywhere. This is because, as we saw about Facebook pages in chapter 2, anyone can make a copy and post the item to his or her blog or Web page. And once a photograph, video, or text has been downloaded to a device held in your hand, it is beyond the capacity of any system on the Web to erase (unless its text is on an Amazon Kindle). The immediacy of new new media and the ease of erasing or preventing access to its contents can disguise this kind of permanence through dissemination and give the impression that everything posted on the Web is easy come, easy go. But, in fact, the potential indelibility of anything posted online may be, literally, its most enduring characteristic.

We might also say that the sovereignty that the blogger has over his or her blog—the freedom from foreign gatekeepers ("foreign" being anyone other than the blogger)—finds its limit not only in the larger system on which the blog resides (Blogspot, Wordpress, whatever—see the upcoming section on blogging platforms), but in the ability of anyone to copy whatever is in the blog, for saving or dissemination.

Comment Moderation

The blogger's sovereignty also relates to gatekeeping in a different way: Although the blogger is not subject to anyone else's gatekeeping, the blogger becomes a gatekeeper in deciding whether to allow comments by others on the blog and, if so, how to moderate them.

The pros and cons of gatekeeping or moderating comments on one's blog are straightforward. Moderating comments, rather than allowing them to be posted automatically, allows the blogger to keep disruptive comments out of the blog. But such moderation also slows the pace of the blog. Unless the blogger is online every minute of the day, an excellent comment, which could spark further excellent comments, could be left waiting for approval.

Is the protection of the blog from undesirable comments worth such a potential slowing and even stifling of worthwhile conversation? It depends on what the blogger and the larger world of readers deem undesirable. Certainly we can see why even strong disagreement with a blogger's political positions, or analysis of a television show, should not be barred from the blog. Indeed, a blogger can usually use such criticisms as a springboard for elaboration of the blogger's initial opinion. "But don't you think mega-funding of candidates is undermining our democracy?" a comment could ask. "No, I do not," the blogger could respond and go on to explain how people can separate truth from falsity regardless of who pays for the message.

But this is all a matter of the blogger's judgment. A comment deemed disruptive by one blogger might be deemed conducive to valuable, multiple discussions by another blogger. Or a given blogger might want no comments at all, preferring the blog to be a one-way rather than an interactive mode of communication.

Bloggers can also install a CAPTCHA system ("Completely Automated Public Turing test to tell Computers and Humans Apart"), which requires commenters to answer a computer-generated question (for example, reproduce a blurry sequence of numbers and letters) designed to distinguish human commenters from automated spam. A CAPTCHA, of course, will not get in the way of a human being bent on entering a nasty or disruptive comment in a blog.

In general, bloggers who want to encourage comments might keep in mind the following principle: Only block or remove comments if you believe they will discourage other comments from you and your readers. A blog without comments is like a flightless bird: The blog may make important contributions or bring satisfaction to its writer, but it will lack one of the signature social characteristics of new new media—interaction with the audience. (But see the discussion of Kathy Sierra in the "Online Gossiping and Cyberbullying" section of chapter 9, "The Dark Side of New New Media," for what can happen when comments become abusive. And see Kennedy, 2012, for the *New Haven Independent* decision to do away with commenting, because it had "skidded to the nasty edges and run off the rails.")

Commenting as the Ubiquitous Greek Chorus

As easy as blogging is, writing a comment in someone else's blog, or any online forum, is even easier. All the commenter needs to do is enter the comment in a blog that already exists. Indeed, entering a comment on someone else's blog can be a very effective way of promoting your own blog. If your comment is about an issue that you are blogging about and you sign your comment—that is, your comment is not anonymous (see the "Anonymity in Blogging" section later in this chapter)—then readers of your comment can easily find your blog. You can encourage this discovery of your blog by including a link to it in your comment, but some bloggers may see this as use of their blog for promotion of other blogs and lodge an objection (either by entering a comment that says "please don't use my blog to promote yours" or by removing your comment—see "Further Tensions Between New New Media and Older Forms" later in this chapter for details).

As a blogger, I welcome comments with links—as long as the comments and links are relevant to the discussion at hand and not spam for gold sold at low prices. Because, whatever the motivation of the commenter, comments that are not spam serve to further what Comenius centuries ago called "The Great Didactic" (1649/1896).

Given that blog entries on new media systems such as *Entertainment Weekly* or *USA Today* regularly draw hundreds of comments—and on new new media amateur blogs (such as mine) anywhere from none to a few to occasionally hundreds of comments per entry—the comment is clearly the most frequent form of sustained written discourse in the new new media world. Comments on active Facebook and YouTube pages can number in the thousands, and are part of this commenting culture. (My 2006 debate with Jack Thompson about violence in video games, put on YouTube in 2007, had more than 3700 comments as of February 2012.)

At their best, comments serve not only as a voice of the people but as conveyors of truth and correction to blog posts, videos, and any item on the Web. In this capacity, commenting epitomizes the democratic alternative to expert driven information that is one of the hallmarks of new new media, and has been developed to a fine art on Wikipedia (see chapter 5). At their worst, comments can be vehicles for trolls to grab attention and can mar or derail an online conversation (see chapter 9 for more). In between, comments are the ubiquitous Greek chorus of the new new media world.

"Is it a fact—or have I dreamed it—that, by means of electricity, the world of matter has become a great nerve, vibrating thousands of miles in a breathless point in time?" Nathaniel Hawthorne's character Clifford asks about the telegraph in *The House of the Seven Gables* (1851/1962, p. 239). It was indeed a fact back then. But not as much as when Marshall McLuhan talked about the "global village" in *The Gutenberg Galaxy* in 1962. And by no means as much as now, when Hawthorne's and McLuhan's visions have achieved their fullest realization in the hundreds of millions of comments on Facebook, YouTube, and 165 million blogs worldwide at any instant.

Comments as Correctors

I try to get my reviews of television shows posted on my *Infinite Regress* blog within a few minutes of the conclusion of the show's episode on television, which serves to maximize the number of people who will read my review.

But such a tight schedule does not always make for a review that is perfectly factual. I make it a point to mention the names of actors and actresses, if they play important roles in a show I am reviewing, but sometimes these may not be available online, either on the show's website or on IMDB (Internet Movie Database).

On October 12, 2007, I reviewed the 12th episode of the first season of AMC's *Mad Men* on my blog. It was an excellent episode, and I mentioned in my review that "my favorite sex/romantic scene in this show was Harry (Isaac Asimov!) (played by Rich Sommer) and that secretary (played by xxxx)." The "Harry" was Harry Crane, who, in my opinion at least, looks a lot like science fiction author Isaac Asimov did in the 1950s and 1960s. (You can see their two photographs side by side at my "Interview with Rich Sommer," 2007.)

But to return to comments as correctors, the reason I wrote "played by xxxx" in the preceding paragraph is that, in my original blog post, I listed the wrong actress. I had looked at IMDB and every site of relevance I could find on the Web. I could find no actress credited with playing beside Rich Sommer on the couch. So I then pored over whatever photos I could find of actresses who played secretaries on *Mad Men* and came up with the wrong actress as having played "that secretary."

The first I learned of my mistake was via a comment in my blog, written about 30 minutes after I posted my review. It read, "Hey, Paul. I read your reviews every week. Thanks for the kind words, and for helping to get the word out. We really appreciate it! An important correction: Hildy is played by Julie McNiven. She deserves full credit for her amazing work!"

And the comment had been entered by none other than Rich Sommer!

We exchanged emails after that, and I interviewed Rich on my *Light On Light Through* podcast by the end of the month.

But, aside from the coolness of blogging about an actor and then being contacted by him on the blog—something that has happened to me more than once and is a good example of the equalization of new new media, in which famous and not-so-famous people can more easily be in touch—the comment by Rich Sommer, with a correction of my misidentification of the actress in his scene, spotlights the important role that comments can serve as correctors in blogging.

The whole world, in principle, is not only reading what you write when you blog but is waiting there as a potential safety net and source of correction for any mistakes you might make. These readers are much like the reader/editors on Wikipedia, except reader/commenters on blogs are likely a more diffuse community, larger but less intent on finding and correcting errors.

Of course, not all comments are helpful, and some might be hostile. But the correction of your review by the very subject of your review, within half an hour of its posting, is something new under the sun of media, unless your review was delivered on a live television broadcast, and the subject of the review happened to have your phone number.

As for Rich Sommer's helpful correction (his comment is still on the page), I changed the wrong name to Julie McNiven as soon as I finished reading his comment, and taking in the larger significance of hearing from a celebrity.

Myspace Message from Stringer Bell of *The Wire*

Everyone is a fan of someone, usually more than one actor, actress, singer, musician, or author. As exciting as it was to hear from Rich Sommer after blogging about him, his was not the most extraordinary and unexpected comment I received from an actor, or from a member of an actor's family, after blogging about the actor. In addition to Rich Sommer, I heard from Len Cariou's wife (via a comment still on the page) after I had blogged in 2007 about how much I had enjoyed his performance in two seasons of *Brotherhood* on Showtime (the character died at the end of the second season) and from the father of Aaron Hart (via email), one of two actors who played Don Draper's little boy in the second season of *Mad Men* in the summer of 2008. But as fortunate as I was with *Mad Men*—hearing from two actors or relatives of actors on the series—and as much as I enjoyed both *Mad Men* and *Brotherhood* (and still enjoy *Mad Men*; *Brotherhood* ended its run in 2008), neither, in my view, achieved the extraordinary quality of *The Wire*, which ran for five seasons on HBO, from 2002 to 2008.

Paramount among *The Wire*'s characters, dominating every scene he was in for the first three seasons (his tenure on *The Wire*) was Stringer Bell, second in command of the drug operation under investigation by the police. An attendee of night classes in economics, a copy of Adam Smith's 1776 *The Wealth of Nations* on his shelf, and as ready to kill if necessary as to worry about inflation, Stringer Bell was no ordinary ghetto drug chief.

In August 2006, when the only blog I was writing was the very occasional *Twice Upon a Rhyme* on Myspace (named after my 1972 album of the same name), I wrote a piece about *The Wire*. The little knowledge I had then of blog promotion led me to post a link and brief summary of the blog post on HBO's "Community" forum about *The Wire*.

A few months later, in the wee hours of a day in late October, I was quickly reading through a batch of "Friend" requests on Myspace. It was late. I was tired. I was not thinking at all about *The Wire*, and although the name Idris Elba seemed familiar enough for me to accept his Friend request without looking at his page, I went on quickly to the other Friend requests and promptly forgot about Idris's—until I received a message from Idris Elba about a week later, in which he told me that he'd read my comments about his acting on *The Wire* a while earlier, thanked me for my support, noted my long involvement in the music business and wondered what I thought of his music. He added that he'd be buying my latest book, *The Plot to Save Socrates*, because it was the sort of novel he liked to read.

I liked his music, especially his hip-hop version of "Johnny Was," so much so that I played it on a special episode of my *Light On Light Through* podcast, "*The Wire* Without Stringer," on November 4, 2006. I received another message on Myspace from Idris Elba a few days later in which he thanked me for dedicating an entire podcast to his work, appreciated my scholarly analysis of his acting and music and what made his character Stringer Bell so compelling, and indicated that his music came from the same place as his acting, except his music was his own script.(This message is currently posted on the right-hand column of my *Light On Light Through* podcast page.)

In the realm of new new media that we all inhabit, it is that easy for someone, anyone, watching television, with computer, now tablet or smart phone, at hand, to strike up a relationship with the star of that television show.

Changing the Words in Your Blog— After Publication

The blogger's authority over the blog pertains not only to the comments but also to the blog post itself, not only before it is posted on the blog but also for as long as it remains on the blog, which could be forever after.

Writing used to be the archetypically immutable medium. Writing with ink or whatever chemical or dye on papyrus, parchment, or paper gave those words life as long as the papyrus, parchment, or paper survived. The words could be crossed out or obliterated, of course, but the obliteration was still observable. Ink could fade, but rarely to the point of being totally illegible. Even erasing the marks of a pencil on paper leaves signs of the erasure.

The printing press heightened this immutability. Under pressure from the Roman Catholic Church, Galileo recanted his views that the Earth revolved around the sun. But the thousands of copies of books expressing his original opinion were not changed with the recantation. The Church won a Pyrrhic victory, and the Scientific Revolution continued (see Levinson, 1997, for more).

That happened in the first decades of the 1600s. This immutability of published writing was still very much in effect at the end of the 19th century, at the end of the Victorian age of printed literacy, when Oscar Wilde famously is supposed to have observed about the process of authoring that "books are never finished, they are merely abandoned" (the quote more likely originates a little later, however, with French poet Paul Valéry in 1933 and is about creating art or writing poetry). But whether of book, poem, or painting, the abandonment was as real as a loved one moving out of the home. Once published, a book or a newspaper article was beyond being changed by the author, except via means of a new edition of a book (as you are reading now of *New New Media*) or an editor willing to publish an amending note by the reporter in the newspaper, neither of which were likely. But that was to radically change with the advent of "word processing" and then online publishing by the end of the next century (see Levinson, 1997). And in our 21st-century age of new new media, bloggers may be seen to have the reverse problem: The easy revision of a blog means it is never really finished and all but impossible to abandon if the blog is on a site under the blogger's control.

Here is how that came to be: In the last two decades of the 1900s, word processing for the first time in history gave writers the capacity to change their written words with no tell-tale evidence of the original. Spelling errors could be corrected in an email prior to sending and ideas could be sharpened in manuscripts with no one other than the writer the wiser.

But email and manuscripts submitted to editors were by and large one-on-one communications. Once a manuscript was printed and published, it was as immutable in the 1980s as were the words wedded to the paper of Galileo's books in the 1600s.

Blogging made the publication as easy to alter as the initial writing. The most innocuous result is that spelling errors are easily correctable, as are missing words. There is no downside to such correction, nothing nefarious. But what about the capacity of any blogger to easily change the material wording and meaning of a blog post after it has been published?

If no one or few people have seen the original, such alterations pose no problem. But what if many people have read the original and commented on it, in whatever media available?

On the one hand, changing a text already extensively commented on can certainly generate confusion. What is Reader "C" to make of a blog post and comment in which Blogger "A" quietly changed the wording of the blog to reflect and remedy a critique made by Commenter "B"? One way Blogger "A" can eliminate any ensuing confusion is to speak up about the change—that is, put a postscript in the blog post, appropriately dated, that explains that a change was made in response to a comment made by Commenter "B." But what if the blogger neglects or decides not to do that?

On the other hand, the greater the number of people who have read and commented on a text, the more difficult for the author to surreptitiously alter the text and pretend the altered text was in the blog post all along. The audience for the initial text thus serves as protection against the changing of the text for purposes of deception, just as the same audience can be a safety net for the blogger by pointing out errors in the blog that can be corrected. (Wikipedia, as we saw in the last chapter, deals with this problem in a more efficient way, providing an easily accessible transcript of every edit made to an article.)

The social group as a guarantor of truth or, at the very least, accuracy, is a check-and-balance that works to the benefit of all new new media and their users.

Long-Range Blogging and Linking

The duration of blog posts for months, in some cases years, after their posting allows for another kind of self-promotion, in which the blogger keeps abreast of comments about his or her post in other blogs on the Web and adjusts the links in the original post to take advantage of these new comments.

Here is an example: In August 2007, I wrote a short item in one of my blogs with four pieces of advice to would-be writers. The item drew many readers (see "Gauging the Readership of Your Blog," later in this chapter, for how bloggers can keep track on a daily or even more immediate basis of the number of readers). A few months earlier, I had begun a podcast—*Ask Lev*—with brief, 3–5-minute bits of advice to writers. At some point a few months after my August 2007 posting, I got an email from a reader saying he was trying to locate my "My Four Rules: The Best You Can Do to Make It as a Writer" blog post but could not find it and instead had discovered my *Ask Lev* podcast, which had answered his questions.

The first improvement of my August 2007 "Four Rules" then occurred to me: put a link in that post to the *Ask Lev* podcast, because readers of the post would be likely to find the podcast of interest. Of course, that could and should have occurred to me when I first wrote the post. But the infinite perfectibility of any blog allowed me to recover and to put in this link months later.

The story continues: In December 2007, I interviewed Dr. Stanley Schmidt, editor of *Analog Magazine of Science Fiction and Fact* (the leading science fiction magazine), for my *Light On Light Through* podcast. That interview drew many listeners, including those on *Analog*'s online site, AnalogSF.com, where it became a topic of conversation. I, of course, kept a happy eye on these online discussions and noticed in October 2008 that someone said one of the best parts of the interview was the advice it gave to writers who wanted to get published in *Analog*. This immediately set off another insert-a-link bell, and I proceeded to put a link to the August 2007 "Four Rules" blog post in the text accompanying my podcast interview with Stan Schmidt. (By the way, you can find the URL to "My Four Rules," 2007, in the Bibliography at the end of this book in case you, too, are desirous of advice on how to become a published writer.)

You can see where this is going: Once you begin to look at not just your blog but the whole Web as your oyster for blog promotion, you have entered a realm in which your words not only do not deteriorate but also can improve with time, as you draw ever more readers from different places to your blog. The key is that, although blogging is usually a solitary process, its promotion is inherently social and thrives on the easy linking of the Web.

Of course, if you are not interested in large numbers of readers, or any readers at all, you can always make your blog private and admit only those readers who meet your criteria. This would deprive your blog of many of the social advantages of new new media, but the preeminent principle is nonetheless that the blogger has complete control over his or her online work and its dissemination (aside from the organization that owns the blog platform).

Usually, the blog will be the continuing creation of an individual. But sometimes the very blog writing itself can be a group activity.

Group Blogging

Entries or articles on Wikipedia are edited by everyone, which is also an option for any blogger who might want to open one or more blog posts to other authors. Such group blogging is a good example of readers literally becoming writers of the very text they are reading.

Writing has traditionally been and usually is an individual effort, in contrast to talking, which usually entails two or more people (it could be argued that talking to yourself is not really talking because no interpersonal communication takes place unless someone overhears you, in which case you are no longer talking only to yourself). The advent of group blogging thus can be seen as a further erosion of the difference between writing and talking, which began when word processing made correction of the written word almost as easy as the spoken and in some ways more effective, because the digitally corrected written word can leave no trace of the original, in contrast to the listener's memory of a spoken error.

But group writing has at least one disadvantage: Unlike a spoken conversation, in which each voice is identifiable as belonging to a separate person (even if we do not know who that person is), nothing in the written word intrinsically connects it to any author. Wikipedia, again, addresses this problem by providing detailed "histories" of every article, in which every edit is clearly identified. Group blogs are usually less sophisticated and often do nothing more than list everyone who has written or edited a given post.

The main benefit of group writing of blogs is that it can increase the sum total of expertise brought to the blog. For example, in December 2008, I started a blog entitled *Educated Tastes* about food, drink, restaurants, recipes, and groceries. Because my expertise in food pertains mostly to consumption, I had a choice of either leaving recipes out of the mix or bringing another writer on board who knew how to cook and write about it. Because my wife excels in both, I invited her to join the blog as a writer.

Whether blogwriting or songwriting or scriptwriting, the same calculus of collaboration applies. If such collaboration adds more to the project than any frustration you might feel from sharing your creative control, then it is worth trying.

Monetizing Your Blog

The commercial essence of the Web has always been that it's free—"only suckers pay for content," as David Carr aptly observed about what succeeds most on the Web in *The New York Times*, back in 2005. That still holds true, and more so than ever, with flourishing, free sites such as *The Huffington Post*, even though newspapers such as *The New York Times* have begun to put much of their content—formerly available for free on the Web—behind "pay walls" to offset loss of income from declining paper sales (literally newspapers on paper) and loss of advertising (see the discussion later in this chapter). But a site being available for free—whether *The Huffington Post* or your own blog—does not mean that you cannot earn money from your blogging.

You can make money from any blog or online site in five general ways:

1. Google AdSense is the grandparent of revenue-making by individuals (you and me) on the Web. You sign up, get "code" to put on your blog, and you're in business. Text, image, and/or video ads, the size and subject and placement of your choosing, appear on your blog. The work required to set this up is easy and less demanding than the writing of most blog posts.

That is the good news. The not-so-good news is that you won't make much money—not enough to retire on or earn a living from and not even enough in a month to buy a decent dinner in New York. An average of 500 to 1000 visitors a day is likely to earn you no more than about $10 per month from Google AdSense, which pays on clicks and impressions, meaning you get paid for the number of people who click on the ads (clicks) or view them (impressions). As is the case with many online ad services, Google AdSense only pays you when your ads have earned a set minimum amount of revenue—in the case of AdSense, $100.

You will likely find that ads about certain topics—usually those that relate in some way to the subjects of your blog posts—attract more clicks on your blog than ads that have nothing to do with the subject of your blog. AdSense automatically runs ads, when available, that relate to the subjects of your posts. Unfortunately, this selection process is keyed only to the subject and can miss the tone or opinion of your blog post. A post on my blog that criticized John McCain in the 2008 presidential campaign attracted Google ads in support of McCain. The same happened with Mitt Romney in 2012. If such ads are not acceptable to the anti-Republican blogger, Google AdSense provides a means of filtering out any ads on specified unwanted subjects. But unless this is done when the ad code is first created, an unwelcome ad can nonetheless appear on the blog. The code, however, can be revised at any time. If I hadn't been so busy, I would have put in filters for ads that went contrary to my political views before I blogged on the subjects. Blogging takes more than compelling writing to make money in a way that stays true to the goals of your blog. It requires careful tending, much like a garden, to limit the likelihood and impact of weeds—that is, ads you don't want to see on your blog.

You might find that video and image ads attract more clicks than text ads. Placement of the ads can also increase your revenue. A text ad at the top of a blog can generate far more hits than attractive image and video ads in the sidebar. But ads placed at the top of the blog give the blog a more commercial look than ads placed in the sidebar. The blogger thus has a choice: Which is more important, appearance of the blog or income earned? Of course, if you want your blog to look as commercial as possible, then your course of action is clear.

The key point in all cases is that you have complete control over the kinds of ads (text, image, video) and where on your blog they are placed, as well as some control over the subject of the ads. You can learn via experiment which combinations look best and which produce the most revenue.

2. Amazon Associates has a different approach. You place ads for Amazon's books and other products on your blog page and get paid a percentage every time someone clicks on the ads and buys something from Amazon. The percentage, as of January 2012, starts at 4 percent for the first 6 sales, increases to 6 percent when sales number 7 or more, increases to 6.5 percent when there are 33 or more sales, and so forth. As an author, I find it valuable to have numerous Amazon ads on my blogs for my own books. But the more general guiding principle for this kind of monetization is not that you need to be an author of books sold on Amazon but a blogger willing to do the little research required to see which books on Amazon relate to subjects of your blog posts.

For example, in a review of an episode of *Lost* in its fourth season, in which time travel played a major role, I not only placed Amazon ads for my own time travel novel, *The Plot to Save Socrates*, but also for such time travel classics as Isaac Asimov's *The End of Eternity* and Robert Heinlein's *The Door into Summer*.

Because Amazon sells much more than books, you can use its Associate services to sell a wide range of products on your site. For example, if you have a blog about food, you could put Amazon ads for foodstuffs, beverages, cutlery, and the like on your blog.

CafePress operates in a somewhat similar way. You design a logo, which can be placed on coffee mugs, T-shirts, and so forth. You place an ad for the item on your blog. CafePress produces an item every time one is ordered—publishing on demand—at no cost to you. CafePress sets its price, and you can add whatever you like, above that price, for your commission. If your logo is some sort of advertising for your blog, you earn not only a commission but also good publicity for every sale.

Unlike Amazon, however, you either need sufficient talent to design an attractive logo for CafePress or will have to hire or persuade someone to design it for you. In contrast, Amazon supplies images of the book covers and all of its products in the ads for your blog.

3. In the case of Google AdSense and Amazon Associates, nothing is changed in the writing of your blogs—the ads are placed at the bottom, the sides, the top, or in the

middle (if you prefer) of your text; it's your choice. PayPerPost, one of several different such operations, offers another kind of approach to making money from your blog: You are paid to write posts on given subjects.

PayPerPost pays anywhere from $5 to $500 or more for blog posts requested by its clients. Your payment depends mainly upon the popularity of your blog—how many readers the advertiser can expect will see your post about the advertiser's subject.

The great advantage of this kind of blog monetization is the money you see in hand from your blog posts. Leading earners on PayPerPost since its inception in 2006 have received more than $10,000 per year for their written-to-order blog posts. It's relatively easy to see hundreds of dollars of income in a year—more than the Google AdSense revenue indicated earlier.

The disadvantage is you may be tempted to write about subjects you otherwise might not want to write about in your blog. This can undermine one of the crucial benefits of new new media and blogging: writing whatever you want, with no gatekeepers to approve or disapprove of your output. The fine line to be walked is writing reviews of products you already know about and like. But this could be difficult: Would you pass up $500 to write a positive post about a product you thought was just okay, not great?

The principle of being honest with your readers can also come into conflict under this kind of monetized blogging. PayPerPost insists as standard operating procedure that all of its assigned posts have a clearly displayed notice that the blog post was purchased or written for hire. As a further safeguard, PayPerPost also requires all participating bloggers to publish at least one nonhired post for every purchased post, which further makes clear to the reader which posts were hired. But several other "blog for money" organizations want otherwise—reasoning, probably correctly, that readers would take the post more seriously if they thought the post came from the blogger's mind and heart and not the advertiser's paycheck. Indeed, even PayPerPost offers a few of these "nondisclosure" opportunities, with the proviso that it did not endorse the approach but would be willing to serve as broker if that is what the advertiser and the blogger both wanted.

Another, related problem can arise from the general topic of the blog post. Favorably reviewing a movie you already saw and liked, or even expected that you would like, is one thing. But what about accepting PayPerPost blogging assignments for political or social issues, in which the assignment requires you to write on behalf of the issue or candidate? Even if you support the issue, and even with the PayPerPost disclosure advisory on assigned posts and no advisory on everything else, taking on such political assignments can cast doubt among your readers that you mean what you say in your nonhired posts. If you want your readers to be 100 percent certain that the political analyses they read on your blog are 100 percent yours, the safest course of action may be to avoid doing any PayPerPost or hired blog posts on political and social subjects. (See also "Bloggers and Lobbyists," later in this chapter.)

4. You can put a PayPal donation widget—a digital money tip jar—either on your overall blog or on any specific blog post. PayPal is in effect an online banking service, which receives payments from other PayPal accounts, as well as traditional credit cards, and makes payments to other PayPal accounts. PayPal account holders can transfer funds from PayPal to their traditional bank accounts.

How much money can a PayPal donation button generate on a blog? Shaun Farrell's 2007 podiobook of my 1999 novel *The Silk Code* provides an instructive example. A podiobook is an audiobook available free, online, in weekly installments, from

Podiobook.com (see chapter 8, "Smaller Potatoes," for details). *The Silk Code* podiobook placed in the top 20 of podiobooks downloaded in 2007 (its exact placement in the top 20 was not revealed). More than a thousand people downloaded all or part of the novel. Farrell received about $100 in the PayPal donation box on his blog page.

But a podiobook is not a typical blog. Because a podiobook appeals to an audience that might otherwise purchase an audiobook, donations to the author (and, in Farrell's case, the narrator) make some sense. In contrast, authors of written blogs tell me they are lucky to receive even a few dollars a year from their tip jars.

5. A fifth way of making money from one's blog draws upon the oldest form of advertising and predates new new media by centuries: You can accept and place ads on your blog, paid for directly by the advertiser. You can make far more money than via Google AdSense—you can charge whatever the market for blog ads will bear, based on the number of people who read your blog—but the price you pay for not going through the Google AdSense middleman is you have to find the advertisers, or they have to find you.

This kind of advertising goes back to the advent of newspapers in the 1500s, 1600s, and 1700s—they were called "pamphlets" back then—and developed as follows: Originally, printers were funded and supported by the monarchs of Europe, and especially fortunate printers were designated "royal presses." But monarchs expected printers to publish stories favorable to the monarchs, and eventually some printers began to chafe under this arrangement.

Merchants with ships laden with goods from the New World provided a way out and indeed a solution that provided the economic basis of democracy. Merchants paid printers to run announcements of their products, what we today call "ads." Other than printing these announcements, the presses could print whatever else they pleased. Printers thereby gained the economic freedom to break free of royal purse strings and political reins. This worked best first in England and then America, which enacted the First Amendment to ensure that the government, even in a democracy, could never control the press. (As I detail in my "The Flouting of the First Amendment," 2005, the First Amendment has not always been adhered to in America; see the "First Amendment" section later in this chapter. See also *The Soft Edge*, Levinson, 1997, for more on the advent of advertising and its political consequences.)

The advertising symbiosis, however—merchants get publicity, printers get money, both are beneficiaries—became a bedrock of American media and continued in the age of radio and television, which went a big step further than newspapers by providing content free of charge to their listeners and viewers. Consumers paid for the receiving equipment—radio or television set—but received the content free. Radio and television stations and networks made money by attracting consumers of the free programming and then selling airtime, or exposure to the audience numbers, to sponsors. The free blog, though it is written like a newspaper article, is therefore more like the traditional broadcast media in terms of being free. And, although one of the hallmarks of new new media content is that it costs the consumer nothing, this characteristic began not with new new media but with older broadcast media. Ironically, although free radio and television continue to be major players in our lives, "teens and young adults cut their radio-listening time in half as they became infatuated with the Internet, cellphones and video games" in the past decade (Lieberman, 2011, who also notes a small "renaissance" for radio in 2009–2011), and the number of network television viewers has been declining on and off for almost two decades, with paid cable and free new new media drawing away audiences (Associated Press, 2008; see also Hibberd, 2011, for TV ownership declining in 2011–2012).

In all such classic cases of paid advertising, the ad is paid for on a cost-per-thousand basis—that is, how many thousands of people will see or hear the ad. Television programs live or die depending on the number of their viewers, as reported by the Nielsen ratings. These ratings are based on statistically valid samples of the total television-viewing public. In contrast, the new new medium of blogging on the Web offers direct counts, not samples, of blog visitors (see "Gauging the Readership of Your Blog," later in this chapter).

But the blog, as we learned earlier, also offers ways not available in print or broadcast media to earn income from an ad—there is no way to click on an ad heard on radio, or seen on television or in a newspaper, unless we're experiencing those old media on the Web. Online ads also can provide knowledge of where the purchase of an online product or service originated by showing the clicked link that resulted in a purchase. This is a much more precise and efficient method of tracking the source of sales than providing a code seen on television when ordering a product by phone, and facilitates the Amazon method of payment, in which the blogger is paid a percentage of the sale.

Television, radio, and newspapers, then, charge for their ads based solely on how many people can be expected to see or hear the ad (the cost-per-thousand, or CPM, formula). In contrast, although blog ads that come directly from advertisers can also work on such a CPM basis, the blogger can also be paid based on the number of clicks and actual purchases resulting from an ad. When payments are made based on number of impressions, or CPM, methods of gauging the readership of one's blog are crucial (see "Gauging," later in this chapter).

These five ways of earning money from your blog—Google AdSense, Amazon ads, PayPerPost, PayPal donations, and direct ad purchases—all pertain to blogs completely under the blogger's control. In the "Blogging for Others" section later in this chapter, we will consider the opportunities for remuneration when you blog for someone else. But, first, let's consider in a little more detail the degree to which any way of monetizing your blog may be incompatible with the communicative and democratizing ideals of blogging.

Is Monetization Incompatible with the Ideals of Blogging?

Not everyone in the blogosphere is happy about the monetization possibilities of blogging. Jeff Jarvis, creator of *Entertainment Weekly* and the well-known *BuzzMachine* blog, put the "problem" he saw with the PayPerPost model as follows: "The advertisers are trying to buy a blogger's voice, and once they've bought it they own it" (Friedman, 2007).

David Sirota, then a senior fellow at the Campaign for America's Future, saw a different kind of harm arising from advertising in blogging. Criticizing a report that Jonathan Martin gave on Politico.com about President-elect Obama's December 7, 2008, appearance on *Meet the Press*—that Obama was "backing off" (Martin's phrase) his campaign pledges on taxes and Iraq—Sirota concluded with the following: "I'm not linking to [Martin's] story because the entire reason the *Politico* made up this outrageous lie is to get people to link to the story and build up traffic which it then uses to attract ad revenue" (Sirota, 2008).

Jarvis, then, sees money as putting literal words in bloggers' mouths—or via their fingers in their blogs—while Sirota sees the desire to increase the number of readers, to increase advertising revenue, as leading to the writing of blogs of "outrageous lies."

Both concerns may be warranted. But let's try to put the pursuit of money by the press in historical context. Why and how did advertising as a source of income for the press arise in the first place? And what damage, if any, has resulted to a free press from this?

As we saw in the previous section, the press adopted advertising in the first place as a means of freeing the press from economic and thus political reliance on the monarchies of Europe. And as far as we know, the press has had but three sources of income, as have media in general, in history.

One income source is government support, which has always translated into government control of the media. Whether Pravda in the Soviet Union or the BBC in Britain or the royal press hundreds of years earlier in that country under Henry VIII, government financing of the press has always made the press an organ of government. In a totalitarian society, this hardly matters, because the government controls everything anyway. In a democracy, government control of the press can undermine the democracy, because it can obstruct the press from being a critic of the government and reporting to the people what the government might be doing wrong. During the Falklands War, to cite just one example, the British government controlled and censored the BBC's reporting on that war (see Levinson, 1997, for details). Indeed, one of the reasons that democracy was able to arise and flourish in England is that printers were able to break free of royal control. Thomas Jefferson, James Madison, and James Monroe understood the crucial role of a free press in a democratic society, which is why they insisted on the First Amendment to our Constitution and its guarantee of a press unfettered by governmental fiat.

A second source of income for media is the purchase or rental of the media by the public. Sales of newspapers, magazines, books, DVDs, CDs, and movie theater tickets (a form of rental) have worked well for many media. But they have not worked very well for newspapers, especially in recent years. *The New York Times* thus loses money on every paper it sells, and *The Village Voice* (a New York progressive, counterculture weekly) dispensed with its price per copy altogether and has been distributed at no charge for the past decade. Newspapers do this because they want to keep their number of readers as high as possible, to attract advertising revenue.

Furthermore, or maybe first of all, to charge for reading a blog would cut far more deeply against the ideal of blogging, and new new media in general, as available to the public for free, than would advertising if needed to keep the blog free. *The New York Times* online went behind a pay wall, but, again, a newspaper online is not a blog or a new new medium for many reasons, so charging for online access is just a continuation of another old medium characteristic. Organizations such as Media Pass allow for easy creation of pay walls, but its clients, including Social Toddlers and Wizzard Media, are online businesses selling know-how, not blogs.

Which brings us to the third source of income for media for the past hundreds of years: advertising. In a Platonically ideal world, perhaps we would not need it—not for blogging or older media such as newspapers and magazines. Independently wealthy bloggers with the best of motives would write just the truth as they saw it and would not contaminate it in either reality or appearance by taking any money for their work. But we do not live in such an ideal realm—in our world, bloggers and people in all media need to eat. I love teaching, but I do not usually do it for no payment, because I do have to pay my mortgage and electricity bills.

And what, specifically, is the evidence of damage done to blogging, either by the PayPerPost approach or the pursuit of advertising? Sirota's post is titled "Politico's Jayson Blair" after the infamous *New York Times* reporter who made up stories and plagiarized (Levinson, "Interview about Jayson Blair," 2003)—and unintentionally brings home a telling point: The "newspaper of record," *The New York Times*, was plagued by "outrageous lies" on its pages by Jayson Blair. Was that because it, too, was pursuing advertising revenue?

The more likely explanation is that there is no cause and effect between advertising and faulty reporting, which arises from the frailties of all human beings, including reporters (though see Nissenson, 2007, for Dorothy Schiff, *New York Post* publisher, killing a story in 1976 because her advertisers objected to it). Nor is there any evidence that PayPerPost blogging has deluded the public with lies. If a post is clearly identified as written to someone else's specification, right before and after posts that are clearly written only to the blogger's specifications, the reader is no more likely to perceive the paid-for post as the blogger's "voice" than the reader of a newspaper is to confuse an ad with the paper's editorial opinion, even though both kinds of confusion do happen.

Photos on Blogs and Photoblogs: Photobucket, Instagram, Flickr, Pinterest

Ads on blogs come in text, images, and video. Amazon ads have images of the books for sale, and Google AdSense offers options for text, image, or video ads, as discussed previously. But images and videos also can be placed on blogs just to make the blogs more interesting, colorful, and spiffy—to illustrate blog posts or just attract viewers—with no ad revenue earned from them.

Many blog platforms (such as Blogspot, see "Different Blogging Platforms" later in this chapter) allow the writer to upload images and videos directly to the blog. In the case of videos, they also can easily be embedded by code available from YouTube and other video sites.

Photobucket is an example of a free site that hosts images. HTML code is generated for every hosted image and can be edited to change the size and placement of the image on your blog. You can align images to the left or right, and the text will wrap around them. Links can also be easily placed in the image code, so that when readers click on the images, they will be taken to the page on the Web in the link. This is the way Amazon and Google image ads work.

Instagram, a relative newcomer (launched in October 2010) initially designed to facilitate photosharing on iPhones and iPads, was purchased by Facebook for one billion dollars in April 2012. The dot.com boom lives in new new media.

Flickr not only hosts images but also works, in effect, as a photographic blog, or a photographic equivalent of YouTube, which attracts viewers to its site, as well as provides content embeddable on blogs. Photobucket and Instagram can be used that way, too. Twitpic and yfrog, as mentioned in chapter 3, are image hosts especially designed to work quickly with Twitter, but their hosted images can also be put on blogs.

Pinterest allows easy capture of any image on the Web, including an image of a video, which then appears on your profile board or pinboard, for repinning and comment by other Pinterest users. Pinterest images can also be uploaded from your computer, embedded on your blog, and tweeted about and placed on Facebook pages via links. Techcrunch named Pinterest "best new start-up of 2011" (Constine, 2012; see also *MarketingProfs*, 2012) and the site had an Alexa rank of #88 in February 2012. Bianca Bosker, writing in *The Huffington Post* (2012), attributes Pinterest's success to its refreshing focus on items (images we like) rather than the burden of reporting on what we are doing (Twitter, Facebook, Foursquare), or a push back against the tide of new new media. If so, Pinterest especially bears further watching (and see Ferraro, 2012, for a critique).

Widgets are a way that blog posts, videos, and links of any kind can easily be integrated into a blog or Web page. As distinct from a "button," which usually links to just one other site, a widget is designed to offer numerous connections. Facebook and Twitter, for example, supply "buttons" or "badges," which allow readers to connect to a specified profile. Amazon supplies widgets, which allow readers to connect to numerous pages on its site.

Widgets are supplied not only by companies such as Amazon to help readers of your blog or Web site see Amazon's products (for which purchases you will be paid a percent-age, if you are monetizing your blog) but also by networks and organizations that are not selling anything. Twitter offers not only buttons but also widgets that allow your readers to see the tweets of specified people, including you or only you, or everyone on Twitter. In all cases, the widgets are supplied for free. They, in effect, act as little building blocks of the Web, apps appearing on your page with a bundle of connections to other websites.

One of the distinguishing characteristics of widgets in contrast to static links is that the links in widgets change, or are "dynamic," based on the purpose of the widget. Amazon has widgets for its products that provide updating links to those products based on the content of blog posts on the same page. For example, if I post a review about *Dexter*, the Showtime television series, my Amazon widget will display the *Dexter* novels and DVDs of earlier seasons. Google AdSense ads work in the same way. Twitter's widgets are constantly updated to show the most recent tweets. I also sometimes have a "Politics" widget on my blog from an organization called "Widget Box," which takes yet a third approach, display-ing headlines with links for the most popular—meaning, most read—political posts on blogs in the "Politics" division of the Widget Box network (divisions exist for television, science, and other categories). Widget Box also provides a widget that lists the posts in your blog with updates; this can be very useful if you have more than one blog and want to attract readers back and forth and, of course, if you can get friends to put your widget on their blogs and Web pages. Blogging platforms such as Blogspot also provide numerous widgets, including one—much like the Twitter widget—that lists and links to the most recent posts of other blogs, which you have entered into your "blogroll."

Note that blogs listed in any Widget Box widget may display Google AdSense or any kind of ads, even if your blog does not. If for some reason you are not only allergic to making money but also to aiding any kind of income generation on the Web, you need to take special care in choosing your widgets.

Gauging New New Media Impact: Statcounter, Alexa, Klout

Unless you blog purely for the pleasure of seeing your writing on a Web page—which is certainly one motivating factor for most writers—you will be interested in how many people are reading your words, and in other statistics that measure the popularity of your blog.

Services such as Statcounter and SiteMeter provide details on the number of people who visit your blog, including raw number of visitors, what pages they read, where the visitors come from (what countries, what Web sites, and so forth), how long they stay on your blog, and where they go when they leave your blog (what exit links they click). The basic services are free, with paying options that provide analyses of larger groups of visitors.

Technorati has been measuring the popularity of blogs in a different way since 2002: how many other blogs have linked to your blog. Further, Technorati, in turn, keeps track of the linkages of all blogs that link to yours. Being linked to 10 blogs with 500 links each is more impressive than being linked to 100 blogs with 5 links each. In the first case, many more readers are likely to see your blog.

Alexa takes another, complementary approach, ranking blogs according to a formula based on number of readers, links, and rates of growth. Google PageRank does something similar but over longer periods of time. Both systems are secretive about the precise "algorithms" they use to determine the rankings, to discourage unscrupulous bloggers and Web site developers from manipulating or "gaming" the data to achieve higher rankings.

Such "gaming" is something we will encounter in other systems that measure popularity or base their listings on popularity. Reddit and Digg, which we will look at in chapter 8, put articles, images, and videos on their front pages based on the number of up or down votes ("Diggs" and "Buries" on Digg) that submissions might receive from readers. This makes such systems especially prone to gaming, as users attempt to inflate the positive numbers by marshalling votes on behalf of given articles.

Klout, a newcomer to new new media measurement (September 2009) with 100 million users by the end of 2011, measures the popularity or impact not of blogs but of bloggers, and their "influence" on Twitter, Facebook, Google+, YouTube, Foursquare, LinkedIn, Flickr, Tumblr (see next section), and Last.fm (a music listening site). Influence is gauged by number of re-tweets, comments on blogs, Facebook, Google+, YouTube, and the like. Users with high Klout scores receive "perks" (I've received perks ranging from a free Subway sandwich to a discount on Leftlane gloves). Because Klout keeps track of so many different systems, it is more difficult to game.

Different Blogging Platforms

My InfiniteRegress.tv blog uses Google's "Blogspot," or "Blogger," platform (launched independently of Google in 1999). In addition to the virtue of being free, it offers a big assortment of blog templates (which determine what the blog looks like—colors, positioning of blog posts and sidebars, for example) or allows you to import and therein design your own template. The Blogspot platform also offers extensive control over comments, including notification of new comments and various moderator tools such as CAPTCHAs. Blogspot also allows multiple blogs by the same or multiple authors, all at no charge.

A key feature of Blogspot—perhaps the most important—is that bloggers have access to the underlying HTML code that determines the look and feel of the blog and allows easy insertion of stat counters and widgets, as discussed in previous sections.

Wordpress (launched 2003) is most like Blogspot, in that it offers a wide variety of features and is free. Amazon and other websites also offer free blog space to their users but with no access to the HTML code and far less control over the blog in general.

At the other end of the spectrum, some platforms offer features equivalent to Blogspot but are not free. Typepad (launched in 2003) charges anywhere from $8.95 (basic service) to $29.95 (premium service) per month. Its main advantage over Blogspot is a more distinctive look (assuming you like that look), and it comes packaged with sophisticated stat counters and other features. Movable Type (launched in 2001) is free for noncommercial use (no ads on your site, and you do not use it to make money); it otherwise costs hundreds of dollars per year. The LiveJournal (launched in 1999) basic blogging account is free but offers "paid" accounts at $19.95 per year. (Typepad, Movable Type, and LiveJournal are all owned by Six Apart.)

Tumblr (launched 2007) and Posterous (launched 2008, sold to Twitter in 2012) are more recent, free platforms, which feature easier integration of videos, images, and anything on the Web with a URL. Tumblr in particular caters to short blog posts, making it a form of microblogging halfway between Twitter and Blogspot, and faster to post to than Blogspot on a smart phone.

In the end, if money is no object, your choice of blog platform will likely be most determined by what you find most attractive or consonant with your image of your blog's purpose. For a cheapskate and on occasion long-winded writer like me, the free cost of Blogspot is irresistible. And I do like its general appearance and the powers I have to sculpt and control the blog. But if you prefer the short burst but want a platform with posts less ephemeral and a little longer than Twitter, go for Tumblr. Or go for both Blogspot and Tumblr, and have them link to one another.

Are Bloggers Entitled to the Same First Amendment Protection as Old-Media Journalists?

Blogging can be serious business, not only in the money that can be made and the ethical issues involved, which we have examined previously, but in its political and social impact and its relationship to older media ranging from newspapers to television. We turn in this section and the remainder of this chapter to a consideration of some of these issues, starting with the question of whether bloggers are protected from government interference under the First Amendment.

The Supreme Court generally sided with newspapers and print media on First Amendment and freedom of the press issues in the 20th century. In *The New York Times* v. Sullivan (1964), the Court severely limited the degree to which the press could be sued for defamation and libel; in *The New York Times* v. the United States (1971), the Court stopped the Nixon administration's attempt to shut down publication of the Pentagon Papers (see Tedford, 1985, for a detailed discussion of these and the other First Amendment cases mentioned in this chapter; see also Levinson, "The Flouting of the First Amendment," 2005).

Broadcast journalism, the other old-media part of the press, has not fared as well. The Fairness Doctrine, introduced by the Federal Communications Commission in 1949, required broadcasters to give balanced coverage to controversial issues. In Red Lion Broadcasting v. Federal Communications Commission (1969), the Supreme Court upheld that doctrine, on the grounds that broadcast stations are necessarily scarce in comparison to print media—only a limited number of stations can fit on the broadcast spectrum, in contrast to no natural or technological limit on the number of newspaper publishers. The FCC decided to abandon the Fairness Doctrine in 1987. But in the interim, on an issue relating more to social satire than journalism, the Supreme Court ruled in Federal Communications Commission v. Pacifica Foundation (1979) that the FCC had a right to tell radio stations not to broadcast comedian George Carlin's "Seven Dirty Words" routine (the reason in this case was that listeners could tune in and accidentally hear such objectionable broadcasts, unlike a deliberate decision to buy a copy of *Playboy*).

New media—or the appearance of old media such as newspapers on the Web—received a major endorsement by the Supreme Court in Reno v. American Civil Liberties Union (1997), in which the Communications Decency Act and Attorney General Janet Reno's attempt to use it to punish Joe Shea for publication of "indecent" language (critical of Congress for passing this law) in an online magazine were struck down as a violation of the First Amendment's protection of the press (see Levinson, 1997, for more). The decision in effect held that an online magazine was more like a newspaper than a radio or television broadcast.

And what of new new media—such as blogging?

Here a battle began and is still being waged over government coercion of the press in an area that may be a bit beyond First Amendment territory: shield laws, which protect journalists from being forced to reveal their sources to prosecutors and courts and do not address the right to publish, per se. The Supreme Court held in Branzburg v. Hayes (1972) that the First Amendment did not give journalists the right to refuse to testify or reveal sources, but Congress and the courts could enact legislation that gave journalists that privilege. Shield law supporters argue that, without such protection, journalists would be unable to do their jobs, because their sources could not rely on any pledge a journalist made to not reveal his or her sources in a story. I agree and was quoted in *USA Today* about *New York Times* reporter Judith Miller's 2005 imprisonment for failing to reveal her sources in the Valerie Plame CIA leak investigation: "It is wrong to jail a reporter for protecting sources, including flawed reporters" (Levinson, quoted in Johnson, 2005). Miller quoted my comment in the opening statement of her testimony to the U.S. Senate Judiciary Committee, Hearing on Reporters' Shield Legislation, on October 19, 2005.

At that time, there was no federal shield law—there still is none—which is why federal prosecutor Patrick Fitzgerald was able to get a judge to put Miller behind bars. Forty states and the District of Columbia currently (as of 2011) have shield laws, but do they—should they—protect bloggers or journalists who blog? Judith Miller reported on the *Fox News Watch* (2008) that, for the first time, more online journalists than print journalists had been arrested around the world in 2008.

The imprisonment of video blogger Josh Wolf in San Francisco in 2006–2007 shows that, for some people, the very phrase "journalists who blog" is a contradiction. Wolf was videotaping a protest in San Francisco in July 2005 about the G-8 Summit taking place then in Scotland. He sold some of his video to local television stations and posted other clips on his blog. A police officer, ironically named Peter Shields, was assaulted at another part of the demonstration, not videotaped by Wolf, and suffered a fractured skull. Wolf was asked by authorities to turn over his videotapes. He refused and was thrown in jail. Commented U.S. Attorney Kevin Ryan in a court filing, "[Wolf] was simply a person with a video camera who happened to record some public events"; U.S. District Judge William Alsup, apparently agreeing, described Wolf as an "alleged journalist." Wolf's attorney, First Amendment advocate Martin Garbus, thought otherwise and indicated, "I would define a journalist as someone who brings news to the public" (see Kurtz, 2007).

Wolf was released in April 2007, after eight months in prison, when prosecutors withdrew their insistence that Wolf had to testify. I concur completely with Garbus and was pleased to produce several blog posts and one podcast (Levinson, "Free Josh Wolf," 2007) as well as a letter to the federal prosecutors on Wolf's behalf. But he nonetheless was deprived of his freedom for eight months.

One way of looking at this case, and the more general issue of whether bloggers are bona fide journalists, is how to best apply Marshall McLuhan's famous aphorism that "the medium is the message" (1964). Applied superficially, we might well conclude, as Prosecutor Ryan did, that the medium of blogging is different from the media of print and broadcasting, as it indeed is, and different enough to negate or not allow journalists in its online ranks. A more accurate analysis, however, would note that there are media within media—that journalism, a form of communication, is a medium that can be presented via other media, such as newspapers, radio, TV broadcasts, and written and video blogs (see Levinson, 1999, for more on media within media). As Garbus observed, the medium or practice of journalism is the bringing of "news to the public." Wolf was clearly working in that medium, within the larger packaging of video blogging.

Wolf's case was likely complicated by the fact that he was not only a blogger but also a nontraditional blogger, in that he was using video rather than text as his medium (media within media: journalism via video via blog). Text blogging, which is what we have been looking at in this chapter, has significant differences from video blogging, including that the text can be written and uploaded and therein disseminated at least a little more quickly, with less technical requirement or savvy than required for videos. But Garbus's definition of what makes a journalist indicates that the capacity for journalism is not among such differences.

Wolf's release might have been a sign that the world of law enforcement was becoming aware of the role of new new media in journalism. But it was Wolf's arrest, instead, that would prove to be a harbinger of massive police mistreatment of citizen journalists six years later, with not only arrests but beatings of reporters using the tools of new new media to tell the world about Occupy Wall Street.

Citizen Journalists, the First Amendment, and Occupy Wall Street

In one sense, the police response to Occupy Wall Street across the United States in the Fall of 2011 was an equal-opportunity abuser of the First Amendment rights of all journalists across the media spectrum: journalists for old media, new media, and new new media, that is, video streaming and tweeting. In New York City, Mayor Michael Bloomberg kept all of the press, including local TV news helicopters, away from his eviction of the protesters from Zuccotti Park on November 15, 2011. Reporters on the ground were shoved and worse. A reporter for the *New York Post*—the 13th oldest continually published newspaper in the United States, founded in 1801 (you can't get much more old media than that), and a politically conservative paper—was put in a choke hold. A journalist working for National Public Radio (NPR) was detained by police (see Stelter & Baker, 2011, for details). Justifiably outraged over this mistreatment of their own, establishment media delivered a letter of complaint to Mayor Bloomberg, written by *The New York Times*, and signed, among others, by the Associated Press, *New York Post, Daily News,*

Thomson Reuters, Dow Jones & Company, and WABC, WCBS, and WNBC local TV news stations (Stelter, 2011). The New York Police Department responded a week later, with a directive read in precincts that police should not interfere with journalists doing their jobs (Associated Press, 2011).

But that was just part of the story. In one of the other parts, police mistreatment of reporters covering Occupy Wall Street continued, with Mayor Bloomberg defending such conduct. In another part, new new media journalists endured worse and more extensive mistreatment by police than did traditional media reporters, even as tweeted-about videos and text reports got the news out to the world when traditional media were handcuffed (figuratively and literally). As Stelter and Baker pointed out, as a result of the police muzzling of traditional reporters, "much of the early video of the police operation was from the vantage point of the protesters. Videos that were live-streamed on the Web and uploaded to YouTube were picked up by television networks."

And the NYPD responded. *The Huffington Post* (Mirkinson, 2011) provided an account of small-press and new new media reporters hit by police with nightsticks, shoved against walls, slammed against barricades, and arrested. The victims were reporters for such sites as *The Daily Caller* and *DNAinfo*—likely unfamiliar to most readers of *The New York Times*, but well known to people who get their news via smart phones and tablets.

According to the preceding accounts, the reporters for the older and newer media mistreated by police had clearly visible credentials. But there were also many others with no credentials, because they were affiliated with no organization at all, but were record-ing and tweeting out the truth for all to see, anyway. We will encounter some of these ultimate citizen journalists and their work in chapter 10, "Politics and New New Media." For now, we can say that the work begun by Josh Wolf—insisting that anyone practicing journalism be protected by the First Amendment, professional affiliation or not—still has a long way to go.

Bloggers and Lobbyists

Another kind of First Amendment blogging issue surfaced in Washington state in December 2008 (*Fox Report with Shepard Smith*), where its Public Disclosure Commission began looking at whether bloggers who are paid to write posts endorsing specific positions are, in effect, lobbyists and therefore subject to the regulations that govern lobbyists (these amount to always disclosing that you are a paid lobbyist).

Horsesass.com blogger David Goldstein argued on the Fox segment that bloggers are entitled to First Amendment protection from any disclosures to the government, including whether they are paid for their blogs and who is paying them. But advertis-ing and lobbying are already under substantial governmental regulation, which insists on full disclosure for lobbyists and truth in advertising for commercials on television, radio, the press, and, indeed, anywhere. In the political sphere, the McCain–Feingold Act (2002) placed limits on campaign financing, including prohibition of ads paid for by corporations and unions, but this restriction was struck down by the Supreme Court as a violation of the First Amendment in Citizens United v. Federal Election Commission (2010).

Before addressing the question of whether bloggers who are hired to write posts endorsing political positions are entitled to First Amendment protections given to the press, we first should ask: Are the lobbying laws and restrictions on advertising themselves in violation of the First Amendment, as the Citizens United decision held about corporate and union ads on behalf of political candidates?

The question regarding advertising and governmental insistence on truth is the easiest to answer, because advertising is clearly a form or part of business, which is itself regulated in numerous ways by the government. False advertising is surely a kind of fraud in business and therefore not really in the same arena as reporting and commenting on public policy or any other subject—which is the job of the press, whether new new media blogs or old media newspapers. Regulation of lobbying is a different issue, part of the goal of making politics in our democracy "transparent," as in obliging candidates for office to reveal their financial contributors. But I am not sure, even aside from blogging, that any government monitoring of election contributions is in the best interests of our democracy. An argument could be made that the best policy is for the government to keep its hands and scrutiny totally off election financing, because such supervision could lead to a party in power taking actions that support its continuing dominance. For that reason, I think the Citizens United decision is a step in the right direction.

But even if, for the sake of argument, we agreed that lobbyist financing should always be made public, there is still the question of whether a blogger being paid to write in favor of a candidate, official, or political position is in effect a lobbyist. A lobbyist usually works on an interpersonal basis, via meetings with the targets of the lobbying (lawmakers and so forth) to convince, cajole, and pressure the targets to vote or act in favor of or against a certain piece of legislation, or to take a certain position on a package or wide range of bills revolving around a central issue, such as global warming. Although production of press releases may well be part of such efforts, the text is just a component of the campaign.

In contrast, a blog post, whether hired or created on the blogger's initiative, exists in its own right on a blog page. A lobbyist may well link to it, reprint it, or include it in campaign materials, but if we are talking about a blog post, and not a press release, the text also has a life of its own. Although it obviously has characteristics in common with advertising and should be identified as a purchased post (as discussed previously in "Monetizing Your Blog"), I would argue that government insistence that the blogger reveal all circumstances of the purchase goes too far and does violate the blogger's First Amendment rights. The publisher paid an advance and pays royalties to me for *New New Media*. Newspapers pay reporters salaries. The name of the publisher is on the title page of this book, and the name of any newspaper is clear to any reader. But other than the IRS getting notified of this income for tax purposes, no one would dream of saying the government has a right to know the specific financial arrangements between my publisher and me, or between a newspaper and its reporters. A blogger being paid to write on behalf of a political cause or candidate should be entitled to the same business privacy. And as for the public being misled to think that a blog post is the blogger's when it is really a purchased opinion, what does it matter whose opinion the post really is? Should not the opinion be assessed on the basis of what the opinion says, not who said it? (See, again, Richards, 1929.)

Anonymity in Blogging

Although bloggers should not be compelled by government to reveal the circumstances of a blog post's creation, good form nonetheless suggests that a blogger should let readers know when a post is hired. This question of what should and should not be revealed about how and why a blog post is written relates to a larger question of anonymity, or whether a blogger (or commenter) should write under his or her real name.

Anonymity is antithetical to journalism; most reporters and documentarians, including Josh Wolf, are all too happy to have their names associated with their work, and, indeed, in old media such as newspapers, a byline is rightly considered crucial in building a career.

But *The New York Times* (Glater, 2008) reported a case in which a district attorney in the Bronx subpoenaed a text blog about New York politics, titled "Room 8," to reveal or help prosecutors discover the identities of several anonymous bloggers. As was the outcome with the Josh Wolf case, the DA's office withdrew the request—this time under threat of a lawsuit by the blog over violation of its First Amendment rights.

The great advantage of anonymous blogging, of course, is that it maximizes the freedom of bloggers to speak or post their minds without fear of reprisal from supervisors, bosses, voters, friends, and family. Anonymous blogging goes even further in this direction than blogging under a pseudonym or a nickname unrelated to the blogger's real name—all anonymous blog posts literally have the same "anonymous" attribution, which defeats any attempt to identify a series of blog posts as the work of a single person, obviously apparent when a post is signed by a pseudonym, even though the real name of the blogger is not known.

Posting without revealing one's identity has a long history on the Web and online communication. When my wife Tina Vozick and I founded Connected Education in the mid-1980s—a nonprofit organization that offered courses for academic credit, completely online, in cooperation with the New School and other land-based institutions of higher education (see Levinson, 1985, 1997)—one of the first things I discussed with a colleague, Peter Haratonik at the New School for Social Research, was whether we should allow anonymous comments in the Connect Ed Café, an online forum for casual discussion. Anonymous comments by students in their online classes were ruled out from the beginning, but we thought that perhaps discussion in the Café would benefit from the opportunity of anonymity by those who wanted it. In the end, we decided against it; people don't like talking to people with "bags over their heads," as Haratonik put it.

But anonymity, and/or pretending to be someone you are not, has evolved into many other uses in blogging and new new media, including not only the capacity to make controversial posts without worry of reprisal but also disruptive, cyberbullying, and cyberstalking comments without revealing one's identity (see chapter 9). Used for such purposes, anonymity serves as a coward's mask for reprehensible behavior.

In an entirely different kind of disruptive application, anonymous and pseudonymous accounts can be employed to boost the popularity of a blog post or anything with a URL on the Web. All the booster needs to do is create multiple accounts. This rears its head on Wikipedia, as we saw in the previous chapter, where "sock-puppets," or accounts created by users to buttress their arguments, can short-circuit or bias attempts to build a consensus among online editors. Anonymous and pseudonymous accounts also aid and abet voting stories up and down on Reddit and Digg, which we will examine in chapter 8.

There may also be a personal disadvantage to both anonymous and pseudonymous blogging for the blogger, in addition to the professional problem of not building your reputation as a writer. I often joke that I would never write under a pseudonym, because I want the girl who sat next to me in seventh grade, and didn't pay much attention to me, to see the error of her ways when she walks into a bookstore—or, nowadays, if she's reading on the Web. The general principle here is that anonymous writing will not assist your quest for fame, if that is what you seek.

Anonymity is obviously easier in text media than audiovisual media, where disguising of voices and images takes a little work, and any muffling of sound or image is obvious. Indeed, anonymous comments are an option on most blogs, although the moderator can block anonymous comments. If a blogger wants to encourage discussion, blocking or removal of a comment merely because it is anonymous may be counterproductive. As a rough, anecdotal statistic of the popularity of anonymous comments on blogs, more than one of four comments on my *Infinite Regress* blog are anonymous.

WikiLeaks and Anonymous

WikiLeaks—founded in 2006, and with no connection to Wikipedia—is technically neither a blog nor a new new medium, but an online publisher of secret and classified documents submitted to it by anonymous sources ("classified" means classified by government as not available for public scrutiny). Venerable media such as *The New York Times*, *The Guardian* (UK), *Le Monde* (France), *El Pais* (Spain), and *Der Spiegel* (Germany) have partnered with WikiLeaks in publishing the documents.

The release of U.S. State Department cables by WikiLeaks and its old media partners in November 2010 provoked a U.S. Department of Justice criminal investigation of WikiLeaks—ongoing as of February 2012—and brought to the front burner questions of whether WikiLeaks was entitled to First Amendment protections. Few disputed that *The New York Times* was—as made clear in the Pentagon Papers case (New York Times Co. v. United States, 1971)—but opponents of WikiLeaks argued that it was not a bona fide organ of journalism, much like the arguments against blogging as journalism.

First Amendment advocates once again begged to differ. I told *The Christian Science Monitor* in February 2011 that the WikiLeaks release of U.S. State Department communiques was akin to the Pentagon Papers, "which was a very important moment in our history because it showed how our government had manipulated the truth and lied to the American people" (Levinson, quoted in Goodale, 2011).

Some supporters of WikiLeaks went beyond words. Anonymous—a group of anonymous "hactivist" groups and individuals who use the name Anonymous—hacked Paypal and old-line credit card companies (Mastercard and Visa) in December 2010, in retaliation for their freezing of WikiLeaks accounts. Arrests soon ensued in England and Holland, and the FBI issued search warrants in the United States but made no arrests. Significantly, although Anonymous was and is anonymous, the founder of WikiLeaks, Julian Assange, is well known. Bradley Manning, a soldier in the U.S. Army, was arrested in March 2010 on suspicion of supplying WikiLeaks with classified information. As of February 2012, he has been set to stand for court-martial.

To be clear, hacking for the sake of disruption, as Anonymous did in protest of the credit card company actions against WikiLeaks, is by no stretch a form of journalism, and therefore not deserving of First Amendment protection. But I would argue that the actions of WikiLeaks and Manning certainly are, in the same way that Daniel Ellsberg's release of the Pentagon Papers and its publication in *The New York Times* and *The Washington Post* was deemed worthy of First Amendment protection by the U.S. Supreme Court.

And since its actions on behalf of WikiLeaks, Anonymous has gone on to do work that certainly is journalism, including video coverage of and trenchant commentary about the Arab Spring and Occupy Wall Street, to which we will return in chapter 10.

Blogging for Others

Although blogging on your own blog is the newest new media use of blogging—that is, the specific kind of blogging that most captures the qualities of new new media and its differences from older media—numerous blogs on the Web permit, invite, and consist of posts written by people who are not the blog's owner. The crucial difference between writing for these kinds of blogs and your own blog, of course, is that you have far less control over how what you write is published on the blogs of others. In its most extreme form, this kind of gatekeeping can decide whether your post will be published. The applicant blogger is in such cases no different from a freelance writer or reporter submitting a story to an online newspaper. But even when the publication of anything you submit is assured, writing for the blogs of others may leave decisions in the hands of others about where on the blog page your post is placed, in what category, and so forth. The blogger may also be deprived of the ability to edit the post after it has been published, remove or moderate comments, keep track of the number of readers, and earn advertising revenue from the blog post. These and other specific limitations of blogging for others differ from blog to blog.

The great advantage of blogging for sites other than yours is that these sites may well have enormously greater numbers of readers than does your blog. *Daily Kos*, for example, had some 5 million readers on Election Day 2008, and averaged hundreds of thousands of visits on weekdays in 2010. Compare those numbers with the readership of *The Wall Street Journal*, the highest circulation (in paper) newspaper in the United States with 2.1 million readers a day in 2010, and *USA Today* with 1.8 million per day, and you can get an idea of the power of the most successful blogs to attract large numbers of readers. (The most readers I've ever had on *Infinite Regress* on a given day was 20,000 for the Season 3 finale of *Lost*, a year after the review was first posted.)

Daily Kos started in 2002, which makes it one of the oldest of the new new media. It publishes "diaries" submitted by registered users (registration is free and open to everyone). Such blog posts cannot be submitted more than once a day. They are listed briefly on the front page—unless they are "Recommended" by *Daily Kos* editors, in which case they are listed on the front page longer—or, even better, "Front Paged" by the editors, in which case the blog post is actually published on the front page (this happened to me just once, out of about 50 submissions, "Take It from a College Prof: Obama's 'Missing' Paper Is Another Conservative Red Herring," 2008). The writer can edit the diary after publication, but there is a public indication that the diary has been edited. Other registered users can make comments—diaries on the front page often get hundreds of comments—but the writer has no power to eliminate, reject, or otherwise moderate the comments. The writer, however, is free to join in such discussions and respond to comments. Diaries can be recommended by readers. Comments can be rated (a form of recommendation), and writers can also post a special comment titled "Tip Jar," which readers can rate and therein show additional approval and appreciation of the diary.

These features of blogging on *Daily Kos* provide an excellent example of a mixture of new new media and new media (or top-down, expert-driven, editorially controlled approaches of older print media applied on the Web). Another of *Daily Kos's* new new media characteristics is that it permits cross-posting, or publishing pieces that have already been published on other blogs, including your own. Not so *Blogcritics* (founded in 2002, acquired by Technorati in 2008), which insists on first publication of all submissions. It adopted this policy in 2007, as a way of maintaining its readership. Google usually puts the earliest publication of a blog at the top of its search results.

Neither *Daily Kos* nor *Blogcritics* pay the writers who post blogs on their sites. But some blog sites do. This, obviously, can add a powerful incentive for writing for the blogs of others. Payment can generally come in one of two ways: payment for publication of the story (either on a per-word or per-story basis) or payment from ad revenues earned from your stories' publication. *Internet Evolution* is an example of a blog site that pays in the first way. *Open Salon* employs the second method. Guess which kind of payment is most likely to provide the most income?

The answer should be apparent in the "Monetizing Your Blog" section. Advertising on blogs generates negligible payment unless your daily readership is in the many thousands. *Open Salon* allows its bloggers to earn ad income directly from Google AdSense. My *Infinite Regress* posts are automatically relayed to my *Open Salon* blog, where they earn about 10–20 percent of the advertising revenue generated on *Infinite Regress*.

In summary, it is worth noting the obvious: All blogs under the control of someone other than you not only can refuse to publish a given piece by you, but also can fire you if you are a regular blogger, or ban you from the blog. *Daily Kos* banned Lee Stranahan in August 2008 (Stranahan, 2008) for cross-posting a piece he had written for *The Huffington Post*, urging John Edwards to tell the truth about his affair first reported in the *National Enquirer*. Stranahan's banning took place before Edwards admitted to the affair, but the truth or falsity of Stranahan's or anyone's post is not the issue that concerns us here. The lesson of Stranahan's banning is that any blog other than your own, regardless of how progressive and writer-driven, can still exercise old-style media control any old time it pleases.

Daily Kos, in terms of the ultimate control it exercises over its pages, is thus no different from *The New York Times*. Given that *Daily Kos* publishes "diaries" written by readers—or, at least in principle, anyone—we can reasonably designate it an example of new new media, in contrast to *The New York Times,* which is an archetypal old medium in journalism (not really "all the news that's fit to print" but "all the news that we the editors of *The New York Times* deem fit to print"), with articles written by assigned, professional reporters, even when published on the new medium of the Web.

But *Daily Kos* is nonetheless very much on the old side of the new new media continuum, if only because of its power to ban any blogger. In a truer or full-fledged new new medium, which arises any time anyone writes a blog under his or her control, the blogger may retire or refrain from blogging but cannot be fired or banned.

Of course, a blogging platform—Google's Blogspot or Six Apart's Typepad or Moveable Type—could refuse for whatever reason to provide or sell a platform to a given blogger. But such refusals seem closer to a telephone company refusing to provide service to a given customer—because of the customer's poor credit, for example—than an editor of a blog banning one of its writers.

Changing the World with Your Blog

As in everything we do in life, we may have different motives for publishing our blogs—and often more than one motive. These could include the joy of writing and having other people read what you write, making money, and changing the world—influencing something real in the world, in politics or science or whatever area—by the words on your blog. Words, after all, can be very powerful. And the power of a blog is unique in comparison to older forms of writing, in that the writing, as we have seen, can be instantly published, which means that anyone, including powerful, important, and famous people, can read it. A significant limitation, however, is that readers, whether famous, important, powerful or not, are not likely to know about a blogger's writing, are not likely to look for it, and are not likely to pay much attention to it if they stumble on it, unless the blogger already possesses some of these qualities—that is, the blogger is powerful, important, famous. Nonetheless, when all factors are taken into the equation, the unknown blogger still has a much better chance of being read by the powerful and famous than the unknown writer in older media, mainly because those older, unknown writers had little chance of being published in the first place.

How do you know if someone important is reading your blog? Stat counters can tell you the IPs—Internet locations—and geographic locations of your readers. These may include the company or school in which their computer is located but not likely their names. Ultimately, the only completely reliable way of knowing who, specifically, has read your blog is when readers comment, link, or refer to your blog in their own blog, or speak or write about your blog in other media.

Rich Sommer's comment on my blog about *Mad Men*, discussed previously, would be a case of someone more famous than I not only reading but also communicating to me and the world on my blog. But the world did not change as a result of this. And, indeed, television reviews are not all that likely to have a big impact on the world.

Political blogs, of course, are different in their potential impact. I have no idea if Barack Obama or any of his close advisers or anyone significant in politics has ever read any of my blog posts, let alone been influenced by them.

But on the early afternoon of September 24, 2008, I published a piece titled "Obama Should Reject McCain's Call to Postpone Friday Debate" on *Infinite Regress* and cross-posted to *Open Salon* and several other sites. This was my response to John McCain's announcement that he was putting his campaign on hold, so he could go to Washington to deal with the financial crisis, and his request to Barack Obama to join him in postponing their first scheduled debate of the 2008 Presidential election.

I "advised" Obama that postponing the debate would be a big mistake, that the financial crisis called for an affirmation of the democratic process, including a continuation of the campaigns and the scheduled debates, not suspending or delaying them.

I was soon pleased to post the following on my blogs:

BREAKING NEWS: 4:47 p.m.: Obama just said that he thinks the debates should go on—that this is precisely a time when the American people need to see what he and McCain would do as President. Good!

And, at 6:00 p.m., Joan Walsh, then editor-in-chief of *Salon* and blogger on *Open Salon*, posted the following comment on my blog:

Paul Levinson speaks, Obama listens! I just blogged on this, too!

Did Obama or any of his advisers actually read my blog? Were they influenced by it? Probably not. Obama's team was far more likely to have read and been influenced by the blog of Joan Walsh, who was not only chief editor of *Salon* back then but also a frequent guest on Chris Matthews' *Hardball* and other news shows on MSNBC. (She is still a frequent guest on MSNBC shows, and is now—in January 2012—editor-at-large at *Salon*.)

But I included this true story of my blogging in this book because it highlights the potential of any post, anywhere on the Web, to be read by a presidential candidate or even the president. And this, too, is one of the hallmarks of new new media: You sit at your computer and type your words, and those words can tip the world in a better direction, or at least the direction you think best. You can be a major editor, a college professor, or a sophomore in college or high school.

A Town Supervisor and His Blog

Paul Feiner, who since 1991 has been town supervisor of Greenburgh, New York (an elected two-year term, in Westchester County, a little north of New York City), is explicit about his reliance on blogging. When I was a guest on his weekly "Greenburgh Report" radio show on WVOX on January 9, 2009, Feiner explained that he finds comments made on his own public blog to be helpful, even crucial, in staying informed of what his constituents are thinking.

Feiner even recognizes the benefits—and drawbacks—of anonymous commenting. "I let people write anonymously on the blog," Feiner told me, even though such commenters can be "very nasty" and "make up stuff." Feiner appreciates the dividends of this: "I'm able to get a sense from my blog [of] what some of the issues and controversies are going to be well before they hit a Town Board meeting...because sometimes people can say what's really on their mind in a blog....If I hadn't had a blog or used the Internet or just relied on newspapers, I would never know what people are saying, not in my presence."

In other words, for officials and political leaders such as Paul Feiner who perceive the advantages of new new media in governing, we might say that "foreblogged" is forewarned or "fore-informed."

"Bloggers in Pajamas"

The political impact of blogging, however, has not been applauded by everyone. Back in September 2004, Jonathan Klein, a former CBS News executive, defended Dan Rather's *60 Minutes* segment about George W. Bush's lack of National Guard service during the Vietnam War, by observing on Fox News that "You couldn't have a starker contrast between the multiple layers of checks and balances [at *60 Minutes*] and a guy sitting in his living room in his pajamas writing" (quoted by Fund, 2004). Klein, who would soon be appointed CNN/USA Network president, was attacking the conservative bloggers who were attacking Rather and CBS. And, although I thought then and now that CBS and Rather were right to run that story (see Levinson, "Interview by Joe Scarborough about Dan Rather," 2005, and Levinson, "Good For Dan Rather," 2007), I certainly did not agree with Klein's myopic "analysis" of blogging, nor with his confidence in the "multiple layers of checks and balances" in mass media journalism. Jayson Blair's several years of fictitious and plagiarized reporting for *The New York Times* had already been exposed. And given the power and reach of the Internet even then, and the way all kinds of information could become available in all sorts of unexpected ways, it struck me that pajamas and living rooms were no impediments to the pursuit and publication of truth.

That is obviously much more the case today, in a world in which tweets from private and public places, by people at all levels of professionalism, provide a constant flow of news. But the "bloggers in pajamas" meme lives on, not only as a justifiably defiant comment on Klein's 2004 statement and any like-minded old-media worshipers still among us—and in the names of successful online news venues (for example, *Pajamas Media*) and well-read independent blogs such as *The Pajama Pundit*—but also in the thinking of conservatives such as Sarah Palin, unsuccessful Republican candidate for vice president in 2008.

Palin, shortly after losing the election, told Greta Van Susteren on Fox News that a lot of the media's negative stories about her were due to their reporting on the basis of "some blogger, probably sitting there in their parents' basement, wearing pajamas, blogging some kind of gossip, or a lie" (Palin, 2008). Palin not only demoted the blogger in pajamas from guy to kid, from living room to basement, but also later switched the focus of her concern from pajamas and parents' basements to anonymity in blogging, asking John Ziegler in the segment of his *Media Malpractice* documentary put on YouTube in January 2009, "When did we start accepting as hard news sources bloggers—anonymous bloggers especially? It's a sad state of affairs in the world of the media today—mainstream media especially, if they're going to be relying on anonymous bloggers for their hard news information. Very scary." (See also Kurtz, 2009.)

In Klein's slight defense, in 2004, new new media were much newer than they are now. *The Huffington Post*, YouTube, and Twitter did not yet even exist, and Facebook was just a few months old. Palin's attack in 2008 was thus more unwarranted than Klein's.

But Palin's contempt for new new media is nonetheless shared by many in the older media themselves. Or as "John Connor," lead character in Fox's *Terminator: The Sarah Connor Chronicles,* sarcastically observed in the 13th episode of its second season (2008): "We all know how reliable bloggers are." That bloggers were mentioned at all on a television series about fictional characters is an indication of how important blogging had become in our lives and culture. But the fact they were cited with disdain shows the degree to which so many people in our real world did then and still do distrust them.

Not coincidentally, Facebook took a lashing in the 10th episode of the same season of *The Sarah Connor Chronicles* (2008), a few weeks earlier, when "Riley," John's girlfriend, lambasted her adoptive family and their obliviousness to the real dangers that awaited them with a remark that all they care about is looking at their "Facebook pages." Meanwhile, over on the premiere of the fifth season of *Weeds* on Showtime in 2009, "Celia Hodes" observed that a Facebook account "would be a waste of time." And "Margene Heffman" on the sixth episode of HBO's third season of *Big Love* in 2009 bad-mouthed yet another new new medium, apologizing that some of the information she had obtained about a Mormon pioneer "may not be right—I got it off Wikipedia."

In incurring this disfavor among some politicians and people who write fiction for older media, new new media continue a tradition that in one way or another afflicted the advent of many nascent media in their time, including the telegraph, motion pictures, and television. *The London Times* delayed printing the news it received about Abraham Lincoln's assassination, because the news was received via telegraph. Motion pictures were considered a "primary school for criminals" early in the 20th century (thus wrote McKeever, 1910). And, first, television and, more recently, video games have been blamed for violence in the real world, on the basis of no reliable evidence, or at best a misunderstanding of correlation (A and B happen together) and causation (A causes B to happen). Just for good measure, television also has been blamed for a reduction in literacy, even though a survey taken in 1978, in the same town in Indiana as in 1944, showed no decline in literacy at all, and book sales have risen through the past 50 years of television. (See Levinson, 1997, for details on the initially distrusting reception of telegraph and motion pictures, the continuing attacks on television, and the status of book sales in the 20th century; Maeroff, 1979, for the Indiana literacy study; and Levinson, 2006, for the confusion of correlation with causation in the "evidence" attempting to link violent video games to violence in the real world.)

The telegraph was replaced in the 20th century by the telephone and, ultimately, by fax and email. But motion pictures and television did just fine, even though the screens on which movies and television shows are viewed are increasingly on smart phones and tablets, the same screens on which blogs are read.

And there are those in old media who see blogging as neither bogeyman nor panacea but subject to the same events that threaten to undermine old and new media, and all of society. Or, as Neil Young put it in his 2009 "Fork in the Road" song, in part about the economic crisis: "Keep on blogging, till the power goes out, your battery's dead, twist and shout."

Blogging cannot in itself cure what ails our society. (No communication can.) Blogging certainly cannot solve economic crises or make peace in the world. But it beats the alternative of saying nothing, and it goes a lot further than saying a word to the person next to you or relying entirely on professional reporters and commentators to say it for you.

Further Tensions Between New New Media and Older Forms

As we have seen and will see throughout this book, media rarely live just in harmony. In fact, media throughout history have both cooperated and competed for our attention and our patronage in a struggle for survival that Charles Darwin would have recognized. The only difference is that, in the Darwinian evolution of media, we humans make the natural selections, or decide which media survive (Levinson, 1979).

The competition between new new and older media is therefore no surprise, and it plays out in the disdain and misunderstanding of new new media by people working in and through older kinds of media, as we saw in the previous section. Another clear example can be found in the attitudes of official television blogs—message boards set up by television networks for discussion, that is, promotion, of their shows—to the posting of comments with links to other blogs. Over the past years, both as promotion for my own blog and as a low-key experiment, I have posted comments on Fox, NBC, CBS, ABC, AMC, TNT, HBO, and Showtime television series pages and blogs. These comments were all signed by me and contained links to my reviews of these same television shows on my own *Infinite Regress* blog.

Moderators from some of these sites occasionally moved or removed my comments, and the Fox *Sarah Connor Chronicles* blog removed my account—that is, blocked me from its blog completely. As of January 2012, all Fox TV official blogs are closed with the following notice—"Our FOX.com community is currently under construction"—but for many years the Fox TV sites advised that "The only links that are allowed are ones to articles about the show, cast, etc., in the mainstream media, or the official sites of the cast. Links to fan sites, personal sites, competing sites, commercial sites, links to download sites, jpgs, MP3s, etc., are not allowed."

In terms of the tensions between new new and older media we have been tracing, we might more accurately put the preceding policy as follows: "The only links allowed on our new media site, about the old medium of television we are promoting, are links to other new media or official sites such as those in the old, mainstream media or official, professional sites about the show, cast, etc. Links to new new media fan sites, personal sites, competing sites, etc., are not allowed."

The hundreds of millions of new new media users show that these media are already part of the "mainstream," but even if those numbers were smaller, a moment's reflection shows how destructive Fox's restrictions were to the purpose of the Fox blogs, which presumably was to promote the television programs. Although links to "unofficial" blogs in comments posted on official blogs may indeed draw readers from the official blogs to the unofficial blogs, the readers of the unofficial blogs are still reading discussions of the television program that is the subject of the official blog.

The phrase "competing sites" in the original statement of the rules shows, in particular, just how illogical and counterproductive this policy is. What is a "competing site"? Is not any site that posts blogs and reviews of the same television series a site not in competition with but in support of the same goal as the official site? A blog site not allied with any television series—such as BuddyTV—might at least have a logical point in forbidding links to other sites, because what these sites want is not necessarily an increase of viewers of any television show but an increase in readers of their site. So might television recap and review sites affiliated with major networks—such as TV.com (CBS) and *Television Without Pity* (NBC)—at least insofar as links to reviews about television series on other networks. I would still disagree with such a strategy—because I think the profusion of links raises all boats in the blogosphere, or all blogs—but I could at least see its logic. (Of the three blogs mentioned, only *Television Without Pity*—perhaps apropos its name—has a tradition of zealously removing links and banning writers for posting them.)

Conceivably, the official blog moderators do not actually read any blog posts with links to other sites and do not click on the external links posted in the official blogs, and as a result assume the external links are nothing more than spam, with no connection to the television show. But, in that case, the old media top-down approach of deciding what gets published, rather than letting all readers become writers and publishers, is still to blame.

For highly successful television shows, such self-destructive actions—or inoculations against the very advantages of viral marketing and promotion—likely will not have much ill effect on the popularity of the shows. But as we move into a world that increasingly expects unfettered participation of viewers—one of the hallmarks of new new media— the difference between a show that gains a reliable audience and a show that does not may well reside in how fully the online discussion boards divest themselves of old media habits. (It may be worth noting, in this context, that *The Sarah Connor Chronicles* was not renewed by Fox for a third season.)

The misunderstanding of new new media by older forms manifests itself in other ways. As *Mad Men*, the AMC television series about early 1960s advertising executives, gained popularity and notice in the first part of 2008, people with names of characters from the show—"Don Draper," "Peggy Olson"—began tweeting. Myspace had for years hosted accounts of users with names ranging from Socrates to Jack Bauer (hero of Fox television's *24*). These, like the Twitter names, are a form of role-playing that people enjoy, and which therefore help promote the show. AMC at first did not see it that way and filed a copyright violation notice that forced Twitter to take down the accounts. Fortunately for all concerned, AMC's ad agency had more new new media savvy than AMC and talked it into backing off (Terdiman, 2008). Don (with 16,000 followers), Peggy (21,000 followers), and the gang are happily tweeting, at least as of January 2012, and *Mad Men* has won numerous Emmys.

The Associated Press and bloggers have been embroiled in a different kind of copyright conflict. AP regularly files "take down" notices to bloggers who extensively quote AP articles without permission and payment. (AP—which as we saw in the "Occupy Wall Street" section joined *The New York Times* and other traditional media in protesting NYPD mistreatment of the press—is a news agency or wire service like Reuters, which sells news reports and stories to newspapers and broadcast media. It has roots going back to 1846 and the advent of the telegraph and is the only surviving international news service headquartered in the United States.) Bloggers retaliated by threatening to boycott AP (Liza, 2008). So far, neither side has annihilated the other, but the battle continues, with AP suing an aggregate online news site, Meltwater, for violation of copyright in 2012, on the grounds that Meltwater charges for access to its service (Ellis, 2012). Copyright continues to be a major bone of contention between old and newer media, as we also saw in chapter 3 regarding YouTube.

But it would also be a mistake to conclude that old media and their practitioners have nothing of value to teach or impart to new new media. We turn now to hard-line, investigative reporting, at the opposite end of the journalistic spectrum from the commentary that thus far has been the mainstay of blogging.

The Need for Old-Media Reporting in an Age of New New Media Journalism

Marshall McLuhan astutely observed back in 1977 that "the Xerox makes everyone a publisher"—but, like his recognition in 1962 that electronic media were turning the world into a "global village," his observation about the Xerox machine was more a prediction, based on a powerful trend he noticed, than a depiction of how the media and the world of that day actually were.

It would take the rise of new new media in general, and the internationally interactive participants they created, for the global village to be fully realized (see the Arab Spring in chapter 10, and my *Digital McLuhan*, 1999). For the global village of the 1960s was neither global (television was a national medium) nor interactive like the residents of a village (television viewers across a nation could not talk to each other, except in very small groups).

As for photocopying creating publishers, almost all of the output of such machines, even today, is also for very small numbers of readers. That limited kind of publishing would finally be surpassed—and in a way that rivaled older publication of newspapers and magazines—only with the advent of blogging, as we have seen in this chapter.

And what of the older vehicles of journalism—*The New York Times*, *The Washington Post*, *The Wall Street Journal*, and other paper press? Their numbers have been declining, in circulation, number of different newspapers, and the size of the newspaper operations that have survived (Perez-Pena, 2008). *The New York Times*'s paper circulation continued to decline in 2010–11, though it is still around a million. These older media have to some extent migrated to the Web. *The New York Times*'s website gets 30 million visitors per day—the most of any online newspaper, twice that of *The Huffington Post*—and has had financial success with its pay wall (charging for online content) along with staunch criticism (see Levinson, 2011; Chittum, 2011). See "themediaisdying," 2009, on Twitter for hourly or more frequent reports about cutbacks, layoffs, and closings in old media. (The title gives cause to think that grammar may be dying, too—"media" is plural for "medium.")

But whatever the ultimate fate of the paper press, there remains, as of April 2012, a crucial resource in older media that newer media such as *Daily Kos*, *The Huffington Post*, and *Politico* have yet to fully re-create for themselves, and thus continue to seek from old media. As Jeff Jarvis noted in an NPR interview back in 2008 about "How Will Investigative Stories Fare in an Era of Layoffs and Slashed Newsroom Budgets?": "Bloggers rely on the resource that mainstream media put into this....The whole business is still in trouble and investigative journalism is in peril...." But David Wood's winning of a Pulitzer Prize in 2012 for his stories in *The Huffington Post* about wounded veterans is a big, promising step in the right direction. As Amy Chozick (2012) observed in *The New York Times*, which won two Pulitzer Prizes in 2012, "the awards to *Politico* and *The Huffington Post* reflect the emerging power of Web-based journalism as it competes with legacy newspapers." (*Politico*'s Pulitzer was for an editorial cartoon.)

Ironically, *Daily Kos* and new new media blogging first achieved prominence as important media of journalism in the aftermath of the failure of old media journalists to report the absence of weapons of mass destruction in Iraq and in general to supply sufficient criticism in reporting the buildup to that war. (*Daily Kos* began in 2002; *The Huffington Post* in 2005.) One could say, cynically, that new new media would do well to field their own investigative reporters, who could not do much worse than the old media professionals on the crucial issue of going to war (see Reilly in Hunter, 2009, for a similar point). That might be all well and good, but given that new new media may not have their own extensive investigative teams fully in place, where would investigative journalism come from, if the older media ceased to exist?

Citizen journalism, as indicated in the "Occupy Wall Street" section, is part of the answer, but the good news from the history and evolution of media is that new media rarely replace, utterly, their ancestors. For every hieroglyphic or silent movie that did not make it into the future—because it could not survive the competition of alphabetic writing in the case of hieroglyphics or talkies in the case of silent movies—hundreds of media, large and small, have taken the path of radio (which amply survived the advent of television) and still photography (which easily survived the rise of motion pictures).

The key, as I alluded to earlier when I said that humans decide the survival of media—and I explain in *Human Replay: A Theory of the Evolution of Media* (1979) and *The Soft Edge: A Natural History and Future of the Information Revolution* (1997)—is that media survive if they uniquely satisfy a human communication need. Radio survives in an age of television because it caters to our need to sometimes hear one thing when seeing something else. Imagine driving down the highway and watching television; if you were the driver, you would not get very far. In addition, the world grows dark every night but never really silent, and our eyes close but not our ears, making hearing without seeing—radio—a quite natural and comfortable kind of communication. In contrast, seeing without hearing does not really exist in our natural perception, and this spelled the end of silent movies when talkies came along. (See the next chapter for more on this "anthropotropic" evolution of media, as I call it, toward more human communication.)

Words on newspaper pages still have their advantages. They are inexpensive in comparison to the cost of any electronic device and its data charges, and easily disposable. As long as such advantages continue in contrast to words on a screen, old media newspapers will survive in some form, which, one hopes, includes some number of investigative journalists. And if and when that advantage fades, presumably most exclusively online newspapers by then will be generating enough steady income to field their own investigative reporters.

Old Media and New New Media Symbiosis: Easter Eggs for *Lost* and *Fringe*

As indicated earlier in this book, not everything in the natural, Darwinian world is competition. Organisms also live in mutually beneficial relations, as do bacteria in our digestive system, which help us digest our food, as we give them a nice warm place to live. Bees eat pollen, which helps plants reproduce, as the bees carry some pollen from one plant to another. And we humans also benefit, doubly, because we like both honey and flowers.

The old medium of television clearly benefits from publicity given to its shows by the new new medium of blogging; the new new medium of blogging benefits from television or any medium that gives bloggers something to write about. News blogs benefit from the work of old print media investigative journalists, while old print and broadcast news media draw upon opinions and analyses expressed in tweets and blogs. And old media such as television shows and newspapers advertise extensively on blogs, just as blogs such as *Television Without Pity* show up on Bravo Television in our living rooms (both are owned by NBC), and Twitter comments appear at the bottom of cable news programs such as *The Dylan Ratigan Show* and *The Ed Show* on MSNBC (see chapter 3 for more on Twitter/TV news anchor integration).

The symbiotic or mutually catalytic relationship of old and new new media is thus undeniable and vibrant. And although conflicts can get in the way of such cooperation—as when an official television blog prevents links to reviews on other blogs—there are also cases in which television deliberately works new new media into its programming and promotion.

The virtual "game" of Second Life—in which users appear as avatars—figured in a *CSI* television episode in 2007, in which characters from the television show pursued an investigation in Second Life and entered there as characters (Riley, 2007; see chapter 8 in this book for more on Second Life). *Lost* tried something even more ambitious, setting up a real website for "Oceanic Airlines"—the fictitious airline which flew the lost flight that started the show—on which users could look for "additional" flights. *Lost*, as well as one of J. J. Abrams' more recent shows, *Fringe*, offer "Easter eggs," or clues on the Web, which fans can then find to gain special insight into the ongoing stories on television.

As *Fringe* Executive Producer Jeff Pinkner told *TV Guide*'s Mickey O'Connor in an online interview (2008), "There are many Easter eggs, several of which have yet to be discovered by anybody—either on the show or out there on the Internet. There's a clue in every episode that tells you what the next episode will be about."

So *Lost* and *Fringe* deliberately seeded the Internet with clues to enhance the viewers' enjoyment of the show, not just by giving them valuable information but also by making the viewers more than viewers, turning them into researchers, and in effect much more active participants in the unfolding fiction of the show. And, to complete the cycle, some of these viewers who were transformed into researchers were so inspired that they blogged about the show. And the cycle continues in the university classroom. Sarah Clarke Stuart's Spring 2009 "The Infinite Narrative: Intertextuality, New Media and the Digital Communities of *Lost*" course at the University of North Florida, for example, used blogs about *Lost* (see Stuart, 2009; Aasen, 2009).

But the symbiotic qualities of new new media go beyond their relationship to older media, online and offline. In the next chapter, we will see how a recent new new medium has built a relationship with the real world itself—with restaurants, street corners, and all manner of places—reversing the possibilities for anonymity and other prime characteristics we have explored in this chapter about the oldest new new medium, blogging.

Foursquare and Hardware

I WAS IN BELLA LUNA, ONE OF MY FAVORITE ITALIAN RESTAURANTS in New York City, around 9 p.m. in September 2011 with Josh Meyrowitz, an old friend, fellow student in New York University's Media Ecology doctoral program in the 1970s, and author of *No Sense of Place* (1986). Josh, who teaches at the University of New Hampshire, was in town for a conference about Marshall McLuhan at Fordham University, where we would both be speaking the next day. As our dinner concluded, I "checked in" on Foursquare. The check-in, or notice of where I was physically at the moment, was instantly relayed to Twitter, and, in turn, to Facebook, LinkedIn, and all the sites that carry my Twitter feed.

Several hours later, I received an email from Sam Fleishman, who was in the same PhD program with Josh and me: "Paul: I, too, was having dinner at Bella Luna on Friday at about 7pm. Give Josh my best. Sam." He had seen my Foursquare check-in on LinkedIn—the new new media résumé site, launched in 2003, with more than 135 million users as of November 2011—where Sam and I are "connected." I hadn't seen Sam since the 1970s, and we narrowly missed seeing each other that night. But Foursquare had almost made that possible. By putting physical places so effortlessly on the Internet, it has changed the basis and impact of place forever—where we happen to be, and its connection to everyone we have ever known in our lives, and people we do not know, depending on how far and wide we allow our check-ins to be spread.

Foursquare and iPhone

Foursquare opened shop in March 2009, and is a creation of Dennis Crowley and Naveen Selvadura. Crowley had previously developed a precursor to Foursquare—Dodgeball—as his master's thesis at New York University, my double alma mater

(BA, PhD). Memo to students in all programs: Take those final projects seriously, you never know what they may engender.

In the case of Foursquare, that would be a new new medium with 15 million users as of January 2012. Relative small fry, in comparison to Facebook and Twitter, but Foursquare is unique in the new new media world, and points the way to the future.

Here is why: Foursquare could not have existed prior to the advent of the iPhone in 2007. Foursquare can live only on a smart phone, tablet, or other truly handheld portable device. You can't even check in with Foursquare on a laptop, without special apps that require the addition of GPS locator capability—which is standard for smart phones and tablets. Foursquare is thus the first new new or social medium intrinsic to the smart phone and its cousins. Had the iPhone not been introduced, or suffered the same failed fate as Apple's Newton a decade earlier, there would be no Foursquare today. In contrast, Twitter and all the other new new media considered in this book work just fine on desktop and laptop computers, as well as smart phones and tablets.

Check-Ins and Truths

The defining action of Foursquare—the equivalent of the tweet on Twitter—is the "check-in," which happens every time someone wants to tell the world, or, at least, "Friends" on Foursquare, where he or she is. The ideal or expectation is that the user indeed be in the place specified in the check-in—the restaurant, movie theater, beach, park, whatever. The GPS—Global Positioning System—in your smart phone or tablet lets Foursquare know where you are in the world, but the system (at least at the beginning of 2012) is not precise enough to see the difference between being in a restaurant or standing right outside it. This adds a new opportunity for online deception—not as profound as sock puppets on Wikipedia and deceptive accounts on other social media, but inimical to the purpose of Foursquare.

Checking in from a place where you are not in reality located is called "cheating" on Foursquare, and highlights the game-like aspects of the system. Users are in continuing competition to become "mayors" of locations, based on the number and recency of check-ins. Users get salutary announcements when they become a mayor, and "bad news" email when another user "steals" that position away. "Badges" are awarded for various milestones, such as number of times you've checked in from a pizza place.

Online games are a major activity on Facebook and elsewhere online. Second Life, the avatar-driven social medium, presents itself as one big game (see the next chapter for more on Second Life). The difference on Foursquare is that the game is not just within the online system, but intertwined with where you are and what you are doing in the world outside. Real life is not only part of this new new media game; it is also the game's object. Further, just as with the "perks" on Klout, success in the Foursquare game can have real-life benefits, including discounts when you show your check-in (hold up your smart phone or tablet for the clerk to see) at frozen yogurt shops such as Go Greenly to American Express discounts in restaurants, supermarkets, and a wide range of establishments.

Privacy and Location

Broadcasting your location obviously can compromise your privacy. What if I hadn't wanted to see Sam Fleishman when I was dining with Josh Meyrowitz in Bella Luna?

There are strategies you can adopt that limit your exposure to unwanted encounters generated by Foursquare check-ins. These are not listed online, but amount to common sense. First, if you don't want anyone else in the world to know where you are, don't check in. Every check-in should be the result of a decision, however quick: Which is more important to you at the moment—the check-in and its possibilities for mayorships and badges, or your privacy in the real world?

In any case, whenever I check in, I always do so when I'm about to leave a location—if in a restaurant, I check in after I pay the check. Had Sam Fleishman been in Bella Luna when I checked in, and I had not wanted to see him, checking in after paying the check would not have helped me. But it would have worked had Sam been in the restaurant and already left before I checked in at the end of my visit. Checking in when you are departing thus limits your exposure.

Of course, beyond not checking in at all and subtler strategies to safeguard privacy, there is the option of not using Foursquare at all, or not using a smart phone or tablet. People in every era have anonymously or famously said no to a new medium of the day—such as Lewis Mumford's refusal to watch television in the 1950s and 60s, and Gore Vidal's eschewal of word processing in the 1980s—which underscores the irreducible human option in adoption of all media. But, that said, there are strong reasons in the evolution of media to conclude that the use of smart phones and tablets, and the mobility and therefore integrations of the digital and physical worlds they encourage, will increase to the point of being standard devices for most people in the world.

The Inevitability of Mobile Media

I wrote in my doctoral dissertation way back in 1979—*Human Replay: A Theory of the Evolution of Media*—that "the wireless, portable evolution of media should continue to the point of providing any individual with access to all the information of the planet, from any place on the planet, indoors and outdoors, and, of course, even beyond the planet itself as communication extends into the solar system and cosmos beyond" (p. 275). And I added on the next page that this system "will eventually give the individual the same unrestrained access to information on the global basis that the individual has always enjoyed to information in the immediate physical environment."

This inevitability of what in 2007 would be called the iPhone flowed from the "anthropotropic" theory of media evolution I devised, developed, and named in *Human Replay* 30 years earlier, and mentioned briefly in chapter 6. As in "anthro" meaning human and "tropic" meaning toward (like plants growing toward the sun, or being "heliotropic"), I discovered that as media evolve—as we invent successive media—they eventually become increasingly human in their performance. The initially still, black-and-white, silent, picture-in-a-frame situation of photography changed both to talking motion pictures with color and still photographs that we can send and receive about as easily as we can speak on the phone. The original telephone itself was an anthropotropic update of the telegraph, which used Morse code, an abstraction of writing, which itself is an abstract—or unnatural representation—of speech. More details about this "anthropotropic" theory are in *The Soft Edge: A Natural History and Future of the Information Revolution* (Levinson, 1997).

The iPhone started to satisfy the longstanding human need to have any and all information, anytime we may want it, wherever we and the information we seek may happen to be. Like all anthropotropic media, the smart phone makes real what we envision in our mind's eye—it brings to the little screen in our hand the newspapers, video clips, Web pages, Friends on Facebook, tweets and blogs that previously we had only been able to think about, to imagine, until we arrived home or in our office or another place that housed a computer. The Rolling Stones' "You Can't Always Get What You Want" may still and always be true for life in general, but smart phones and tablets have made it much less so for information.

The Necessity of Hardware

Smart phones and tablets are obviously physical pieces of equipment, and bring to the fore another point that may be obvious but nonetheless warrants mention: You cannot have media, old, new, or in between, without equipment or hardware. Thoughts require brains to think, communicate, and retain them. Information not contained in brains requires devices to create, store, communicate, receive, and retain the information. In the realm of old media, books and newspapers require paper and printing presses. Radio and television require broadcast towers (and sometimes satellites) and receiving sets—that is, radios and televisions.

Equipment, devices, hardware of one sort or another also play a crucial role at two points of the new new media process. First, the system—Facebook, Twitter, YouTube, Wikipedia, Foursquare—or software has to live on some central computer. Because such hardware is invisible to the user, who sees and hears only the new new media system, there is no need to address that underlying hardware in this book. Interested readers can consult numerous sources—for example, Wikipedia servers (2012), Justin Smith (2008), Layton and Brothers (2007)—that examine the complex "servers" that make not only new new media but also old media and many other things, such as banking, run in our world today.

At the other end of the spectrum, however, we have the technologies through which people read, write, see, hear, and produce new new media—the devices, in other words, that we hold in our hands or at least address with our hands or voices when we work and play with new new media. A desktop, laptop, or cellphone-like device is engaged any time someone reads or writes a blog, views a video on YouTube, or sends and receives a tweet.

All of those devices existed before the advent of new new media—they were and still are the hardware of older new media, such as iTunes, Amazon, and *The New York Times* online. But the portable devices—laptops and cellphones—played an especially important role in new new media even before the advent of smart phones and tablets (see Levinson, *Cellphone: The Story of the World's Most Mobile Medium*, 2004, for the evolution of mobile media up until that time). Whether you're messaging a friend on Facebook, looking something up, editing on Wikipedia, or commenting about a video on YouTube, the capacity to do this at any time and from any place of your choosing stems from the laptop and cellphone and is one of the cardinal features of new new media.

The introduction of the first iPhone in July 2007, however, when the engines of new new media were already well underway, captured and catapulted this marriage of mobility and user control. We could say that, with the iPhone, for the first time, we had a technology specifically designed to enable not just new media but new new media literally at the user's fingertips, any place the user happened to be.

Twitter was from its outset in 2006 intrinsically mobile—the capacity to tweet from cellphones and smart phones was and is a defining characteristic of the system.

Wikipedia started to "go mobile" in 2008—meaning a free "application" became available for the iPhone, which enabled fast browsing online of Wikipedia (Pash, 2008). This was a prelude to "Wikipedia Officially Launches Mobile Version" at the end of 2008, when Wikipedia put up a version of itself especially suited to iPhone and mobile access. Blogspot has offered "Blogger on the Go" since 2005 and Google has had an "AdSense for Mobile Content" since 2007. Myspace has had mobile applications since 2006, as has Facebook since 2007. YouTube was a highlighted application of the very first iPhone released in 2007. Foursquare was a logical outgrowth of all of this.

Mobile new new media applications and mobile devices spur each other in an obvious, powerful mutually catalytic relationship: The better the mobile application, the more incentive to have a cool mobile device, and the better the mobile device, the greater the incentive for new new media to develop cool new mobile applications. But unlike the free new new media systems—Facebook et al.—the mobile hardware does cost money, sometimes a lot, and when it does not, the mobile device can require plenty of money for "data plans," that is, the transmission of text, images, sound, and videos to, through, and from the new new media.

The Price of Mobility

Money has always been the sticking point, the burden of electronic media—going back to radio and television and the monetary trade-off of electronic with print media. The music and talk we hear on radio are free, the programs we watched on television prior to cable were free—unlike books and newspapers—but not so the price of the radio or television receiver, which in the case of television cost far more than any book or newspaper.

New new media continued this electronic tradition, but with the rise of mobile media are losing a great piggybacking advantage of operating on equipment that consumers already owned and were using for older new media such as email. When someone uses a desktop to blog, access YouTube, Wikipedia, Facebook, or Twitter, all aspects of these new new media activities are free, including the hardware, if the user already owns the desktop. In contrast, the move to applications on mobile media works against this lack of expense and its advantages, if the mobile medium has to be purchased and if its use requires a monthly subscription and data plan. Further, some of the applications on mobile media—including games such as the wildly successful Angry Birds (500 million downloads and 12 million copies sold from Apple as of 2012)—are not free ($4.95 for Angry Birds). In the case of Foursquare, which is free, if you do not already own a smart phone or tablet, one must be acquired to easily check in from your favorite hangout.

Are expensive smart phones and tablets on a collision course with what one observer several years ago aptly called "this freaky land of free…the Web" (Anderson, 2008)? Plain old cellphone sales did drop more than 12 percent in the last quarter of 2008, but sales of smart phones were up by as much as 70 percent in North America in 2009 (Reardon, 2009).

By the end of 2011, however, smart phone sales were "sluggish" (King, 2011)—but tablet sales (dominated by Apple's iPad) were "explosive" (Arthur, 2011). This suggests that the appeal of new new media via mobile applications is so strong as to be fueling the growth of one or another kind of mobile device—whether smart phone or tablet—counteracting the reduction of disposable income that has accompanied the economic recession since 2008. More check-ins on Foursquare are clearly in our future.

If the ascension of mobile devices and the new new media they enable are recession-proof, think of how they'll do in boom times.

The New New Media Exile of Useless Places

I was in an elevator a few years ago that almost got stuck. It stopped for a split second between floors, shuddered, and then resumed its upward journey. But it got me to thinking about how mobile media have made every place more useful than it used to be. A stalled elevator, a car stuck in a traffic jam, a seat in a doctor's office when you're waiting endlessly for an appointment—a tablet or a smart phone in your hand makes all of those formerly useless places useful.

The result is that we are enjoying increasing discretion and control over our lives and our activities. The investment of portable devices with new new media means that we have a vast array of options when we happen to be in a useless physical place—read or write a blog, promote it, look at a video on YouTube, read or write on Wikipedia, wish a Friend happy birthday on Facebook, and so forth. These situations are in effect the flip side of the Foursquare requirement of a mobile device to check in from some place you want to be. The mobile device also makes a place where you don't want to be located amenable not only to check in to Foursquare, if you like, but any place else on the Web.

Increasingly, we do nothing only when we want to do nothing, not when circumstances dictate that we waste our time.

Smart Phones in the Car, in the Park, and in Bed

When I wrote *Cellphone* (2004), I discussed and analyzed in detail the way that the mobile phone cut the umbilical cord of the landline phone in our homes and places of business and allowed us to roam in the outside world, on foot or in cars, and stay in touch, via voice or text, with anyone we pleased. The general principle was that the cellphone liberated us from the home or office, and the specific consequence I explored was how this freedom had moved us outdoors.

The new new media available on smart phones and tablets are, of course, available outside the home or office—and Foursquare check-ins are usually not from the home or the office—but given the tweets, YouTube videos, blogs, and Facebook Friends we might wish to access, and the blogs and tweets we might wish to write, the bed has also become one of our prime new new media locations. And, indeed, the bed and the park are almost equidistant from the desk, as significantly different from the desk, in different directions. Mobile devices have made the circumstances in which we engage new new media more private (the bed) as well as more public (the park).

The car has been a popular place for use of electronic media outside the home and the office since Transitone introduced the first car radio in 1929 (Levinson, 2004). But radio turns out to be a special case, at least for the driver, because the listener can look at and concentrate on something else while listening. In contrast, watching a television show or a YouTube video on an iPhone while driving a car would be a quick way to end that ride in the worst possible way: Our eyes cannot be in two places, cannot look carefully at two or more things at the same time. Neither, for the same reasons, can a driver safely read a newspaper online or a blog or consult Wikipedia, let alone write and edit. Car passengers, on the other hand, can safely read, write, view, or otherwise interact with all new new media via tablets and smart phones.

To what extent will this increasing availability of new new media outside the home and office lead to their actual use in cars, beds, parks, and the like? Reading books and newspapers on park benches is a time-honored tradition, which certainly suggests that reading, writing, and viewing new new media in public has a bright future. Because none of the new new media, except recording a podcast, require talking, new new media on smart phones have an advantage over cellphones in not disturbing anyone in the vicinity (see Levinson, 2004, for cellphone etiquette). Internet cafés and wi-fi in Starbucks can be seen as the first step of new new media in public—a step in a short journey that is already well underway from the laptops in Starbucks to mobile devices anywhere and everywhere.

Batteries as the Weak Spot

The weak spot of all mobile electronic media, as far back as the transistor radio in the 1950s, is the battery. The first 2007 iPhones, for example, had batteries that lasted only 30 minutes depending on the task—watching a video, talking on the phone, working on the Web. The iPhone 4 in 2010 extended that average to 4 hours and 30 minutes. Laptops have notoriously short battery charges, and cellphones are chronic in going silent due to an exhausted battery.

The solution resides in what we saw about the enduring advantage of reading paper rather than screens in the previous chapter—paper requires only the light of the sun, or any artificial source in the vicinity, to be readable. Ultimately, smart phones and tablets will have "batteries" that can be recharged by sun or any ambient light. As is usually the case with new technologies that free us from less convenient earlier technologies, such "smart batteries" will likely cost a lot more than our current "dumb" ones. But once they become standard, the battery will no longer be the weak link of mobile media.

iPhones, iPads, Bluetooth, and Brains

Media convergence—two or more media, starting with different capabilities, developing intersecting and overlapping functions to the point that they are almost the same medium, or a single medium with expanded functions—has been recognized for decades as an important principle of media evolution (see Levinson, 1997).

Smart phones evolved from cell phones—phones through which we talked and texted developed into phones through which we could also work and play on the Web. iPhones, BlackBerrys (which began as mobile email devices), and Androids are examples of smart phones. Tablets evolved from laptops—mobile computers, which at first required modems and then wi-fi, progressed into even lighter computers that provided the same data plans and easy Internet access as smart phones. iPads and Kindles are examples of tablets—both have easy Web access, with Kindles having special capacities for book delivery and reading. The main current differences between smart phones and tablets is that smart phones allow for phone calls and have smaller screens and keyboards than do tablets. But the capacity for voice communication via Skype, Google, and other Internet applications means that tablets are becoming even more like smart phones. Both also have similar capacities for video recording and video conversation.

The next step, already well underway for all mobile media, will be for new new media devices to become even smaller and lighter than they are now. Buckminster Fuller's (1938) "dymaxion principle," which holds that new technologies get ever smaller and more powerful—more from less, in terms of power (more) and size (less)—has never been as well borne out as with 21st century mobile media.

But this all begins with the human brain, which, at just over a kilogram of mass in adult size, is both the primordial oldest and ultimate new new medium. Our brains read, write, view, and hear—receive and produce all the content of new new media—not to mention think, feel, believe, dream, imagine, and much more. And, as I indicated in my 2007 interview on *The Alcove with Mark Molaro* (where I first spoke publicly about "new new media"), that triumph of multitasking which is our brain is likely, at some point in the future, to be where at least some of us initiate via digital embeds in the brain what we produce for new new media. And it will also be the place where some of us directly receive the words and images and sounds of new new media, without that content first being processed by our eyes and ears. Bluetooth hands-free technology is but the first step in that direction—which, given the difference between an external device such as eyeglasses and even contact lenses versus an implant in the brain, is nonetheless still a long way off from public acceptance, whatever its scientific feasibility.

Over on YouTube, where that interview now can be found, one commenter offered an opinion that people would not be likely to embrace implants.

But that was no ultimate problem, I replied. The essence of new new media is choice.

We turn in the next chapter to a variety of additional choices in new new media—systems that once were titans in new new media or at least bigger than they are today in 2012. Human selection made them less prominent and popular, but still significant in the evolving world of new new media.

Smaller Potatoes

THE BREAKNECK SPEED OF MEDIA EVOLUTION IN THE 21ST CENTURY has left some major new new media in the dust, or at least not as prominent as they were just a few years ago. They nonetheless merit some of our attention, both for what they still do now and for what they tell us about how our leading new new media in 2012 rose to their current position.

Myspace

All media, new and old, are intrinsically social. Even ancient hieroglyphics required at least two people—one to write, one to read—as does all communication, if it is to be communication. A word spoken or written to oneself, unheard or unseen by anyone, may be just as real as the proverbial tree falling in a forest with no one around, but it is not communication.

New new media all heighten this crucial social aspect of communication in one way or another. Wikipedia would be unworkable without groups of editors, and a blog with no comments would technically still be a blog but much more like an online, one-way magazine or newspaper than a blog. Old media such as printed newspapers, of course, publish letters to the editor, but these enjoy a much smaller role in the daily life of a newspaper than do comments in a blog.

But some new new media not only increase the social component, but make it the main thing the new new media do. Working in groups may be essential for Wikipedia, but the reader/editors in these groups do not think of themselves or categorize each other as "Friends," certainly not offline but not even the online kind. In contrast, the basic component of Facebook, as we saw, is not the article or editor as on Wikipedia, not the video as on YouTube, not the tweet on Twitter, or the check-in on Foursquare. The basic, defining component of Facebook is the Friend.

But Myspace was there first.

The Origins of Online "Friends"

Myspace—known at first and for most of its existence as MySpace and then briefly as My[_____]—was launched in August 2003 by Brad Greenspan (then CEO of e-Universe), Tom Anderson, Chris DeWolfe, and Josh Berman, also with e-Universe. Myspace built on the social dynamics of America OnLine, CompuServe, message boards, forums, and computer conferencing (see Levinson, 1985 and Levinson, 1997; Ryan, 2008; and Vedro, 2007; for details), but Greenspan saw the key new new media value, as did Friendster (actually before Myspace, in 2002), of not charging for accounts. Rupert Murdoch's News Corp. purchased Myspace for $580 million in July 2005. It was from then through 2008 one of the two behemoths of online social media (along with Facebook, which in that period was smaller than Myspace). Myspace had more than 300 million accounts in its heyday. It was sold to music and movie star Justin Timberlake and Specific Media in 2011; it had shrunk to a tenth of that size by then, with only 30 million users.

Myspace's tagline from 2003 to 2009—the equivalent of *The New York Times*' "all the news that's fit to print," Fox News' "fair and balanced," and YouTube's "broadcast yourself"—was "a place for friends." It was dropped when Myspace began to focus on "social entertainment"—that is, music (see the *"Myspace Music and New New Media"* section). How truthful was Myspace's erstwhile slogan? Was it as accurate a description of Myspace as "broadcast yourself" is for YouTube? Or was it more like *The New York Times*' classic blurb, on its front page since 1897, which, as we saw in chapter 6, disguises the fact that what gets into its pages is not all the news that's fit to print but all the news that the editors at *The New York Times* deem fit to print. Fox's 1998 slogan is more subjective and thus less easy to refute—what, exactly, does "fair" mean—but no one except Fox would characterize its lineup of anchors and commentators as "balanced" between left and right, or even Democratic versus Republican points of view.

And what of "Friends" on Myspace? As we saw with "Friends" on Facebook, a purely online Friend has only one significant thing in common with offline, in-person friends—a sharing of one or more keen interests. But on Myspace, this coincidence of interest took an ugly turn.

"Cyberbullying" on Myspace

The capacity of any user to take on a completely false identity—false not only in name but also in gender and age—opens up all kinds of possibilities for abusive and dangerous behaviors. No medium—old or new—is immune to abusive, dangerous, and criminal uses, and in the next chapter we will examine some of the misuses and abuses that arise from false identities and other aspects of new new media. But the Lori Drew "cyberbullying" Myspace case is so intrinsically an example of what can go very wrong with online "Friends"—how a social medium can be used to kill or can result in a "Friend's" death—that we will consider that perversion of a social medium here.

To begin with, the Lori Drew case was not a straightforward instance of cyberstalking, in which someone, usually with a false name and picture, befriends someone else on a social new new medium—usually a vulnerable, young teenage girl—with the goal of arranging a meeting with this new "Friend," in person, for whatever unfortunate purpose. The remedy for this sort of cyberstalking is to never meet a person face-to-face whom you know only online, unless it is in a very public, safe place.

Nor was this a typical case of cyberbullying, in which one or more people harass an individual for the purpose of embarrassing, ridiculing, or humiliating the victim (see the next chapter).

The Lori Drew cyberbullying instance was something different, although it occurred because of the same inability of anyone to know who their online "Friends" really are, unless they already know them offline.

The background of the case is as follows: According to 49-year-old Lori Drew, her 13-year-old neighbor, Megan Meier, was spreading nasty rumors about Drew's daughter. Lori Drew exacted revenge. She created the false identity of "Josh Evans" on Myspace and there befriended Megan Meier. "Josh" pretended to fall in love with Megan. And when the 13-year-old was convinced of "his" love, Josh/Lori had email sent to Megan that said "the world would be a better place without you." Megan, who suffered from depression, hung herself (Masterson, 2008).

Local prosecutors were unable to get an indictment against Drew in Missouri, where she and Megan Meier lived. But federal prosecutors were able to indict her in Los Angeles (headquarters of News Corp/Fox, which then owned Myspace) on three counts of illegally accessing computers (misdemeanors) and one felony count of conspiracy under the Computer Fraud and Abuse Act. The jury found her guilty of the first three, lesser charges.

As Kim Zenter pointed out in Wired.com (November 26, 2008), the prosecution was based on a "novel" equation of the use of Myspace to harass (in violation of its "terms-of-service" agreement) and "hacking" as prohibited under the federal law. Although Myspace concurred with the prosecution, numerous legal experts and civil libertarians objected (Zenter, May 15, 2008), and although I almost always agree with them (see my "Flouting of the First Amendment," 2005), in this case, I did not. I think the verdict, even for just the misdemeanors, created an important precedent. Using false identifies for fun, role-playing, and nondeceptive commercial activity is fine. But using a false identity to abuse someone—especially an adult abusing a child—would be harassment not protected under the First Amendment. A federal judge, however, did not see this issue in that way and overturned the guilty verdicts in 2009.

In some ways, the most disturbing part of what happened to Megan Meier is that she did not fall prey to "traditional" cyberstalking—she did not die because she foolishly met an online Friend in person at some private place. Indeed, she did nothing wrong or foolish at all—other than falling in love with a "boy" on Myspace.

What can we do to protect our children from this kind of potentially deadly abuse?

Other than keeping them offline completely or forbidding them to be "Friends" with anyone they do not already know—neither of which is likely to succeed in practice—the only remedy is to hold adults accountable, as the jury did with Lori Drew, but the appeals judge ultimately did not.

But children can also be abusive to other children online, and, in the end, there is no law or enforcement that can completely protect us from our worst instincts, expressed in new new media, old media, or anyplace else.

New New Media Provide Medicine for Cyberbullying

Within a few days after I posted a blog on Myspace about Megan's awful story (Levinson, 2008), I received a message from a publicist, alerting me to a song that had just been written and released, "Shot with a Bulletless Gun" by the Truth on Earth band. The song begins, "I try to explain what it feels like when you're shot in the back of your mind with a bulletless gun by a kid that you don't even hardly know . . ." (written by band members Serena, Kiley, and Tess).

The band put up a Web page, http://truthonearthband.com/, which, in addition to an MP3 of the song and its lyrics, had a link to where you could "Read Facts about Cyber Bullying." The band consisted of three teenaged sisters (by 2012 a little older). Their musical influences include "Crosby, Stills and Nash, Creedence Clearwater, Lynyrd Skynyrd, Jethro Tull, Eric Clapton, and Santana"; their stated social influences include Martin Luther King, Jr., and Mahatma Gandhi.

Truth on Earth says its "main goal is to raise consciousness to a level where, over time, everyone can become part of the solutions instead of just living the experience of the problems."

I would say the band is an example of new new media providing a remedy for its own worst ills—in this case, cyberbullying. It's not a cure but a medicine that might help keep this abuse of new new media in check by alerting people to its dangers. (See "*Myspace Music and New New Media*" and "Podcasting" later in this chapter for more on the Truth on Earth band and podcasting.)

Myspace began losing users in 2008, a decline from which it has yet to recover. Although no scientific poll was done about why people left Myspace, it's fair to say that what happened to Megan Meier made Myspace an unattractive and uncool place to be.

Myspace as One-Stop New New Media Cafeteria

With some new new media systems, the question of the purpose of the system—what the new new medium does—is easily answered. Wikipedia is an encyclopedia, YouTube shows videos, and Blogspot (obviously) hosts blogs. With others, such as Twitter, the answer is not as obvious. To say what Twitter does is encourage tweets is tautological, and raises the further question of what is a tweet? That can be answered as a brief expression of opinion, emotion, whatever, but that is a longer answer than encyclopedia or video.

The answers for Myspace—and now Facebook—are longer for a different reason. Both did and do so many different things, as much or more as real friends might do together offline, that the best answer would be neither had nor have a single main purpose or function. Myspace in its prime offered a smorgasbord of services, including private messages, bulletins or group messaging to all of one's Myspace Friends; blogging; posting of photographs, videos, and music; IMing; and groups devoted to common interests.

The posted photographs, videos, music, and text of various sorts appeared on the Myspace member's "Profile" page, which served as a cyber calling card or one-stop advertisement on behalf of the user's vanity, social status, or online and offline professional pursuits.

Facebook has inherited and expanded this multiplicity of services, while Myspace has concentrated its focus on music.

Myspace Music and New New Media

Myspace's "music pages" were especially revolutionary. The traditional path to becoming a successful recording artist was to come to the attention of a record company's "A & R" people—"Artists and Repertoire"—which could happen at a live performance or by sending your "demos" (demonstration recordings) to the record company. The concert was usually the preferred method, because it gave the record company a way of gauging the public's interest in the potential recording artist.

The "music pages" on Myspace, initiated in 2005, offered a different approach: Set up an account on Myspace, on a special kind of page, which showcased MP3s of your music. Invite people on and off Myspace to come over and listen—for free. Build up your Friends list. And when the time was right, let a record company know about all the excitement your music page was generating.

This can now be seen as a classic new new media approach: The musician, the potential recording artist or group, need no longer rely on an agent to get into a club, and on the club to book the musician for a performance, just so a record company can see what impact the artist has on the audience. The recording artist, instead, could create a club or place for performance right on Myspace and thereby eliminate several levels of middlemen or experts.

Myspace music pages accommodate a wide array of genres and artists. Only a few have leveraged their Myspace profiles to go from unknown to superstar—as Justin Bieber did with YouTube—but that Myspace had this great an impact on anyone and the popular culture is notable.

Kate Nash, a native of Dublin, Ireland, started her Myspace page early in 2006. She then "found a manager for herself before proceeding to look for producers for her music" (Wikipedia, 2012). Her first single, produced in Iceland, had a limited 1000-copy release in 2006. Meanwhile, her Myspace fan base grew. Her songs had more than 26 million free plays on Myspace as of 2012. Meanwhile, her *Made of Bricks* album had gone "platinum" (sold one million copies) and hit No. 1 in the United Kingdom in 2007.

Londoner Lily Allen "created an account on Myspace and began posting demos in November 2005" (Wikipedia, 2012). She attracted fans and mainstream press interest, notably a piece in the U.K.'s *Guardian* (Sawyer, 2006). Her single "Smile" was No. 1 in the United Kingdom a few months later, and her album *Alright, Still* has sold more than 3.3 million copies. Her songs had more than 72 million free plays on Myspace as of 2012.

Sean Kingston, born Kisean Anderson in Miami, Florida, and raised in Kingston, Jamaica, used Myspace to ignite his musical career in a slightly different way. He explains (2007) that he sent messages to his target, record producer Jonathan J. R. Rottem, numerous times a day for weeks on Myspace, after Kingston had joined in the summer of 2007. Rottem was intrigued, took Kingston on, and the results speak for themselves. Kingston has since had No. 1 songs in the United States, Canada, and Australia (Wikipedia, 2012), and more than 114 million free plays of his songs on Myspace as of 2012.

More than eight million music pages competed for attention on Myspace as of January 2008 (Techradar, 2008), and almost none of those had the success of Nash, Allen, or Kingston. But others have found smaller benefits to their careers on Myspace.

Truth on Earth, whose music we encountered earlier as an antidote to cyberbullying, established a Myspace page in April 2008—some nine months before the group's publicist contacted me—and its songs had nearly 14,000 plays as of January 2012. (As comparison, my songs on Myspace received nearly 5000 plays as of January 2012.)

Truth on Earth participates in just about every new new medium considered in this book, with pages and accounts on YouTube (videos on their "channel" with 32,000 views as of 2012), Twitter (1400 followers), Facebook (a Musician/Band page with more than 90,000 "Likes"), a blog on Blogspot, and several social media not discussed here, including "I Like." Their music is for sale on Amazon and iTunes—70 percent of the money they make goes to social causes. Truth on Earth has not yet broken into the mainstream, but Myspace's music pages certainly helped keep the band in the game, especially in their crucial early days.

Other music sites in competition with Myspace—offering Profile Pages to which artists can upload their music—include Soundcloud (founded 2008, with 5 million users as of January 2012) and Reverbnation (founded in 2006, with a million users in 2011). In both cases, the users are musicians, bands, or someone in ownership of copyrights for MP3s (the same for Myspace musicians). Last.fm (2002) is primarily a music listening site, with 30 million users, some fraction of which are artists with pages for their music; Spotify launched in 2008, had 10 million listener users in 2011, and was aggressively promoting its premium services (listeners pay for music) at the end of 2011 (Pham, 2011).

Myspace Poetry

I titled this section "Myspace Poetry," not as a lyrical way to describe a relationship or some kind of writing one might find on Myspace, but to call attention to a use of Myspace blogs by a self-selected group of poets (all truly new new media producers are self-selected).

Lance Strate is a colleague at Fordham University—in fact, as Chair of the Department of Communication and Media Studies in 1998, Lance first brought me to teach at Fordham. We are friends as well as colleagues—both graduates of New York University's Media Ecology PhD program, where we both studied under Neil Postman at different times—and, in those capacities, we talked frequently about new new media and their impact. Indeed, as I mentioned in the Preface to the first edition of this book, it was during a discussion I was having with Lance in the Fall of 2007 when I was Chair, about the unsuitability of the name "new media" for one of our major tracks of study, that I realized the name "new new media" would be much a better description of blogging, YouTube, Wikipedia, and so forth.

Lance had joined Myspace just a few months earlier, after a year or so of casual discussion with me about the value of Myspace for promoting scholarly groups. (Lance was then also president of the Media Ecology Association, a group he and I and several others founded in 1998.) Early one evening in July 2007—Lance and I were teaching graduate classes that summer—Lance walked into my office and said something along the lines of "I finally did it." He was referring to a blog he had just started, on July 4, 2007, on Myspace. Unlike another blog Lance had earlier started on Blogspot (also under my benevolent coaxing), Lance told me that this blog on Myspace was likely to consist of his poetry.

Lance had never published any poetry before. In the field of poetry, he is an epitome of the nonprofessional new new media producer. By December 2008, Lance had published 150 poems on his Myspace blog. They had received more than 13,000 comments and more than 66,500 views from hundreds of Friends, most of whom also had poetry blogs on Myspace. Some, such as Larry Kuechlin, also have published "chapbooks" of their poetry— real books made of paper—that can be purchased on Amazon.

In January 2009, Lance and several of his colleague Myspace poets took another kind of step from Myspace to real space, or from the realm of new new media to the world of old media in the world at large. They announced the creation of NeoPoiesis Press, whose purpose was to bring to the world's attention poetry and other written and artistic work expressing the energy and vision of the new digital landscape (NeoPoiesis, 2009). They have since published 14 paper books of poetry, 2 books of fiction (including Robert K. Blechman's Twitter-written novel in 2012, mentioned in chapter 3 of this book), and 1 nonfiction tract—a mixing of new and old media, which typifies an increasing number of new new media activities.

The general pattern is this: (1) New new media arise as alternatives to new and old media, as blogging did to newspapers printed and online, YouTube did to television, Wikipedia did to printed encyclopedias, and so on. (2) New new media create groups, businesses, and products that go back to the old media, offline world, and achieve success there, as Tucker Max did when he put his blog posts into a best-selling book (2006), YouTube has done with its videos increasingly shown on broadcast and cable television newscasts, and NeoPoiesis Press has been doing for its books of poetry, fiction, and scholarship.

We turn now to online indexes of news, which had significant impact on the U.S. 2008 election, and now help get news out about Occupy Wall Street and the U.S. election of 2012.

Digg and Reddit

If Wikipedia was conceived as an online encyclopedia, also used nonetheless as an online newspaper, Digg was conceived by Kevin Rose, Owen Byrne, Ron Gorodetzky, and Jay Adelson in 2004 as an index for all news published on the Web, but it soon came to serve as an instantly updating digest of news, or an online newspaper of newspapers. Along with Reddit, founded by Steve Huffman and Alexis Ohanian in 2006, and at least half a dozen other online news-listing services (such as BuzzFeed, Fark, and StumbleUpon), the articles that appear on Digg are published elsewhere online and selected—in the case of Digg, "Dugg"—by readers to appear on its front pages. At its height, Digg was the biggest and most influential of these sites—number 32 in the top 100 American online sites as listed by Alexa in June 2008. Digg's ranking had dropped to #272 in February 2009. It was back up to #179 by January 2012, but behind Reddit at #114, which Digg had once surpassed.

As CNET News reported in May 2008, "with the 2008 presidential election on the way, Digg has caught on among another very vocal set of news junkies: the political crowd. It's helped boost the site's numbers for sure: Digg now boasts 230 million page views per month, 26 million unique visitors, and 15,000 stories submitted per day" (McCarthy, 2008). The U.S. presidential election of 2012 is beginning to have the same salutary effect—on Reddit as well as Digg.

Reddit has likely moved solidly ahead of Digg because Reddit became a major news site for Occupy Wall Street reporting in the Fall of 2011, with a "sub-Reddit" devoted completely to posting links to stories and tweet-like headlines about Occupy Wall Street developments. Reddit also joined Wikipedia in the one-day shutdown of services in protest of the Stop Online Piracy Act (SOPA) in January 2012. The House and Senate versions of the bill were soon after shelved. (I supported the Reddit shutdown but had qualms about the Wikipedia pause in service, because I didn't want the online ency-clopedia unavailable to students in need of its articles—see Levinson, "Is Wikipedia Wrong," 2012.)

Digg and Reddit operate essentially in the same way. Registered users can post anything with a URL—any blog post, online newspaper article, photograph, video—on Digg or Reddit. All users can Digg or Bury as many posts as they like, or vote the item Up or Down on Reddit. The names of those actions mean just what they sound like: Diggs and Ups are approvals; Buries and Downs are dislikes of posted links.

When a post or submission receives an undisclosed number of Diggs, and no minimum number of Buries (Digg keeps this Digg/Bury algorithm secret), the submission becomes "Popular," and reaches the front page of Digg. The same happens with Reddit.

Users also can comment on a submission, and the number of comments also works on behalf of a submission getting on the front page. Comments can be supportive or critical of a submission and are themselves subject to Digg/Bury or Up/Down voting. Digg has extensive integrations with Twitter and Facebook, with an option for all of a user's activities on Digg to show up on the user's Facebook page. Reddit's "share" options extend only to email (as of January 2012).

Thus, to return again to *The New York Times*' "all the news that's fit to print," Digg and Reddit publish on their front pages all the submissions endorsed by their readers—in contrast to the way *The New York Times* and all old media online and offline really select stories, which is by their small groups of editors.

But the Digg/Reddit method itself does not always function in complete accordance with its ideal. As is the case with Wikipedia and all nonexpert-directed new new media, Digg and Reddit are subject to abuse or "gaming"—users teaming up to get stories to the front page, rather than endorsing what they genuinely see as worthy.

This is an abuse as old as democracy itself: The more that any process, government, or publication is open to the will of the people, the more vulnerable it is to small groups of people using the democratic levers to make the process work in their favor. In government, we call this process "lobbying." In new new media, including Digg and Reddit, it is called "gaming." In the following sections, we examine some of Digg and Reddit's democratizing techniques, how they have been utilized by "gamers," and what impact both the democratizing and the gaming may have had on the world at large.

Shouting, Paying for Diggs (and Buries)

In principle, stories are supposed to be promoted or demoted on Digg and Reddit according to the assessments of each individual reader. In practice, Diggs and Buries in the past on Digg were often amassed via deliberate campaigns of readers. As is the case with the "meat puppet" problem on Wikipedia (sock puppetry is always unethical), a question always remained as to the validity of such sought-after Diggs and Buries: Would the Digger (or Burier) on his or her own have been moved to Digg or Bury the story? Is the mere fact that the Digg or Bury occurred after the reader received a solicitation enough to invalidate the Digg or Bury?

Digg itself has not been consistent in its response to solicited Diggs and Buries. A powerful feature on Digg from 2007–2009 allowed users to "Shout" to up to as many as 200 "Friends." Such Shouts could encourage Diggs or Buries. (Encouraging Diggs was a little easier, because the default Shout was "sharing." To elicit Buries, the shouter had to attach a brief note urging a Bury.) Digg retired the Shout feature in May 2009, and encouraged Diggers to continue shouting about Digg stories on Twitter and Facebook, via buttons provided on Digg's pages (Milian, 2009).

Of concern to the Digg administration, then, was not Digg's own "Shouting" feature or informal sharing and promotion of Digg stories on Twitter and Facebook, but deliberate campaigns on and off the system to Digg or Bury stories, including operations purported to deliver X number of Diggs for a given story for $1 or more per Digg (Newitz, 2007). A blogger might be tempted to use such a service, not only to obtain more readers, but for the advertising revenue that a monetized blog with a larger number of readers could generate.

And the numbers were considerable. Of the 10 stories written by me and posted on my blogs that went "Popular" on Digg in 2007–2008 (on PaulLevinson.net, which I later merged with *Infinite Regress*), the least number of additional readers attracted to my blog was 15,000, and the most was 50,000. But in terms of book sales and advertising income received from that number of visitors, having "Popular" articles on Digg did not generate enough income to retire on, and it would not even have been enough to purchase Diggs (assuming a minimum number of 150 Diggs at $1 each to get the article to the front page, though most articles back then actually took at least 200 to 300 Diggs to be promoted to the front).

But Digg is by no means averse to promotion of Digg stories off the Digg website. It provides a variety of "buttons" and widgets that bloggers can put directly on their sites, with the result that readers can Digg a story directly from the blog. Reddit also does that. Some blogs, such as *The Huffington Post* and Blogcritics.com, have long had widgets indicating which of their stories are surging on Digg and Reddit at any moment.

These were the ethical bottom lines, then, for promoting stories on Digg: Stories promoted on websites on which the stories appear and stories promoted (and trashed) to and by "Friends" on Digg were fine. Stories promoted and trashed by groups outside Digg, especially if an exchange of money was involved, were not. And, of course, sock puppets set up to Digg or Bury stories was a practice that, as on Wikipedia, was also not allowed on Digg, but, as is the case on Wikipedia, no doubt did take place until uncovered (see Saleem, 2006 and Saleem, "Ruining the Digg Experience," 2007, for analysis and cautions about gaming Diggs).

Or, as Digg advises in its posted "Terms of Use" (2011): Digg is not to be used "with the intention of artificially inflating or altering the 'digg count,' blog count, comments, or any other Digg service, including by way of creating separate user accounts for the purpose of artificially altering Digg's services; giving or receiving money or other remuneration in exchange for votes; or participating in any other organized effort that in any way artificially alters the results of Digg's services." Reddit's Terms of Service has similar language.

But with all this concern about the authenticity of Diggs, what impact have they had in the nondigital, offline world?

Ron Paul vs. Barack Obama on Digg

Stories about Ron Paul, a contender in the Republican presidential primary campaign in 2007–2008 (as well as in 2011–2012) were enormously popular on Digg. CNET News reported in August 2007 that he "enjoys about 160,000 mentions on Digg.com, more than the next four most popular candidates combined" (McCullagh, 2007), but also advised that "Paul's poll numbers award him less than 2 percent of the vote among Republican candidates." And, in fact, Ron Paul obtained fewer than 5 percent of the votes in Republican primaries in most states in 2008. Stories about Barack Obama were also highly popular on Digg—though, during the times of the primaries, not as successful as Ron Paul's Digg numbers. Why did Obama succeed in real, offline politics, while Ron Paul did not?

The easy explanation that Ron Paul's success on Digg was inflated, while Obama's was not, is probably not correct, because, although we have no reliable, proven knowledge about what either of the candidates' supporters did to promote their candidate on Digg, there is no reason to think that Ron Paul's supporters did anything more or different from Obama's.

Ron Paul's high profile on Digg did attract much more general attention than Obama's, precisely because Paul was so low in offline polls and primary votes. First heralded and decried by various observers as a "fringe politician" taking "over the Web" (Spiegel, 2007), Ron Paul's success on Digg soon came under more serious analysis by social media practitioners such as Muhammad Saleem, who wrote in July 2007 that he was at first surprised by Ron Paul's popularity on social media sites and believed it to be a genuine example of online democracy at work but now thought otherwise. The cause for this change of opinion was an analysis by Ron Sansone (2007), another social media analyst, whose investigation convinced Saleem that Paul's "apparent popularity was simply a result of mass manipulation" on Digg, or encouragement of Ron Paul supporters on various websites to join Digg and vote up Ron Paul stories. Saleem later noted (November 2007) that "Ron Paul submissions can now get over 100 diggs in an hour" and that Digg Shouting had exacerbated this problem.

But Ron Paul's supporters responded throughout 2007 that, if anything, more stories about their candidate should have made the front page of Digg, and did not because they were hit by an anti-Ron Paul "Bury brigade" (Jones, 2007). Mainstream online media such as Wired.com had been reporting about possible "Bury brigades," or organized efforts to vote down a variety of articles posted on Digg (not just about Ron Paul), for several months (Cohen, 2007), and, ironically, insofar as Ron Paul, Saleem had offered screenshot "proof" of Bury brigades at work, several months earlier (February 2007), concluding that although Buries are "supposed to be used to remove superfluous or irrelevant content from Digg, the mechanism is often abused to remove useful and insightful content by malicious users for self-serving and vindictive reasons."

Obama, for his part, was recognized early on and throughout the 2007–2008 contests as the other Internet candidate (Stirland, 2007; VanDenPlas, 2007), and in the general election as the Internet candidate, period (see chapters 4 and 10 for more). One observer at the end of August 2008 noticed multiple stories about Obama on Digg "having over 2 thousand votes on them and hundreds of comments" (Gladkova, 2008), or easily being at the top of the front page. An article in *Business Week* from the same time reported that "Obama's people may ask you to Digg an article that is favorable to Obama or critical of his opponent" (Hoffman, 2008). But, interestingly, such reports stopped short of claiming that Obama's supporters had outright gamed the system. Scott VanDenPlas's report from a year earlier sums up the enduring perception about the successes of Ron Paul and Barack Obama on Digg: "Paul's surge seems to be more manufactured, based on rigging the democratic systems of the web to return results favorable to the supported candidate. Obama's support has more of an organic feel with power in numbers" (VanDenPlas, 2007).

But what was the difference between being asked "to Digg an article that was favorable to Obama" (Hoffman, 2008) and "manipulation" of Digg to benefit Ron Paul

(Sansone, 2007)? As an alternative to the "Ron Paul gamed the system and Obama did not" explanation of why Ron Paul's excellent showing on Digg bore such meager results in the primaries while Obama's excellent showing on Digg correlated with his getting the Democratic nomination and going on to win the 2008 general election, let me offer an hypothesis that does not have to do with the ethics and sincerity of pro-Paul and pro-Obama Diggers, but with their ages.

Users must be 13 years of age to register on Digg, and registration is needed to submit articles, Digg or Bury, comment, and so forth. The registration process, however, does not insist on any proof of age, so it is a safe assumption that children under the age of 13 were submitting stories in 2007–2008, Digging, and so forth on Digg. But even if the 13-year-old requirement were 100 percent honored, that would leave five years of people—ages 13 to 17—who could Digg stories but not vote in primary or general elections.

That discrepancy is probably the best place to start looking for why a political candidate could do splendidly on Digg—have stories about him or her dominate the Digg front pages—but fail, and by large margins, in actual elections. Socialmediatrader.com reported that, in a snapshot analysis of Diggs on January 11, 2008, Ron Paul had the greatest number of Diggs in popular or front-page stories—close to 3000, some 50 percent more than the candidate with the second-biggest number, Hillary Clinton with close to 2000. The other candidates were just hundreds of Diggs below Hillary Clinton. Rudy Giuliani was third, Mike Gravel fourth, Dennis Kucinich fifth, Mike Huckabee sixth—all ahead of Barack Obama, who had only the seventh-greatest number of Diggs, a little under 1500, on front-page stories about him, on this day. John McCain was in eighth place, with about 100 fewer Diggs than Obama. This was eight days after the January 3 Iowa caucuses, in which Obama came in first for the Democrats and Hillary third, while Ron Paul came in fourth or about midway in the field of Republicans. In the January 8, 2008, primary in New Hampshire, Clinton came in first for the Democrats, McCain first for the Republicans, and Ron Paul fifth. Clearly, the January 11 Digg activity was already way out of synch with what was happening in caucuses and primary voting booths, most especially concerning Ron Paul.

Was this because Ron Paul's supporters were already gaming Digg, while Barack Obama's supporters were not, at least not at that point in the primaries? That may have been a contributing factor, but let's look at the discrepancy between Diggs and the results in the primaries from another angle. Obama's campaign clearly worked the "grassroots" well enough to win in Iowa and come in second in New Hampshire. Ron Paul's campaign did poorly in both states. This means that Obama's campaign galvanized a far greater number of people who caucused or voted, age 18 or above, than did Ron Paul's campaign. Let's assume that a similar percentage of those Obama and Paul voters—anywhere from 0 to 100 percent—found their way to Digg, or were already on Digg at the time of the primaries. An alternate explanation to Paul's supporters gaming or manipulating Digg is that, in addition to the age 18 or older supporters, Ron Paul also had a large number of supporters on Digg ages 13 through 17, or even younger, and that theirs were the Diggs that lifted Ron Paul's articles so high up on the front page.

But how was it that Barack Obama, the widely acknowledged "youth" candidate, as we saw in chapter 4 about YouTube (see Wertheimer, 2008; Baird, 2008), did not attract large numbers of 13- to 17-year-old supporters of his own to Digg? The answer, I would suggest, is that Obama's campaign wisely focused on people aged 18 to 30, who could go out and caucus or vote. Ron Paul's campaign had no equivalent grassroots operation and did the best it could with extensive Internet promotion, which reaches people below the age of 18 as easily as people above that voting age. Obama's 2007–2008 Internet campaign, in other words, built on the foundation of a powerful in-person campaign directed at potential voters and partnered with it. Ron Paul's campaign started with the Internet and never got beyond it.

No scientific statistics exist for the age of Digg users. But a poll reported in September 2006 shows 5 percent of Digg users were between the ages of 13 and 16, 22 percent ages 17–20, 28 percent ages 21–24, 20 percent ages 25–28, and so forth (Ironic Pentameter, 2006), which certainly indicated a tilt toward younger users and a significant percentage (more than 5, fewer than 27 percent) of Diggers under 18. Another impression, widely shared (at least insofar as mental age or sophistication), was "that the average age of Digg users is about 15" (MacBeach, 2008).

I thus think there is sufficient reason to conclude that, as an alternative to the "gaming" effect, or at least a more significant factor, the below voting age of Ron Paul's supporters on Digg resulted in his success on Digg and failure at the polls. Obama's campaign concentrated from the outset on young voting-age people, who helped propel him to first- and second-place finishes in the primaries and eventually to a position on Digg almost as powerful as Ron Paul's and, ultimately, to a revolutionary victory in the general election. Ron Paul, in contrast, never succeeded off of Digg and the Internet in 2007–2008. He was defeated in the primaries not by the failure of gaming on Digg to translate into votes but because Digg demographics had insufficient correlation to the demographics of American voters.

Ron Paul would do much better in the 2012 Republican primaries, getting percentages in the teens or higher in some of the primaries and caucuses, in contrast to the four or fewer percent he received in 2008. This was likely due, at least in part, to some of his underage supporters on Digg in 2008 growing up into voting age by 2012. Ironically, Digg itself was a far less important factor in the 2012 than the 2008 presidential election. But the older media, which work in a symbiotic relationship with new new media regarding politics and elections, played a prominent role in both Ron Paul campaigns.

Ron Paul and the Older Media

The possible gaming by Ron Paul's supporters in 2007–2008, and their likely young age, figured in a similar story off of Digg, in the older medium of television and its coverage of the primary campaigns and debates.

ABC-TV neglected to mention on at least one occasion that Ron Paul came in first in its postdebate poll. It removed comments from Ron Paul supporters on its online board and then proceeded to shut it down. And ABC also showed a lone Ron Paul supporter before the 2007 Iowa straw poll, in contrast to big crowds for Mitt Romney, when in fact Ron Paul had big crowds of supporters, too (see Levinson, "Rating the News Networks," 2007, for a summary of these and other network shortcomings in their coverage of Ron Paul, with links). CNBC removed a postdebate poll that Ron Paul had won (Wastler, 2007; see also Levinson, "Open Letter to CNBC," 2007). Sean Hannity denigrated Ron Paul's first-place finish in another postdebate poll on Fox, as due to repeat dialing by a small number of supporters, in contrast to Alan Colmes, who insisted on reporting Ron Paul's first-place result without spin (Hannity & Colmes, 2007; see also Levinson, "Hannity & Colmes Split," 2007).

Although commentators such as MSNBC's Lawrence O'Donnell maintained that Ron Paul would never get the 2012 Republican nomination (for example, on MSNBC's coverage of the South Carolina GOP Primary results on January 21, 2012), this sort of criticism was far different from claiming Ron Paul's supporters were gaming the system, or from not mentioning that Ron Paul had won a poll. In general, Ron Paul's coverage in the old media in 2012 was no different from that received by other candidates. Perhaps producers in the older media were more attuned, by 2011–2012, to the fact that Ron Paul's success online in 2007–2008 was predominantly real, not gamed.

Obama was generally spared such dismissive treatment by the old media in even 2007–2008, but MSNBC's Chuck Todd, at that time the station's professional pollster, discounted Obama's success in a postdebate poll on that cable network as due to his supporters dialing repeatedly on cellphones in responding to the poll (Levinson, "Now Obama's Poll Results Are Denigrated," 2007).

Hannity may have had cellphones in mind, too, and he and Todd may have been right that cellphones were the medium that propelled Paul and Obama to victories in the phone polls—but not because of repeat dialing or the same small number of supporters casting numerous phone votes. A 15-year-old, after all, who cannot vote in a primary, could respond via cellphone to a postdebate poll as easily as a 25-year-old. And although I would not put it past supporters of any candidate to cast repeated votes in a postdebate poll, apparently that was not possible with the Fox texting poll on October 22, 2007—I tried to vote twice, as a test to see what would happen, and my second vote was not counted. Of course, I could have cast additional votes on different phones or texted my friends to vote for my candidate on their phones. But the explanation for Ron Paul's success in postdebate phone polls may well be much the same as for his success on Digg: some gaming and manipulation, no doubt, but the younger-than-voting-age of the callers was also likely a significant factor. Because Obama in 2008 did as well in the primaries as in postdebate polls, his success in the phone polls requires no further explanation, though it is likely that under-voting-age people cast phone votes for him as well.

Reddit in the Real World and on the Big Screen

Reddit has had its own increasing impact on politics in the real world. Its Occupy Wall Street "subReddit"—a Reddit devoted completely to a given topic—had more than 30,000 readers as of January 2012, links to a dozen other Occupy Wall Street websites off Reddit, and hundreds of daily new links on its front pages. The Occupy Wall Street subReddit serves in effect as an online hub for reports of OWS-related events and news.

Occupy Wall Street can be seen as a resurgence of direct democracy, as indicated earlier in this book, and will be explored in more detail in the concluding chapter. But Reddit has also had a direct impact on the workings of representative democracy in the United States.

In January 2012, Reddit readers voted Up to the front page what was in effect an online petition to raise money for Representative Paul Ryan's (R-WI) opponent in the 2012 election. The reason: Ryan was ambiguous in his position on the Stop Online Piracy Act (SOPA). The result: Ryan soon came out with a statement saying he did not support the bill (which was subsequently shelved). In the previous month, Reddit readers had voted Up a petition with similar goals—to get people to cancel their GoDaddy accounts, in disapproval of GoDaddy's support of SOPA. The result was the same: GoDaddy withdrew its support of SOPA. GoDaddy sells Internet domain names—such as InfiniteRegress.tv and PaulLevinson.net—so Reddit's success with both GoDaddy and Paul Ryan shows its influence in both the online and offline worlds.

And one user is having a series of comments he made on Reddit made into a movie. James Erwin wondered on Reddit, "Could I destroy the entire Roman Empire during the reign of Augustus if I traveled back in time with a modern U.S. Marine infantry battalion?" The idea appealed to Warner Brothers, who are making it into an historical science fiction movie entitled *Rome, Sweet Rome* (Couts, 2011)—continuing a new tradition of new new media as a source for movies and television shows, including *Julie & Julia* (2009), based in part on Julie Powell's blog, and the short-lived CBS-TV 2010–2011 show *$#*! My Dad Says*, based on Justin Halpern's Twitter feed "Shit My Dad Says," which was also the basis of the best-selling book *Sh*t My Dad Says*. (The three different titles are themselves a study in freedom of expression in 21st century media, with new new media being the most free, and television the least, due to fear of advertiser and FCC disapproval.)

Reddit's users also have used Reddit to promote an online cause very close to their hearts and interests: Reddit itself. A story on the front page of Reddit on December 25, 2008—in the top 20, in fact, with 3378 Up votes and 1170 Down votes for a net of 2258 "points," as well as 843 comments—was titled "So Who Else Here Left Digg for Reddit?" (ILeftDiggforReddit, 2008). The gist of the comments was that Digg was terrible and Reddit was wonderful, and Reddit had either already buried or soon would bury Digg.

The first comment offered a history of that user's experience—starting on Digg, then using both Digg and Reddit, and finally settling just on Reddit. The commenter complained about needing to amass a large number of "Friends" on Digg to get a posting to the front page. The second comment observed that Reddit was for smart people and Digg for people not so endowed.

But Reddit's far worse Alexa ranking of #5122, in comparison to Digg's #294, in December 2008 told a different story—back then. Three years later, the 2008 comments had become prescient, with Reddit at #115 and Digg #189 on Alexa. (But see Rucker, 2012, for a claim that Digg could surge again in 2012.)

Reddit, then, represents another successful integration of the digital and physical real world, which is becoming an increasing hallmark of new new media. Such integration was far less in residence in 2008, when Ron Paul's success on Digg had no analog in the real world, and Foursquare had just come into existence.

In the next section, we consider a new new medium totally immersed in the digital realm, with few offline connections. Its diminished importance since 2008 may reflect the growing convergence of digital and physical worlds in our time.

Second Life

It was cold and raining in New York City, early on a Sunday evening in December 2007. I did a reading from my novel *The Plot to Save Socrates*, to an international audience—people from Romania and other places overseas, as well as the United States—and not a raindrop hit me as I traveled to the reading. That's because I did not do it in this world but in Second Life.

In Second Life, avatars not only read aloud from their books to audiences of avatars, but they also do lots of other things we ordinarily do in our flesh-and-blood lives. Avatars get their hair styled, buy clothes and land, dance, make love, do all manner of business, and run shops. I had just opened a "virtual" bookstore, the "Soft Edge Book Shop" on Book Island in Second Life. My rent was paid in "Linden dollars," which were purchased by real U.S. dollars and came to about $5 per month. My store was stocked with covers of all of my books—some 15 of them—which visitors could click on and see reviews of the books, as well as links through which they could read more about the books and buy them on real-life Amazon. I did my reading to a crowd of about 40 avatars who were standing right in front of the bookstore, as my avatar sat in a rocking chair on the porch of the store. It was a nice, old-fashioned bookshop—in a world that could not have existed when such shops were on the main streets of our small towns.

I have since closed my shop—I could no longer afford the time to tend it—but if it were still open, it would no doubt have a cover of this very book, *New New Media*, on one of its walls. (See Kremer, 2008, for a summary of authors who have given readings, established two-dimensional offices and bookstores, and conducted other professional writerly activities in Second Life.)

Everything in life has precedents, and Second Life is no different. People have been chatting online now for decades—back before anyone even talked about new media, let alone new new media—ever since the French Minitel system in the 1980s (Levinson, 1997). Texting is still essential to communication in Second Life, as tweeting is to most new new media, but Second Life in 2007 added voice chat capabilities. You can find an avatar to dance with and select a script—you can waltz or boogie or whatever—and you chat either via text or voice and watch your avatars dance on the screen.

Second Life residents use Linden dollars to purchase land, objects, skin, and scripts that animate the avatars. Linden dollars (named after Linden Labs, which created Second Life under Philip Rosedale's supervision in 2003, and continues to develop and administer the community of about one million as of 2011) can either be purchased with real dollars, via PayPal, or earned from other residents in Second Life. In December 2008, $1 US purchased about 250 L (Linden) dollars (down to about 200 Linden dollars as of January 2012). I decided to make my books available only for purchase on Amazon via U.S. dollars, in part because I was interested in the Second Life/real-life interface—how permeable was the boundary between the two, how success in Second Life could translate into success in real life—and in part because it is always better for an author if his or her books sell through a bookstore and money goes back to the publisher, from whom the author receives royalties. In that way, your advance from the publisher can be repaid, and the publisher can be impressed with the sales of your book, which make additional printings and contracts for subsequent books more likely.

About a week before my first Second Life reading at the bookstore, I did a Sunday afternoon reading as a guest on Adele Ward's Second Life "Meet the Author" series. This reading was "televised" live in Second Life on SLCN.tv—Second Life Cable Network (since renamed Treet.tv)—but soon became available to everyone on the Web at the SLCN.tv website. (I also embedded copies and excerpts of this video on my blogs and posted excerpts on YouTube; see Levinson, Reading from *The Plot to Save Socrates*, 2007.)

The availability of Second Life "off world"—or on computer, smart phone, and tablet screens in real life, or RL, as the residents say—is part of the intermingling of Second Life and the rest of the Internet, if not the offline world as in Foursquare. I was also interviewed by Esther DeCuir in a Second Life newspaper for an article about my Soft Edge Book Shop. Like the SLCN.tv interview, the article in SLNN—Second Life News Network—was available to everyone on the Web, not just in Second Life (DeCuir, 2007; SLNN closed in 2009). Like my Amazon book links, these news and television operations indicated the extent to which Second Life worked (and still works) with the rest of the online world.

Selling books from a virtual bookshop, with chairs and tables and photos on the walls, however, feels more like selling books at an author's reading in a real bookstore than IMing from a Web page with images of my books. One night, my avatar was standing in front of my shop. Another avatar was walking by and stopped to look at the big book cover of *The Plot to Save Socrates* that was slowly spinning on the first step in front of the shop. We chatted for a few minutes about the book, and then the customer clicked on the Amazon link and purchased it. I told him where he could mail my novel—in the real world—if he wanted me to autograph it. This felt so close to being in a real bookstore, I could almost feel the texture of the book in my hand.

More than any of the other new new media we have examined in this book, the avatars and animation and sounds of Second Life make it seem more like an alternative than adjunct to our lives—a third place, different from our lives away from computers and smart phones (precious little time for the latter), yet also different from the work we pursue and the fun we have via our computers and smart phones. But, of course, Second Life is nonetheless a part of our real lives, exists in the same online matrix as all the other new new media, and ultimately proves its mettle to the extent that it can make a difference in our real-life activities of fun, love, politics, and business.

History and Workings of Second Life

Second Life had about 15 million users as of September 2008, five years after its creation, but many of them were not active. The figure of 1 million active users in 2011 is therefore not fully comparable, other than indicating a significant decline in the population.

Like Facebook, Twitter, and all successful new new media, joining Second Life—becoming a member or "resident"—is free. But unlike the other new new media, spending money in the form of Linden dollars, as we saw earlier, is an essential part of Second Life. Perhaps that expense, in a time of worldwide recession, was in part responsible for the reduction of Second Life's resident numbers.

Here's how Second Life works: After joining, you can choose a male or female avatar (regardless of your actual gender) and then select a body type, precise facial attributes ranging from plumpness of lips to facial hair, and clothes. All of this is free. But the nature of the free clothing, and even the facial attributes and hairstyles, mark the new resident as a "newbie." This is where the spending starts. Residents can purchase just about anything, ranging from a kick-ass earring to a great-looking backside, for modest to large amounts of Linden dollars.

In one sense, Linden dollars are play money like Monopoly game money—and residents indeed frequently refer to their experiences as "playing" Second Life. But because Linden dollars can be purchased by real U.S. dollars and many international currencies and converted at the going rate back into dollars or the international currencies, spending Linden dollars in Second Life can quickly become serious and even big business. *Business Week* reported that Ailin Graef (under the avatar name of "Anshe Chung") made more than a quarter of a million U.S. dollars in Second Life as of May 2006 (Hof, 2006), and Reuters' Second Life bureau said Chung had announced Second Life "real estate" assets worth $1 million US at the end of November of that year (Reuters, 2006). Reuters also indicated that 58 Second Life residents were making in excess of $5,000—a spike in Second Life profits—but by April 2008, *The Alphaville Herald* (a Second Life newspaper, unaffiliated with Linden Labs) reported that Second Life had posted the lowest ever growth in profit per capita in the first quarter of 2008

(Holyoke, 2008). This turned out to be the beginning of the big decline of all things Second Life.

But this much is still clear: Given the easy exchange via PayPal of Linden dollars and non-Second Life currencies (i.e., "real" currencies, associated with real countries), what is the difference between Linden dollars and Australian or Canadian dollars, from the standpoint of an American, or the difference between Linden dollars and American or Canadian dollars, from the standpoint of an Australian? From the point of view of a person in any country, Linden dollars are no different from any other foreign currency—or, the only difference is that Linden dollars work in a virtual realm, easily and nearly instantly accessible from just about any country in the world, via desktop, laptop, smart phone, or tablet.

Second Life and Real-Life Interface

Real life—what we do in the physical world when we're not interacting on a computer or cellphone—figures in, or lurks behind, everything we do online. Did mybarackobama .com result in more votes for Barack Obama in 2008? There is no way we can conduct a controlled experiment and restage that election without Obama's websites and all the other new new media.

Second Life, apropos its development by Linden Labs, can be considered an ongoing laboratory for investigating such online/real-world impacts. Every time someone clicked on a link in my Soft Edge Book Shop in Second Life and then bought one of my novels on Amazon, that Second Life denizen was moving from the new new medium of Second Life to the new medium of Amazon, on which an interaction—a purchase, in this case, with real, not Linden, dollars—resulted in a hardcover or paperback copy of my novel being shipped to the Second Life buyer's real-world home or place of business. In my case, alas, those digital/real world interfaces were not enough to make any of my books best sellers. And the general decline of Second Life earnings indicated earlier shows I wasn't the only one not making a bundle "in world."

But if business is the most easily quantifiable kind of Second Life interaction with real life, it is by no means the only one. We consider several other Second Life activities with real-world impact in the following subsections, ranging from educational seminars to sex.

A Seminar in Second Life

Given the voice capabilities of Second Life, we could say that any time an avatar talks to a group of other, assembled avatars, the first avatar is conducting a live-streaming audio seminar, or webinar.

But some Second Life events are more explicitly seminars or webinars than others. In a typical reading from one of my science fiction novels that I conducted in Second Life, announcements were sent to various communities in Second Life, as well as to my Friends on Second Life. They received those announcements in their message boxes on Second Life, and/or via their real-life email, if they had enabled that option. In reality, these flesh-and-blood people were invited to attend my reading via their avatars on Second Life. The "game" or experience of Second Life, however, is so realistic—so effortlessly extended to the real world—that it could also be reasonably said that avatars and personas received the invitation in their real-world email.

Indeed, I also announced the reading in my "off-world" online communities—on Facebook, Myspace, and on my blogs—and invited off-world friends in these social media, and via Gmail, to the reading. The invitation included instructions on how to get a free Second Life account and the location—or "coordinates"—of the reading and details on how to get there, from any point of entry in Second Life. When logging on to Second Life, your avatar appears at the last place in which it was located (when you log on for the very first time, you find yourself in an area where you can create and clothe your avatar).

The last names of every avatar or denizen on Second Life are provided by Second Life. "Aeon," "Latte," and "Freenote" are examples of the many possible last names. If someone wishes to disguise totally a true, offline identity on Second Life, this can easily be accomplished by creating a first name that has no connection to your real-life name— "Star Aeon" or "Tasty Latte." This, indeed, is by far the most common way that names are created on Second Life and underscores the fact that, of all the social media considered in this book, Second Life is by far the most anonymous. In the cases of Facebook and Twitter, you can create an account under a fictional name if you wish. In the case of Second Life, you have to go out of your way to have an avatar name that has any connection to your real-life name. The way to do that is to create a Second Life first name that consists of your real-life names. If you ever run into a "PaulLevinson Freenote" on Second Life, that would be me.

A fine assemblage of avatars convened for my appearance at Adele Ward's "Meet the Author" event on Sunday, December 9, 2007, at 2 p.m. SLT (Second Life Time, which is the same as Pacific time). It was held in a beautiful venue—the Town Center in a sim (or virtual place) by the name of Cookie. The invitees and I were given the "coordinates" of the Town Center, which enabled us either to log on directly to that virtual place or "teleport" there from someplace else in Second Life. "Teleporting" is an instant way to move from one place to another in Second Life. Other, slower options are flying and walking. Members of my audience arrived in all three ways.

Before I began the reading, attendees chatted among themselves, via text or voice, as they arrived. There were seats on which the avatars could sit, and they were encouraged to do so—not only out of courtesy to the avatars, who, of course, could feel no pain or tiredness, but because standing required more computing power from Second Life to keep the simulacrum intact (you can see the seated audience a few minutes into the interview in Levinson, Reading from *The Plot to Save Socrates,* 2007). A week before the reading, Adele had explained to me—via her "Jilly Kidd" avatar (Adele Ward is her real name, and she is a real poet who lives in London)—that the Town Center venue could only support a maximum of 45 to 50 avatars. (Other venues can support as many as several hundred avatars. "Support" is the Second Life computing power needed to maintain the "sim" or virtual imagery, which can crash if the number of avatars exceeds Second Life bandwidth required for the sim.) I had estimated, based on the number of invitations distributed and the number of attendees I had attracted to other online events not in Second Life, that my reading would attract a maximum of 30 avatars. I thus was very happy with the 36 avatars I counted in the audience as I took my place on the stage—more is always better for an author, as long as the event is not in Second Life, and the number of attendees shuts down the system (not Second Life as a whole but the specific audiovisual part of the system or sim where the reading is conducted). Of course, an in-person bookstore can attract an audience that exceeds its seating, but that's what standing room is for, and overflow audiences do not shut down the brick-and-mortar bookstore.

"Arton Tripsa" (an historical fiction writer from Australia in real life), "aurel Miles" (a writer from Vancouver, Canada, in real life, with no "L" for Laurel in her Second Life first name), "Kenny Hubble" (a professor in real life, also from Canada—more about Kenny follows), "iodach Gumbo" (an author from Romania, in real life, who created a lowercase avatar first name), "Kelsey Mertel" (an American author living in Greece, in real life), and "Dreame Destiny" (a publisher in real life from Australia), as well as "Polaris Snook," "Tinkerer Melville," "Edward Russell," "Toria Mumford," and "Zeropoint Thielt"—virtual beings whose real names and real-life locations I still do not know—were some of the avatars who walked, flew, or teleported in to my reading, in a pageantry of color, feathers, and costumes that exceeded anything you might find even at a *Star Trek* convention. But one thing that readings in Second Life and real life do have in common—they are likely to be well attended by other authors and, if the author giving the reading is a professor, by another professor and a student or two as well.

As indicated, "Starr Sonic" and her crew at SLCN.tv videotaped the reading. As of January 2012—four years after the reading in Second Life—the video clips of the reading I posted on YouTube and Blip.tv have received more than 6000 views. Thirty-six avatars at the live reading in Second Life, and more than 6000 views on YouTube and Blip.tv four years later, gives a good indication of the power of the Web outside Second Life, and YouTube in particular, in comparison: An event on Second Life put on YouTube has drawn almost 200 times the number of original virtual attendees or viewers. YouTube gives immortality—or at least, durability—to Second Life as well as real-life events.

Kenny Hubble, Second Life Astronomer

In real life, Ken Hudson is Managing Director of the Virtual World Design Centre at the Loyalist College in Canada. Not surprisingly, Ken has a keen interest in Second Life; it was his invitation to interview me about new new media in his Second Life Media Ecology symposium (Levinson, Interview by Ken Hudson, 2007) that brought me to Second Life in the first place in November 2007 and resulted in the "birth" of PaulLevinson Freenote.

One of Ken Hudson's other keen interests has always been astronomy. Hence his Second Life name, "Kenny Hubble." Kenny created the Caledon Astrotorium and The Caledon Astronomical Society, which looked upward via telescope, orrery (look that up!), and balloon rides to the stars in Second Life, 2008–2010. Caledon is a virtual place or sim—like Cookie Town Center and Book Island—but constructed to look and feel like a Victorian corner of the city, the kind of place that Charles Dickens or Charles Darwin might have strolled through on a sparkly wintry evening. Kenny told me he not only loved astronomy and looking at the heavens, but also looking at it with the sense of wonderment that he associates with Victorian eyes and minds, their belief in the progress of science, and the joy of new discovery. (I share his admiration of this aspect of Victorian culture.) The CAS's explanatory text explained that it operated "the planetarium as a public service to the citizens of Caledon and of Second Life. The Society holds regular events, including readings, lectures, discussions, demonstrations, social events, and other astronomically related activities" (Hudson/Hubble, 2008; see also Merlot, 2008).

A planetarium, if you think about it, is an ideal real-world place to build in Second Life. The images you see at the Hayden Planetarium, in New York City, are just that—images, brilliantly constructed, to give you the illusion that you are looking at this or that part of the night sky. We might even say, looking at the Hayden or any real-world planetarium through retro eyes, that we are seeing the stuff of Second Life, created decades earlier—or in the case of the Hayden Planetarium, which opened in 1935, more than 75 years before Second Life was possible on our little computer and smart phone screens. Unlike what we see through the Hubble Telescope, including raw photographs of what the Hubble sees—which is the cosmos as it is—Kenny Hubble's Caledon Astrotorium and planetariums in the real-world show artistic renderings of the cosmos. A photograph, of course, may be part of a Second Life, or a planetarium's, presentation. But the milieu in both environments is always more than photographic.

Ken Hudson told me (via Facebook message, December 26, 2008) that his Caledon Astrotorium received "over 100 visitors per week—many just use the space to relax in the stars. . . ." Not relax "looking or gazing at" the stars, but, relax "in" the stars. This is the "total immersion" I mentioned earlier. It is the total immersion in the medium McLuhan spoke of (see Levinson, 1999), without ever knowing Second Life.

And if you wanted more immersion in the stars in Second Life, you might have teleported over to the Van Gogh Museum in Second Life (Museum closed since 2009), walked out on the terrace, and seen the night sky cool and blazing with Van Gogh's "The Starry Night." And if not just Van Gogh but also Don McLean's "Starry Starry Night" was now in your head, there was Robbie Dingo's off-world page, "A Second Life Machinima" (Dingo, 2007), which as of January 2012 is still available. You do not need to be in Second Life to see this: "Shot on location in Second Life then post-produced," Dingo explains. "Ever looked at your favorite painting and wished you could wander inside?" (See Au, 2007, for further details about the creation of the video.) Dingo's video also lives on YouTube—again, the closest we have to media immortality.

And although art on Second Life requires access to Second Life or another online medium such as YouTube to be fully appreciated, the principles of digital art that come to life on Second Life have also migrated via other digital media to the real world. Sondro Kopp paints portraits of people who sit for him from afar, via Skype. As he explained on CNN (2012), "Monet would have gone completely bananas through Skype," because the essence of Impressionism, whether Van Gogh or Monet, was capturing not reality but the light that brings us its images.

Sex in Second Life

Not everything in Second Life is astronomy and painting. As is the case in real life, sex flourishes in all of its forms in Second Life.

Whether an assignation with a prostitute, a pick-up in a bar, or making love at home next to the fireplace with your Second Life spouse, sex in the virtual realm always requires two components: body parts and scripts.

The body parts are just what you would expect. You purchase breasts, derrières, and genitalia, which are available in all shapes, colors, and sizes. You "wear" them—that is, make them part of your avatar—as you would an article of clothing or a piece of jewelry. "That's a nice ass you're wearing" can be a literal compliment, more than a metaphor, in Second Life.

You can purchase body parts for yourself or give them to your lover. A woman avatar I interviewed in Second Life told me that she brought a man home to her Second Life bedroom, gave him a "script" for sex (see the next paragraph), and was not pleased to see when the man took off his clothes that he had a "Louisville Slugger" or baseball-bat–sized penis. "I gave him something more suitable," she said.

But body parts, as they are in real life, are just the beginning, or prerequisite, for sex in Second Life. All unusual movement of avatars in Second Life, any motion beyond walking, waving, flying, and teleporting (flying and teleporting are intrinsic to Second Life), are made possible by "scripts" of special programs to control or guide the avatar. Some scripts come in objects. If you see a chair and you want your avatar to be seated, you click on the "sit" option or script that is embedded in the image of the chair, and, voilà, your avatar is seated. Other scripts can be purchased or given to you by other avatars. If your avatar goes to a nightclub, you may well be offered scripts to do all kinds of dances. Your avatar and your avatar partner can rumba, waltz, or twist the virtual night away.

Sex scripts sometimes come packaged in beds or other "love furniture," or they can be offered by a potential partner. They vary as to length and the specific sexual activity desired. The specific moves programmed in these scripts represent the limit of your choice and control of the sexual act in Second Life. You can choose the script. But once you and your partner are in the script, you can't decide to shift positions or even hold a kiss a little longer. Spontaneity, in other words, is scripted.

How much would such body parts and scripts cost a Second Lifer looking for love? Typical ads posted in December 2008 from such major vendors as Animation Sensations and Henmations offered everything from beds to gazebos and hot tubs, with hundreds of animations (scripted moves for your lucky avatar) for every erotic position imaginable. These virtual *Kama Sutras* even offered realistic skin textures, and sofas for groups of lovers, all set to appropriate music, and all designed to make the Second Life sexual experience as authentic as possible. The prices ranged from L$550 to L$230,000 for someone who wanted to set up shop and retail all of the preceding. The cost of $550 L was about $20 US.

As is the case with all cybersex—going back to the French Minitel system in the 1980s and its origination of online sex via texting (see Levinson, 1992)—sex in Second Life has the advantage of not conveying sexually transmitted disease or resulting in unwanted pregnancy. But it is also prone to the drawback of all virtual or online social activity, sexual or otherwise: Unless you already know the real-life person running the avatar, you have no way of knowing the gender and age of that real-life person.

"Lost" in Second Life

The relationship between real, off-world life (life either offline or on systems other than Second Life) and Second Life flows both ways. Not only do denizens of Second Life make money, or try to make money, which can be converted into real currencies, but they bring into Second Life all manner of media and issues from real life, ranging from what I did with my books, to supporters of political candidates meeting via their avatars for discussions of how to work for their election in the real world, to groups on Second Life devoted to the appreciation of television shows seen in the real world.

"*Lost* in Second Life" refers to a group of devotees of the *Lost* television show in Second Life and not to being lost in Second Life, though one might say that some of the inhabitants of Second Life are lost in it, even though they may feel they have really found their truest lives in the game of Second Life. In May 2007, around the time of the extraordinary Season 3 finale (which I have described as one of the best hours ever on television, see Levinson, "*Lost*'s Season 3 Finale," 2007), several *Lost* fans began construction of a virtual *Lost* island in Second Life. Their goal was to create a place, similar to the island on the television program, where their avatars could meet and discuss the program. They later also created a website away from Second Life, sl-LOST.com, where they tell the story of their Second Life group and island. It is a story—a true story—of surprises and heartbreaks and redemptions, including a disappearing island, that almost rivals the story in the television series.

One of the deepest realities of Second Life, as we have seen, is that everything costs money. This means that, whether you want to set up a bookshop to sell your books or create an island to talk about *Lost*, someone has to pay Linden dollars, either in rental or purchase of the property, or someone in Second Life has to be willing to give you use of such property for free. My first bookstore, on Book Island, off Pulitzer Square in Second Life, cost me about $5 US a month in rental. I was later offered a free bookstore in another place in Second Life, The Artists' Village, so I closed the first one and opened the second version of The Soft Edge Book Shop. After about four months, the landlord disappeared and with it all of the stores on her island, including my bookshop. Another deep reality of Second Life is the intrinsic impermanence of its structures and creations (see the Kenny Hubble section). Although I could have reopened the bookstore elsewhere in Second Life—and may still do so, someday—I decided I was too busy (in part, with writing the first edition of this book) to reopen the store at that time.

The *Lost* group in Second Life encountered a similar problem of the rug—or island—being pulled out from under them. As they explain on their website, the original financial backer and owner of the island vanished one day in October 2007 without warning or explanation. The island was reopened in November 2007—not by the long-gone owner but by the administration of Second Life—"for 24 hours in order for members of the group to collect the items they made." The homeless-in-Second-Life group eventually found new backers and new headquarters, giving this true saga a happy ending. But the value of having a website, off of Second Life, was amply demonstrated. Before their second *Lost* island was created in Second Life, the website served as a way of keeping the group together. I got to know the group when it published an interview with me in January 2008, about *Lost*, conducted by one of the group's leaders (which, however, ironically vanished from the group's off-world website). I also visited the new headquarters in Second Life in 2008.

But why was it so important for this *Lost* group to meet via their avatars in Second Life, when they already had a Web page and could easily have IM'd about *Lost*, out of Second Life, as much as they liked? The answer gets, again, at the immersive appeal of Second Life versus the rest of the Web: When you're in Second Life, you feel, much more than on other nonsimulation sites on the Web, as if you are really in your community. The combination of the moving graphics and voices, the way you can move your avatar through this environment, creates a powerful illusion that you are actually in—rather than observing, listening to, or reading about—the Second Life world.

Lost was by no means the only old-medium television show to have a life, or at least an adventure, in Second Life. CBS's *CSI-NY*'s (fictional) agents entered Second Life to pursue someone who killed a Second Life denizen, in "real life," in a case of cyberstalking—that is, the victim was a fictitious flesh-and-blood person who in this television drama was playing the Second Life avatar. Viewers were "encouraged to join Second Life and investigate the case by following a link on the CBS website," as Duncan Riley explains in "*CSI: NY* Comes To Second Life Wednesday" (2007).

Second Life thus represents the epitome of a world of its own in a new new medium. You can pause a video on YouTube, stop editing on Wikipedia, leave your profile page on the screen and grab a bite to eat without missing too much on Facebook, but to leave the screen when you are connected to Second Life is, literally, to leave your avatar frozen or sleeping—that is what you, via your avatar, will look like to all the other avatars in your vicinity—and, of course, your avatar will neither see nor hear anything they say or do.

In contrast, Twitter and Foursquare allow you to work and play online without missing a bite in the real world—as does a podcast, which like all acoustic media, is designed to be listened to when you are doing something else. We examine this archetypal multitasking new new medium in the next section.

Podcasting

Historically, the recording and dissemination of images preceded the same for sound. Photography was developed by Daguerre in the 1830s, in contrast to the phonograph invented by Edison in 1876. Motion pictures, also invented by Edison—as well as the Lumière Brothers in France and William Friese-Greene in England, more or less independently—also preceded Marconi's radio in 1901 by more than a decade (see Levinson, 1997, for further details). Indeed, if we take cave paintings as a form of recorded images, we have this visual medium preceding any acoustic recording, as far as we know, by some 30,000 years. (The music box precedes the phonograph by less than a century.)

On the other hand, radio in 1901 certainly preceded the invention of television in 1927, and the commercial success of radio in the 1920s presaged the commercial success of television by at least 20 years.

And at this current stage—the year 2012—of the digital age, recording, editing, and dissemination of sound-only programs is still a bit easier than webcasting, YouTube, and the new new media recording, editing, and dissemination of audiovisual content. This is because editing audio is easier than editing video, where disruptive jump cuts usually need to be avoided. (Videorecording and live streaming are as easy as audio recording and streaming.)

The new new media recording and dissemination of sound—music, interviews, soliloquies—is known as podcasting. The "casting" part comes from broadcasting, or the widespread casting (from the broad casting of seeds in farming) or dissemination of first sound by radio and then images and sound via television. The "pod" comes from iPod, which was the device via which podcasts were first intended to be heard.

But podcasts are now easily available on any computer, smart phone, tablet, and indeed in cars, via Bluetooth connections to phone banks that play podcasts. Because radio, available in automobiles since Transitone in the late 1920s, and more recently just a click away on the Web, presents the same kinds of programs as found on podcasts, we could say that podcasts and radio are converging.

Except, the important fact remains that radio programs are professionally produced, whereas podcasts—like all new new media—can be made and disseminated by anyone.

In December 2008, a new member of Podcastalley.com, a social site for podcasters and listeners, asked if anyone could explain the characteristics and benefits of a podcast. I replied as follows, "It's an audio or audio-visual program you can get, for free, over the Web. Its advantage is that the podcast comes straight from the podcaster and does not have to meet whatever the requirements of radio and television broadcast producers. This means that the podcast can be more original and idiosyncratic, and the podcast does not have to attract x number of listeners or viewers in order to continue—that is completely up to the podcaster" (Levinson, "Response to 'What Is A Podcast,'" 2009).

How Is a Podcast Made?

You need a microphone and a sound-recording program to make a podcast. Like most new new media software, sound-recording programs can be purchased (such as Sound Forge, which I use) or found for free on the Web (Audacity would be an example). The commercial programs usually have a few more bells and whistles than the freebies, but the free programs certainly do the job.

Recording a podcast that sounds good takes a little talent, as well as a decent-sounding voice (unless the podcaster is going for a quirky sound). But mistakes, coughs, and other acoustic errors can usually be edited out with ease, and professional and free programs (the Levelator would be an example) can be used to improve the voice quality and reduce undo fluctuations in loudness and softness. (Editing out a cough in a video can be difficult, if you do not want a sudden shift of images or a jump cut.)

Podcasts vary in length from a few minutes to a few hours long. The longer the podcast, the bigger the file required to store it and the more bandwidth required to disseminate the podcast on the Web. Recordings can be stored in a variety of acoustic formats, ranging from uncompressed WAV files to highly compressed MP3s. The MP3s, in turn, can range from 64 kbs compression, which has the sound quality of talk you might hear on the radio, to 320 kbs, which provides crystal-clear CD-quality sound. The greater or more detailed the kbs compression of the sound file, the more space will be needed to store the file and the more bandwidth to disseminate it.

Once recorded, the podcast has to be uploaded someplace on the Web, from which it can be disseminated to the world—or to anyone with a computer, iPod, or smart phone.

Blueprint for a Podcast

Although a podcast requires more production than writing a blog, it shares the blog's and all new new media's advantage of being doable, capable of being produced, without needing anyone else's permission. Unlike the "showrunner" of a television series, or the person who first came up with the idea for the television show, or even the radio producer who has to run ideas through the station's program director, the podcaster can move from conception to production in hours or days, and sometimes minutes.

Here's an example of a podcast I produced a few years ago: an episode of *Light On Light Through* about cyberbullying. As I mentioned in the Myspace section earlier in this chapter, the publicist for the Truth on Earth band contacted me shortly after I had posted a blog on Myspace in late November 2008 about cyberbullying. The band wanted me to know about its new song "Shot With a Bulletless Gun," which I immediately realized was an example of the Internet's musical medicine for the new new media abuse of cyberbullying.

After I heard the song, I was thinking about what I could do to help promote it and asked the band members if they would like to be interviewed on *Light On Light Through*. They agreed. I called the band via Skype, via a process known as VOIP, or voice over IP. The connection sounded fine and cost nothing. I had a microphone and earphones—my standard podcasting gear. The band, which consisted then of three young women, Serena, Kiley, and Tess, used the built-in microphone and speaker system of their Mac. I used another free program, "Hot Recorder for VOIP" to record the program. (But I needed an "Audio Conversion for Hot Recorder" program, which I had purchased the year before for $15, to translate the Hot Recorder file into a WAV file I could use to make the podcast.)

The interview took 15 minutes and included a live performance of a new song by the band about homeless people. The band had emailed an MP3 of "Bulletless Gun" to me to be included in the podcast. The recording of the interview had good sound quality (you never know for sure with recordings until you play them back). The entire process, at that point, including the recording, had taken about 45 minutes.

I recorded an introduction and brief discussion of the problem of cyberbullying—an oral rendition of my written blog—the next day. I inserted my "bumper" music, at the very beginning and end of the podcast. It is a riff taken from "Looking for Sunsets (in the Early Morning)," the lead song from my 1972 album, *Twice Upon a Rhyme*. I spiced up the podcast with sound effects here and there and added a few commercials for my novels, *The Silk Code* and *The Plot to Save Socrates*. (I did not insert any paid commercials—see *"Advertising on Podcasts"* later in this section.) I did add several "promos," or free ads for other podcasts, at the end of my podcast. After the podcast was totally assembled, I ran it through another free program, the "Levelator," which as I mentioned earlier equalizes, or gives equivalent tone and volume, to all the pieces of the podcast. This is especially important when the podcast consists of different parts, recorded in different ways, as was the case with this episode of *Light On Light Through*, which consisted of just my voice (at the beginning); my interview with Serena, Kiley, and Tess; a studio-recorded MP3 of "Shot With a Bulletless Gun"; and the band's live performance of "Where You Sleep Tonight."

All of this took less than an hour. And the podcast was then ready for distribution.

Podcast Storage and Distribution: Players, iTunes, and RSS Feeds

Before a podcast can be disseminated—or listened to on laptops, iPods, smart phones, and tablets—it has to be uploaded from the producer's computer to a storage site on the Web. Such sites function much like blog sites, except the "posts" are acoustic podcasts. Blog posts sometimes accompany the podcasts on such sites and can be read before, after, or during the playing of the podcasts. If the podcast is also delivered via a "feed" to iTunes or some other system from which the podcast can be downloaded for free for listening, the blog posts can be automatically set or "coded" to accompany the podcast, so as to be readable on the iPod or smart phone's screen. Podcast storage sites usually do that unless set otherwise.

As is the case with blog sites, podcast storage sites are either free or "rentable" under a variety of options. My *Levinson News Clips* podcast, which started as brief, 5-minute commentaries on media and political news but soon developed into brief reviews of television shows, is housed on Mevio.com, for free. My *Ask Lev* podcast, which provides 5 to 10 minutes of advice for writers, is hosted on TalkShoe.com, also for free. Mevio and TalkShoe on occasion insert their own ads at the beginning and/or end of the podcasts they host, and Mevio offers some of its podcasters opportunities to earn advertising income (see *"Advertising on Podcasts,"* later in this section). There are also ads on their websites that house your podcast—that is one of the ways those sites earn revenue. My *Light On Light Through* podcast, usually about 30 minutes in length and devoted to various aspects of popular culture and politics, can be found at Libsyn.com, which charges me $15 per month and can cost as little as $5 or as much as $75 per month (as of January

2012) depending on how many podcasts and what length and compression you want to store on the system. There are half a dozen other podcast hosts available, free or for hire.

Why would a podcast producer pay for storage rather than use a free site? Libsyn offers highly detailed, much better statistics on podcast dissemination than do the free sites. A podcaster is interested not only in how many times a podcast has been listened to but also via what means of dissemination, and the podcaster prefers such information updated on an immediate or close-to-immediate basis. Libsyn does both, as well as providing a blog environment for posts about the podcasts that is available on the HTML design level to the podcaster, which gives the podcaster more control over the look and feel of the blog, including the capacity to add Google AdSense, Amazon, and the whole range of possible advertising revenue available for bloggers (see "Monetizing Your Blog" in chapter 6).

Once the podcast is housed on a site, the most straightforward way of attracting listeners is by posting links to the podcasts, in all possible places on the Web, just as a blogger would for a blog. As of January 2012, my *Light On Light Through* podcast (87 episodes) received more than 210,000 plays, *Levinson News Clips* nearly 600,000 plays (400 episodes), and *Ask Lev* (68 episodes) more than 40,000. More than 90 percent of the podcasts were heard on any one of several "podcast players" I have on my *Infinite Regress* blog and the podcast pages themselves.

A podcast player is in effect a kind of widget that contains links to the MP3s of each podcast episode stored on your podcast-hosting service. Libsyn, Mevio, and Talkshoe automatically provide their own links to every blog post on their pages with a podcast. They also provide players that can be put on other blog pages and websites. At the same time, Big Contact offers "feed players" that can be put on any blog pages and websites, including Libsyn's. I have both kinds of podcast players, and several others, on all blogs and podcasts over which I have HTML control (see "Blogging for Others" in chapter 6 for more).

Of the other 10 percent of my podcast plays, nearly 9 percent were via iTunes, and the other 1 percent on smaller "aggregation" or distribution systems such as Zune. Thus, nearly 99 percent of my listeners either heard my podcast by direct link (90 percent) or via iTunes (9 percent).

In all cases, the podcast was free to the listener, which, unsurprisingly, is one of its appeals. Indeed, iTunes, which functions as an old medium, or an old medium in the new medium of the Web when it charges for its music, performs much more like a new new medium when it provides podcasts (and vidcasts, which are podcasts with not just sound but images) for free. These can be heard either by logging directly onto iTunes and searching for the podcast or by subscribing to the podcast on iTunes.

But how does the podcast get from the producer's host site (Libsyn) to iTunes? RSS, an acronym for Real Simple Syndication, does the heavy lifting. Podcast hosts provide easy ways of getting a podcast series onto iTunes. The host sends out a feed— an RSS feed—which iTunes or in fact any RSS receiver can pick up. In the case of iTunes, the podcast producer has to first submit a description of the podcast, with its unique RSS feed (provided by the hosting service), to iTunes. Once accepted by iTunes—and I don't know of any podcast which was ever rejected (in contrast to iTunes' stringent gatekeeping for record labels and other vendors of music)—each episode of the podcast automatically appears on iTunes, brought there by the RSS feed. Other podcast distributors work the same way, although podcasts do not have to go through a formal submission process.

Case Study of Podcast Success: Grammar Girl

Mignon Fogarty started her *Grammar Girl* podcast—more formally, *Grammar Girl's Quick and Dirty Tips for Better Writing*—in July 2006, the year in which podcasting first emerged as an important new new medium. Four months later, in November 2006, *Grammar Girl* had received more than one million listens (Lewin, 2006). The number had grown to more than 40 million by January 2012, and Mignon had appeared on CNN and the *Oprah Winfrey Show*. *Grammar Girl* is often in the top five most-listened-to podcasts on iTunes, and Fogarty's paperback book based on the podcast, *Grammar Girl's Quick and Dirty Tips for Better Writing*, was No. 9 on *The New York Times*' best-seller listing in August 2008. Her *Grammar Girl's 101 Misused Words You'll Never Confuse Again* was on *The Washington Post's* best-seller list in July 2011. These accomplishments are another example of the power of new new media to call the shots in traditional modes of public presentation. Fogarty was a science writer before she started the podcast, and the success of *Grammar Girl* made her a star.

But how did a show about split infinitives and infelicitous adjectives become so popular? Bloggers such as Tucker Max (2006) have had best-selling books, understandable due to the raw sexual nature of the content in Max's case, but a show about grammatical subtleties? We might think that just about everyone is interested in improving his or her grammar, so the show had a big potential audience, but that's probably not the reason for *Grammar Girl's* success and not even true in the first place. Indeed, had Fogarty presented her podcast idea to a radio station, it is unlikely that the show would have been given a broadcast spot—I am not aware of any show on commercial radio about grammar. The enormous success of *Grammar Girl* thus can likely be explained by something else: the capacity of podcast listeners to receive useful lessons in grammar, in a way that seems like fun because the delivery is still so new. (See Levinson, 1977, for more on the debut of technologies as toys.) It's both valuable and enjoyable, in other words, not just to hear a witty show about grammar but also to hear it on your iPod or computer or smart phone at a time of your choosing.

Podcasts on Smart Phones and in Cars

RSS feeds can also bring podcasts to sites that disseminate sound in ways very different from iTunes. Podlinez.net, for example, assigns each podcast series a telephone number. When one calls that number, the most recent episode of the podcast is played. (The basic service is, as of January 2012, free to the podcaster and the listener, with several more sophisticated options for sale.)

Availability via phone opens up all sorts of additional possibilities for podcast dissemination and reception. My Prius has a Bluetooth connection for my BlackBerry, which works even for a non-smart cell phone, and plays the voice of the person I'm talking to right out of the radio speakers. I can call the Podlinez phone number and the podcast will play on the car radio. Thousands of podcasts are available in this way.

Stepping back and looking at the larger picture of this media environment, what we have with podcasts that can be heard through car radios is a co-option, or merging, of the digital (podcast) and broadcast (radio) ages—or yet another integration of old media (radio) and new new media (podcast).

The result is a very different kind of "radio" in the car. The traditional broadcast radio comes into the car via a professional production, broadcast from a big central facility, at a specified time. The podcast on the car radio can be produced from a rocking chair—mine often are—and is uploaded to a website that produces an RSS feed. It then becomes available to the listener any time he or she chooses to call the Podlinez number. In both the production and the reception end, the sound program has been greatly democratized. This is the beginning of a much larger co-option of old by new new media, which will include YouTube on televisions in living rooms (Orlando, 2009) and podcasts on car radios without cellphones. Aereo, which provides broadcast television on smart phones, tablets, and laptops (Carter, 2012) is another step in this co-option from the opposite direction (old media on new new media devices).

Traditional broadcast radio and podcasts do have a very significant characteristic in common: both are free. But podcasting also provides another kind of free-of-charge acoustic program, one which otherwise would have to be paid for by the listener: the podiobook.

Podiobooks

Audiobooks are still a small part of the book publishing industry. February 2011 statistics reported $90.3 million for e-book sales (exceeding paper books) versus $6.9 million for audio books (Ogasawara, 2011). But audiobooks have their undeniable advantages. If a driver wants to enjoy a book while driving, certainly an audiobook is preferable, and far safer, than opening a book and reading it, whether e-book or paper.

Audiobooks come in various configurations: just narrated or the parts more performed, with sound effects and music or not, abridged or complete. Depending on the length and production, audiobooks cost more or less the same as a hardcover or expensive trade paper book, usually between $15 and $30.

Tee Morris and Evo Terra came up with an alternative a few years ago: "podiobooks," or audiobooks available in sequential episodes, a chapter or two per episode. Like all podcasts, these podiobooks are free. Readers, however, are encouraged to make donations to the authors and/or narrators, via PayPal, with the Podiobook.com site keeping 25 percent of the proceeds. (See also *Podcasting for Dummies*, 2nd edition, 2008, by Tee Morris, Chuck Tomasi, and Evo Terra for more on their approach to podcasting.)

Shaun Farrell produced and narrated a podiobook of my 1999 science fiction novel, *The Silk Code*, in 2007. The novel was already well known in science fiction circles—it had won the Locus award for best first science fiction novel—but there's nothing as appealing as something for free, especially when alternative versions cost money. The podiobook placed in the top 20 downloaded in 2007 (Podiobooks did not provide exact rankings for the top 20).

Poor economies make free content even more appealing. In January 2009, *Time* magazine wondered if podiobooks were "publishing's next wave," noting that "book sales are down; MacMillan has laid off employees, as have Random House and Simon & Schuster; and Houghton Mifflin Harcourt has suspended the purchase of most new manuscripts" (Florin, 2009). Evo Terra told me via email that more than 1.3 million episodes from podiobooks had been downloaded as of January 2012.

Podcasts and Copyright: Podsafe Music

But providing content for free to the audience—whether podcasts or blogs—can be difficult if the producer has to pay for part of that content. This problem usually does not arise in blogging, where quotes from other sources can be worked into the blog, without payment, under Fair Use, and it certainly doesn't arise when a podcast consists of just the podcaster talking. But what if the podcaster wants to play some music? Fair Use only applies when a small segment of the original is used. In the case of a track of music, the usual practice is to play all of it.

The problem of how to pay songwriters for performances of their music first arose and was dealt with almost a century ago in the dawn of radio. ASCAP (American Society of Composers, Authors and Publishers, created in 1914) licensed music for live performances and expanded to radio. BMI (Broadcast Music, Inc., created in 1940) did the same for radio, and now ASCAP and BMI both license music for broadcast on radio and television. I am a member of both organizations, as a songwriter. ASCAP distributed $845 million to its members in 2010, and BMI distributed $796 million that year.

ASCAP and BMI collect such monies as "performance rights" fees, payable by radio and television stations and networks. Given the billions of dollars of profit earned by television and radio every year, payments to ASCAP and BMI are not excessive.

Where does this leave podcasters? They can earn money from advertising (see "Advertising on Podcasts," later in this section), which could pay for music performance rights, but what if a podcaster wants to play music but runs no advertising? Should these podcasters violate the copyright of recording artists and songwriters, and play their music without compensation? This problem of copyright and compensation is the podcasting equivalent of what I called the "Achilles' Heel of YouTube" in chapter 4—the violation of copyright in numerous videos posted on YouTube. My solution to YouTube's problem was that copyright should be relaxed, to allow posting of any content online that does not remove the creator's attribution or earn money for the poster without the creator's permission (much the same as what Creative Commons advocates).

Podcasting came up with another, partial solution. Adam Curry, whose pioneering championship of podcasting in 2004, after a career as an MTV "veejay," earned him the moniker of "Podfather" (Jardin, 2005), created the "Podsafe music" network in 2005 (Sharma, 2005). Its idea is that artists and songwriters upload their music to the Podsafe network, where it is made available, free of charge and without giving up the copyright, to podcasters, for the sole purpose of being played on a podcast. The artists get publicity and the podcasters get free music in this symbiotic relationship. (Yes, I have about half a dozen of my recordings in the Podsafe network. I was pleased when one of my least-known songs, "Snow Flurries," by Levinson and Krondes, 1969, was played on Erin Kane and Kristin Brandt's popular *Manic Mommies* podcast in February 2007.)

But the Podsafe solution is partial because podcasters might well still want to play a Beatles recording, or music by anyone who wants a performance fee for a podcast play. At present, such podcasters have a choice of playing the music in violation of copyright or earning enough via advertising revenues to pay a performance fee, if they prefer not to produce the podcast at a financial loss.

Advertising on Podcasts

Advertising on podcasts—or podcasters making money from ads placed in their podcasts—is more like the traditional television and radio approach to advertising than Google AdSense, Amazon Affiliate, and similar kinds of advertising on blogs that we examined in chapter 6.

The way most podcasts obtain paid advertising on their podcasts is via affiliation with a monetizing podcasting community, or, in more old-fashioned terms, an organization that acts as a broker or middleman between advertisers and podcasters. These can be podcast-hosting sites such as Mevio, or services devoted purely or mostly to advertising deals, such as the "Blubrry" community, run by Raw Voice. Both offer a variety of advertising deals to their podcasters. They come in two general types.

1. GoDaddy.com—the place where most domain names are registered and well known to the general public through its saucy Super Bowl ads—and many other well-known companies ranging from car rental to home improvement offer commission ad deals. The podcaster is given talking points and asked to talk in his or her own voice for 30 to 60 seconds about the sponsor. The pitch ends with a unique code, "xxx Levin" or "podcast xxx," that the listener is told to use when ordering anything from the sponsor in response to the special deals offered in the ad. The podcaster is paid a flat fee for every sale made in response to the ad—$10 or $20 or whatever number of dollars—or a flat percentage, depending on the nature of the promotion. Such ad campaigns can generate thousands of dollars per month for podcasters.

This commission approach can also work with ads that are recorded by the advertiser and given to the podcaster, or with ads that the podcaster reads verbatim from specific scripts provided by the advertiser. Many advertisers, however, prefer the podcaster to deliver the ad with his or her own words and style, because that endows the ad with a more personal quality and can be more effective with the podcaster's loyal listeners. Late-night radio, such as the *Long John Nebel Show* in New York City, used that kind of personal rendition of ads for years. But most current radio shows, such as the Bob Shannon show on WCBS-FM Radio in New York City, play ads in which the disc jockey, in this case Bob Shannon, reads from a script verbatim.

2. A very different kind of ad buy, based not on commissions for actual sales but on the number of people who hear the ad, is also offered by Mevio and by Raw Voice to podcasters. The ad itself can be prerecorded, spoken verbatim from a script, or ad-libbed by the podcaster from talking points provided by the advertiser—just as with the commission ads—but, unlike the commission approach, the podcaster needs to report the number of people who heard the podcast. As is the case with advertising in old media newspapers and broadcast media, the podcaster is paid on a cost-per-thousand basis. Mevio keeps its own tally of these statistics. Blubrry (Raw Voice) provides its own "counter" for numbers of listens—sometimes also referred to as downloads, even though the podcast can also be listened to live, and live listens count the same as downloads. Note that number of listens is not the same thing as number of people who have listened, because one person, of course, can listen to a podcast more than once, but I am using these measures here interchangeably, because the best that any stat counter can do is keep track of the IP addresses from which a podcast is accessed. One person, if he or she wants, can obviously listen to the same podcast more than once from different IP addresses. Five thousand listens or downloads in a given period of time can earn more than $500 from ads paid for on a cost-per-thousand basis.

This payment for number of listens which is equivalent, in blogging, to payment for impressions or views of ads, in contrast to payment for clicks or clicks with purchases—is clearly a more reliable source of revenue than payment for actual sales, or commissions. There is no guarantee that any of a podcaster's listeners, however many they may be, will go on to buy the advertised product or service. Why, then, would any podcaster choose the commission method?

Part of the answer is that the podcaster usually has no choice. Advertisers are reluctant to waste time on a podcast with just a handful of listeners—not the time needed to plan the ad campaign but the accounting time required to determine the negligible payment for the small number of listeners. In contrast, commission payment requires no accounting and no reports, other than keeping track of the special promotion codes that already accompany online sales made in response to the ads.

But another part of the answer is that a small audience of listeners, highly responsive to a commission advertising campaign, can generate far more income for the podcaster than an ad campaign for a larger audience with a payout based on the number of listeners. For example, 30 listeners out of an audience of 1000 purchasing a product or service with a $20 commission would yield the podcaster $600, in contrast to a $10 payment for every thousand listeners and an audience of 3000, which would net the podcaster only $30. In other words, the commission podcaster would earn 20 times as much as the cost-per-thousand colleague, even though the commission podcast had only one-third the audience. Of course, the commission mode of payment is nonetheless more of a gamble, because the commission podcaster's audience might not make even a single purchase.

This brings into play another question, the answer to which can also help explain why a podcaster goes with either a commission or a CPM (cost per thousand) approach, and, indeed, why podcasters with small numbers of listeners can still take on ads on a CPM basis. The question is why would a podcaster go with an ad broker or an ad-providing site rather than working with advertisers directly?

First, ad brokers take a substantial portion—as much as 30 percent or more—from all ad revenues earned by podcasters who play ads that come from their deals. That might be reason enough for any podcaster to want instead to work directly with the advertiser—except, most podcasters have little or no knowledge about whom to contact for ad deals.

Even if the podcasters did, the ad broker helps in an additional way, of special benefit to the podcaster with a small number of listeners. The ad broker or ad-providing podcast host negotiates deals with advertisers who want, for example, 10,000 listens, by people listening to a podcast on a topic of value to the advertiser, say, a podcast about movies and television, which would be a good place for Netflix to place advertising. The advertiser does not care if these 10,000 listens come from one podcast or a thousand podcasts—all that counts are the statistics that accurately show that the ad was listened to or downloaded 10,000 times (or via 10,000 IPs). Thus, a podcaster with just 100 listeners in the period of time covered by the deal (which could be a week, a month, or several months) can get a piece of this action. If $1000 is earned from the 10,000 listens, the podcaster with just 100 listens would earn $10 for participation in this deal (or, actually, $7, after deduction of the ad broker's cut).

Podcast ad brokers and ad-providing hosts usually require the podcaster to agree not to work directly with an advertiser who has come to the podcaster through the broker's service. This seems only fair, to protect the broker, and is another reason direct deals with advertisers are rare for most podcasters. Some ad brokers also insist that their podcasters take on no ads other than those provided by the broker. But should a podcaster be fortunate enough to be solicited directly by an advertiser, in a way that does not conflict with any agreements between podcaster and ad broker, the podcaster would be wise to consider it.

There is just about no downside to running advertising on your podcast, other than the amount of time it might take to report the statistics. This is usually just a few minutes, and even this is not needed if the ad broker or ad-providing podcast host provide their own statistics.

But some listeners and podcasters might see one other, less tangible aspect as a drawback to running ads on podcasts. The ad, unless it is a public service ad, makes the podcast "commercial." The podcast, of course, would still be available free of charge and, in that very important sense, would be noncommercial, whether it included ads or not. But for some people, myself not included, who regard noncommerciality—not making money from a creative work—as an ideal in itself, an ad on a totally free podcast could be seen as a betrayal.

Free promo exchanges—advertisements for podcasts that podcasters exchange and play on their respective podcasts at no charge—can be an attractive option for those who eschew any kind of commercial advertising. Or they can be and are often played along with paid-for ads. The *Mike Thinks News* podcast plays both, as do my *Light On Light Through*, *Levinson News Clips*, and *Ask Lev* podcasts. The free promo exchange in podcasting works the same as link exchanges in blogging. Podcasters would like their promos to be on as many other podcasts as possible. But because every promo for your podcast played on another podcast requires you to play a promo for the other podcast on your podcast, you need to make sure the promos do not dominate your podcast show.

Live Streaming

Podcasts can be considered a form of publishing—sound rather than text and, in the case of vidcasts (podcasts with video, which we will examine in the next section), publishing of audiovisual productions. But sound can also be "streamed" live on the Web, in which case the podcast becomes a form of broadcasting, or Internet radio.

Indeed, traditional broadcast radio has been live streaming online for at least eight years. WCBS Radio in New York City, which commenced broadcasting (as WAHG) in September 1924, began "simulcasting" online at the end of 2004. You could not ask for a better example of an old medium joining the new media world, much as traditional print newspapers such as *The New York Times* have online venues. When I was interviewed every Sunday morning from 2006–2008 about media, politics, and popular culture on KNX Radio (see Levinson, "The KNX 1070 Interviews," 2007)—the CBS all-news station in Los Angeles—the broadcast was simulcast online, and the majority of email I received was from listeners nowhere near Los Angeles. This globalization, one of the key features of new media, and thus new new media, is one of the main advantages of an old medium simulcasting online. The other would be that you can hear it on your computer, or via an app on your smart phone or tablet, which can make listening easier and more discreet than turning on a radio in your office. But unlike true new new media, a radio broadcast simulcast on the Web is subject to the same top-down control as radio broadcast the old-fashioned way. When KNX decided in 2008 that it wanted to feature CBS news people and commentators rather than outside professors, my regular weekly interviews on KNX concluded (and were replaced by occasional interviews with me). In contrast, a podcast series, whether recorded or simulcast, ends when the podcaster decides—there is no boss other than the creator in the realm of new new media. (Of course, a podcast that is a copy or adjunct of a cable TV or traditional mass-media show—such as by CNN's Piers Morgan or MSNBC's Rachel Maddow, both of whom do podcasts—can be terminated if and when the network so decides.)

BlogTalk Radio, launched in August 2006, offers live streaming and podcast archiving, and features anyone who comes forward with an idea, a microphone, and a computer connection. As the BlogTalk Radio website (2009) correctly notes, "Finally, a 16-year-old expressing her views and passions from Jacksonburg, Ohio, could secure quality air time alongside famous personalities." David Levine (2008) said it was the "newest form of new media; the audio version of the Internet blog." And, indeed, BlogTalk Radio is five months younger than Twitter and its March 2006 debut (though by 2009 not younger than Foursquare, which came online a year after Levine's article), and it is an "audio version" of a blog. But straight-up podcasting would be a better example of an audio blog, because the most distinctive characteristic of BlogTalk Radio is that it is live streaming, which would make it most like a live blog (a blog written and posted in real time, as commentary to a live event like a baseball game).

Talkshoe is BlogTalk Radio's main competition. It has roots that go back to April 2005 but was launched in its current form in June 2006, or two months before BlogTalk Radio. The main difference between the two is that Talkshoe paid its producers a small amount for every listener and download (in the case of its podcasts), though Talkshoe "paused" this "cash" program in June 2008, and as of January 2012 this "pause" has been permanent. In contrast, BlogTalk Radio started an advertising revenue-sharing program for its producers in January 2008, which pays both on audio ads inserted in the live streams and podcasts, and on banner ads placed on the Web pages for the radio programs. (Talkshoe also offers ad deals for its podcasts, similar to Blubrry's.) The bottom line, financially, is that Talkshoe's per-listener/download fees were a more reliable source of revenue. (See Talkshoe, 2009, for more details.)

Talkshoe hosts my recorded *Ask Lev* podcast. Unlike BlogTalk Radio, which offers podcasts only as recordings of its live-streamed shows, Talkshoe also offers the option of a stand-alone, recorded podcast with no live streaming (as is the case with podcasts on Libsyn and Mevio). *Ask Lev* was brought to Talkshoe by the *10-Minute Lesson* network, which received a percentage of my *Ask Lev* earnings for the first year.

As of January 2012, I have not hosted any live radio shows on BlogTalk Radio or Talkshoe. (I did participate as a guest on Shaun OMac's BlogTalk Radio show about *Journeyman* in the Fall of 2007, on the Gypsy Poet's BlogTalk Radio show in May 2009, and on Máia Whitaker's show on Talkshoe in February 2008.) The reason I have not hosted a live show is that I do not want to be locked into a specific time; I value the podcaster's power to record the podcast at times of the podcaster's choosing. This highlights one of the prime decisions of all new new media producers—live blogging versus "regular" blogging, live conversations on Twitter versus posting of one-liners for later reading, and live streaming of audio (and visual) versus podcasting and vidcasting. The choice goes back more than a decade, to the first expression of new media in the late 1980s and early 1990s, and the advantages of IMing, or instant messaging, and chatting versus email. The two methods, of course, both have their advantages—just as did live conversation versus letter writing in a world before email—which is why social media such as Facebook provide both IMing and email-like messaging. The producer of a new new medium live show on BlogTalk Radio and Talkshoe can have the show recorded and saved as a podcast with no additional work needed. But the podcast recording of a live show might lack some of the sound effects and production values of a podcast recorded from scratch—just as a film of a theatrical performance will be different from a film made as a film in the first place. This means that someone who is weighing whether to produce a live-stream show or a podcast still needs to decide which is more consonant with what the producer wishes to create. (See "Occupy Wall Street" in chapter 10 for video live streaming as an essential news medium.)

Similar issues arise with live, interactive streaming for education, or webinars.

Webinars and the Move to Vidcasts

A live-streamed radio show need not be interactive—the show could be streamed without any callers or input from anyone other than the producer—but every live-streamed new new media show I've ever heard has featured callers, who connect to the show online, via VOIP or via telephone. In contrast, although broadcast radio can and does integrate callers into its simulcast programming, these calls come into the radio station, that is, into the source of the broadcast in the offline world, not via the Internet (unless the caller is using a VOIP phone to reach the radio station's control room). Thus, another difference between new new media live streaming and old media streaming on the Web is that the new new media live streaming can easily feature call-ins from people anywhere in the world, at no charge to them.

Call-ins via computer are the essence of webinars—seminars conducted on the Web—which can be distinguished from live-streaming lectures in which the call-in is not crucial to the presentation. A typical webinar, conducted via Go To Meeting, ReadyTalk, or any number of similar organizations, begins with a preparatory email sent to one or more participants, with a specific time and link to click to get to the webinar. As is the case with podcasts, the webinar can be conducted via the computer's speakers and microphone, but the sound exchange is more clear and private when the caller has earphones or earbuds and uses a more professional microphone. The moderator or webinar leader can see who has logged on to the webinar site and can test the connections.

In a typical webinar, the moderator controls who can talk—the same as in a call-in show on BlogTalk Radio. But unlike BlogTalk Radio and Talkshoe, where the Web page is secondary and the talk is primary, the Web page in the case of the webinar is just as important as the talk. In a full multimedia webinar, the moderator will in effect conduct a tour of the Web page, play videos, show graphics, and demonstrate programs. The participants will see all of this on their computer, smart phone, or tablet screens, will hear the moderator describe what is happening in the videos and other multimedia, and will be able to ask and answer questions. Text chat boxes are usually available, in case the audio fails or if the moderator or participants want to communicate something more easily written than spoken, such as a URL. If the moderator and user have webcams, the webinar can be video, but this is not essential to the webinar, unless some visual characteristic such as what the webinar participants are wearing is germane to the subject of the webinar.

Podcasts, as indicated earlier, can have video with sound rather than sound only. Usage varies as to what they are then called—vidcasts or just podcasts. The "podcast" appellation probably makes more sense, because the "pod" is neither intrinsically audio nor video but derives from iPod. The most logical designations would therefore seem to be that podcasts can be either vidcasts or audiocasts, but terminology that catches on may not necessarily be the most logical.

And, indeed, whatever they are called, vidcasts posted on YouTube and iTunes are increasingly more prominent in our culture than audio podcasts, which, in many ways, have taken second place under vidcasts as the cutting edge of podcast media, just as radio did vis-à-vis television in broadcast media. The Vatican, Queen of England,

and U.S. President YouTube channels discussed in chapter 4 are essentially recorded (non-live-streaming) vidcasts. On the more amateur, consumer-become-producer level, sites such as Mevio prefer vidcasts over audio podcasts as recipients of their ad deals. The blueprint for production of a vidcast is essentially the same as for an audio podcast, with additional work and talent needed for lighting, image-framing, and video editing for the vidcast.

Webinars, whether audio or video, can be conducted for business, education, or fun. If the user's computer has a big enough memory, then email and other regular functions of the computer can be accessed during the webinar. But the power of users' and moderators' laptops or desktop computers is the weak link of webinars. In the dozens of webinars I have attended (the majority of which have been on Second Life—see the previous section), there has rarely been a time when one or more of the participants has not gone silent and needed to log back on to resume participation. Webinar software also limits the number of participants.

Webinars and their educational uses can be seen as one of the loftier applications of new new media. Of course, a private or closed webinar can be conducted on any topic— including a planned criminal activity. In the next chapter, we turn to "The Dark Side of New New Media."

CHAPTER 9

The Dark Side of New New Media

I HAVE FOR DECADES BEEN DELIVERING A LECTURE TO MY CLASSES, and at conferences and symposia, titled "Guns, Knives, and Pillows." The lecture seeks to answer the question of whether some technologies are inherently good or bad in their use and impact on people.

I start with guns—they kill and wound people and are implements of crime. Indeed, they help make some violent crimes possible. So the gun is bad, right? It is a weapon that we would be better off without. But what if someone uses a gun as a weapon to stop or prevent a crime? Or not as a weapon against humans at all but as a way of getting food? Or as a technology of sport? Or, again as a weapon, but to defend our nation against violent attack? These cases make it clear that, although we might argue that the world as a whole would be better off without guns, we cannot consider them only or exclusively devices of evil.

Okay, then, what about the other side—can we think of a technology that is consistently, solely good? Is there a device with no ill effects? How about a pillow? It is soft, comfortable, and helps us sleep. So far, so good. But a pillow can also be used to murder someone via suffocation. This means that the pillow can be used to accomplish something that is not so good. Just as the gun cannot be considered solely a "bad" technology, neither can the pillow be considered solely good. Guns and pillows are actually a lot alike, in that they can each be used for good or bad.

Perhaps the problem is that we are looking at weak examples. How about stronger, more powerful technologies? Nuclear energy, atomic power, started off with a pretty bad reputation—atom bombs and nuclear weapons. Even that, however, had a morally ambiguous component; historians are still arguing about whether President Harry Truman was right to drop the atom bomb, twice, on Japan. On the one hand, it soon brought the world, in the Cold War that followed, to the brink of atomic destruction. And it killed many innocent civilians in Japan. On the other hand, the Japanese government was insisting on continuing the war, which would have meant the death of some additional number of American soldiers, had the bomb not been dropped. And Japan did attack the United States to start the war in the first place, not vice versa. Further, in addition to those ethical controversies, nuclear energy has been put to indisputably good use as a source of energy to generate electrical power and in medicine via radiation therapy. Nuclear energy thus turns out to be like guns and pillows, too, with both good and bad results for humanity.

Can we think about any stronger example of a good technology? How about medicine, which, based on its understanding of microbes and viruses, cures or reduces the damage of illness? Unfortunately, that same technology can and has been turned into a weapon arguably as dangerous as nuclear weapons—germ warfare. This indeed was used in World War I and by Saddam Hussein against Iran and his own people in Iraq, but even Adolf Hitler, fearing it could be used against German troops, refrained from using it in World War II. So medical technology ends up in the same category as guns, pillows, and nuclear energy: All can be used for good and bad purposes.

All technologies, indeed, are best described, in their capacity for good or bad, as knives. A knife can be used to cut food, which is good, and to stab an innocent person, which is bad. The determining factor in whether the knife—or whatever the technology— is used for good or bad turns out not to be the technology but the human being or group of humans using the technology.

In this chapter, we look at how the knives of new new media, which up until this point we have examined mostly with an eye to their advantages, can be used in the wrong hands for bad. Unfortunately, but not surprisingly, the evidence is that they can. We thus consider how the very advantages of new new media, when understood by people with evil intentions, can be used to hurt us.

Pre-New New Media Abuses: Bullying, Flaming, and Trolling

Some misuses and abuses of Web life predate new new media and were already part of the older new media constellation from which new new media arose.

Email, as is the case with any kind of communication, can be used to harass and cyberbully. Lori Drew used Myspace's message system to send the deceptive "the world would be better off without you" note (see the previous chapter), but it could just as easily have been sent via any email. And, indeed, email is used to convey all manner of spam and scams, ranging from easy ways to increase your sexual assets; to offers to entrust millions of dollars in your safekeeping by some desperate widow on the other side of the world, in order to get your bank account information; to messages urging you to immediately log on to your PayPal account, designed to get you to unknowingly give up your password to someone who would clean out your account.

Confidence games, of course, predate the Internet. There were probably Cro-Magnons who charmed the prehistorically naïve out of their best shells and furs. But the absence of a face and voice in email has long made it especially well-suited for all kinds of swindles.

Bullying was probably going on in Cro-Magnon circles as well—it certainly has long been a distressing feature of our schoolyards. Faceless, voiceless names on the Web have made bullying easier to mete out, too.

But bullying in a schoolyard or any physical place is usually more dangerous than cyberbullying, because physical intimidation is involved and can escalate into a "beat down." And, as we saw in chapter 4, YouTube, unfortunately, has given physical bullies an additional inducement, by providing a worldwide audience for uploaded videos of the beatings. Victoria Lindsay, a 16-year-old girl in Lakeland, Florida, was hospitalized in March 2008 after receiving a severe beating from six teenage girls, who videotaped it and told police they were responding to "trash" that the victim had posted about them on Myspace. "Police say the teens planned to post the video on YouTube," Rich Phillips reported on CNN.com (2008). He noted that "the idea of girls administering a vicious beating so they can post the video online may seem shocking, but it's becoming an increasingly common scenario, according to experts and news reports." The suspects were offered plea bargains in November 2008 (Geary, 2008).

The new new medium of YouTube thus can act as an accelerant for the ancient abuse of physical bullying. But it can also act to diminish additional bullying, after the video is posted on YouTube. The one drawback of bullying in person—disadvantage for the bullies, benefit for potential and actual victims and the world at large—is that the bullies can usually be clearly identified. This, obviously, does not stop bullies who want to see themselves on YouTube, but it does help police catch them (and, as Manjoo, 2008, suggests, potential bullies could even be deterred by the thought that the police might see them on a YouTube video made by some onlooker—see chapter 4 for more on such possible remedial effects of YouTube). Physical bullying, cyberbullying, flaming, and all such abuses flourish in anonymity.

Flaming goes back to the very origin of online communication in the 1980s; I noticed it in the first online class I taught for the Western Behavioral Sciences Institute in September 1984. The students were CEOs in business and public service, along with several Army generals, and we all used Kaypro II CP/M computers and 300 to 1200 bps modems to communicate. In this case, people did use their real names—we had met several months earlier in an in-person seminar, and the lack of pseudonymic cover likely restrained the flaming. But it was there, nonetheless, in comments entered late at night, when one student would be far harsher in criticism of another student than these business and public service executives had ever been as in-person students years earlier, or as business executives at the time of the online course. I realized back then that the synapse between anger and the expression of it was a lot shorter and quicker when it went to fingers over a keyboard than to tongues in in-person conversation (see Levinson, 1997; and Strate et al., 2003; and Barnes, 2012; for more).

The synapse only gets shorter and more grievous when real names and identities are unknown. Here is a user's assessment of the flaming she witnessed of another user on a popular conspiracy theory site in November 2008: "You hide your mediocrity and spew your rancor from behind your anonymity and attack/accuse/berate someone who could surely tear your ass up if he were similarly cloaked." This analysis of flaming accords double importance to the incendiary nature of anonymity: It emboldens the flamers yet restrains the victim (who is not "similarly cloaked") from responding in kind. And this makes perfect, unfortunate sense. Although the flamers and targets are both beyond in-person, physical range, and the flamers are encouraged by that distance to give vent to their anger or grievance, the target, using his or her real name, takes heightened care in commenting and responding, because those comments will leave a record directly traceable to the real-life commenter.

Trolling, which also goes back to the origins of online communication in the 1980s, is usually anonymous for much the same reason. But users can troll under their real names as well, as when a political troller writes comments for the purpose of inflaming and angering those with different or opposite political opinions. On my blog posts in support of Barack Obama in the 2008 presidential campaign, I encountered in the comments section many Republican or conservative trollers who were proud to use their real names.

But what constitutes a comment made by a troll versus a comment made by someone with a genuinely different opinion, political or otherwise? Sometimes it is difficult to tell the difference, but the defining characteristic of a troll's comment is that it is intended to evoke an angry reaction, not dialogue. "Obama will work with those who share his Islamic terrorist religion to destroy the United States" is what a troll's comment looks like. (Mattathias Schwartz notes in "The Trolls Among Us," 2008, that a troll has long been defined as "someone who intentionally disrupts online communities.") In contrast, "Obamacare will seriously damage heath care in America, and put the nation in further debt" could well be an example of a point made in a continuing dialogue.

Genuine attempts at dialogue invite rational response—or a reply that employs some kind of logic or offers evidence in support of its view—and this suggests a strategy to combat trolling. "Do not feed the troll" is the advice offered by many an online discussant in an attempt to silence or mute a disruptive commenter. Because the goal of the troller is to disrupt an online conversation by directing attention away from the conversation and toward the troll, starving the troll for attention makes sense. (See Sternberg, 2012, for more on trolling, especially its history in the 1990s.)

Ironically, flaming can arise from a genuine attempt at dialogue, when one or more people in the conversation lose their temper. In contrast, trolling is a deliberate attempt to extinguish a dialogue. Trollers may be more incorrigible than flamers, whom I have seen apologize and sometimes leave an online forum completely after regretting their initiation and pursuit of a flame. Nonetheless, the Pew Research Center found that "negative behavior, such as trolling, seems to remain an admissible exception to at least 85% of SNS [social network site] users" (Northendom, 2012)—that is, trolling, when it occurs, does not disrupt a satisfactory new new media experience for at least 85 percent of users.

Online Gossiping and Cyberbullying

Online gossiping also has roots in earlier digital and offline media but brings us more fully into the realm of social new new media. Cyberbullying, which usually entails a group of online users "ganging up" on another user and talking "trash" or otherwise ridiculing and embarrassing the target, feeds on online gossip and can be fanned by flaming. (The Lori Drew/Megan Meier case is not really an example of cyberbullying, even though it was extensively reported as cyberbullying in the media, which is why I have used the term in connection with that case in this book and online. But it is, rather, an example of cyberstalking—by an adult of a teenager. See the "Cyberstalking" section.)

Online gossiping has colorful roots in newspapers, which reach back at least as far as Walter Winchell in the 1920s. As in all things new new media, the difference between Walter Winchell's columns in the *New York Daily Graphic* (and later in the *New York Mirror*) and online gossip leading to cyberbullying is that Winchell, Ed Sullivan, and Louella Parsons dished gossip about celebrities, whereas online gossip is often about the kid sitting next to you in class. JuicyCampus.com, in operation from 2007 to 2009, bragged that its "posts are totally, 100% anonymous" and inveighed its users to "give us the juice"—that is, juicy tidbits about people on campus, which may or may not be true. When I logged on to the site in 2008, I found this on the front page about a student at a major university: "really loose girl." Searching on another university, I found this gossip from a few days earlier: "What do you think about this girl? I heard she has a tattoo of a pussy cat right below her panty line." Forty-three percent of the seven people who voted on this entry agreed that it was true.

Online gossiping hardens into cyberbullying when the nasty messages are directed at the target, so the target sees them, and the people sending the messages work intentionally or unintentionally not as disparate individuals but as a group. I-Safe (2009) reported for the 2003–2004 school year that "42% of kids have been bullied while online," a figure that held constant through 2007–2008, with the National Crime Prevention Center indicating that "40% of all teenagers with Internet access have reported being bullied online" during that year (Cyberbully Alert, 2008). Ryan Halligan, age 13, committed suicide in October 2003 after a combination of in-person and instant-message bullying (Associated Press, 2007). Because Myspace did not go online until August 2003, and Facebook not until February 2004, the stability of the 40 percent number between 2003–2004 and 2007–2008 suggests that Myspace and Facebook inherited cyberbullying from earlier social media such as instant messaging and chat rooms. Indeed, I-Safe indicated with its 2004 survey that "savvy students are using Instant Messaging, e-mails, chat rooms and websites they create to humiliate a peer." By 2008, Cyberbully Alert included Myspace: "Chat rooms, MySpace, email, instant messaging and other online tools have all helped create the cyber bullying epidemic." The epidemic would soon spread to other new new media.

Phoebe Prince, 15 years old, committed suicide in January 2010, after cyberbullying so relentless that taunting comments were left on her Facebook page even after her death (James, 2010). By September 2010, Twitter and video streaming had enabled cyberbullying that led to another suicide—of 18-year-old Rutgers University freshman Tyler Clementi—whose gay sexual encounter was secretly captured on video and publicly streamed and tweeted about (Pitts, 2010). Clementi's roommate Dharun Ravi was tried and found guilty of invasion of privacy and bias intimidation (Allen & Ali, 2012).

The remedies advised by I-Safe are the same as those for traditional schoolyard bullying: A victim should let school officials and/or parents or a trusted adult know about the bullying and contact the police if physical harm is threatened—with the additional advice, especially appropriate for targets of cyberbullying, to block the bullies' online accounts and keep copies of all harassing messages. But in Tyler Clementi's case, there wasn't really enough time for that—the damage was done the instant the video was streamed. The immediacy of the new new media world, which is such an advantage in so much that it does, also is an advantage to those who wield it for ill.

One of the goals of responding to cyberbullying is to stop it before it escalates into cyberstalking, which can take the abuse out of the virtual schoolyard, into someplace more dangerous. Kathy Sierra received harassing comments on her *Creating Passionate Users* blog, initially ranging from "banal putdowns to crude sexual garbage," which then turned violent, with posts such as "...i hope someone slits your throat...." (Walsh, 2007). Sierra stopped writing her blog, "cancelled all speaking engagements," and added that "I am afraid to leave my yard" (BBC, 2007). *Creating Passionate Users* continues as a comment-only public record of Sierra's earlier blogging (Sierra, 2007). Her case serves as a disquieting example not only of the dregs of humanity who bully but that cyberbullying can target adults and professionals and veer into a kind of cyberstalking that makes the victim afraid to leave her own yard.

Cyberstalking

If cyberbullying is usually a group activity, cyberstalking is usually solitary, just as is stalking by a psycho or some other kind of obsessed or maladjusted individual in the real world. The essence of cyberstalking is persistent, unwanted online monitoring or contact of the target, to the point of obsession (see Netlingo, 2009). And just as stalking in the real world can be much more dangerous than traditional schoolyard bullying, so can cyberstalking have a worse impact than cyberbullying. Lori Drew in effect stalked Megan Meier—first with feigned affection, then a vicious comment—and Megan Meier took her own life (see previous chapter). More common examples of cyberstalking entail a stalker with real, unrequited affection or obsession for the target. A U.S. Bureau of Justice Statistics advisory in 2009 reported that "3.4 million persons identified themselves as victims of stalking during a 12-month period in 2005 and 2006." Further, "more than one in four stalking victims reported that some form of cyberstalking was used, such as email (83 percent of all cyberstalking victims) or instant messaging (35 percent)." Myspace and Facebook were still but a year or two old when those people fell prey to cyberstalking. As with cyberbullying, cyberstalking has migrated from IMing and chat rooms to the specific, highly publicized venues of social media.

"Enhancing Child Safety & Online Technologies: Final Report" (Internet Safety Technical Task Force, 2008)—a task force of which Facebook, Myspace, Linden Labs (Second Life), Google, Yahoo, and 25 other major cyberplayers were members—highlights the conduciveness of social media for cyberstalking: "Contrary to popular assumptions, posting personally identifying information does not appear to increase risk in and of itself. Rather, risk is associated with interactive behavior" (p. 20). The recourse for targets of cyberstalking is the same as for victims of cyberbullying: Let responsible, trusted people know, including police, if any physical threats are made.

Foursquare, unfortunately, can provide an ideal tool for those who want to take their cyberstalking to the real world. So does Google Earth, in a different way. Many an address typed into the system yields a photograph literally of a nearby house on a street, replete with yard signs and cars parked in the driveway. The house being close by and not the address itself is a security precaution, as is the photograph being a few years old, but the camera angle can be shifted to actually show your house, which means that the whole world can see whether your lawn was mowed. And a stalker who knows what car you drive can easily see right where you live.

And Google maps can also be used by terrorists.

Tweeting and Terrorism

Let's begin by looking at how new new media can assist not terrorists but the combating of terrorists and the reporting of terrorism and its aftermaths in the real world.

New new media helped, and even played a crucial role, in the initial reporting of the Mumbai massacre on November 26, 2008. Adrian Finnigan on CNN International early the next day described how he had heard on his Facebook account from a friend in Mumbai, with word that he was okay and details on what he was seeing. James Winston, a Facebook "Friend" (see chapter 2), IM'd me on November 28, 2008, that his "best friend just moved to Mumbai a couple of weeks ago. He lives about two miles from the Taj Hotel. Facebook let me know he was safe." Meanwhile, Finnigan also reported that

Twitter was buzzing with brief messages from people near the hotels that were under attack in Mumbai.

John Ribeiro (2008) provided similar news that the "Micro-blogging site Twitter is also being used to pass on information, or to just express feelings about the terrorist attack, and sometimes about the inadequate coverage of the crises by some Indian TV channels"—more evidence of new new media providing a dimension not available via old broadcast media—in this case, providing direct, personal information about a terrorist massacre. Just as students had sent email from the Tiananmen Square massacre of 1989, letting the world and the mass media know what was happening, so did Twitter and Facebook in 2008 provide much-needed windows onto what had happened in Mumbai.

At times during the three-day crisis, the old media of television provided no coverage at all. On the final night of November 28, 2008, as the Taj Mahal Hotel still burned and Indian commandos were readying their final assault, MSNBC ran canned programming—its "Doc Bloc" with unrelated footage several years old—and Fox interspersed its coverage of Mumbai with reruns of *The O'Reilly Factor* and Greta Van Susteren's *On the Record*. Only CNN provided live, continuing coverage (see my "MSNBC Runs Canned 'Doc Bloc,'" November 28, 2008, for further details; see also the discussion of "Stop the Doc Bloc" in chapter 2). Fortunately, people interested in learning what was happening in Mumbai could consult Twitter, where updates were posted more often than once a minute from onlookers in Mumbai.

Some of the tweets I noticed, just seconds apart in the early morning, New York time, of November 28, 2008, follow: "Indian officials are big on bulllshit, weak on results"; "What guns are our commandos using???"; "100 trapped at Trident"; "this whole thing stinks, our govt have left us as sitting ducks, throw UPA [political party in power in India] out"; and "Japan had terrorist strike in past, China is blessed to have neighbors like us, we are not that fortunate." Twitter advised that 216 new tweets on this subject had arrived in the 30 seconds it took me to capture the preceding tweets. Of course, there is no guarantee that those blurbs all came from Mumbai—though Twitter would have had a record of the IP addresses, if the source of the tweets needed confirmation.

But no system is perfect. As Stephanie Busari pointed out on CNN.com/asia (2008), "Someone tweets a news headline, their friends see it and retweet, prompting an endless circle of recycled information" on Twitter.

Twitter would go on to play a crucial role in what can be perceived to be the beginning of the Arab Spring—with the U.S. State Department asking Twitter not to go down as scheduled for a few hours of maintenance during the unsuccessful Green Revolution in Iran in 2009. We will explore this and the use of Twitter in democratizing other countries in further detail in the next chapter (see also chapter 3), and Twitter's January 2012 announcement that it might censor tweets in some countries.

But Twitter, to return to the evil use of new new media that is the subject of this chapter, can also be an effective tool in the hands of terrorists. Busari notes that "it was suggested via Twitter that terrorists were using the medium to gain information about what Indian security forces were doing." And this does not address the possibility, even the likelihood, that Twitter and other social new new media could have been used by the terrorists in the planning of their attacks.

Indeed, a U.S. Army report of October 16, 2008, expresses the concern that Twitter "could theoretically be combined with targeting" by terrorists (Musil, 2008). The Army report does not point out, however, that Twitter offers no digital communication that could not already be accomplished by group email, IMs, and chat rooms. But Twitter and its facility for rapidly creating de facto groups of "Followers" undeniably makes the mobilization and deployment of any group easier—including groups of terrorists. The upside for civilization is not only that law enforcement and security can similarly tweet, but also, in the event that Twitter is used by terrorists or criminals, Twitter would have a record of those communications, for subsequent pursuit and conviction of the terrorists.

New new media thus can be employed for abusive social activities ranging from virtual school bullying to worldwide terrorism. We look next at how new new media can abet a more conventional kind of crime.

The Craigslist Bank Heist

Almost sounds like the name of a movie, doesn't it? But it's real, and, even if Craig's didn't quite rob the bank, it was used to hire "a dozen unsuspecting decoys" (see King5.com, 2008) to help the real bank robber get away in a heist that took place on September 30, 2008, at a Bank of America branch in Monroe, Washington.

Now, my wife and I have used Craigslist to do good things. Not long after the bank heist was reported, we used Craig's to purchase a nice La-Z-Boy loveseat for $75. But like the knives of all media, the no-cost ads sell just about anything people want to buy and sell, including not only loveseats but also (until not too long ago) prostitutes (see Lambert, 2007; Abelson, 2009) and, in the case of the Bank of America in Monroe, accomplices in a bank robbery.

The robber's plan was quite ingenious. Have a dozen people, dressed just like you, standing in front of the bank. This little flashmob would dilute the value of what eyewitnesses told the police. "I came across the ad that was for a prevailing wage job for $28.50 an hour," one of the decoys explained to King5.com. He was instructed to wear a "yellow vest, safety goggles, a respirator mask…and, if possible, a blue shirt"—the same outfit as the robber, who made good his escape through a nearby creek.

He was, however, arrested a few weeks later—DNA did him in (see Cheng, 2008, for details). I guess this shows that biological code is still more powerful than digital code. Or, as my character, NYPD forensic detective Dr. Phil D'Amato, says in my 1999 science fiction novel, *The Silk Code,* "DNA is the ultimate dossier" (quoted in Gerald Jonas's *New York Times* review, 1999).

It's fun to take a break in this dark chapter with such an amusing, true story. But the unyielding, grim reality is that the criminal use of new new media can serve up death and destruction. The accused "Craigslist Killer" Philip Markoff, arrested in April 2009 on charges of murdering a masseuse obtained through Craigslist, brings home once again the perilous, frightening side of new new media. Yet, as Leslie Harris (2009) noted, "What if the criminal in question had lured his victims using newspaper classifieds? Would we be calling this the *Boston Globe Killer*?" Her apt point is that killers trolling the media for victims are hardly an invention or unique consequence of new social media. Still, their abuses, whether unique or in common with older media, must be studied, understood, and protected against, where possible. Markoff, for his part, committed suicide in 2010 before his case could come to trial.

Spam

We come near the end of this tour of the dark side to the least destructive but most prevalent despoilers of online systems: conveyors of spam, not just in email but also in blog comments. In its most common new new media form—comments about gold jewelry or something else utterly irrelevant to the subject of the blog post—spam is like an online mosquito bite, digital graffiti, which distracts from the reading of the blog and may annoy the reader but otherwise does no harm.

Indeed, the main ill effect of spam is the extra work it imposes on bloggers and Web administrators who want to eliminate it, and the impediment that protective measures installed by bloggers can have upon nonspamming commenters. As we saw in Chapter 6, CAPTCHAs are a common defense against spammers, but these make legitimate commenters go through an additional hoop to enter their comments. A blogger interested in a no-holds-barred political discussion might choose to leave a blog unmoderated, to encourage immediate entry of comments and rapid response, but this would also leave the blog open to spam having no connection to the blog.

Facebook, Twitter, and all social media suffer from similar annoyances. Spam tweets with a link to a page selling a usually dubious product or service can be sent to anyone's account. Twitter allows reporting of such spam, which automatically removes the spamming tweet and blocks the spammer. Facebook allows users to be tagged, which means their names can be associated with any text, image, or video. The taggee can remove the tag, or hide or delete the item from his or her timeline. Facebook privacy settings allow selection of who can tag you—"Friends," family, everyone—but using this option could result in not being tagged when you might want that. Myspace has long been vulnerable to unwanted comments on the member's profile comment section—these can be removed as well as marked as spam. YouTube has similar options for comment pages on videos, including the uploader choosing not to allow comments at all.

One vulnerability that spammers have on these systems, but not when they post spam on individual blogs not situated on some central social system, is that Facebook and the rest can and do cancel the accounts of spammers. New accounts can be created easily enough, but the spammer is at least slowed down a little.

"Blog spam" is a phrase that applies to something a little different from the just-noted spam. In general, "blog spam" is a derogatory assessment of the worth of a blog post, and it sometimes refers to a blog post whose only goal—as least as perceived by the person who calls it "blog spam"—is to lure readers for the purpose of earning Google AdSense revenue, or clicking on some other ad or link associated with the blog. Digg has yet an additional usage of the "blog spam" appellation, which refers to a news article that has taken a story from a previously posted article, with an eye toward drawing readers to the new post. This might also be called plagiarism, except the new post might even give credit to the earlier source of the story.

Stepping back a little and looking at new new media as part of the larger constellation of all human communication, we can see that spam is just the digital equivalent of noise, or the most common example of noise (in media theory, any interference with communication), that afflicts all media. In the case of older media such as newspapers, noise occurs every time the newspaper prints something that is false. Noise can occur when the ink smears or when we get distortion on our television screens (see Levinson, 1988, for more on the Shannon-Weaver model of communication, and noise). Similar kinds of noise can occur with false information on blogs and Wikipedia, or when any online system or laptop or smart phone encounters technical difficulties. But the power that new new media gives all consumers to become producers creates a new kind of noise—a noise deliberately created and posted by a user.

In the old media world, and indeed in the physical world as well, noise has long been recognized as never totally reducible or capable of elimination. You introduce a new system for improving storage and transmission of music—MP3s—and this creates new intellectual property problems. Every remedy for one kind of noise opens up the system for a new kind of noise. As a form of new new media noise, spam is likely also impossible to eliminate entirely, at least not without incurring a new form of new new media noise. Fortunately, the price of spam on blogs is usually not too high to pay.

Or, put otherwise, one form of noise that new new media are especially not likely to eliminate, or even effectively control, is the digital trespass of spam—because, to truly and effectively eliminate spam, the new new medium would have to be so heavily controlled as to no longer be a new new medium. (See also chapter 4, Wikipedia, for intrinsic new new media capabilities of identifying and removing noise.)

Old Media Overreaction to New New Abuses: The Library vs. the Blogger

We have been tracing throughout this book the antagonism (as well as the mutual dependence) of various old media to new new media—antagonism that looks at new new media as unworthy competition and alternatives to old media. Press and broadcast media critiques of bloggers—not the content of given blogs, which is fair game, but the process of blogging itself—are the seminal example. Denunciations of "bloggers in pajamas" discussed in chapter 6 are indicative of the ridicule and scapegoating, going beyond rational criticism, that bloggers have been subjected to. New new media have not been above wielding similar attacks on themselves, as we saw in chapter 2, when Facebook banned photos of women nursing their babies.

But the underlying tension is greatest between old and new new media, and it comes to the surface whenever any real wrongdoing on or by new new media is involved. Cyberbullying and cyberstalking are justifiably big stories in all news media—old, new, and new new—because they can lead to real life-and-death situations, and therefore need to be known by everyone. But the tension also erupts when there is no real wrongdoing in the new new media, only the incorrect perception of it.

Twanna A. Hines writes in "I'm a Writer, Not a Child Pornographer" (2008) that she showed up for "a hard day's work" with her laptop at the Mid-Manhattan branch of the New York Public Library, where she liked to do her writing, to find that access to her blog had been banned. The reason? She writes in her blog about "dating, sex and relationships...about men who wear thongs, technology, and sex." The library advisory indicated that sites that depict obscenity, child abuse, and materials "harmful to minors" could be blocked.

None of these were depicted on Hines's site, and, indeed, after someone else contacted the library and complained that access to her site was blocked, the library removed the block. But what does the fact that her site had been blocked at all say about the role of libraries in our new new media world?

A frequent critique of personal computers, going back to the 1980s (see Levinson, 1997), is that people who spend time on them are cutting themselves off from "real life"—that is, in-person, interactions with other human beings. This argument might claim today, for example, that shopping in a Barnes and Noble would be better or healthier than buying books on Amazon, because in a Barnes and Noble you deal with real people, not pixels. Facebook would be seen as exacerbating this perceived problem, by offering digital social alternatives for a variety of in-person interactions. And as we saw in chapter 4 in the Vatican's statement accompanying the Pope's YouTube channel, the Vatican has indeed expressed this concern about social media.

Looking at the case of Hines in this context of virtual versus in-person interactions, we can see that she sought to be out among real people, in a public library, when she was practicing her new new media craft of blogging. And this made the New York Public Library uncomfortable, because of the content of her blog. To be clear, she was not using a library computer, just its wi-fi Internet connection. If we agreed with the library that the materials on Hines's blog were not suitable for children, was there no better method to protect them from the site? Rather than blocking out everyone else, including the author herself, perhaps the library could have required some special code to access such sites, one given only to people showing proof of age.

One hopes that libraries will use these kinds of solutions in the future. But in the present age of misunderstanding and suspicion of new new media, including not only by old media but also their repositories in venerable institutions of free societies such as libraries, the simple banning or blocking of the new new media access is, unfortunately, the easy remedy.

Twanna Hines says she continues to love the New York Public Library and quotes T. S. Eliot that "the very existence of libraries affords the best evidence that we may yet have hope for the future of man." That future will be a little better assured when libraries show a little better comprehension of media that are increasingly rivaling and supplanting the books on their shelves as the library's intellectual stock and trade.

As with going out to the movies rather than watching television, or dining in a restaurant rather than at home, the eventual future of libraries will reside in providing places that offer social advantages not found at home, along with all the informative avenues available at home, to lure people out of their homes with their laptops. But to the degree that all of the world's books may someday be available for free via smart phones and tablets, the library will be any place we can sit comfortably and read, be it café or park bench.

In the next and concluding chapter, we see how the political process here and around the world has combined both the best of new new media and their inextricable interaction with the offline world.

CHAPTER

Politics and New New Media

Eric SCHMIDT, CURRENTLY EXECUTIVE CHAIRMAN AND THEN ALSO CEO of Google, immediately agreed with Arianna Huffington—founder of *The Huffington Post*—when she said Barack Obama won the presidency in 2008 because of the Internet. Schmidt was a guest on *The Rachel Maddow Show* on MSNBC, where Huffington was filling in for Maddow, on November 17, 2008, 13 days after Election Day.

Since then, new new media have played important roles in the rise of the Tea Party and the midterm 2010 election in the United States, and in the Arab Spring around the world, where Twitter, YouTube, and Facebook continue to play a vital role. New new media have also been a mainstay in Occupy Wall Street protests here in the United States and abroad, and are a major part of the strategies of both the Democratic and Republican Parties in the 2012 presidential election underway in the United States as of this writing.

Barack Obama, New New Media, and the 2008 Election

The perspective of *New New Media*, of course, is that Huffington and Schmidt were completely right. Blogging, the oldest of the new new media, was well established in 2004. But Facebook, Twitter, and YouTube did not even exist then. Howard Dean, the Internet candidate in 2004, lost in the primaries. Barack Obama, the Internet candidate in 2008, won the primaries and the general election. Although many other factors no doubt played a role, that comparison is as clear an indication of media influence as Nixon doing better than JFK among radio listeners in their 1960 debates, JFK doing better than Nixon among TV viewers of those same debates, more people watching the debates than hearing them on television, and JFK winning the election.

How might new new media, had they then existed, have helped Howard Dean in 2004? The "Dean scream"—given by the candidate in a speech to his Iowa supporters after coming in third in the state's 2004 caucuses—is widely said to be the beginning of his undoing. The so-called scream was replayed extensively on television, with sage, sarcastic commentary from news anchors and experts. What if YouTube had been online then, and the clip with the VP scream had been uploaded there, for all to see, without the cable news commentary? You can see it now—search on YouTube for "Dean Scream" (2004)—does it seem that bad to you?

New new media encourage people to think for themselves. In the 2008 election, they also encouraged people to act—do more than support and eventually vote for a candidate—to actually work for a candidate.

I volunteered for Eugene McCarthy's presidential campaign and his effort to stop the war in Vietnam in 1968. That was the last time I had worked for any national candidate until 2008, when I registered at mybarackobama.com. I occasionally posted a blog on that site and from time to time logged on to keep apprised of various campaign developments. But for two days prior to Election Day 2008 and on Election Day itself, I logged on to do something else. My wife also logged on—the last time she had worked for a national candidate had been when we'd worked together for Eugene McCarthy.

The site provided names and phone numbers of Obama supporters. You could locate supporters in many states via a map on the site. We chose Pennsylvania, because the McCain campaign had been saying it was its "last stand"—that is, a state crucial to any chance of a John McCain victory, which we wanted to thwart.

It took about an hour for each of us to call about 50 different Obama supporters. We each encountered some wrong numbers and left voicemail for many people who were not at home. But we each managed to speak to dozens of supporters, from Philadelphia to the other side of the state—all from the convenience of our living room, a little north of New York City. After each phone call, we filled out a brief form on the site, where we indicated if we had made contact and noted the result—if the supporter was still planning on voting for Obama, or if he or she knew where the polling place was located, for example. Then we proceeded to do the same for Ohio, another crucial state.

Keith Goodman of the Obama campaign sent out the following email two days after the election, to everyone who had made calls for Obama: "I wanted to thank you for helping us make an astounding 1,053,791 calls on Election Day. I know it wasn't easy, and many of you kept calling long after you were tired and your voice had grown hoarse, but your calls to get our supporters out to the polls helped tip the scales in key battleground states like Florida and Ohio. Together we did it!"

New new media, as we have seen, change readers into writers all the time. In making those million calls on behalf of Obama's election, readers and writers on mybarackobama .com had been briefly transformed into active campaign workers.

New New Media VP Announcement Misstep

Before we go too far down the misty road of hindsight that Obama did everything right, at least regarding new new media in the 2008 campaign, we need to note that his campaign was not infallible in its use of new new media. The single biggest misstep was likely its announcement in July 2008 that it intended to let the world know about Obama's choice of vice presidential running mate only via email to people on Obama's list of contributors. This was an attempt to reward his supporters by giving them a special preview, to the explicit initial exclusion of media such as television, radio, and newspapers—or the old media press.

This announcement was ill-advised for at least two reasons. First, there were, obviously, many members of the traditional press on this email list, and they could easily have transmitted Obama's choice to their old media channels instantly. Second, the previewing of anything to be done on new new media, any new new media strategy, runs contrary to the viral new new media principle of making the event seem as if it happened spontaneously, not via high-level, top-down strategy (see Levinson, "Announcing Obama's Choice Through Email Not Good Idea," 2008). As it was, word of Obama's choice of Joe Biden first broke on the old medium of CNN—and the much-heralded email announcement actually came hours later, when it was anticlimactic and no longer breaking news.

Inauguration and After on the Internet

CNN reported a four-fold increase in the number of live-streamed videos viewed on Barack Obama's January 20, 2009, Inauguration Day, in comparison to Election Day November 4, 2008, viewing—some 21.3 million in a nine-hour period through midafternoon on Inauguration Day versus 5.3 million all day on Election Day. *The New York Times* also reported that "Internet traffic in the United States hit a record peak at the start of President Obama's speech as people watched, read about and commented on the inauguration, according to Bill Woodcock, the research director at the Packet Clearing House, a nonprofit organization that analyzes online traffic" (Vance, 2009, which also provides details on CNN video viewing; Internet traffic and viewing of online videos surpassed Obama's for the Michael Jackson memorial in July 2009, see Hibberd, 2009).

It was no surprise that a lot of this traffic and viewing got stalled, as the Web and its carriers struggled to meet the demand. But such problems are healthy growing pains and the best stimulus for improving the hardware infrastructure on which all new new media depend.

Obama's new administration took control of whitehouse.gov—the official Presidential website—right after the noon hour of the Inauguration. The change not only in president but approach is a textbook example of the difference between new and new new media. Under the George W. Bush administration (2001–2009), the site provided information—in the words of one observer, mainly "links to press releases, speeches, and propaganda documents" (Manjoo, 2009). The new rendition of the site was no less propagandistic but promised to be more interactive. Its first blog post, on January 20, 2009, proclaimed that "One significant addition to whitehouse.gov reflects a campaign promise from the President: we will publish all non-emergency legislation to the website for five days, and allow the public to review and comment before the President signs it." That pledge, however, was already broken for 10 out of 11 pieces of legislation by April 2009 (Harper, 2009; see also Maddow, 2012, for an equivalent list of promises broken by Republicans in the House of Representatives in the 2011–2012 congressional term). Like all things new new media, interactivity and transparency in governance is better just done than promised.

There is also an argument that, in a democracy, elected officials should do what they think best—follow their intellects and their consciences—and let the people demonstrate their approval or not in the next election. ("A leader's relevant decision makers should be his heart and mind, not his political consultants and Gallup poll readouts," as Messerli, 2006, observes.) In our day and age of constant consultation of polls, this ideal, to the extent that it was ever held, has been mostly abandoned. New new media may well have the effect, for better or worse, of pushing that principle ever further out of play. They certainly have facilitated, as we will see later in this chapter (in the Occupy Wall Street section), a rise of direct democracy, which challenges the effectiveness of all representative democracy, Democratic or Republican, here in the United States and around the world.

The President and the BlackBerry

Not everyone in the new administration of 2009 was happy about new new media. The story broke 11 days after the election that prospects did not look good for Barack Obama to continue personally sending and receiving email once he got into the White House (Zeleny, 2008). The problem of hacking into the president's email was raised, as well as the Presidential Records Act, which requires all presidential communications to be eventually available for public review.

I blogged at the time that I thought depriving the president of email, especially in this day and age, was a bad idea (Levinson, "Keeping Obama with His Email," 2008).

The "President and the BlackBerry" turned out to be a story in four parts, with a happy ending:

1. Surely a system could be devised that would automatically record all email that the president sends and receives. Come to think of it, isn't that what happens on every Gmail or any email account anyway?

More important, should not a president be able to communicate in whatever way is most effective for him or her? A person in such a position, who is comfortable with current technology, needs to be able to devote maximum attention to thinking and communication, without having to be handicapped by using old-fashioned paper, telephone, and other systems. Email has grown astronomically in the past decade for good reason: It has all the advantages of writing—permanence—and yet it is as immediate as speech. Plus, it is global and easily searchable. (See Levinson, 1997, for more on the evolution and advantages of email.)

And then there is the question of mindset: Should not a president be able, if at all possible, to continue to use a communications system with which he or she is already very comfortable and accustomed?

This raises an issue fundamental to the evolution and adoption of all media. As we begin and continue to employ any new—or new new—medium, we come to rely on it as we would our eyes, ears, mouths, and fingers. As Marshall McLuhan (1964) famously put it, media act as our "extensions"—as surrogates for the communicating parts of our bodies and brains.

Taking email away from anyone so accustomed to using it would thus be the equivalent of a psychological amputation. The president should be the last person we would want to undergo such draconian and counterproductive treatment.

2. Barack Obama himself offered a very new-new-media–savvy argument in favor of keeping his BlackBerry—short for unfiltered email contact with the world—in an interview as president-elect with Barbara Walters on November 26, 2008. "I'm negotiating to figure out how can I get information from outside of the 10 or 12 people who surround my office in the White House," Obama told Walters. "Because one of the worst things I think that could happen to a president is losing touch with what people are going through day to day" (Obama, November 26, 2008). In a January 7, 2009, interview with John Harwood on CNBC-TV, Obama said the same thing, adding, in

Charlton Heston-and-gun fashion, that "they would have to pry" the BlackBerry out of his hands. In other words, at the same time as the president-elect was assembling not just a team of rivals but a team of the best experts in foreign and domestic policy he could find, he was also fighting to keep his lines of communication at least somewhat open to the world at large of non-experts—or open to the logic of blogging, Wikipedia, Twitter, and the revolution of non-expert opinion—which is the democratizing hallmark of new new media ("every consumer a producer"). Actually, a better name for such "non-experts" would be "non-appointed experts," because the public at large was not likely to have the president's BlackBerry phone number or his email address—but, presumably, some experts outside the appointed ranks might well know how to contact the president, and making that easier and more direct is certainly a step in the right, democratizing direction. In addition, that same device would enable the president to reach out himself, not just receive advice.

Or, as Mike Allen, chief political correspondent for Politico.com, told Norah O'Donnell on MSNBC on November 26, 2008, "people [read: appointed experts] are reluctant to tell the truth to their boss...let alone a president of the United States." Whether president of the United States or town supervisor—like Paul Feiner—who, as we saw in chapter 6, relies on anonymous comments in his blog to keep informed—our leaders and representatives can all benefit from new new media connections to people outside the realm of appointed advisers.

3. Norah O'Donnell reported on MSNBC on January 18, 2009, two days before Obama's inauguration, that the "lawyers" had informed Obama and his team that they would be able to keep their BlackBerrys but not their instant messaging. The lawyers thought that IMing could make "embarrassing" messages available to hackers. If the concern, however, was salty language, such as that spoken by then White House Chief of Staff Rahm Emanuel, the cat was already well out of the bag (see rahmfacts.com for many examples).

4. And on January 21, 2009, Marc Ambinder reported in *The Atlantic* online that "Obama Will Get His BlackBerry," albeit with "a super-encryption package," but nonetheless for "routine and personal messages." An excellent example of human beings—in this case, the president—running our technologies, rather than letting concerns about their possible problems run us.

Off and Running

So the new administration in 2009 was off and running on all new new media cylinders. As we saw in earlier chapters, the president would go on to have an active Twitter account and regularly post YouTube videos. But as Obama successfully struggled against the forces of legal caution and inertia to keep his BlackBerry, his staff discovered upon moving into the White House that its telecom was stuck in a "technological dark ages" (Kornblut, 2009; Patterson, 2009), with no Facebook or Twitter, not even Gmail.

Law has always been among the slowest elements of society to embrace new media. Verbal contracts were considered more binding than written documents until the printing press standardized writing. Digital contracts have been a problem for decades, with questions arising over what constitutes a valid and binding signature if it is not produced by pen on paper (see Wright and Winn, 1998, for some early details).

But law sooner or later does catch up to technology, as do most people in politics. By February 2009, new new media were breaking out all over, especially in political circles.

Republicans tweeted during meetings with President Obama (Goddard, 2009). John McCain, no longer a presidential candidate but still a Republican senator from Arizona, had a busy Twitter account. The stage was set for a Republican resurgence, buoyed by new new media and the Tea Party, that swept Republicans into an overwhelming majority in the House of Representatives.

The Tea Party and Twitter in 2010

Ron Paul's success on Digg and other new new media in 2007–2008 did not translate into votes in primary elections, as we saw and analyzed in chapter 8 (Digg section). But the online support was real—not, for the most part, the result of gaming new new media, as the older media wrongly supposed—and in 2009 this was transformed into hundreds of Tea Party demonstrations across America, most in protest of tax policy and Obama's proposed health care law.

Twitter was a key facilitator of these protests (see Nationwide Tea Party Coalition, 2010). By the November 2010 midterm national election, not only Twitter but the whole array of new new media helped propel Tea Party candidates—that is, Republicans with Tea Party views and support—into office.

In Massachusetts, for example, where Democratic hero and icon Ted Kennedy's U.S. Senate seat was up for special election due to his death the summer before, Republican Tea Party candidate Scott Brown "had a more effective strategy of using social networking tools including Facebook, Twitter, and YouTube to promote his campaign and connect with supporters" than did his Democratic opponent Martha Coakley (Emerging Media Research Council study, reported by Davis, 2010). Among the differences in new new media engagement as of January 2010:

> *Facebook Fans: Brown (70,800), Coakley (13,529)*
>
> *YouTube Video Views: Brown (578,271), Coakley (51,173)*
>
> *Twitter Followers: Brown (9,679), Coakley (3,385)*

Among politicians already in office, another study cited in the same article "found that Republican lawmakers are taking advantage of the Twitterverse significantly more than their Democratic counterparts. In the House, GOP lawmakers send out 529% more tweets than Democrats."

Brown soon joined them in the Senate, beating Coakley 52 to 47 percent in the usually Democratic state. He was the first Republican to be elected to the U.S. Senate in Massachusetts in almost 40 years (the previous Republican was Edward Brooke, elected in 1972).

When the November 2010 midterm national election came around, in which all members of the House of Representatives were up for election, the Republicans made good their Twitter advantage, and took control of the House with a majority of 241 to 192 for the January 2011–December 2012 session. Sixty-six members of the Republican majority formed the Tea Party Caucus. Obama's health care plan and the repeal of the "don't ask don't tell" policy in favor of equality for gays in the military had already been passed by Congress and signed into law by the president. But those would be the last pieces of major, pathbreaking legislation Obama and the Democrats would get through Congress in the first three years of his presidency. The new new media revolution that had facilitated Barack Obama's election in 2008 had now done the same for his opponents.

Is this giving too much credit to new new media? Consider this: In the national election of 2000 for the House of Representatives (before new new media) Democrats received 47 percent and Republicans 47.3 percent of the popular vote. In the election of 2004 (still before YouTube and Twitter, and with Facebook in its infancy), Democrats received 46.6 percent and Republicans 49.2 percent. In the House election of 2008, with Barack Obama and therefore the Democrats having the new new media advantage, Democrats received 53.2 percent and Republicans 42.5 percent in a near landslide victory. But just two years later in 2010, with Republicans clearly more in command of new new media than the Democrats, the landslide was all but completely reversed, with the Republicans getting 51.6 percent over the Democrats' 44.5 percent.

New new media have proven to be equal opportunity providers of political advantage.

The Arab Spring and Media Determinism

The year 2010 would have one more political revolution in part indebted to new new media—actually not one but three revolutions and more than a dozen other major and minor protests, beginning in 2010 but resulting in new governments in the three revolutions in 2011, and happening not in the United States but the Arab world—hence, the Arab Spring.

Indeed, the unsuccessful "Green Revolution" in Iran in 2009 can be seen as the beginning of the Arab Spring, even though Iran is not an Arab nation. So significant did the U.S. State Department view Twitter to be in getting word out to the world about that protest, that it asked Twitter to cancel a systemwide maintenance shutdown that had been planned for a night expected to be crucial in Tehran (see chapter 3).

The protests that began in Tunisia on December 18, 2010—considered the official commencement of the Arab Spring—had better results. The regime was overthrown on January 14, 2011, including the dissolution of its police, and a Constituent Assembly was elected on October 23, 2011. Although opinions differ on the precise significance of Twitter and YouTube in facilitating the successful revolution, most observers agree that they played important roles in coordinating actions on the ground and getting real-time reports out to the world (Ingram, 2011).

No one doubts the role of Facebook and Twitter in the Egyptian revolution that began January 25, 2011, and resulted in the resignation of Hosni Mubarak on February 11. Wael Ghonim's anti-Mubarak Facebook page was a trigger and rallying point for the revolution. "This revolution started online," he told CNN, "this revolution started on Facebook." Protesters held up signs in Arabic thanking Facebook and Twitter after Mubarak's departure (Evangelista, 2011; see also Levinson, "Marshall McLuhan, North Africa, and Social Media," 2011).

But the success in Egypt turned out to be shorter-lived than in Tunisia. Protesters were back in the streets a year later, outraged that nothing had really changed with Mubarak gone. The Egyptian military "threw Mubarak under the bus, then got back to business as usual," an American colleague who lives in Cairo told me, explaining that their domestic policies hadn't changed at all.

The revolution in Libya, which began February 15, 2011, was worse in process but better in results than Egypt's. Not only were new new media not enough, but neither were the protesters in the streets in Libya—Muammar Gaddafi's overthrow on August 23 and death on October 20, 2011, required massive NATO military intervention by air, and 25,000–30,000 lives lost (in contrast to 226 in Tunisia and 846 in Egypt; see The Arab Spring, Wikipedia, for details on these and the other Arab Spring protests, including in Syria, where, as of March 2012, the government and the protesters were locked in conflict). The better result in Libya is that, unlike in Egypt, there is apparently a thorough rebuilding of the government taking place.

The question of just how significant were and are the new new media in these uprisings can be better assessed by bearing in mind a distinction made by the concepts of "hard" versus "soft" determinism. In hard determinism, A is all that is necessary to cause B. If A spills a pail of water over B's head, that is all that is necessary for B to get wet (this is also known in science as a "sufficient" condition). But the relationship between, say, an elevator and a skyscraper is different. You couldn't have a skyscraper without an elevator or some sort of automatic lifting device, but you also need steel girders and other kinds of construction technology for skyscrapers to be built and to work. The elevator, in other words, is a necessary condition, not a sufficient condition for the skyscraper, and we call this kind of relationship "soft" determinism. When media are said to be responsible for a development in society, we're talking about soft determinism. This is what McLuhan had in mind when he wrote that there would have been no Hitler without radio, and no JFK elected as president in 1960 without television (McLuhan, 1964), and what I and others mean when we say there would have been no Arab Spring without new new media (see Levinson, 1997, for more on hard versus soft media determinism). It also was what NBC correspondent Harry Smith was thinking when he said of "The Revolution of the White Snow"—the Russian version of the Arab Spring, also known as "The White Revolution," ongoing since the summer of 2011—that "if no Facebook, there's no revolution" (Smith, 2012).

This cause-and-effect between new new media and freedom around the world is what makes Twitter's announcement in January 2012 that it now had the capacity to "withhold content from users in a specific country" so surprising and disquieting. Twitter mentioned the banning of "pro-Nazi content" in France and Germany as a policy it would like to accommodate, but, as Jon Bershad pointed out in *Mediaite* (2012), what if Twitter for whatever reason shut off the tweets of people struggling for freedom in the Middle East or anywhere in the world? In contrast, Google redirected its search engine from China to Hong Kong in 2010, rather than allowing searches on its system to be subject to Chinese censorship (Drummond, 2010).

Twitter did indicate that the rest of the world would be able to see the censored tweets, but the "freedom to connect"—Jerry Edling's (2011) apt description of the necessity of new new media for political freedom in today's world—applies to getting the message out not only to the world at large but also among the people struggling for freedom themselves.

The same applies to Occupy Wall Street.

Occupy Wall Street and the Resurgence of Direct Democracy

The first inkling I had that the Arab Spring would have ramifications that went beyond the Arab world, and would lead to protests not against dictators but elected leaders in representative democracies, was when I was in Barcelona in May 2011, to give a lecture at the McLuhan Centenary Conference at the Centre de Cultura Contemporània. My wife and I, strolling on the Rambla a few blocks from the Centre, saw protests about the economic conditions—Spain, like most of Europe and democracies in the West, was in the grip of the current recession. Later that evening, we asked Cristina Miranda de Almeida, one of the conference organizers, what the protesters wanted—a change in government? Were they campaigning for an opposition party? Not really, we were told. The protesters just wanted to call attention to unfair economic policies.

The Indignatos in Spain mounted protests throughout the country, gathering supporters and reporting to the world via Twitter and Facebook. It didn't take too long—July 13, 2011—for the Adbusters Media Foundation in Canada to propose a peaceful protest about the destructive effects of corporate greed, to take place on Wall Street, the symbolic and in many ways literal capital of capitalism and its corporate abuses (Berkowitz, 2011).

And that protest started two months later, in September 2011. As the Occupations continued, several things became increasingly clear:

1. The old media were misunderstanding the movement. I was asked on a panel on Fox-NY TV on October 27, 2011, why Occupy Wall Street had not come out with a list of demands. I explained that the need for a headline, for a lead story, was a characteristic of old media, and that media such as Twitter and Facebook, unhindered by space and time restrictions (limited pages in newspapers, limited minutes in newscasts), could present a more realistic multiplicity of demands. In the case of Occupy Wall Street, these ranged from ending usurious bank rates for students who needed extensions for repayment of their loans to helping people with mortgages underwater (owing more on their mortgage than their property was currently worth).

2. The police were abrogating the First Amendment rights of people to peaceably assemble, and the First Amendment rights of the press in all of its forms to report on Occupy Wall Street (see chapter 6 for more on this).

3. Occupy Wall Street was not interested in fielding candidates for the 2012 election (see Seltzer, 2012, for more)—making OWS, in this respect, very different from the Tea Party. (See also Aldous, 2011, for a comparison of OWS and Tea Party Twitter behavior—Tea Party tweets were fewer in number and less frequent than their OWS counterparts, but Tea Partiers were more likely to follow each other's accounts, making them a more "tightly knit" de facto group than OWS on Twitter.)

This point about elections, I think, gets at the most fundamental truth about Occupy Wall Street, and fuels the others. Occupy Wall Street is not particularly interested in the 2012 election, because it is at its core a protest against elections and representative democracy itself. As Adbusters' Kalle Lasn, quoted at the top of Wikipedia's Occupy Wall Street article, puts it: "When the financial meltdown happened, there was a feeling that, 'Wow, things are going to change. Obama is going to pass all kinds of laws, and we are going to have a different kind of banking system, and we are going to take these financial fraudsters and bring them to justice.' There was a feeling like, 'Hey, we just elected a guy who may actually do this'" (Eifling, 2011). And when that didn't happen, and the inspiration of the Arab Spring and the Indignatos did, Occupy Wall Street was born. (See Hazen, Lohan, and Parramore, 2011, for detailed analysis of the beginnings of Occupy Wall Street; see also Levinson, 2011, "Occupy Wall Street Chronicles"; and see also Lawson, 2012, for a list of scholarly articles investigating "Social Media and Protest," including The Arab Spring and Occupy Wall Street.)

To return to a perspective discussed in the first chapter, it is not surprising that the old media did not and still do not understand Occupy Wall Street—the press was the right hand of the representative democracy that arose in the Renaissance and then in America. But the freedom of press insisted upon in the First Amendment was not to protect the representative democracy in America, and not even the press—it was to protect the people, whom Jefferson, Madison, and Monroe correctly saw as always on the edge of endangerment by the government the people had elected. When the police pepper spray peaceful demonstrators, as they did in California, or rough up both demonstrators and the press, as they did in New York City, they are the very agents of representative democracy Jefferson and his colleagues most feared. In this crucial area, the interests of the Tea Party in respecting the Constitution and Occupy Wall Street in bypassing representative government to address the damages wrought by greed are one and the same.

But how far away are we actually from bills being debated and voted upon by citizens via Facebook and Twitter instead of elected representatives and senators in Congress? On the one hand, the new new media, as we have seen throughout this book, allow for far more input by individuals than older media controlled by editors and producers. On the other hand, the new new media, as we also have seen, are ultimately controlled by people beyond the user's control—by the owners of Facebook, Twitter, YouTube, and the rest. This would make the new new media, as they currently are, ultimately unsuitable as vehicles of direct democracy. What might eventually be required is a Facebook-like system run by the government, and specifically designed to maximize discussion and voting (see Straus, 1991, 2001, for thoughts on direct democracy via the Web, prior to Facebook and new new media). But any governmental system—like the current voting system itself, vested, as per the Constitution, in the states—has problems of its own.

Iceland made forays into direct democracy facilitated by new new media in 2011, with a new constitution written with citizen input via Facebook and YouTube and a "direct democracy website" that allows citizens to easily communicate with their MPs (representatives) on proposed legislation (IceNews, 2011). But as Sorin Adam Matei (2011) pointed out, the final decisions regarding the new constitution were reached not via consensus as on Wikipedia but by executive fiat—or in the same way that voters got to have their questions posed to candidates in the first YouTube debates on CNN in the United States in 2008 (the questions were selected from voter submissions by CNN—see chapter 4).

Here in the United States, the Americans Elect organization is seeking to have candidates chosen on the Internet on the ballot in every state in the 2012 election (they have candidates in 30 states as of January 2012—see Heilemann, 2012, for details). This would direct-democratize the primary electoral process—certainly a good first step—but not the general election nor the actual workings of government, as in Iceland.

Meanwhile, new new media themselves are almost daily evolving to more directly democratic, less top-down structures. I interviewed Tim Pool, who has live streamed much of the Occupy Wall Street protest in New York (Timcast on UStream), in one of my classes at Fordham University in January, 2012 (see also Levinson, 2012, "Timcast"). He pointed out that the best way to report to the public via video is via live streaming—not in edited clips that we see in the old television media. But Pool's view that "we've got to get rid of the idea of editing" applies to YouTube, as well, which is neither live nor usually even a recording of an unedited video stream. Whether edited by a traditional media producer or the individual with the video camera in a phone, the result is an adulterated presentation of what actually happened in front of the camera.

But live streaming is still a long way from replacing or even competing with YouTube, which had more than 500 million users in 2011 in comparison to UStream's 2 million. In the U.S. presidential election of 2012, YouTube will undoubtedly be the big new new media video player, and representative democracy the electoral mainspring.

The U.S. Election of 2012

Mitt Romney all but wrapped up the 2012 Republican nomination for president in April 2012. Prior to that, however, there was serious speculation that the 2012 Republican nominating convention might be "brokered"—that is, not enough delegates would be chosen in support of any candidate in the primaries to give that candidate enough delegate votes to win the nomination on the first ballot in the convention. Prior to 2012, the last time a Republican convention had been brokered was 1940.

Thomas Dewey received 49.9 percent of the vote in the 1940 Republican primaries, but the nomination went to Wendell Willkie, whose supporters used radio—the new medium in those days—to create and convey the impression of surging support at the convention (Gizzi, 2012; see also Peters, 2005). Romney in many ways was the antithesis of a new new media candidate. He outspent his rivals in the primaries on mass media advertising by 10 to 1, and offered a stream of gaffes—calling attention to his wealth—that were fodder for Twitter and YouTube, and worked against him in the 2012 primaries. But he nonetheless was on his way to securing the Republican presidential nomination at the end of April 2012.

What does this tell us about the role of new new media in 2012 American politics? Romney was certainly not the choice of anyone with any sympathies for Occupy Wall Street, nor was he favored by even the Tea Party. The only conclusion is that the role of new new media in the 2012 Republican primaries was not decisive.

But neither was it negligible. Orrin Hatch, Republican senator from Utah, failed to win enough votes in the primary in that state to avoid a run-off election—the first one in his career in the Senate since 1976. His opponent was a Tea Party candidate. Hatch went on to win the run-off election, but his Republican colleague Dick Lugar of Indiana—also in the Senate since 1976—was not so fortunate. He was trounced by his Tea Party favored opponent in the primaries, and became the first six-term senator to lose a primary battle since 1952.

Meanwhile, Occupy Wall Street, though yet to have major political impact in 2012, achieved a significant victory in May: A citizen photojournalist arrested during an OWS demonstration in New York City on New Year's Day 2012 for blocking traffic was found not guilty in Manhattan Criminal Court. The key piece of evidence in this acquittal of Alexander Arbuckle and triumph of the First Amendment was UStream video provided by none other than Tim Pool (Robbins, 2012). As has been the case since Rodney King in 1991, the video camera in the hands of a citizen serves as an effective check on abuse of official power.

At least two things now seem clear regarding the general presidential election in the Fall of 2012. The Republicans will continue to make as much good use of new new media as they did in 2010, and did not in 2008. And older media, especially cable television and talk radio, will continue to have an impact. The revolution in new new media is now bestowing equal opportunities for Democrats and Republicans, progressives and conservatives, Obama and Romney—and indeed people affiliated with no political party—as Facebook, Twitter, YouTube, and even newer media continue not to preempt but transform and work right alongside older media in our political world, and in all aspects of our lives.

bibliography

Note: URLs listed in this Bibliography were confirmed as working as of February 2012.

Aasen, Adam (2009). "ABC's *Lost* is required viewing for students in UNF course," *Florida Times-Union*, 12 May. http://www.jacksonville.com/lifestyles/2009-05-11/story/abcs_lost_is_required_viewing_for_students_in_unf_course

Abelson, Jenn (2009). "Craigslist drops erotic services ads," *Boston Globe*, 14 May. http://www.boston.com/business/technology/articles/2009/05/14/craigslist_drops_erotic_services_ads/

Ahmed, Mural (2008). "Apple threatens to shut down iTunes over royalty hike," (London) *Times Online*, 1 October. http://technology.timesonline.co.uk/tol/news/tech_and_web/article4859885.ece

Aldous, Peter (2011). "Occupy vs. Tea Party: what their Twitter networks reveal," *New Scientist*, 17 November. http://www.newscientist.com/blogs/onepercent/2011/11/occupy-vs-tea-party-what-their.html

Allen, Jonathan, and Ali, Aman (2012). "Dharun Ravi found guilty of hate crimes for spying on gay Rutgers roommate," Reuters, 16 March. http://www.reuters.com/article/2012/03/16/us-crime-rutgers-idUSBRE82F0VP20120316

Allen, Lily (2005). Myspace music page, 7 November. http://www.myspace.com/lilymusic

Allen, Mike (2008). Interview by Norah O'Donnell, MSNBC-TV, 26 November.

Alter, Jonathan (2008). Conversation with Keith Olbermann about YouTube, *Countdown*, MSNBC, 9 June.

Ambinder, Marc (2009). "Obama will get his BlackBerry," *The Atlantic*, 21 January. http://marcambinder.theatlantic.com/archives/2009/01/obama_will_get_his_blackberry.php

Anderson, Chris (2008). "Free! Why $0.00 is the future of business," *Wired*, 25 February. http://www.wired.com/techbiz/it/magazine/16-03/ff_free

Arnold, Gin (2008). "Missing in action—Olbermann and Maddow," *Op-Ed News*, 17 November. http://www.opednews.com/maxwrite/diarypage.php?did=10837

Arthur, Charles (2008). "Censor lifts UK Wikipedia ban," *The Guardian*, 9 December. http://www.guardian.co.uk/technology/2008/dec/09/wikipedia-iwf-ban-lifted

_____ (2011). "iPad to dominate tablet sales until 2015 as growth explodes, says Gartner," *The Guardian*, 22 September. http://www.guardian.co.uk/technology/2011/sep/22/tablet-forecast-gartner-ipad

ASCAP (American Society of Composers, Authors, and Publishers) (2008). *2007 Annual Report*. New York: ASCAP. http://ascap.com/about/annualReport/annual_2007.pdf

Associated Press (2005). "Wikipedia, Britannica: a toss-up," 15 December. http://www.wired.com/culture/lifestyle/news/2005/12/69844

_____ (2007). "States pushing for laws to curb cyberbullying," 21 February. http://www.foxnews.com/story/0,2933,253259,00.html

_____ (2008). "Network television viewership plunges by 2.5 million people, data shows," 9 May. http://www.foxnews.com/story/0,2933,270965,00.html

_____ (2008). "Thomson Reuters reports lower profit on costs of a merger," *The New York Times*, 12 August. http://www.nytimes.com/2008/08/13/business/13thomson.html

_____ (2011). "Let journalists work, city police are ordered," *The New York Times*, 23 November. http://www.nytimes.com/2011/11/24/nyregion/new-york-police-are-ordered-to-let-journalists-work.html?_r=1

Au, Wagner James (2007). "Remake the stars," *New World Notes* blog, 18 July. http://nwn.blogs.com/nwn/2007/07/remake-the-star.html#more

Baez, Joan (1966). Performance of Bob Dylan's "With God on Our Side," in Stockholm, Sweden, video. http://www.youtube.com/watch?v=Pih1hVdflnQ

Baird, Derek E. (2008). "Youth vote 2008: how Obama hooked Gen Y," *Barking Robot* blog, 1 December. http://www.debaird.net/blendededunet/2008/12/youth-vote-2008-how-obama-hooked-gen-y.html

"Barack Obama (One Million Strong for Barack)" (2007). Facebook group. http://www.facebook.com/group.php?gid=2231653698

"Barack Obama (Politician)" (2012). Facebook page. https://www.facebook.com/barackobama

Barlow, Perry (1955). "Another Radio to the Attic," *The New Yorker*, cover, 22 October. http://www.tvhistory.tv/1955_Oct_22_NEW_YORKER.JPG

Barnes, Susan (2012). *Socializing the Classroom: Social Networks and Online Learning*. Lanham, MD: Lexington Books.

Bennett, Shea (2011). "Twitter: the fastest-growing social network," *MediaBistro*, 8 September. http://www.mediabistro.com/alltwitter/twitter-growth-july-2011_b13482

Berkowitz, Ben (2011). "From a single hashtag, a protest circled the world," *Brisbane Times* (Australia), 19 October. http://www.brisbanetimes.com.au/technology/technology-news/from-a-single-hashtag-a-protest-circled-the-world-20111019-1m72j.html

Bershad, Jon (2012). "#Betrayal: Twitter announces that it will begin letting governments censor tweets," *Mediaite*, 27 January. http://www.mediaite.com/online/betrayal-twitter-announces-that-it-will-begin-letting-governments-censor-tweets/

Big Love (2009). Season 3, Episode 6, HBO TV series, 22 February.

Blechman, Robert (2012). *Executive Severance* (novel). Houston, TX: NeoPoiesis Press.

BlogTalkRadio (2009). "About BlogTalkRadio." http://www.blogtalkradio.com/about.aspx

BMI (Broadcast Music, Inc.) (2007). "Broadcast Music Inc. announces record-setting royalty distributions," 4 September. http://www.bmi.com/press/releases/BMI_revenues_release_2007_final_9_4_07.doc

Bodnar, Kipp (2011). "The ultimate Google+ cheat sheet," *Hubspot* blog, 30 August. http://blog.hubspot.com/blog/tabid/6307/bid/23765/The-Ultimate-Google-Cheat-Sheet.aspx

Boskar, Bianca (2012). "The secret to Pinterest's success: we're sick of each other," *The Huffington Post*, 14 February. http://www.huffingtonpost.com/2012/02/14/pinterest-success_n_1274797.html

British Broadcasting Company (BBC) (2007). "Blog death threats spark debate," 27 March. http://news.bbc.co.uk/1/hi/technology/6499095.stm

_____ (2009). "Pope launches Vatican on YouTube," 23 January. http://news.bbc.co.uk/2/hi/europe/7846446.stm

Buggles, The (1979). "Video Killed the Radio Star," recording, Island Records.

Bureau of Justice Statistics (2009). "3.4 million people report being stalked in the United States," U.S. Department of Justice, 13 January. http://www.ojp.usdoj.gov/bjs/pub/press/svuspr.htm

Busari, Stephanie (2008). "Tweeting the terror: how social media reacted to Mumbai," CNN.com/Asia, 27 November. http://edition.cnn.com/2008/WORLD/asiapcf/11/27/mumbai.twitter/index.html

Butler, Samuel (1878/1910). *Life and Habit.* New York: Dutton.

Carpenter, Hutch (2009). "Karl Rove is on Twitter," *I'm Not Actually a Geek* blog, 9 January. http://bhc3.wordpress.com/2009/01/10/karl-rove-is-on-twitter

Carr, David (2005). "Why you should pay to read this newspaper?" *The New York Times*, 24 October. http://www.nytimes.com/2005/10/24/business/24carr.html

Carter, Beth (2012). "Introducing Aereo: one small step for cord cutting, one giant leap of faith," *Wired,* 14 February. http://www.wired.com/epicenter/2012/02/aereo-cord-cutting/

Catch Up Lady blog (2007). "Dick in a box grabs Emmy nod, NBC's YouTube mea culpa complete," 23 July. http://catchupblog.typepad.com/catch_up_blog/2007/07/dick-in-a-box-g.html

Chansanchai, Athima (2012). "Pope to debut personal Twitter account," *Digital Life on Today*, 27 February. http://digitallife.today.msnbc.msn.com/_news/2012/02/27/10517820-pope-to-debut-personal-twitter-account

Cheng, Jacqui (2008). "Crowdsourcing Craigslist bank robber nabbed on DNA evidence," *ars technica*, 7 November. http://arstechnica.com/tech-policy/news/2008/11/crowdsourcing-craigslist-bank-robber-nabbed-on-dna-evidence.ars

Chittum, Ryan (2011). "Audit notes: Newsstand success, Paywalls and tacos, *WSJ* on debt collectors," *Columbia Journalism Review*, 23 December. http://www.cjr.org/the_audit/audit_notes_newsstand_success.php

Chozick, Amy (2012). "2 Pulitzers for Times; Huffington Post and Politico win," *The New York Times*, 16 April. http://www.nytimes.com/2012/04/17/business/media/2012-pulitzer-prize-winners-announced.html

Cohen, David (2007). "Hunting down Digg's Bury Brigade," *Wired*, 1 March. http://www.wired.com/techbiz/people/news/2007/03/72835

Cohen, Noam (2008). "Delaying news in the era of the Internet," *The New York Times*, 23 June. http://www.nytimes.com/2008/06/23/business/media/23link.html

Collins, Barry (2008). "IWF lifts Wikipedia ban," *PCPro*, 10 December. http://www.pcpro.co.uk/news/242013/iwf-lifts-wikipedia-ban

Comenius, Johann Amos (1649/1896). *Didactica Magna*. Translated by M. W. Keatinge as *The Great Didactic*. London: Adam and Charles Black.

Constine, Josh (2012). "Congratulations Crunchies winners!" *TechCrunch,* 31 January. http://techcrunch.com/2012/01/31/crunchies-dropbox/

Couts, Andrew (2011). "Warner Brothers to film screenplay that started as a Reddit comment," *Digital Trends*, 14 November. http://www.digitaltrends.com/movies/warner-brothers-to-film-screenplay-that-started-as-a-reddit-comment/

Crocker, Chris (2007). "Britney fan crying ('Leave Britney Alone')," 11 September, video. http://www.youtube.com/watch?v=LWSjUe0FyxQ

Cyberbully Alert (2008). "Cyber bullying statistics that may shock you!" 27 August. http://www.cyberbullyalert.com/blog/2008/08/cyber-bullying-statistics-that-may-shock-you

Dahl, Melissa (2008). "Youth vote may have been key in Obama's win," MSNBC.com, 5 November. http://www.msnbc.msn.com/id/27525497/

Davis, Susan (2010). "Atwitter in Mass.: Brown's social media strategy tops Coakley's," *The Wall Street Journal*, 19 January. http://blogs.wsj.com/washwire/2010/01/19/atwitter-in-mass-browns-social-media-skills-top-coakleys/

Dawkins, Richard (1976). *The Selfish Gene*. New York: Oxford University Press.

_____ (1991). "Viruses of the mind" in *Dennett and His Critics: Demystifying Mind*, ed. Bo Dahlbom. Cambridge, MA: Blackwell, 1993. http://modox.blogspot.com/2007/12/memes-viruses-of-mind-or-root-of.html

Dean, Howard (2004). "Howard Dean's scream," 19 January, video. http://www.youtube.com/watch?v=D5FzCeV0ZFc

DeCuir, Esther (2007). "Soft Edge bookstore to showcase works of Paul Levinson," *Second Life News Network*, 4 December. [Site defunct.]

Deneen, Sally (2011). "The Facebook age," *Success*, 1 April. http://www.successmagazine .com/the-facebook-age/PARAMS/article/1287/channel/22

Dewey, John (1925). *Experience and Nature*. Chicago: Open Court.

"Dick in a Box" (2006). Featuring Justin Timberlake and Andy Samberg; written by Andy Samberg, Akiva Schaffer, Jorma Taccone, Asa Taccone, Justin Timberlake, Katreese Barnes; produced by The Lonely Island for *Saturday Night Live*; 16 December, video. http://www.youtube.com/watch?v=WhwbxEfy7fg

Dickinson, Tim (2006). "The first YouTube election: George Allen and 'Macaca'," *Rolling Stone*, 15 August. http://www.rollingstone.com/politics/blogs/national-affairs/ the-first-youtube-election-george-allen-and-macaca-20060815

"Digg Terms of Use" (2012). http://digg.com/tou

Dingo, Robbie (2007). "A Second Life machinima," *My Digital Double* blog, 16 July. http://digitaldouble.blogspot.com/2007/07/watch-worlds.html Video: http://blip.tv/file/get/RobbieDingo-WatchTheWorlds570.mov Video: http://www.youtube.com/watch?v=vV1YbWBSXS8

Donnelly, John M. (2009). "Congressman Twitters an Iraq security breach," *CQ Politics*, 6 February. http://www.cqpolitics.com/wmspage.cfm?docID=news- 000003026945

Drummond, David (2010). "A new approach to China: an update," *The Official Google Blog*, 22 March. http://googleblog.blogspot.com/2010/03/new-approach-to- china-update.html

Dumbach, Annette E., and Newborn, Judd (1986). *Shattering the German Night*. Boston: Little, Brown.

Dunlop, Orrin E., Jr. (1951). *Radio & Television Almanac*. New York: Harper & Bros.

Edling, Jerry (2011). "Freedom to connect," *Mountain Runner*, 28 January. http:// mountainrunner.us/2011/02/freedom_to_connect/

Eifling, Sam (2011). "Adbusters' Kalle Lasn talks about Occupy Wall Street," *The Tyee*, 7 October. http://thetyee.ca/News/2011/10/07/Kalle-Lasn-Occupy-Wall-Street/

Eisenstein, Elizabeth (1979). *The Printing Press as an Agent of Change*. New York: Cambridge University Press.

Elba, Idris (2006). Private messages to Paul Levinson, on Myspace, 28 October and 7 November.

Ellis, Justin (2012). "Is the AP suing an aggregator or a search engine in the Meltwater case?" *Nieman Journalism Lab*, 15 February. http://www.niemanlab.org/2012/02/ is-the-ap-suing-an-aggregator-or-a-search-engine-in-the-meltwater-case/

Evangelista, Benny (2011). "Facebook, Twitter and Egypt's upheaval," *SF Gate*, 13 February. http://www.sfgate.com/cgi-bin/article.cgi?f=/c/ a/2011/02/12/BUGN1HLHTR.DTL

Feiner, Paul (2009). Interview with Paul Levinson, *The Greenburgh Report*, WVOX Radio, 9 January. Also included in Levinson, Paul (2009), "Conversation."

Ferraro, Nicole (2012). "Feeling disinterest for Pinterest," *Internet Evolution*, 14 February. http://www.internetevolution.com/author.asp?doc_id=239237

_____ (2012). "Google+ defenses get childish, illogical," *Internet Evolution*, 28 February. http://www.internetevolution.com/author.asp?doc_id=239855

Finin, Tim (2008). "Mobile texting now more popular than calling in US," *UMBC ebiquity*, 29 September. http://ebiquity.umbc.edu/blogger/2008/09/29/mobile-texting-now-more-popular-than-calling-in-us/

Finnegan, Adrian (2008). Report on November 2008 Mumbai massacre and Facebook, CNN International, 27 November.

Fleetwoods, The (1959, 2007). "Come Softly To Me" and "Mr. Blue," originally released in 1959 on Dolphin Records, performance on *American Bandstand* 1959, live performance 2007, videos.
http://www.youtube.com/watch?v=DgJwm9erBaQ
http://www.youtube.com/watch?v=vclkm6nsnWY
http://www.youtube.com/watch?v=AgQl6Rxk_uM

Florin, Hector (2009). "Podcasting your novel: publishing's next wave?" *Time*, 31 January. http://www.time.com/time/arts/article/0,8599,1872381,00.html

Fogarty, Mignon (2008). *Grammar Girl's Quick and Dirty Tips for Better Writing*. New York: Holt.

_____ (2011). *Grammar Girl's 101 Misused Words You'll Never Confuse Again*. New York: St. Martin's Griffin.

Fouhy, Beth (2008). "Obama to pioneer Web outreach as President," *USA Today*, 12 November. http://www.usatoday.com/news/topstories/2008-11-12-1697755942_x.htm

Friedman, Josh (2007). "Blogging for dollars raises questions of online ethics," *Los Angeles Times*, 9 March. http://articles.latimes.com/2007/mar/09/business/fi-bloggers9

Frith, Holden (2008). "So iTunes won't be closing after all," (London) *Times Online*, 3 October. http://timesonline.typepad.com/technology/2008/10/itunes-wont-clo.html

Fuller, Buckminster (1938). *Nine Chains to the Moon*. Carbondale, IL: Carbondale University Press.

Fund, John (2004). "I'd rather be blogging," *The Wall Street Journal*, 13 September. http://www.opinionjournal.com/diary/?id=110005611

Geary, Jason (2008). "Plea deals offered in video beating case," *The Ledger*, 18 November. http://www.theledger.com/article/20081118/NEWS/811180269

Gergen, David (2008). Guest on CNN, election night coverage, 4 November.

Giles, Jim (2005). "Special report: Internet encyclopaedias go head to head," *Nature*, 14 December. http://www.nature.com/nature/journal/v438/n7070/full/438900a.html

_____ (2008). "Do we need an open Britannica?" *The Guardian*, 20 June. http://www
.guardian.co.uk/technology/2008/jun/20/wikipedia

Gill, Andy (2007). "Famous five: why the Traveling Wilburys are the ultimate
supergroup," *The Independent,* 19 June. http://www.independent.co.uk/arts-
entertainment/music/features/famous-five-why-the-traveling-wilburys-are-the-
ulimate-supergroup-453788.html

Gizzi, John (2012). "The last time Republicans had a 'brokered convention'," *Human
Events*, 21 February. http://www.humanevents.com/article.php?id=49657

Gladkova, Svetlana (2008). "Barack Obama uses the power of social media noticed
by mainstream media," *profy*, 25 August. http://profy.com/2008/08/25/
barack-obama-uses-power-of-social-media/

Glater, Jonathan D. (2008). "At the uneasy intersection of bloggers and the law,"
The New York Times, 15 July. http://www.nytimes.com/2008/07/15/technology/
15law.htm

Goddard, Taegan (2009). "Republicans Twitter meeting with Obama," *Political Wire*
blog, 28 January. http://politicalwire.com/archives/2009/01/28/republicans_
twitter_meeting_with_obama.html

Gold, Matea (2008). "Obama's 30-minute ad attracts 33 million viewers," *Los Angeles
Times*, 31 October. http://articles.latimes.com/2008/oct/31/entertainment/
et-obama31

Golijan, Rosa (2012). "The Pope explains the power—and danger—of Twitter,"
Digital Life on Today, 24 January. http://digitallife.today.msnbc.msn.com/_news/
2012/01/24/10225535-the-pope-explains-the-power-and-danger-of-twitter

Golobokova, Yulia (2008). "YouTube as an alternative medium of political communication," final paper for "Media Research Methods," Graduate School of Arts and
Sciences, Fordham University, Paul Levinson, professor, Dec. 17. http://sites
.google.com/site/ygolobokova/youtube-research-proposal-paper

Goodale, Gloria (2011). "WikiLeaks: is there a future for the website without Julian
Assange?" *The Christian Science Monitor*, 24 February. http://www.csmonitor
.com/USA/2011/0224/WikiLeaks-Is-there-a-future-for-the-website-without-
Julian-Assange

Greene, Brian William (2012). "Steven Spielberg's KONY 2012 connection."
US News & World Report, 9 March. http://www.usnews.com/news/blogs/
washington-whispers/2012/03/09/steven-spielbergs-kony-2012-connection

Grimes, Sara (2008). "Campus Watch: statistics support youth vote turnout,"
The Daily blog, 12 November. http://dailyuw.com/news/2008/nov/12/
campus-watch-statistics-support-youth-vote/

Grossman, Lev (2006). "Time's Person of the Year: You," *Time,*13 December. http://
www.time.com/time/magazine/article/0,9171,1569514,00.html

_____ (2009). "Iran Protests: Twitter, the medium of movement," *Time*, 17 June.
http://www.time.com/time/world/article/0,8599,1905125,00.html

Gumpert, Gary (1970). "The rise of mini-comm," *Journal of Communication, 20*, pp. 280–290.

Guynn, Jessica (2011). "Google+ may reach 400 million users by end of 2012," *Los Angeles Times*, 27 December. http://latimesblogs.latimes.com/technology/2011/12/google-may-reach-400-million-users-by-end-of-2012.html

Hafner, Katie (1999). "I link, therefore I am: a Web intellectual's diary," *The New York Times*, 22 July. http://www.nytimes.com/library/tech/99/07/circuits/articles/22lemo.html

Hall, Edward T. (1966). *The Hidden Dimension*. New York: Doubleday.

Hannity, Sean and Colmes, Alan (2007). Different interpretations of Ron Paul's first-place finish in post-debate poll, Fox News, 22 October, video. http://www.youtube.com/v/hDwDIj5ahuY&rel=1

Harper, Jim (2009). "The promise that keeps on breaking," CATO Institute, 13 April. http://www.cato.org/pub_display.php?pub_id=11449

Harris, Leslie (2009). "Because 'Classified Ad Killer' doesn't have the same ring," *The Huffington Post*, 24 April. http://www.huffingtonpost.com/leslie-harris/because-classified-ad-kil_b_190965.html

Harrison, George (1971, 2002, 2006). Performances of George Harrison's "While My Guitar Gently Weeps" at Concert for Bangladesh, 1971, George Harrison, Eric Clapton; at Memorial Concert for George, 2002, Eric Clapton, Paul McCartney, Ringo Starr, Dhani Harrison; at Rock 'n' Roll Hall of Fame Induction (Posthumous) of George Harrison, 2006, Tom Petty, Jeff Lynne, Prince. (See also McCartney, Paul.)
Videos: http://www.youtube.com/watch?v=T7qpfGVUd8c
http://www.youtube.com/watch?v=zNp45m92e1M
http://www.youtube.com/watch?v=cYl942_I3Wo

Hawthorne, Nathaniel (1851/1962). *The House of the Seven Gables* (novel). New York: Collier.

Hayes, Michael (2012). "'Obama Girl' releases new video for 2012 election, tells President: 'You'd better step up'," *Mediaite*, 15 February. http://www.mediaite.com/online/obama-girl-releases-new-video-for-2012-election-tells-president-youd-better-step-up/

Hazen, Don; Lohan, Tara; and Parramore, Lynn (Eds.) (2011). *The 99%: How the Occupy Wall Street Movement Is Changing America*. San Francisco, CA: Alternet Books.

Heil, Bill, and Piskorski, Mikolaj Jan (2009). "New Twitter research: men follow men and nobody tweets," *Conversation Starter*, Harvard Business Publishing, 1 June. http://blogs.harvardbusiness.org/cs/2009/06/new_twitter_research_men_follo.html

Heilemann, John (2012). "The third-party rail," *New York Magazine,* 22 January. http://nymag.com/news/politics/powergrid/americans-elect-2012-1/

Hibberd, James (2009). "MSN gets record traffic during Jackson memorial," *The Hollywood Reporter*, 7 July. http://www.hollywoodreporter.com/blogs/live-feed/msn-record-traffic-jackson-memorial-51842

_____ (2011). "Nielsen report: TV ownership declines," EW.com (*Entertainment Weekly*), 30 November. http://insidetv.ew.com/2011/11/30/tv-ownership-declines/

Hines, Twanna A. (2008). "I'm a writer, not a child pornographer," *The Huffington Post*, 31 December. http://www.huffingtonpost.com/twanna-a-hines/im-a-writer-not-a-child-p_b_154584.html

Hof, Robert D. (2006). "My virtual life," *Business Week*, 1 May. http://www.businessweek.com/magazine/content/06_18/b3982001.htm

Hoffman, Auren (2008). "It takes tech to elect a President," *Business Week*, 25 August. http://www.businessweek.com/technology/content/aug2008/tc20080822_700775.htm?campaign_id=rss_tech

Holyoke, Jessica (2008). "Lowest profit per capita growth ever in Q1 2008," *The Alphaville Herald*, 29 April. http://foo.secondlifeherald.com/slh/2008/04/state-of-the-ec.html

Horn, Leslie (2012). "Super Bowl 2012 breaks two Twitter records," *PC Mag*, 6 February. http://www.pcmag.com/article2/0,2817,2399868,00.asp

Hudson, Ken ("Hubble, Kenny") (2008). "Caledon Astronomical Society." http://agni.sl.marvulous.co.uk/group/CaledonAstronomical20Society [Site defunct.]

_____ (2008). Facebook message to Paul Levinson, Dec. 26.

Hunter, Mark (2009). "Twestival, swearing, and Cameron Reilly," *Podcastmatters Social Media* podcast, 6 February. http://socialmediapodcast.tumblr.com/post/76150739/edition-2-twestival-swearing-and-cameron-reilly

IceNews (2011). "New direct democracy website opens in Iceland," 19 November. http://www.icenews.is/index.php/2011/11/19/new-direct-democracy-website-opens-in-iceland/

ILeftDiggforReddit (2008). "So who else here left Digg for Reddit?" *Reddit*, 25 December. http://www.reddit.com/r/reddit.com/comments/7ll45/so_who_else_here_left_digg_for_reddit/

Ingram, Mathew (2011). "Was what happened in Tunisia a Twitter revolution?" *Gigaom*, 14 January. http://gigaom.com/2011/01/14/was-what-happened-in-tunisia-a-twitter-revolution/

Innis, Harold (1951). *The Bias of Communication*. Toronto: University of Toronto Press.

Internet Safety Technical Task Force (2008). "Enhancing child safety & online technologies: final report," Berkman Center for Internet & Safety at Harvard University, 31 December. http://cyber.law.harvard.edu/pubrelease/isttf/

Ironic Pentameter blog (2006). "How old is Digg's median user?" 14 September. http://ironic-pentameter.blogspot.com/2006/09/how-old-is-diggs-median-user.html

I-Safe (2009). "Cyber bullying: statistics and tips." http://www.isafe.org/channels/sub.php?ch=op&sub_id=media_cyber_bullying

"I've Got a Crush on Obama" (2007). Video featuring "Obama Girl" Amber Lee Ettinger, produced by Ben Relles for BarelyPolitical.com, song written and sung by Leah Kauffman, 13 June, video. http://www.youtube.com/watch?v=wKsoXHYICqU

James, Susan Donaldson (2010). "Immigrant teen taunted by cyberbullies hangs herself," ABC News, 26 January. http://abcnews.go.com/Health/cyber-bullying-factor-suicide-massachusetts-teen-irish-immigrant/story?id=9660938#.TyLcRsVA8wU

James, William (1890). *The Principles of Psychology*. New York: Henry Holt.

Jardin, Xeni (2005). "Audience with the Podfather," *Wired*, 14 May. http://www.wired.com/culture/lifestyle/news/2005/05/67525

Jarvis, Jeff (2008). Interview about investigative journalism in peril, *On the Media*, National Public Radio (NPR), 15 August, transcript. http://www.onthemedia.org/transcripts/2008/08/15/01

Johnson, Peter (2005). "'Times' report: Miller called her own shots," *USA Today*, 16 October. http://www.usatoday.com/life/columnist/mediamix/2005-10-16-media-mix_x.htm

Johnson, Steven (2009). "How Twitter will change the way we live," *Time*, 15 June, pp. 32–37.

Jonas, Gerald (1999). Review of *The Silk Code* by Paul Levinson, *The New York Times*, 28 November. http://www.nytimes.com/books/99/11/28/reviews/991128.28scifit.html

Jones, Alex (2007). "Ron Paul beats Digg Bury Brigade," *Prison Planet*, 21 May. http://www.prisonplanet.com/articles/may2007/210507paulbeats.htm

Jordan, Tina (2008). "Domestic book sales see slight decline in May," AAP (The Association of American Publishers), 11 July. http://www.publishers.org/main/PressCenter/Press_Issues/May2008SalesStats.htm

Kane, Erin, and Brandt, Kristin (2007). "Welcome to Hollywood," *Manic Mommies* podcast, 18 February. http://www.manicmommies.com/2007/02/welcome-to-hollywood/

Kaplan, Benjamin (1966). *An Unhurried View of Copyright*. New York: Columbia University Press.

Kells, Tina (2009). "Wikipedia ponders editorial reviews after Kennedy death post," *Now Public*, 26 January. http://www.nowpublic.com/tech-biz/wikipedia-ponders-editorial-reviews-after-kennedy-death-post

Kennedy, Dan (2012). "In New Haven, a crisis of confidence over user comments," *Nieman Journalism Lab*, 15 February. http://www.niemanlab.org/2012/02/in-new-haven-a-crisis-of-confidence-over-user-comments/

Kenski, Kate; Hardy, Bruce; and Jamieson, Kathleen Hall (2010). *The Obama Victory: How Media, Money, and Message Shaped the 2008 Election*. New York: Oxford University Press.

Kerry, John (2008). Speech at Democratic National Convention, Denver, CO, 27 August, video. http://www.youtube.com/watch?v=dO2PAm4iCtE

King, Rachel (2011). "Smartphone sales growth sluggish as Samsung soars" (survey), *ZDNet*, 4 November. http://www.zdnet.com/blog/btl/smartphone-sales-growth-sluggish-as-samsung-soars-survey/62664

King5.com (2008). "Armored truck robber uses Craigslist to make getaway," 1 October. http://www.king5.com/topstories/stories/NW_100108WAB_monroe_robber_floating_escape_TP.ce3930c1.html [New URL: http://www.king5.com/news/local/60055547.html]

Kingston, Sean (2006). Myspace music page, 7 July. http://www.myspace.com/seankingston

_____ (2007). "Kingston's MySpace success," contactmusic.com, 6 September. http://www.contactmusic.com/news.nsf/article/kingstons%20myspace%20success_1042855

Kirk, Jeremy (2008). "Wikipedia article censored in UK for the first time," *PC World*, 8 December. http://www.pcworld.com/article/155112/wikipedia_article_censored_in_uk_for_the_first_time.html

Kopp, Sondro (2012). Interview on CNN about painting through Skype, 19 February.

Kornblut, Anne E. (2009). "Staff finds White House in the technological Dark Ages," *The Washington Post*, 22 January. http://www.washingtonpost.com/wp-dyn/content/article/2009/01/21/AR2009012104249.html

Kremer, Joan (2008). "The start of a central information source for writers in Second Life," *Writers in the Virtual Sky* blog, 31 December. http://www.writersinthevirtualsky.com/the-start-of-a-central-information-source-for-writers-in-second-life/

Krieger, Lisa M. (2008). "Protesters to Facebook: breast-feeding does not equal obscenity," *San Jose Mercury News*, 26 December.

Krupp, Elysha (2008). "Wikipedia, Britannica battle over credibility," examiner.com, 10 August. http://washingtonexaminer.com/local/2008/08/wikipedia-britannica-battle-over-credibility/75050

Kurtz, Howard (2007). "Jailed man is a videographer and a blogger but is he a journalist?" *The Washington Post*, 8 March, p. C01. http://www.washingtonpost.com/wp-dyn/content/article/2007/03/07/AR2007030702454.html

_____ (2009). "Online, Sarah Palin has unkind words for the press," *The Washington Post*, 9 January, p. C01. http://www.washingtonpost.com/wp-dyn/content/article/2009/01/08/AR2009010803620.html

Lambert, Bruce (2007). "As prostitutes turn to Craigslist, law takes notice," *The New York Times*, 4 September. http://www.nytimes.com/2007/09/05/nyregion/05craigslist.html

Lavigne, Avril (2007). "Girlfriend," 27 February, video. http://www.youtube.com/watch?v=cQ25-glGRzl

Lawson, Sean (2012). "Social media & protest: a quick list of recent scholarly research," 27 January. http://www.seanlawson.net/?p=1425

Layton, Julia, and Brothers, Patrick (2007). "How MySpace works," *HowStuffWorks*. http://computer.howstuffworks.com/myspace.htm

Leibovich, Mark (2008). "McCain, the analog candidate," *The New York Times*, 3 August. http://www.nytimes.com/2008/08/03/weekinreview/03leibovich.html

Leitch, Will (2009). "How tweet it is," *New York Magazine*, 8 February. http://nymag.com/news/media/54069/

Levine, David (2008). "All talk," Condé Nast Portfolio.com, 26 February. http://www.portfolio.com/culture-lifestyle/goods/gadgets/2008/02/26/Internet-Talk-Radio

Levinson, Paul (1972). *Twice Upon a Rhyme*, music recording, LP, HappySad Records; CD reissue, Seoul, South Korea: Beatball Music, 2008; vinyl reissue, UK: Whiplash Records, 2010.

_____ (1977). "Toy, mirror, and art: the metamorphosis of technological culture," *Et Cetera* journal, June. Reprinted in *Technology and Human Affairs*, L. Hickman & A. al-Hibris (Eds.), St. Louis, MO: Mosby, 1981; *Philosophy, Technology, and Human Affairs*, L. Hickman (Ed.), College Station, TX: Ibis, 1985; *Technology As a Human Affair*, L. Hickman (Ed.), New York: McGraw-Hill, 1990; Levinson, Paul, *Learning Cyberspace: Essays on the Evolution of Media and the New Education*, San Francisco: Anamnesis Press, 1995.

_____ (1979). *Human Replay: A Theory of the Evolution of Media,* PhD dissertation, New York University (University Microfilms Int. #79 18,852).

_____ (1985). "Basics of computer conferencing, and thoughts on its applicability to education," excerpted from "The New School Online," unpublished report, January. Reprinted in Levinson, Paul (1995). *Learning Cyberspace*. San Francisco: Anamnesis Press.

_____ (1986). "Marshall McLuhan and computer conferencing," *IEEE Transactions of Professional Communication*, 1 March, pp. 9–11

_____ (1988). *Mind at Large: Knowing in the Technological Age*. Greenwich, CT: JAI Press.

_____ (1992). *Electronic Chronicles: Columns of the Changes in our Time*. San Francisco: Anamnesis Press.

_____ (1997). *The Soft Edge: A Natural History and Future of the Information Revolution*. New York and London: Routledge.

_____ (1998). "The Book on the Book," *Analog Science Fiction and Fact*, June, pp. 24–31.

_____ (1999). *Digital McLuhan: A Guide to the Information Millennium*. New York and London: Routledge.

_____ (1999). *The Silk Code* (novel). New York: Tor.

_____ (2003). Interview about Jayson Blair and *The New York Times*, *World News Now*, ABC-TV, May 11.

_____ (2003). *Realspace: The Fate of Physical Presence in the Digital Age, On and Off Planet*. New York and London: Routledge.

_____ (2004). *Cellphone: The Story of the World's Most Mobile Medium*. New York: Palgrave/Macmillan.

_____ (2004). Interview by Bill O'Reilly about journalists having private lives, *The O'Reilly Factor*, Fox News, 23 January, video. http://www.youtube.com/watch?v=uSOytS96YhI

_____ (2005). Interview by Joe Scarborough about Dan Rather and "Docu-Gate," *Scarborough Country*, MSNBC, 16 February, transcript: http://www.sff.net/people/paullevinson/scar021605.html
video: http://www.youtube.com/watch?v=VmvzYfY_gJA

_____ (2005). "The Flouting of the First Amendment," Keynote Address, Sixth Annual Media Ecology Conference, Fordham University, New York City, June 23. Reprinted in *Explorations in Media Ecology* (Vol. 5, No. 3), 2006, pp. 199–210, and in *Paul Levinson's Infinite Regress* blog, July 12, 2007. http://paullevinson.blogspot.com/2007/07/flouting-of-first-amendment-transcript.html

_____ (2006). Debate on *Squawk Box* with Jack Thompson about violence and videogames, CNBC-TV, 22 June, video. http://www.youtube.com/watch?v=-XtWV-tIeVg

_____ (2006). *The Plot to Save Socrates* (novel). New York: Tor.

_____ (2006). "*The Wire* and *The Wealth of Nations*," *Twice Upon a Rhyme* Myspace blog, 13 August. http://blogs.myspace.com/index.cfm?fuseaction=blog.view&friendID=17346415&blogID=155375148

_____ (2006). "*The Wire* without Stringer," *Light On Light Through* podcast, 4 November. http://paullev.libsyn.com/index.php?post_id=148095

_____ (2007). "First YouTube/CNN Presidential debate," *Paul Levinson's Infinite Regress* blog, 23 July. http://paullevinson.blogspot.com/2007/07/first-youtubecnn-presidential-debate.html

_____ (2007). "Free Josh Wolf," *Light On Light Through* podcast, 10 March. http://paullev.libsyn.com/index.php?post_id=190952

_____ (2007). "Good for Dan Rather: CBS deserves to be sued," *Paul Levinson's Infinite Regress* blog, 19 September. http://paullevinson.blogspot.com/2007/09/good-for-dan-rather-cbs-deserves-to-be.html

_____ (2007). "Hannity & Colmes split over Ron Paul's 1st place in Fox's latest post-debate poll," *Paul Levinson's Infinite Regress* blog, 22 October. http://paullevinson.blogspot.com/2007/10/hannity-colmes-split-over-ron-pauls-1st.html

_____ (2007). Interview by Ken Hudson (Kenny Hubble), "Media Ecology seminar in Second Life," 5 November, video. http://blip.tv/file/475397

_____ (2007). Interview by Mark Molaro, *The Alcove*, 27 November, video. http://www.youtube.com/watch?v=aqZNGYit3kY

_____ (2007). Interview with Rich Sommer, *Light On Light Through* podcast, 28 October. http://paullev.libsyn.com/index.php?post_id=271587

_____ (2007). Interview with Stanley Schmidt, *Light On Light Through* podcast, 1 December. http://paullev.libsyn.com/index.php?post_id=283468

_____ (2007). "Marshall McLuhan as micro blogger," *Paul Levinson's Infinite Regress* blog, 9 October. http://paullevinson.blogspot.com/2007/10/marshall-mcluhan-as-micro-blogger.html

_____ (2007). "My four rules: the best you can do to make it as a writer," *Light On Light Through* blog, 26 August. http://paullev.libsyn.com/index.php?post_id=249175

_____ (2007). "Now Obama's poll results are denigrated by a professional pollster," *Paul Levinson's Infinite Regress* blog, 1 November. http://paullevinson.blogspot.com/2007/11/now-obamas-poll-results-are-denigrated.html

_____ (2007). "Obama Girl applauded in my class at Fordham this afternoon," *Paul Levinson's Infinite Regress* blog, 21 September. http://paullevinson.blogspot.com/2007/09/obama-girl-applauded-in-my-class-at.html

_____ (2007). "Open letter to CNBC about taking down post-debate poll won by Ron Paul," *Paul Levinson's Infinite Regress* blog, 12 October. http://paullevinson.blogspot.com/2007/10/open-letter-to-cnbc-about-taking-down.html

_____ (2007). Phone-in guest on Shaun OMac's BlogTalkRadio show, *TV Talk*, 23 October. http://www.blogtalkradio.com/stations/bc/SHAUNOMACRADIO/blog/2007/10/24/Journeyman-rocks-Shaun-OMac-Radio

_____ (2007). "Rating the news networks in their campaign coverage," *Paul Levinson's Infinite Regress* blog, 21 September. http://paullevinson.blogspot.com/2007/09/rating-news-networks-in-their-election.html

_____ (2007). Reading from *The Plot to Save Socrates* at *Meet the Author*, with interview by Adele Ward, Second Life, SLCN.tv (Second Life Cable Network), 9 December, video. http://blip.tv/paul-levinson-on-media-writing-science-fiction-and-freedom/talking-about-media-philosophy-and-the-plot-to-save-socrates-in-second-life-543073

_____ (2007). "Republican YouTube/CNN debate in Florida," *Paul Levinson's Infinite Regress* blog, 28 November. http://paullevinson.blogspot.com/2007/11/republican-youtubecnn-debate-in-florida.html

_____ (2007). "Republicans now thumb their noses at YouTube as well as evolution," *Paul Levinson's Infinite Regress* blog, 27 July. http://paullevinson.blogspot.com/2007/07/republicans-now-thumb-noses-at-youtube.html

_____ (2007). Review of *Brotherhood,* Season 1 finale, *Paul Levinson's Infinite Regress* blog, 3 December. http://paullevinson.blogspot.com/2007/12/brotherhood-season-2-finale.html

_____ (2007). Review of *Lost,* Season 3 finale, *Paul Levinson's Infinite Regress* blog, 23 May. http://paullevinson.blogspot.com/2007/05/lost-season-3-finale-flashforwards.html

_____ (2007). Review of *Mad Men* 1.12, *Paul Levinson's Infinite Regress* blog, 12 October. http://paullevinson.blogspot.com/2007/10/mad-men-11-admirable-don.html

_____ (2007). "RIAA's monstrous legacy," *Paul Levinson's Infinite Regress* blog, 13 July. http://paullevinson.blogspot.com/2007/07/riaas-monstrous-legacy.html

_____ (2007). "The KNX Sunday morning interviews," *Paul Levinson's Infinite Regress* blog, 30 June. http://paullevinson.blogspot.com/2007/06/knx1070-sunday-morning-interviews.html

_____ (2007). "The secret riches of the panda," *Light On Light Through* blog, 30 July. http://paullev.libsyn.com/index.php?post_id=240416

_____ (2008). "Announcing Obama's choice through email not good idea," *Daily Kos*, 11 August. http://www.dailykos.com/storyonly/2008/8/11/154117/227/164/566307

_____ (2008). "Cyberbullying mom on MySpace got just what she deserved," *Twice Upon a Rhyme* Myspace blog, 27 November. http://blog.myspace.com/index.cfm?fuseaction=blog.view&friendID=17346415&blogID=452143917

_____ (2008). "George's guitar gently weeps through the ages," *Paul Levinson's Infinite Regress* blog, 15 June. http://paullevinson.blogspot.com/2008/06/harrisons-my-guitar-gently-weeps-ala.html

_____ (2008). Interview by KnitWitch (Máia Whitaker), *KnitWitch Zone* podcast, 26 February. http://www.talkshoe.com/talkshoe/web/talkCast.jsp?masterId=28497&cmd=tc

_____ (2008). "Katie Couric, Hero of the Revolution," *Paul Levinson's Infinite Regress* blog, 13 November. http://paullevinson.blogspot.com/2008/11/katie-couric-hero-of-revolution.html
cross-posted on *Open Salon*: http://open.salon.com/content.php?cid=43629

_____ (2008). "Keeping Obama with his email," *Paul Levinson's Infinite Regress* blog, 16 November. http://paullevinson.blogspot.com/2008/11/keeping-president-obama-with-his-email.html

_____ (2008). "MSNBC runs canned doc bloc as Mumbai burns," *Paul Levinson's Infinite Regress* blog, 28 November. http://paullevinson.blogspot.com/2008/11/inane-msnbc-programming-on-friday-eve.html

_____ (2008). "Obama should reject McCain's call to postpone Friday debate," *Paul Levinson's Infinite Regress* blog, 24 September. http://paullevinson.blogspot.com/2008/09/mccains-to-postpone-fridays-debate-i.html
cross-posted on *Open Salon:* http://open.salon.com/content.php?cid=21963

_____ (2008). Review of *Mad Men*, 2.4, *Paul Levinson's Infinite Regress* blog, 18 August. http://paullevinson.blogspot.com/2008/08/mad-men-24-betty-and-dons-son.html

_____ (2008). "Superb speeches by Bill Clinton and John Kerry," *Paul Levinson's Infinite Regress* blog, 27 August. http://paullevinson.blogspot.com/2008/08/superb-speeches-by-bill-clinton-and.html

cross-posted on *Open Salon*: http://open.salon.com/blog/paul_levinson/2008/08/27/
superb_speeches_ by_b_clintonkerry_-_tv_shows_just_bills
Daily Kos: http://www.dailykos.com/storyonly/ 2008/8/28/577065/-The-Cable-
All-News-Networks-Diss-John-Kerry

_____ (2008). "Take It from a college prof: Obama's 'missing' paper is another
Conservative red herring," *Daily Kos*, 25 July. http://www.dailykos.com/
storyonly/2008/7/25/16275/4548/308/557010

_____ (2008). "Unburning Alexandria" (novelette). *Analog Science Fiction and Fact*,
November, pp. 116–133.

_____ (2008). "Where have Olbermann and Maddow disappeared to?" *Paul Levinson's
Infinite Regress* blog, 19 November. http://paullevinson.blogspot.com/2008/11/
where-have-olbermann-and-maddow.html

_____ (2009). "Conversation with Greenburgh NY Town Supervisor Paul Feiner
about blogging, Obama, and Caroline Kennedy," *Light On Light Through*
podcast, 16 January. http://paullev.libsyn.com/index.php?post_id=423351

_____ (2009). Interview by The Gypsy Poet, *Gypsy Poet Radio*, BlogTalkRadio,
17 May. http://www.blogtalkradio.com/Gypsypoet/2009/05/17/Gypsy-Poet-
Radio-Presents-Paul-Levinson

_____ (2009). "New new media vs. the mullahs in Iran," *Paul Levinson's Infinite
Regress* blog, 16 June. http://paullevinson.blogspot.com/2009/06/new-new-
media-vs-mullahs-in-iran.html

_____ (2009). Response to "What is [a] podcast," PodcastAlley.com, 8 January.
http://podcastalley.com/forum/showthread.php?t=145349

_____ (2009–12). "What's newer than *New New Media*," *Paul Levinson's Infinite Regress*
blog. http://newnewmediabook.com

_____ (2011). "First Presidential Twitter press conference," *Paul Levinson's Infinite
Regress* blog, 11 July. http://paullevinson.blogspot.com/2011/07/first-
presidential-twitter-press.html

_____ (2011). Interview by Janet Babin, "NYT online: from free to fee,"
Marketplace Tech, 24 January. http://www.marketplace.org/topics/tech/
nyt-online-free-fee

_____ (2011). "Marshall McLuhan, North Africa, and social media," lecture at
St. Francis College, Brooklyn, NY, 23 February, video. http://blip.tv/paul-
levinson-on-media-writing-science-fiction-and-freedom/marshall-mcluhan-
north-africa-and-social-media-4862814

_____ (2011). "Occupy Wall Street Chronicles, Part 1," *Paul Levinson's Infinite Regress*
blog, 30 November. http://paullevinson.blogspot.com/2011/11/occupy-wall-
street-chronicles-part-1.html

_____ (2011). "Occupy Wall Street Panel," *Good Day Street Talk*, Fox-NY TV,
22 October. video: http://www.youtube.com/watch?v=_MgQEVFHhS4

_____ (2011). Quoted about WikiLeaks in Goodale (2011).

_____ (2012). "In defense of KONY 2012," *Paul Levinson's Infinite Regress* blog, 9 March. http://paullevinson.blogspot.com/2012/03/in-defense-of-kony-2012.html

_____ (2012). "Is Wikipedia wrong to go dark for SOPA protest?" *Mediaite*, 17 January. http://www.mediaite.com/columnists/is-wikipedia-wrong-to-go-dark-for-sopa-protest/

_____ (2012). "Rick Santorum's Wikipedia page is locked," *Paul Levinson's Infinite Regress* blog, 19 February. http://paullevinson.blogspot.com/2012/02/rick-santorums-wikipedia-page-is-locked.html

_____ (2012). "Timcast on UStream doing great covering NYPD violation of First Amendment tonight," *Paul Levinson's Infinite Regress* blog, 1 January. http://paullevinson.blogspot.com/2012/01/timcast-on-ustream-doing-great-covering.html

_____ (2012). "Why The Monkees are important," *Mediaite*, 29 February. http://www.mediaite.com/online/why-the-monkees-are-important/

Levinson, Paul, and Krondes, Jim (1969). "Snow Flurries," Lady Mac Music, demo recording by Louis Caraballo, Paul Levinson, and Peter Rosenthal. Played on Kane and Brandt (2007).

Lewin, James (2006). "Podcast goes from zero to one million downloads in four months," *Podcasting News*, 28 November. http://www.podcastingnews.com/2006/11/28/podcast-goes-from-zero-to-one-million-downloads-in-four-months/

Lieberman, David (2011). "In a renaissance for radio, more listeners are tuning in," *USA Today*, 21 March. http://www.usatoday.com/money/media/2011-03-21-Radio-listeners-growing.htm

Liza (2008). "Netroots' bloggers boycott of Associated Press is working," *culturekitchen* blog, 16 June. http://culturekitchen.com/liza/blog/netroots_bloggers_boycott_of_associated_press_is_w

Lloyd, M. Paul (2010). "Oldest 'writing' found on 60,000-year-old eggshells," *Focus Magazine*, 4 March. http://sciencefocus.com/forum/oldest-writing-found-on-60-000-year-old-eggshells-t700.html

MacBeach (2008). Comment to Alex Chitu's "The unlikely integration between Google News and Digg," *Google Operating System* blog, 23 July. http://googlesystem.blogspot.com/2008/07/unlikely-integration-between-google.html

MacManus, Richard (2012). "Top ten YouTube videos of all time," *Read Write Web*, 9 January. http://www.readwriteweb.com/archives/top_10_youtube_videos_of_all_time.php

Maddow, Rachel (2012). "John Boehner is bad at his job," MSNBC-TV, 24 February.

Madison, Lucy (2011). "Brownback apologizes after Twitter dust-up," CBSNews.com, 28 November. http://www.cbsnews.com/8301-503544_162-57332320-503544/brownback-apologizes-after-twitter-dust-up/

Madrigal, Alexis (2011). "Should employers be allowed to ask for your Facebook login?" *The Atlantic*, 19 February. http://www.theatlantic.com/technology/archive/2011/02/should-employers-be-allowed-to-ask-for-your-facebook-login/71480/

Maeroff, Gene (1979). "Reading achievement of children in Indiana found as good as in '44," *The New York Times*, 15 April, p. 10.

Malkin, Bonnie (2008). "Pakistan ban to blame for YouTube blackout," *The Daily Telegraph*, 25 February. http://www.telegraph.co.uk/news/uknews/3356520/Pakistan-ban-to-blame-for-YouTube-blackout.html

Manjoo, Farhad (2008). "Don't blame YouTube, MySpace for teen beating video," *Machinist* blog, Salon.com, 4 April. http://machinist.salon.com/blog/2008/04/08/myspace_beating/

_____ (2009). "I do solemnly swear that I will blog regularly," *Slate*, 20 January. http://www.slate.com/?id=2209275

Marder, Rachel (2007). "Two students sued for illegal downloading," *The Justice*, 12 July. http://www.thejusticeonline.com/home/index.cfm?event=displayArticle&ustory_id=7461e8a8-4bea-4883-af39-1ee5a8ac8fb2&page=1

MarketingProfs (2012). "What's driving Pinterest's amazing growth," 21 February. http://www.marketingprofs.com/charts/2012/7173/whats-driving-pinterests-amazing-growth

Masterson, Michele (2008). " 'Cyberbully' mom closer to learning her fate," *ChannelWeb*, 26 November. http://www.crn.com/software/212200723

Matei, Sorin Adam (2011). "Why Iceland's new draft constitution was not written by crowdsourcing and why this is a good thing, too," *I Think*, 30 July. http://matei.org/ithink/2011/07/30/why-icelands-new-draft-constitution-was-not-written-by-crowdsourcing-and-why-this-is-a-good-thing-too/

mavrevmatt (2008). Comment on Alex Chitu's "The unlikely integration between Google News and Digg," *Google Operating System* blog, 23 July. http://googlesystem.blogspot.com/2008/07/unlikely-integration-between-google.html

Max, Tucker (2006). *I Hope They Serve Beer in Hell*. New York: Citadel.

McCain, John (2008). Speech delivered in Louisiana, *Politico*, 13 June, transcript: http://www.politico.com/news/stories/0608/10820.html video: http://www.youtube.com/watch?v=A7RuX4pQPLY

McCarthy, Caroline (2008). "Who will reign over Digg: Obama or Jobs?" *The Social*, CNET News, 12 May. http://news.cnet.com/8301-13577_3-9942496-36.html

McCartney, Paul (2004). Performance of George Harrison's "All Things Must Pass" in Madrid, Spain, video. (See also Harrison, George.) http://www.youtube.com/watch?v=cYl942_I3Wo

McCullagh, Declan (2007). "Ron Paul: the Internet's favorite candidate," CNET News, 6 August. http://news.cnet.com/Ron-Paul-The-Internets-favorite-candidate/2100-1028_3-6200893.html

McCullagh, Declan, and Broache, Anne (2007). "Blogs turn 10—who's the father?" CNET News, 20 March. http://news.cnet.com/2100-1025_3-6168681.html

McKeever, William A. (1910). "Motion pictures: a primary school for criminals," *Good Housekeeping*, August, pp. 184–186.

McLuhan, Marshall (1962). *The Gutenberg Galaxy*. New York: Mentor.

_____ (1964). *Understanding Media*. New York: Mentor.

_____ (1977). "The laws of the media," with a preface by Paul Levinson, *Et Cetera* journal, *34, 2*, pp. 173–179.

McLuhan, Marshall, and Fiore, Quentin (1967). *The Medium Is the Massage*. New York: Bantam.

Merlot, Miss (2008). "The Caledon Astrotorium grand opening party," 21 March. http://merlotzymurgy.blogspot.com/2008/03/caledon-astrotrorium-grand-opening.html

Messer-Kruse, Timothy (2012). "The 'undue weight' of truth on Wikipedia," *The Chronicle of Higher Education*, 15 February. http://chronicle.com/article/the-undue-weight-of-truth-on/130704/

Messerli, Joe (2006). "Why polls shouldn't be used to make decisions," *Balanced Politics,* 25 January. http://www.balancedpolitics.org/editorial-the_case_against_polls.htm

Meyrowitz, Joshua (1986). *No Sense of Place*. NY: Oxford University Press.

Milian, Mark (2009). "Digg: Don't shout, use Twitter and Facebook instead," *Los Angeles Times,* 26 May. http://latimesblogs.latimes.com/technology/2009/05/digg-shout-share.html

Miller, Judith (2005). U.S. Senate Committee on the Judiciary, Hearing on Reporters' Shield Legislation, 16 October. http://judiciary.senate.gov/hearings/testimony.cfm?id=1637&wit_id=4698

_____ (2008). Appearance on *Fox News Watch*, 6 December.

Milton, John (1644). *Areopagetica.*

Mintz, Jessica (2009). "iTunes price cut: Apple announces tiered system, DRM-free tunes," *The Huffington Post*, 6 January. http://www.huffingtonpost.com/2009/01/06/itunes-price-cut-apple-an_n_155660.html

Mirkinson, Jack (2011). "Occupy Wall Street November 17: journalists arrested, beaten by police," *The Huffington Post*, 17 November. http://www.huffingtonpost.com/2011/11/17/occupy-wall-street-nov-17-journalists-arrested-beaten_n_1099661.html

"Mitt Romney (Politician)" (2012). Facebook page. https://www.facebook.com/mittromney

Morris, Tee; Tomasi, Chuck; and Terra, Evo (2008). *Podcasting for Dummies*, 2nd edition. New York: For Dummies/Wiley.

Mumford, Lewis (1970). *The Pentagon of Power*. New York: Harcourt, Brace, Jovanovich.

Musil, Steven (2008). "U.S. Army warns of Twittering terrorists," CNET News, 26 October. http://news.cnet.com/8301-1009_3-10075487-83.html http://www.fas.org/irp/eprint/mobile.pdf

"My Box in a Box" (2006). Featuring Melissa Lamb, written and produced by Leah Kauffman and Ben Relles, song performed by Leah Kauffman, 26 December, video. http://www.youtube.com/watch?v=3xElIik0Ys0

Nadelman, Stefan (2008). "Food Fight," written, directed, animated by Nadelman, 27 February, video. http://www.youtube.com/watch?v=e-yldqNkGfo

Nash, Kate (2007). Myspace music page, 18 February. http://www.myspace.com/katenashmusic

Nathan, Stephen (2007). "The Glowing Bones in the Old Stone House," *Bones,* Season 2, Episode 20, directed by Caleb Deschanel, Fox-TV, 9 May.

Nationwide Tea Party Coalition (2010). "About us." http://www.nationwidechicagoteaparty.com/about.php

Nature magazine, editors (2006). "Encyclopaedia Britannica and Nature: a response," *Nature*, 23 March. http://www.nature.com/press_releases/Britannica_response.pdf

NeoPoiesis Press (2009). Myspace page. http://www.myspace.com/neopoiesispress

NetLingo (2009). "Cyberstalker." http://www.netlingo.com/word/cyberstalker.php

Newitz, Analee (2007). "I bought votes on Digg," *Wired*, 1 March. http://www.wired.com/techbiz/people/news/2007/03/72832

Nissenson, Marilyn (2007). *The Lady Upstairs: Dorothy Schiff and the* New York Post. New York: St. Martin's.

Northerndom (2012). "Troll essay: Internet attitudes and personal EXP," *Adventures with Media of the Social Variety* blog, 18 February. http://northerndom.wordpress.com/2012/02/18/troll-essay-internet-attitudes-and-personal-exp/

Obama, Barack (2008). Interview by Barbara Walters, *Barbara Walters Special*, ABC-TV, 26 November.

_____ (2009). Interview by John Harwood, CNBC-TV, 7 January.

O'Brien, Terrence (2008). "Teen lands in jail after posting baby-tossing video on YouTube," *Switched*, 3 July. http://www.switched.com/2008/07/03/teen-lands-in-jail-after-posting-baby-tossing-video-on-youtube/

O'Connor, Mickey (2008). "*Fringe*: our burning questions answered!" Interview with Jeff Pinker, *TV Guide*, 11 November. http://www.tvguide.com/News/Fringe-Burning-Questions-58392.aspx

O'Donnell, Lawrence (2012). Coverage of 2012 Republican South Carolina primary, MSNBC, 21 January.

O'Donnell, Norah (2009). Report about Barack Obama and BlackBerry, MSNBC, 18 January.

Ogasawara, Todd (2011). "eBook sales up 202%. Audio book sales up 36.7%," *Social Times* 18 April. http://socialtimes.com/ebook-sales-up-202-audio-book-sales-up-36-7_b58151

Olander, Eric (2011). "#ASKOBAMA: The US President's first ever Twitter news conference," *France 24*, 11 July. http://www.france24.com/en/20110711-2011-07-11-twitter-obama-facebook-internet

Orlando, Carlos (2009). "'YouTube for Television' to launch via Sony and Nintendo," *infopackets*, 27 January. http://www.infopackets.com/news/business/google/2009/20090127_youtube_for_television_to_launch_via_sony_and_nintendo.htm

Orlowski, Andrew (2006). "Nature mag cooked Wikipedia study," *The Register*, 23 March. http://www.theregister.co.uk/2006/03/23/britannica_wikipedia_nature_study/

Palin, Sarah (2008). Interview by Greta Van Susteren, Fox News, 11 November. http://www.foxnews.com/story/0,2933,449884,00.html

_____ (2008). Interview by Katie Couric, *CBS Evening News*, 30 September, video. http://www.youtube.com/watch?v=xRkWebP2Q0Y

Pash, Adam (2008). "Wikipanion brings Wikipedia to your iPhone or iPod Touch," *lifehacker*, 20 August. http://lifehacker.com/400664/wikipanion-brings-wikipedia-to-your-iphone-or-ipod-touch

_____ (2008). "Wikipedia officially launches mobile version," *lifehacker*, 15 December. http://lifehacker.com/5110289/wikipedia-officially-launches-mobile-version

Patterson, Ben (2009). "White House stuck in 'technological Dark Ages'," *The Gadget Hound*, 22 January. [Site defunct.]

Pepitone, Julianne (2012). "Encyclopedia Britannica to stop printing books," *CNN Money*, 13 March. http://money.cnn.com/2012/03/13/technology/encyclopedia-britannica-books/index.htm

Percival, Ray (2012). *The Myth of the Closed Mind: Understanding Why and How People Are Rational*. Chicago, IL: Open Court.

Perez-Pena, Richard (2008). "Newspaper circulation continues to decline rapidly," *The New York Times*, 27 October. http://www.nytimes.com/2008/10/28/business/media/28circ.html

_____ (2009). "Keeping news of kidnapping off Wikipedia," *The New York Times*, 28 June. http://www.nytimes.com/2009/06/29/technology/internet/29wiki.html

Pershing, Ben (2009). "Kennedy, Byrd the latest victims of Wikipedia errors," *The Washington Post*, 21 January. http://voices.washingtonpost.com/capitol-briefing/2009/01/kennedy_the_latest_victim_of_w.html

Peters, Charles (2005). *Five Days in Philadelphia: The Amazing "We Want Willkie!" Convention of 1940 and How It Freed FDR to Save the Western World*. Jackson, TN: Public Affairs.

Petroski, Henry (1999). *The Book on the Bookshelf*. New York: Knopf.

Pham, Alex (2011). "Spotify's plan: get users hooked, then ask them to pay for music," *Los Angeles Times*, 10 November. http://articles.latimes.com/2011/nov/10/business/la-fi-ct-facetime-spotify-20111110

Phillips, Rich (2008). "Suspects in video beating could get life in prison," CNN.com, 11 April. http://edition.cnn.com/2008/CRIME/04/10/girl.fights/index.html

Pitts, Byron (2010). "Gay student's death highlights troubling trend," CBS News, 30 September. http://www.cbsnews.com/stories/2010/09/30/eveningnews/main6916119.shtml

Polipop (2012). "Glease," Obama Girl parody of *Grease* and *Glee*, 14 February, video. http://www.youtube.com/watch?v=CLDvv7S5qMA&list=PL58EBB4E12AD8688C

Popkin, Helen A. S. (2009). "Activism evolves for the digital age," MSNBC.com, 19 June. http://www.msnbc.msn.com/id/31432770/ns/technology_and_science-tech_and_gadgets/

Powell, Colin (2008). Interview by Fareed Zakaria, *GPS*, CNN, 14 December, transcript. http://transcripts.cnn.com/TRANSCRIPTS/0812/14/fzgps.01.html

Rahm Emanuel Facts (2009). Website. http://rahmfacts.com

Raphael, J. P. (2008). "Wikipedia censorship sparks free speech debate," *PC World*, 10 December. http://www.washingtonpost.com/wp-dyn/content/article/2008/12/08/AR2008120803188.html

Reardon, Marguerite (2009). "Smartphones offer hope in declining cell phone biz," CNET News, 4 February. http://news.cnet.com/8301-1035_3-10156897-94.html

"Reuters, Adam" (2006). "Surge in high-end Second Life business profits," Reuters, 5 December. http://secondlife.reuters.com/stories/2006/12/05/surge-in-high-end-second-life-business-profits/

Rheingold, Howard (2003). *Smart Mobs: The Next Social Revolution*. New York: Basic.

Ribeiro, John (2008). "In Mumbai, bloggers and Twitter offer help to relatives," *PC World*, 27 November. http://www.pcworld.com/article/154621/in_mumbai_bloggers_and_twitter_offer_help_to_relatives.html

Richards, I. A. (1929). *Practical Criticism*. London: K. Paul.

"Rick Santorum (Politician)" (2012). Facebook page. https://www.facebook.com/ricksantorum

Riley, Duncan (2007). "CSI: NY comes to Second Life Wednesday," *TechCrunch*, 20 October. http://www.techcrunch.com/2007/10/20/csiny-comes-to-second-life-wednesday/

Roark, James L.; Johnson, Michael P.; Cohen, Patricia Cline; Stage, Sarah; Lawson, Alan; and Hartmann, Susan M. (2007). *The American Promise*. Boston: Bedford/St. Martin's Press.

Robbins, Christopher (2012). "Citizen journalist arrested during OWS march fights city & wins," Gothamist, 15 May. http://gothamist.com/2012/05/15/journalist_arrested_during_ows_marc.php

Rose, Carl (1951). "What's That, Mama?" cartoon, about a radio in the attic, *The New Yorker*, 28 July.

Rove, Karl (2009). "Back in Washington..." Twitter, 14 February. http://twitter.com/karlrove

Rucker, J. D. (2012). "Why Digg's rebound is significant to every social media site today," *Fast Company*, 25 February. http://www.fastcompany.com/1819997/why-diggs-rebound-is-significant-to-every-single-social-media-site

Russell, Jason (2012). *Kony 2012*, video. http://www.youtube.com/watch?v=Y4MnpzG5Sqc

Ryan, Jenny (2008). "The virtual campfire: an ethnography of online social networking," thesis, Master of Arts in Anthropology, Wesleyan University.

Ryan, Paul (2012). "Paul Ryan opposes SOPA after Reddit pressure," RT.com (Russian television), 10 January, video. http://www.youtube.com/watch?v=qIzA_UItA8g

Saffo, Paul (2008). "Obama's 'cybergenic' edge," abcnews.com, 11 June. http://abcnews.go.com/Technology/Politics/Story?id=5046275

Sagan, Carl (1978). *The Dragons of Eden*. New York: Ballantine.

Saleem, Muhammad (2006). Interview by Tony Hung, "Insights from an elite social bookmarker," *BloggerTalks*, 14 November. http://www.bloggertalks.com/2006/11/muhammad-saleem-insights-from-an-elite-social-bookmarker/

_____ (2007). "Ron Paul supporters need a lesson in social media marketing," *Pronet Advertising*, 6 July. http://www.pronetadvertising.com/articles/ron-paul-supporters-need-a-lesson-in-social-media-marketing34389.html

_____ (2007). "Ruining the Digg experience, one shout at a time," *Social Media Strategy for New Entrepreneurs*, 31 October. http://muhammadsaleem.com/2007/10/31/ruining-the-digg-experience-one-shout-at-a-time/

_____ (2007). "The Bury Brigade exists, and here's my proof," *Pronet Advertising*, 27 February. http://www.pronetadvertising.com/articles/the-bury-brigade-exists-and-heres-my-proof.html

_____ (2007). "The Social Media Manual—read before you play," *.docstoc*, 20 November. http://www.searchengineland.com/the-social-media-manual-read-before-you-play-12738

Sansone, Ron (2007). "Digg dirt: exposing Ron Paul's social media manipulation," *iAOC* (International Association of Online Communications) blog, 3 July. http://www.iaocblog.com/blog/_archives/2007/7/3/3068799.html

Sawyer, Miranda (2006). "Pictures of Lily," *The Guardian / The Observer*, 21 May. http://www.guardian.co.uk/music/2006/may/21/popandrock.lilyallen

Schmidt, Eric (2008). Guest on "The Rachel Maddow Show," MSNBC-TV, 17 November.

Schonfeld, Erick (2009). "Twitter surges past Digg, LinkedIn, and NYTimes.com with 32 million global visitors," *TechCrunch,* 20 May. http://www.techcrunch .com/2009/05/20/twitter-surges-past-digg-linkedin-and-nytimescom-with-32-million-global-visitors/

Schwartz, Mattathias (2008). "The trolls among us," *The New York Times,* 3 August. http://www.nytimes.com/2008/08/03/magazine/03trolls-t.html

Scorsese, Martin (2005). *No Direction Home,* movie documentary about Bob Dylan. Paramount.

Seltzer, Sarah (2012). "Occupiers aren't running for office. They have their sights set higher," *The Washington Post,* 13 January. http://www.washingtonpost.com/ opinions/occupiers-arent-running-for-office-they-have-their-sights-set-higher/ 2012/01/12/gIQA0rPwwP_story.html

Shapiro, Phil ((2011). "Should I protect my tweets?" *PC World,* 22 February. http://www.pcworld.com/article/220287/should_i_protect_my_tweets .html

Sharma, Dinesh C. (2005). "Podcast start-up creates music network," CNET News, 23 August. http://news.cnet.com/Podcast-start-up-creates-music-network/ 2100-027_3-5841888.html

Sharp, David (2008). "Audio book sales are booming—what makes them so great?" *LinkSnoop,* 26 December. http://www.linksnoop.com/more/181076/ Audio-Book-Sales-Are-Booming-What-Makes-Them-So-Great/

Shawn, Eric (2008). Report about Facebook groups, Fox News, 1 December.

Sierra, Kathy (2007). "My favorite graphs…and the future," *Creating Passionate Users* blog, 6 April. http://headrush.typepad.com/

Silversmith, David (2009). "Google losing up to $1.65M a day on YouTube," *Internet Evolution,* 14 April. http://www.internetevolution.com/author.asp?id=715&doc_ id=175123&

Sinderbrand, Rebecca, and Wells, Rachel (2008). "Obama takes top billing on U.S. television," CNN.com, 29 October. http://edition.cnn.com/2008/POLITICS/ 10/29/campaign.wrap.spending/index.html

Sirota, David (2008). "The Politico's Jayson Blair," *Open Salon,* 7 December. http:// open.salon.com/content.php?cid=57773

Sklar, Rachel (2007). "A crush on Obama, and an eye on the prize," *The Huffington Post,* 16 July. http://www.huffingtonpost.com/2007/07/16/a-crush-on-obama-and-an-e_n_53057.html

Smith, Harry (2012). Report on "The Revolution of the White Snow" in Russia, *Rock Center,* NBC-TV, 29 February.

Smith, Justin (2008). "Facebook infrastructure up to 10,000 Web servers," *Inside Facebook* blog, 23 April. http://www.insidefacebook.com/2008/04/23/ facebook-infrastructure-up-to-10000-web-servers/

Smith, Shepard (2008). *Fox Report with Shepard Smith,* Fox News, 2 December.

Socialmediatrader (2008). "What would happen if the US elections were held on Digg?" 18 January. http://socialmediatrader.com/what-would-happen-if-the-us-elections-were-held-on-digg/

Spiegel, Brendan (2007). "Ron Paul: how a fringe politician took over the Web," *Wired*, 27 June. http://www.wired.com/politics/onlinerights/news/2007/06/ron_paul

Staples, Andy (2012). "For top football recruits, behavior on social media has consequences," *Sports Illustrated,* 24 January. http://sportsillustrated.cnn.com/2012/writers/andy_staples/01/24/recruits.social.media/index.html

Stelter, Brian (2011). "News organizations complain about treatment during protests," *The New York Times*, 21 November. http://mediadecoder.blogs.nytimes.com/2011/11/21/news-organizations-complain-about-treatment-during-protests/

Stelter, Brian, and Baker, Al (2011). "Reporters say police denied access to protest site," *The New York Times,* 15 November. http://mediadecoder.blogs.nytimes.com/2011/11/15/reporters-say-police-denied-access-to-protest-site/

Sternberg, Janet (2012). *Misbehavior in Cyber Places: The Regulation of Online Conduct in Virtual Communities on the Internet.* Lanham, MD: University Press of America, in press.

Stirland, Sarah Lai (2007). "News recommendation site launches 'Digg the Candidates': Ron Paul & Obama end up on top," *Wired*, 21 November. http://blog.wired.com/27bstroke6/2007/11/news-recommenda.html

"Stop the 'Doc Bloc' on MSNBC" (2008). Facebook group. http://www.facebook.com/group.php?gid=49254779160

Storm, Darlene (2011). "Army of fake social media friends to promote propaganda," *Computer World*, 22 February http://blogs.computerworld.com/17852/army_of_fake_social_media_friends_to_promote_propaganda

Stranahan, Lee (2008). "Markos, John, & Elizabeth: how *Daily Kos* keeps swallowing the Kool-Aid," *The Huffington Post*, 12 August. http://www.huffingtonpost.com/lee-stranahan/markos-john-elizabeth-how_b_118343.html

Strate, Lance (2007). *BlogVersed*, Myspace blog. http://blogs.myspace.com/index.cfm?fuseaction=blog.view&friendID=176504380&blogID=284027048

Strate, Lance; Jacobson, Ron; Gibson, Stephanie (Eds.) (2003). *Communication and Cyberspace*. Cresskill, NJ: Hampton.

Straus, Donald B. (1991). "Intuition—a human tool for generalizing," *Journal of Social and Biological Structures*, 14/3, pp. 333–352.

_____ (2001). "Referenda: can this crippled citizen voice be converted into an educated roar?" *Loka Alert*, 1 February. http://www.loka.org/alerts/loka_alert_8.1.htm

Stuart, Sarah Clarke ("swampburbia") (2009). "The infinite narrative: intertextuality, new media and the digital communities of *Lost*," syllabus, University of North Florida course, Spring. http://lostinlit.wordpress.com

Suellontrop, Chris (2008). "The Kerry surprise," *The New York Times*, 28 August. http://opinionator.blogs.nytimes.com/2008/08/28/the-kerry-surprise/

Sullivan, Andrew (2008). "The Kerry speech," *The Daily Dish*, 28 August. http://andrewsullivan.theatlantic.com/the_daily_dish/2008/08/the-kerry-speec.html

Szalai, Georg (2012). "Facebook files for IPO, looks to raise $5 billion," *The Hollywood Reporter*, 1 February. http://www.hollywoodreporter.com/news/facebook-files-ipo-5-billion-financials-mark-zuckerberg-profit-286384

Talamasca, Akela (2008). "Second Life on an iPhone," *Massively*, 13 February. http://www.massively.com/2008/02/13/second-life-on-an-iphone/

Talkshoe (2009). "New to Talkshoe?" http://www.talkshoe.com/se/about/TSAbout.html

Teachout, Zephyr; Streeter, Thomas; et al. (2008). *Mousepads, Shoe Leather, and Hope: Lessons from the Howard Dean Campaign for the Future of Internet Politics*. Boulder, Co., and London: Paradigm.

Techradar (2008). "Facebook, MySpace statistics," 11 January. http://techradar1.wordpress.com/2008/01/11/facebookmyspace-statistics/

Tedford, Thomas (1985). *Freedom of Speech in the United States*. New York: Random House.

Terdiman, Daniel (2008). "AMC decides to allow fans' 'Mad Men' Twittering," CNET News, 27 August. http://news.cnet.com/8301-13772_3-10027152-52.html

Terminator: The Sarah Connor Chronicles (2008). Season 2, Episode 10, Fox TV, 24 November.

_____ (2008). Season 2, Episode 13, Fox TV, 15 December.

The New Millennium: Science, Fiction, Fantasy (2000). Fox News special, 1 January.

Themediaisdying (2009). http://www.twitter.com/themediaisdying

Time (2008). Magazine cover, 24 November.

TMZ staff (2006). "'Kramer's' racist tirade caught on tape," *TMZ*, 20 November. http://www.tmz.com/2006/11/20/kramers-racist-tirade-caught-on-tape/

Tossell, Ivor (2008). "Teeny-tiny Twitter was the year's big story," *Globe and Mail*, 25 December. http://www.theglobeandmail.com/servlet/story/RTGAM.20081225.wwebtossell1226/EmailBNStory/Technology/home

Trippi, Joe (2004). *The Revolution Will Not Be Televised: Democracy, the Internet, and the Overthrow of Everything*. New York: William Morrow.

Truth on Earth Band (2008). "Shot with a Bulletless Gun," recording. http://www.truthonearthband.com/song_bulletlessgun.html

Valéry, Paul (1933). "Au sujet du cimetière marin," reprinted in *Oeuvres de Paul Valéry*, Paris: Gallimard, La Pléiade, 1957.

Vamburkar, Meenal (2012). "How Kony 2012 is raising awareness, but also raising questions," *Mediaite*, 8 March. http://www.mediaite.com/online/how-kony-2012-is-raising-awareness-but-also-raising-questions/

Van Grove, Jennifer (2009). "One giant leap for Twitterkind; Mike Massimino tweets from space," *Mashable*, 12 May. http://mashable.com/2009/05/12/first-tweet-from-space/

Vance, Ashlee (2009). "Online video of inauguration sets records," *The New York Times*, 20 January. http://www.nytimes.com/2009/01/21/us/politics/21video.htm

VanDenPlas, Scott (2007). "Ron Paul, Barack Obama, and the digital divide," *morefishthanman* blog, 21 May. http://www.morefishthanman.com/2007/05/21/ron-paul-barack-obama-and-the-digital-divide/

Vargas, Jose Antonio (2007). "On Wikipedia, debating 2008 hopefuls' every facet," *The Washington Post*, 17 September. http://www.washingtonpost.com/wp-dyn/content/article/2007/09/16/AR2007091601699_pf.html

Vedro, Steven (2007). *Digital Dharma*. Wheaton, IL: Quest Books.

Wales, Jimmy (2009). Interview by Mark Molaro, *The Alcove*, 26 May, video. http://www.youtube.com/watch?v=e1t88Bul5is

Walsh, Joan (2007). "Men who hate women on the Web," *Salon*, 31 March. http://www.salon.com/opinion/feature/2007/03/31/sierra/

_____ (2008). Comment on Paul Levinson's "Obama should reject McCain's call to postpone Friday's debate," *Open Salon*, 24 September. http://open.salon.com/content.php?cid=21963

Washington Post, The (2008). "President-elect Obama's first YouTube address," 15 November. http://voices.washingtonpost.com/44/2008/11/15/president-elect_obamas_first_y.html

Wastler, Allen (2007). "An open letter to the Ron Paul faithful," *Political Capital with John Harwood* blog, CNBC.com, 11 October. http://www.cnbc.com/id/21257762

Weeds (2009). Season 5, Episode 1, Showtime TV series, 8 June.

Weiner, Anthony (2011). Transcript of resignation speech, 16 June. http://www.nbcnewyork.com/news/local/Weiner-Admits-Confesses-Photo-Twitter-Relationships-123268493.html

Weist, Zena (2009). "Twitterers: how old are you?" *Nothin' but SocNET*, 21 February. http://nothingbutsocnet.blogspot.com/2008/02/twitterers-how-old-are-you.html

Wellman, Barry (2008). "I was a WikiWarrior for Barack Obama," *CITASA*, 8 November. http://list.citasa.org/pipermail/citasa_list.citasa.org/2008-November/000057.html

Wertheimer, Linda (2008). "Age likely to be key factor in Presidential campaign," National Public Radio, 24 June. Also, quoted in full in Liasson, Mara (2008), "Parsing the generational divide for Democrats," National Public Radio, 1 May. http://www.npr.org/templates/story/story.php?storyId=91853809

White House Blog, The (2009). "Change has come to WhiteHouse.gov," 20 January. http://www.whitehouse.gov/blog/change_has_come_to_whitehouse-gov/

Wikipedia (2012). "Category: Wikipedia behavioral guidelines." http://en.wikipedia.org/wiki/Category:Wikipedia_behavioral_guidelines

_____ (2012). "Kate Nash." http://en.wikipedia.org/wiki/Kate_Nash

_____ (2012). "Lily Allen." http://en.wikipedia.org/wiki/Lily_Allen

_____ (2012). "Sean Kingston." http://en.wikipedia.org/wiki/Sean_Kingston

_____ (2012). "The Arab Spring." http://en.wikipedia.org/wiki/The_Arab_Spring

_____ (2012). "The Traveling Wilburys." http://en.wikipedia.org/wiki/The_Traveling_Wilburys

_____ (2012). "Virgin Killer" (Scorpions album, with nude girl on cover). http://en.wikipedia.org/wiki/Virgin_Killer

_____ (2012). "Wikipedia." http://en.wikipedia.org/wiki/Wikipedia

_____ (2012). "Wikipedia: Conflict of interest." http://en.wikipedia.org/wiki/Wikipedia:COI

_____ (2012). "Wikipedia: Identifying reliable sources." http://en.wikipedia.org/wiki/Wikipedia:Identifying_reliable_sources

_____ (2012). "Wikipedia servers." http://en.wikipedia.org/wiki/Wikipedia#Software_and_hardware

Winfield, Nicole (2009). "Vatican 2.0: Pope gets his own YouTube channel," Associated Press, 23 January. http://seattletimes.nwsource.com/html/businesstechnology/2008662245_apeuvaticanyoutube.htm

Wortham, Jenna (2008). "'Puppy Torture' video sparks outrage, military investigation," *Wired*, 4 March. http://blog.wired.com/underwire/2008/03/puppy-torture-v.html

Wright, Benjamin, and Winn, Jane K. (1998). *The Law of Electronic Commerce*, 3rd edition. Aspen, Co.: Aspen Law & Business.

Young, Neil (2009). "Fork in the Road," song. http://www.youtube.com/watch?v=m7L7XsHKCVs

Zeleny, Jeff (2008). "Lose the BlackBerry? Yes he can, maybe," *The New York Times*, 15 November. http://www.nytimes.com/2008/11/16/us/politics/16blackberry.html

Zenter, Kim (2008). "Experts say MySpace suicide indictment sets 'scary' legal precedent," *Wired*, 15 May. http://blog.wired.com/27bstroke6/2008/05/myspace-indictm.html

_____ (2008). "Lori Drew not guilty of felonies in landmark cyberbullying trial," *Wired*, 26 November. http://blog.wired.com/27bstroke6/2008/11/lori-drew-pla-5.html

Ziegler, John (2009). "Media Malpractice," film documentary, videoclip. http://www.youtube.com/watch?v=qXnG8rxOdvQ

Zunes, Stephen (2009). "Iran's history of civil insurrections," *The Huffington Post*, 19 June. http://www.huffingtonpost.com/stephen-zunes/irans-history-of-civil-in_b_217998.html

Zurawik, David (2008). "Is Obama the first 'cybergenic' candidate?" *Baltimore Sun*, 12 August. http://www.mediachannel.org/wordpress/2008/08/12/is-obama-the-first-cybergenic-candidate/

index

permalinks, 59, 83, 84
Perry, Rick, 47
Petty, Tom, 54, 55
Pew Research Center, 164
"Phil D'Amato", 68, 69, 168
Philippines, 1, 38
Phillips, Rich, 163
phonograph, 47, 54, 148
Photobucket, 97
photography, 10, 16, 22, 27, 30, 54, 84, 86, 97, 115, 120, 129, 133, 145, 148, 166
Pinkner, Jeff, 117
Pinterest, 10, 97–98
plagiarism, 60, 97, 111, 169
Plame, Valerie, 101
Playboy magazine, 101
Plugh, Mike, 18
Podcast Pickle, 11
Podcastalley, 148
podcasting, 6, 8, 9, 11, 17, 30, 32, 34, 57, 86, 88, 89, 90, 102, 124, 129, 148–160
podiobooks, 93, 94, 153
Podlinez, 152, 153
Podsafe music, 153–154
Poelz, Felix, 23
poetry, 88, 131, 132
Poland, 20
Politico.com, 95, 97, 115, 176
polls (opinion) and politics, 42, 45, 50, 134, 135, 137, 138, 173, 174
Polytechnic University (New York), 22
Pool, Tim, 181, 182
Pope Benedict XVI, 30, 62, 63, 171
pornography, 27, 170
   see also sex
Posterous, 100
Powell, Colin, 77
Powell, Julie, 139
Pownce, 34
Pravda, 96
Prince (recording artist), 55
Prince, Phoebe, 165
printing press, 2, 32, 54, 59, 82, 88, 121, 176
Prius (Toyota), 152
"promo" exchanges, 150, 157
Public Broadcasting Service (PBS), 3, 48, 61
Public Disclosure Commission (Washington state), 103
Pulitzer Prize, 11, 115

Q

Queen Elizabeth II, 62, 63, 159

R

radio, 2, 5, 11, 32, 37, 38, 40, 45, 49, 50, 56, 74, 75, 83, 94, 95, 101, 102, 103, 110, 115, 116, 121, 122, 123, 124, 148, 149,
152, 153, 154, 155, 157, 158, 159, 172, 174, 179, 182
rahmfacts.com, 176
Rambla, La (street), 180
Random House, 153
Rather, Dan, 110
Ravi, Dharun, 165
Recording Industry Association of America (RIAA), 61
"reliable locatability", 59, 77, 78, 83
Relles, Ben, 42, 46, 51
Reno, Janet, 101
Republican Party, 9, 43, 44–45, 46, 47, 92, 111, 127, 134, 136, 137, 164, 172, 174, 175, 177, 178, 182
Reuter, Julius von, 82
Reuters, 33, 103, 114, 141
Reverbnation, 8, 33, 131
Revolution of the White Snow, 179
Ribeiro, John, 167
Richards, I. A., 69, 104
Richards, Michael, 46
Richter, Diana, 26
Riley, Duncan, 147
"Robbie Dingo", 145
Rock 'n' Roll Hall of Fame, 55
Rolling Stones, The, 55, 121
Roman Catholic Church, 63, 80, 88
   see also Vatican
Romania, 139, 144
Rome, ancient, 1, 54, 139
Rome, Sweet Rome (movie), 139
Romney, Mitt, 16, 33, 44, 45, 69, 91, 137, 182
Roosevelt, Franklin Delano (FDR), 45, 49, 50
Rose, Carl, 56
Rose, Kevin, 132
Rosedale, Philip, 140
Rosenthal, Peter, 23
Rove, Karl, 32
RSS, 151, 152, 153
Russell, Jason, 50
Russert, Tim, 58, 74, 75, 76
Russia, 63, 179
   see also Soviet Union
Rutgers University, 165
Ryan, Kevin, 101, 102
Ryan, Paul, 138

S

Saffo, Paul, 9, 45
Sagan, Carl, 23
Saleem, Muhammad, 135
Salon, 11, 53, 110
   see also Open Salon
"Sam Spade", 68
"samizdat video", 1, 38, 64

PAUL LEVINSON'S eight nonfiction books, including *The Soft Edge* (1997), *Digital McLuhan* (1999), *Realspace* (2003), *Cellphone* (2004), and *New New Media* (2009), have been the subject of major articles in *The New York Times*, *Wired*, and *The Christian Science Monitor*, and have been translated into 10 languages. His science fiction novels include *The Silk Code* (1999, winner of the Locus Award for Best First Novel), *Borrowed Tides* (2001), *The Consciousness Plague* (2002), *The Pixel Eye* (2003), and *The Plot To Save Socrates* (2006). His short stories have been nominated for Nebula, Hugo, Edgar, and Sturgeon Awards. Paul Levinson appears on MSNBC, Bloomberg West, The History Channel, Fox News, NPR, and numerous national and international TV and radio programs. His 1972 LP, *Twice Upon a Rhyme*, was reissued on mini-CD by Big Pink Records in 2009 and was reissued in a vinyl repressing by Sound of Salvation/Whiplash Records in December 2010. He reviews the best of television in his InfiniteRegress.tv blog, writes political and media commentary for *Mediaite*, and was listed in *The Chronicle of Higher Education*'s "Top 10 Academic Twitterers" in 2009. Paul Levinson has a PhD from New York University and is Professor of Communication & Media Studies at Fordham University in New York City.